D1588734

Aratus and the Astronomical Tradition

Classical Culture and Society

Series Editors
Joseph Farrell and Robin Osborne

Aratus and the Astronomical Tradition

Emma Gee

OXFORD
UNIVERSITY PRESS

OXFORD
UNIVERSITY PRESS

Oxford University Press is a department of the University of Oxford.
It furthers the University's objective of excellence in research,
scholarship, and education by publishing worldwide.

Oxford   New York
Auckland   Cape Town   Dar es Salaam   Hong Kong   Karachi
Kuala Lumpur   Madrid   Melbourne   Mexico City   Nairobi
New Delhi   Shanghai   Taipei   Toronto

With offices in
Argentina   Austria   Brazil   Chile   Czech Republic   France   Greece
Guatemala   Hungary   Italy   Japan   Poland   Portugal   Singapore
South Korea   Switzerland   Thailand   Turkey   Ukraine   Vietnam

Oxford is a registered trade mark of Oxford University Press
in the UK and certain other countries.

Published in the United States of America by
Oxford University Press
198 Madison Avenue, New York, NY 10016

Library of Congress Cataloging-in-Publication Data
Gee, Emma, 1970–
Aratus and the astronomical tradition / Emma Gee.
    p.   cm.
Includes bibliographical references and index.
ISBN 978-0-19-978168-3 (hardcover : alk. paper)
1. Aratus, Solensis. Phaenomena. 2. Aratus, Solensis—Influence.
3. Astronomy, Ancient, in literature. 4. Didactic poetry, Greek—History and criticism.
5. Lucretius Carus, Titus. De rerum natura. I. Title.
PA3873.A7G44   2013
881'.01—dc23   2012036874

9 8 7 6 5 4 3 2 1

Printed in the United States of America
on acid-free paper

Endpiece is Copernicus *De Rev.* f.9v, courtesy of Special Collections, St Andrews University Library.

Dedication

Here is the skeleton of a leaf, a childish gift,
Not without residual beauty, if you imagine
It was made from gold wire, like ancient jewellery.
Maybe you set it on your desk for a while, as a specimen,
alongside your lighter and the mouse (the dead kind).

Then, perhaps, you put it in a book,
And there it lies, in its papery grave,
Amidst the carnage of U-boats and torpedoes,
The ashy flecks of those whose bones were never found.

Perhaps you will discover it some day
And wonder who gave it you,
And how it was they knew you were the tree.

The leaf grew, tough and green,
Further away than you imagine:
A place undiscovered not long ago,
Where a child followed the creek up,
Striding, stooping, on hands, knees, belly,
To the source, where everything above is tree
And rainbow slick glosses the dark, dark earth
Where the cattle never tread—
A loved, unbearable place.

Why did you keep it so long, when after all
I dreamed I said goodbye, to the land, to you,
My Keeper of the Leaf?

haec tibi Arateis multum vigilata lucernis
    carmina, quis ignes novimus aerios,
levis in aridulo malvae descripta libello
    Prusiaca vexi munera navicula.

'I have brought you this poem, which teaches us to recognize the fires in the sky. Aratus kept vigil over it for a long time with his lamp. It is written in a tiny book made of smoothed mallow bark, and I brought it as a gift in a little boat from the land of King Prusias.'

Epigram by Cinna, 57–6 BC, my translation

CONTENTS

PREFACE AND ACKNOWLEDGMENTS

Not many of us get not just a second but also a third chance. Although this book was written under the aegis of the University of St Andrews, I have three sets of colleagues to thank, those from Exeter and Sydney as well as St Andrews. I would like to single out two colleagues without whose help this book would never have been written: Frances Muecke and Chris Gill. Both placed invaluable opportunities in my way, and were assiduous in making sure I followed them up. To them I owe my career as well as my book.

I would like to thank all my colleagues in St Andrews, especially Greg Woolf and Stephen Halliwell. The former caused me to have faith, the latter spurred me on by his judicious scepticism. Peter Wiseman, with his challenge to prove that Lucretius really was influenced by Cicero's *Aratea*, is responsible for Chapters 3 and 4. I hope they are an appropriate offering.

Many colleagues willingly took on the unenviable task of reading chaotic and incomprehensible drafts. Peter Wiseman read material that was later to become Chapters 3 and 4, and debunked most of the nonsense (any that remains is, needless to say, my own). Richard Hunter and Michael Reeve read parts of the book and were generous in their time and comments. Greg Woolf reined in Chapter 6 before any damage was done. Many colleagues helped with bibliography in areas where my own knowledge is sketchy: Greg Woolf, Richard Hunter, Alex Long, Félix Racine, Roger Rees, to name a few. I also warmly thank all those Aratus scholars who attended the conference at St Andrews in June 2010 and shared their ideas.

Much praise and appreciation are due to the series editors Joe Farrell and Robin Osborne. Joe acted as ad hoc reader of tedious first drafts and stayed in close touch throughout. I would like to thank Stefan Vranka, Sarah Pirovitz and Natalie Johnson for their efficiency and patience in the face of my needless anxieties and 'goldfish moments'. The comments of the anonymous reader for the press were invaluable.

I could not have written this book at all without my friends. I would like to thank all of them but I only name two: Gillian Galbraith and Miranda Macdonald. Despite their own commitments they have responded tirelessly to trivia. My son Hal has kept me alive during the process by his endless humour and inventiveness, although I am afraid that he may have been more aware than I would have wanted that I was writing a book. Finally, the book's dedicatee. You know who you are.

ABBREVIATIONS

BTL = Tombeur, P., *Bibliotheca Teubneriana Latina*, Centre Traditio Litterarum Occidentalium, Turnhout: Brepols, CD ROM

EANS = Keyser P.T., and G.L. Irby-Massey edd. (2008), *The Encyclopedia of Ancient Natural Scientists*, London: Routledge

LRE = Jones, A.H.M. (1964), *The later Roman Empire, 284–602: a social, economic and administrative Survey*, Oxford: Blackwell

OCD[3] = Hornblower, S. and A. Spawforth edd. (2003), *The Oxford Classical Dictionary*, third edition, Oxford/New York: Oxford University Press

PanLat = *Panegyrici Latini* ed. Nixon, C., and B. Rodgers (1994), *In Praise of Later Roman Emperors: the* Panegyrici Latini, Berkeley: University of California Press

PW = Pauly, August Friedrich von, and G. Wissowa, edd. (1893–1978), *Paulys Real-Encyclopädie der classischen Altertumswissenschaft*, Stuttgart: Metzler, 49 vols.

Aratus and the Astronomical Tradition

Introduction

PARAMETERS

The skies speak first to the poetic, not the scientific, imagination.

—Kuhn 1957: 7

Introduction

If you ask someone how the Greeks and Romans saw the world, you will often get back the answer that they thought that the sun went around the earth. This is true, but only broadly speaking: there were competing, powerful, and long-lived views about the universe with which modernity might be more comfortable, if those views had not become occluded, mostly in late antiquity and the Middle Ages.

We assume that Copernicus is the big break between ancient and modern astronomy. In fact, Copernicus is less radical than modernity chooses to give him credit for: a tipping point rather than a paradigm shift.[1] He was the heir to, and exponent of, ancient astronomy, and brought the system developed in antiquity to a point of departure from which our view of the solar system, and eventually of the universe, could be re-orientated. The 'Copernican revolution' was a consequence of his postulate that it was the motion of the *earth* which accounted for the apparent motion of the sun, stars, and planets. This was the starting point—only that—for a heliocentric view of the world. It was not at first 'factual', nor was the need for a reassessment of the motion of the sun vis-à-vis the earth necessarily its primary impetus. Even if it had been, this idea, like those of atoms and multiverses, is not without ancient precedent. Scientific debate was as vivid in antiquity as it is now.

There is no unbridgeable gulf between our view of the world and Aratus', though the *Phaenomena* was written around 276 BC and under the assumption the earth is the centre of the universe. Nonetheless, when we pick up Aratus' *Phaenomena*, we should not do it thinking we know what to expect. We need to come to the

3

text having shrugged off the baggage of the 'scientific revolution', or at least shifted it about a little. Then it may be that we can understand to a greater extent the baffling popularity of this text.

Aratus

Scholarship is widespread and broadly consensual about the main issues surrounding Aratus' text: that it was written after about 276 BC, perhaps at the court of the Macedonian king Antigonus Gonatas; that it was, in the tradition, characterized as a poetic rendition of one or more prose works of Plato's contemporary, the astronomer Eudoxus; but that, in terms of its language, it looks back to much earlier poetic models, and in terms of its philosophy it gravitates towards Stoicism.[2] Perhaps the best recent restatement of the issues surrounding our text, both a summary and a *praeteritio*, is Volk (2010) pp. 197–8, sounding the appropriate note of caution:

> The ancient biographical evidence[3] . . . does not allow us to construct a coherent picture of the intellectual and political context of Aratus' work. It is reasonably well established that the poet spent time in Athens consorting with early Stoics such as Zeno and Persaeus, and that he accepted an invitation to the court of Antigonus Gonatas in the early 270s. Yet we are unable to trace the influence of specific individuals or circumstances on Aratus' poetry. As for the literary affiliations of the *Phaenomena*, the work's apparent originality may to some extent be a mirage: it is possible that Aratus was the first to write a scientific didactic poem based on prose sources, but we know next to nothing of the didactic poetry of the fourth century, and what appears to be an innovation may well have been part of an ongoing trend.[4]

We should not allow ourselves to become mired in the finer details of these issues to the detriment of the text. I want a reader who comes to Aratus unprejudiced by biographical fallacy or excess of scholarship. Of course we should orient the text in terms of periodicity (contemporary with the 'Alexandrian' poets Callimachus and Apollonius, with all that entails in terms of language, style, and scholarship) and we ought to know something about the preoccupations of the Hellenistic 'age' in which it was written (bookishness, paradoxically combined with an interest in the natural world verging on the prurient, as manifest in the 'scientific' works of Eratosthenes, the anatomical dissections of Erisistratus, or the growth of 'paradoxography' or interest in natural wonders). This goes for each of our translations of Aratus: we should situate each of them, as far as possible and with due scepticism, in their cultural contexts. Cultural ambience is important. It tells us about the concerns each author brings to Aratus' text and can elucidate the reasons for choosing to react to the *Phaenomena* in the first place. Beyond this, we should allow certainties as to what we are dealing with to dissolve, happily and without consequence for our direct approach to Aratus' text and the successive texts it generated, as they stand, in and of themselves.

'Popularity'

Why was Aratus so popular? The popularity of Aratus' text has been the subject of much scholarship, some of it ostentatiously reluctant: 'One of the tasks which any historian of Hellenistic literature must look upon as providing a definition of the term "thankless," is to explain why the *Phaenomena* of Aratus, which seems in most of its parts tedious, was so enormously popular from the third century BC until at least the fourth of our era.'[5] Scholars who do not confess bafflement resort to over-kill. Lewis (1992) for instance painstakingly enumerates no fewer than six explanations for Aratus' popularity (its value for astrology, astral religion, mythology, Stoicism, astronomy, literature) before going on to enunciate her own (pedagogy). The question of popularity in Aratean scholarship stifles the life out of the text.

Why should Aratus' popularity be a problem? If it is a problem it is one for scholars, not for readers: to the latter, the beauty and intellectual transparency of Aratus' text is self-evident. I will, nonetheless, suggest an answer to the 'problem' of Aratus' popularity. My answer does not cancel out all previous suggestions, but it is a different sort of answer: a philosophical one, which situates Aratus as a cardinal point in the scientific tradition of the West.

We need to look first at how the phenomenon of Aratus' popularity manifests itself. At the risk of joining the categorization camp, you might say that his popularity comes out in several ways: (i) translation; (ii) 'tags'; (iii) the literary verdict; (iv) scholia or commentaries on the text. First, translation. 'In antiquity alone, Aratus' poem enjoyed extraordinary success and inspired at least twenty-seven commentaries . . . and four translations into Latin.'[6] This is to understate the case. To the three extant translations, those of Cicero (c.89 BC), Germanicus (c.14–17 AD), and Avienus (c.360 AD), may be added at least three more ancient translations of Aratus' work or substantial portions of it. These are Varro of Atax's *Ephemeris* (mid first century BC[7]), Virgil's translation of the weather-signs in the first book of the *Georgics* (early 30s BC[8]), and Ovid's *Phaenomena* which, if an early work of the poet, might date to c.23 BC (Ovid was born in 43 BC).[9] The first and last of these are all but lost. In addition, Manilius, writing an astrological didactic poem in around 14 AD, paraphrases *Phaenomena* 19–558 in his description of the universe (*Astronomica* 1.255–808).[10] To this spread of 'translations' we can add several more from the Middle Ages and early modern period: the early medieval Aratus Latinus;[11] the translation in the 1523 printed edition of Ceporinus; the 1535 translation by the German humanist Joachim Camerarius; and the reception of Aratus in the *De Sphaera* of the Scottish polymath George Buchanan (1506–82).[12] A verse translation has been published as recently as 2010.[13]

Secondly, the practice of referencing Aratus by using some 'tag' from the *Phaenomena*, either in the original or translated, was extremely widespread. St Paul is a perpetrator of this technique, in *Acts* 17.28, where, addressing the Athenians, he shows himself adept at ancient literary citation practice: ὡς καί τινες τῶν καθ' ὑμᾶς ποιητῶν εἰρήκασιν, Τοῦ γὰρ καὶ γένος ἐσμέν, 'As even some of your own poets have said, "For we too are his offspring"' (Aratus *Ph.* 5, τοῦ γὰρ καὶ γένος εἰμέν). Paul assimilates Aratus' Zeus to the Christian god in a way the Athenians will understand, and brings himself in from the religious fringe to the centre of Greek literary culture. There is good precedent for citation in Roman literature as well. Only a little earlier than Paul, Ovid in *Metamorphoses* 10.148–9 translates line 1 of the *Phaenomena*: *ab Iove, Musa parens, carmina nostra move* ('From Jupiter, parent Muse, begin our song' = *Phaenomena* 1, ἐκ Διὸς ἀρχώμεσθα, 'Let's begin from Zeus'). Here the character Orpheus, a legendary poet, is inscribing his song in the tradition of teaching about the universe (cosmological didactic). This tradition is best represented by Aratus. You did not need to translate the whole of Aratus' poem to show yourself a follower of that tradition. Citation by 'tag', usually Aratus' opening phrase, is a shorthand way of doing it.

Related to this is the tradition of what we might call 'the literary verdict.' In this idiom, the reader has not only read Aratus but is in a position to make a value judgment. The tradition begins in Alexandria in Aratus' own century. Callimachus wrote an epigram praising the literary qualities of Aratus' poem; this was translated into Latin by the poet Cinna in the first century BC.[14] This tradition is also represented in Rome by Cicero, *De oratore* 1.69:

> etenim si constat inter doctos, hominem ignarum astrologiae ornatissimis atque optimis versibus Aratum de caelo stellisque dixisse; si de rebus rusticis hominem ab agro remotissimum Nicandrum Colophonium poetica quadam facultate, non rustica, scripsisse praeclare, quid est cur non orator de rebus eis eloquentissime dicat, quas ad certam causam tempusque cognorit?

> 'Indeed, if learned men agree that Aratus, a man ignorant of astronomy, who nonetheless wrote about the sky and the stars in a poem as excellent and as well crafted as can be, and Nicander of Colophon, a man vastly removed from agricultural life, wrote poetry about it which was anything but "rustic," is there any reason why an orator should not discourse most eloquently on things which he has mugged up for a particular case or occasion?' (my translation).

Cicero (himself an advocate and orator) is positioning himself on the topic of expertise, using two examples of poets who wrote on 'science', Aratus and Nicander (the latter second century BC). It is not often enough pointed out that his judgement of Aratus is favourable seen in this light. An orator is an expert in amassing and conveying knowledge to a purpose: in this he is every bit as good as Aratus and Nicander (who were the best there is).

Ovid too praises Aratus in his literary wrap at *Amores* 1.15.16, *cum sole et luna semper Aratus erit* ('Aratus will always be up there with the sun and moon'). Ovid's whistle-stop tour of earlier literature culminates with himself of course—he absorbs the qualities of the 'greats' he lists, among whom Aratus represents poetry about the sun and moon ('cosmological didactic', as in the case of Ovid's Orpheus in *Metamorphoses* 10), and is playfully located alongside the sun and moon themselves for his afterlife apotheosis.

The other side of the coin comes from Quintilian, *Institutio oratoria* 10.1.55: *Arati materia motu caret, ut in qua nulla varietas, nullus adfectus, nulla persona, nulla*

cuiusquam sit oratio; sufficit tamen operi cui se parem credidit ('Aratus' subject is
devoid of life, to the extent that there is no variety, no emotion, no characterisation,
and no speech by anyone. But he is at least equal to his own level of artistic aspira-
tion', my translation).[15] Perhaps Quintilian either disliked Aratus as a teaching text,
or misconstrued the passage from Cicero's *De oratore* as disapproving, and thought
he was following the great man's lead. We should not be guided by the curmud-
geonly Quintilian any more than by modern scholars who have followed him.

Finally, there is what you might call the 'paratextual' tradition. This is the tradition of scholia or interpretative writings designed to be read alongside the text.
Aratus' *Phaenomena* is one of the most heavily annotated works of antiquity. A
taxonomy of the scholia and introductory works has only partly been written.[16]
There were scholia on the *Ph.* from within a century of its composition. The earliest
scholiastic works on the *Ph.*, the commentaries of Hipparchus and Attalus, date
from the second century BC.[17] The commentaries of Hipparchus and Attalus are
succeeded by Theon (c. first century BC), from whom one of the extant traditions of
scholia arises.[18] There is also a body of scholia drawn from so-called Edition Φ.
According to Martin this edition was perhaps disseminated in the second or third
centuries AD, and consisted of a text of the *Phaenomena* supplemented by various
introductory texts.[19] It is this or a similar tradition which finds is successors in the
early modern printed editions of Aratus, which present the text with various interpretative appurtenances alongside. It is more than likely that Camerarius, who
translated Aratus into Latin in 1535, was using a composite edition, which contained Aratus' text, various Latin translations, including those of Germanicus and
Avienus, and the scholia on Aratus. This was possibly the Aldus edition of 1499.[20]
It is probable that Copernicus was also reading such a text (see below, Epilogue).

'Phenomena'

From its inception, then, the *Phaenomena* was weighed down by the panoply of
readership.[21] Aratus' *Phaenomena* was not—apparently—a revolutionary text in
itself. Neither was Copernicus'.[22] Yet both texts have a huge impact, and both start
a revolution, Copernicus' a noisy one, Aratus' a quiet revolution. The answer to
Aratus' 'popularity' lies in the peculiar construction of Western cosmology.

To understand this we need to shed any preconceived notions of what the text is
about, notions which limit its ambit. These come into play from our first reading of the
work's title. It is unfortunate, in terms of our preconceptions, that Aratus' work has
had, from antiquity, the title *Phaenomena* (Eng. 'Phenomena'), a title apparently inherited from one of its prose sources, a work of the same name by Plato's pupil Eudoxus.

The title *Phaenomena* has been in use since at least the second century BC. It was
shared with one of the works of Plato's pupil Eudoxus (c.410–c.355 BC), whose
'Phaenomena' is named by Hipparchus (writing c.150 BC): ἀναφέρεται δὲ εἰς τὸν
Εὔδοξον δύο βιβλία περὶ τῶν φαινομένων, σύμφωνα κατὰ πάντα σχεδὸν
ἀλλήλοις πλὴν ὀλίγων σφόδρα. τὸ μὲν οὖν ἓν αὐτῶν ἐπιγράφεται Ἔνοπτρον, τὸ

δὲ ἕτερον Φαινόμενα ('Two books about the phenomena are attributed to Eudoxus, agreeing with one another on almost everything except in a very few cases. One of them was entitled *Enoptron*, the other *Phaenomena*,' Hipparchus 1.2.2). Hipparchus also tells us (1.1.8) that Aratus wrote the *Phaenomena* following the order of Eudoxus: τῇ γὰρ Εὐδόξου συντάξει κατακολουθήσας τὰ Φαινόμενα γέγραφεν. . . .[23]

The title itself could prejudice modern readers. In modern usage, 'A phenomenon (from Greek φαινόμενον), plural phenomena, is any observable occurrence.'[24] Aratus' *Phaenomena* must, we think, be about 'Things You See': the observable map of the heavens. We should immediately contest this assumption, on several grounds. First is the idea that a 'phenomenon', as the term is used in science, is based on a set of data from observation, and can be mapped, measured, qualified and quantified in a straightforward way.[25] In fact, 'phenomenon'/'phenomena' is one of several related terms which ought to be subjected to scrutiny.[26] Phenomena are not in a direct sense 'what you see', but the inference of a general formulation from scattered data.[27] Phenomena are mediated through the data which are observed.[28] The phenomena themselves are not directly observable, but a system thought to underlie the data. We are already several steps away from an understanding of 'phenomena' as the material of observation.

To work back another step, how do we come by the preconception that 'phenomena' are what we can see? The history of this usage is long. According to the *OED*, the first English attestation of 'phenomena' (or its equivalent, the transliterated Greek *phainomena*) in the sense of 'what we observe' occurs in Francis Bacon's *Advancement of Learning* (1605).[29] In *The Advancement of Learning* 2 I 3[r], Bacon comments on the commensurability of outcome between the traditional and Copernican models of the universe as ways of accounting for 'the phenomena':

> For as the same *phainomena* in Astronomie are satisfied by the received Astronomie of the diurnall Motion, and the Proper Motions of the Planets, with their Eccentriques and Epicycles, and likewise by the Theorie of Copernicus, who supposed the Earth to move; & the Calculations are indifferently agreeable to both: so the ordinarie face and viewe of experience is many times satisfied by several Theories and Philosophies . . .[30]

In this passage of the *Advancement of Learning*, Bacon used an expression, 'the *phainomena* . . . are satisfied', which we know better as 'saving the phenomena.' In his *Essays*, 'Superstition,' 0 I[r], Bacon uses the expression to ridicule the attempts of astronomers to assign a geometric model to planetary motion: '. . . Like Astronomers, which did faigne Eccentricks and Epicycles, and such Engines of Orbs, *to save the Phenomena*, though they knew, there were no such things. . . .'[31] At its first adoption into English, '*phainomena*'/'phenomena' apparently refers to the observed motion of the heavenly bodies, specifically that of the planets.

The early modern usage of *phainomena*, which we have inherited, privileges *one* ancient meaning of the verb φαίνομαι (*phainomai*, 'to appear'), which *phainomena* comes from: that of sense-data, things which appear to our senses. Bacon's usage can be paralleled from Aristotle, *De Caelo* 293a23–27. Criticizing the Pythagoreans,

Aristotle remarks, Ἔτι δ' ἐναντίαν ἄλλην ταύτῃ κατασκευάζουσι γῆν, ἣν ἀντίχθονα ὄνομα καλοῦσιν, οὐ πρὸς τὰ φαινόμενα τοὺς λόγους καὶ τὰς αἰτίας ζητοῦντες, ἀλλὰ πρός τινας λόγους καὶ δόξας αὑτῶν τὰ φαινόμενα προσέλκοντες καὶ πειρώμενοι συγκοσμεῖν. ('Further, they make up another earth opposite to this one, which they give the name "anti-earth," not seeking their theories and explanations in relation to the apparent facts, but dragging the apparent facts towards, and endeavouring to co-ordinate them with, certain of their theories and opinions,' trans. Leggatt 1995). In this passage, Aristotle is opposing φαινόμενα, things which are manifest, that is, visible in the heavens, with λόγοι, 'theories'. The first are true, the latter can be fictive.

So, Bacon's catchphrase 'to save the phenomena' refers in particular to *planetary* phenomena, the motions of the planets which you observe, which need 'saving' in respect of how you theorize their apparent motions. The expression was coined by interpreters of Aristotle's works.[32] The sixth-century commentator on Aristotle, Simplicius, used it in this way, quoting Sosigenes, a peripatetic philosopher of the second century AD, who (apparently) got it from Eudemus (c.370–300 BC):[33]

μὴ δυνάμενοι δὲ δι' ἀκριβείας ἑλεῖν, πῶς αὐτῶν διακειμένων φαντασία μόνον ἐστὶ καὶ οὐκ ἀλήθεια τὰ συμβαίνοντα, ἠγάπησαν εὑρεῖν, τίνων ὑποτεθέντων δι' ὁμαλῶν καὶ τεταγμένων καὶ ἐγκυκλίων κινήσεων δυνήσεται διασωθῆναι τὰ περὶ τὰς κινήσεις τῶν πλανᾶσθαι λεγομένων φαινόμενα. καὶ πρῶτος τῶν Ἑλλήνων Εὔδοξος ὁ Κνίδιος, ὡς Εὔδημός τε ἐν τῷ δευτέρῳ τῆς Ἀστρολογικῆς ἱστορίας ἀπεμνημόνευσε καὶ Σωσιγένης παρὰ Εὐδήμου τοῦτο λαβών, ἅψασθαι λέγεται τῶν τοιούτων ὑποθέσεων Πλάτωνος, ὥς φησι Σωσιγένης, πρόβλημα τοῦτο ποιησαμένου τοῖς περὶ ταῦτα ἐσπουδακόσι, τίνων ὑποτεθεισῶν ὁμαλῶν καὶ τεταγμένων κινήσεων διασωθῇ τὰ περὶ τὰς κινήσεις τῶν πλανωμένων φαινόμενα.

'Not being able to grasp with precision how what occurs in the heaven is only the *appearance* of their condition [that of the planets] and not the truth, the astronomers were content to find out on what hypotheses the phenomena concerning the stars which are said to wander could be preserved by means of uniform, ordered, circular motions. And, as Eudemus recorded in the second book of his astronomical history (and Sosigenes took this over from Eudemus), Eudoxus of Cnidos is said to be the first of the Hellenes to have made use of such hypotheses, Plato, as Sosigenes said, having created this problem for those who had concerned themselves with these things: on what hypotheses of uniform and ordered motions could the phenomena concerning the motion of the planets be preserved?'[34]

Used this way, 'saving the phenomena' means constructing a mathematical model of planetary motion which corresponds to the apparent movements (φαινόμενα) of the planets and therefore 'saves' them from being left out of any *system*.

The planets are the fly in the ointment in any system of the universe as observed from earth. What you see (*phainomena*) is *not* what you get: it is the reverse of appearance. The planets *seem* to move unpredictably. Some juggling of observational data is needed to make it square with the interpretative model, if you are going to slot the planets into an orderly system. The need to massage the planets to bring fact into line with theory is what provoked the Copernican revolution.[35] The planets also explode the notion of the priority of observation over theory. You may think that after Copernicus' theory of the moving earth the planets ceased to be a problem for astronomy. But 'Copernicus did not solve the problem of the planets'.[36] It was only in the seventeenth century, with systematic sets of observations using the newly invented telescope, that the data began to come into line with the theory, even though 'The Copernicans . . . had *anticipated* the sort of universe that the telescope was disclosing'.[37] The Copernican universe itself, abstract and incomplete to that point, began to adapt to the new 'reality'. Observation, in the case of the planets, comes *after* theory.

To return now to the modern usage of 'phenomena', the *OED* defines '"To save the phenomena," tr. Gr. σώζειν τὰ φαινόμενα', as 'to reconcile *the observed and admitted facts* with some theory or doctrine with which they appear to disagree' (my emphasis). It hinges on a definition of τὰ φαινόμενα, the phenomena, as (a) observable and (b) factual. But φαίνομαι has two meanings. In ancient usage it can signify *either* what appears to the senses, *or* what is 'mentally manifest'.[38] In the passage of the *De Caelo* quoted above, Aristotle uses τὰ φαινόμενα for the *observable* motion of the heavenly bodies, but in other places even he uses it differently. He used the same term to mean something fictive at *Rhetoric* 1402a6-8, ψεῦδός τε γάρ ἐστιν, καὶ οὐκ ἀληθὲς ἀλλὰ φαινόμενον εἰκός, καὶ ἐν οὐδεμιᾷ τέχνῃ ἀλλ᾽ <ἦν> ἐν ῥητορικῇ καὶ ἐριστηκῇ ('. . . for it is a lie, not a true but an apparent phenomenon, and one which does not exist in any skill except rhetoric and argumentation', my trans.; text of Ross 1959). Here φαινόμενον is equivalent to a 'lie' (ψεῦδος), something counter-factual (οὐκ ἀληθές), a 'likely story' (φαινόμενον εἰκός). This is at the opposite end of the spectrum of meaning of φαίνομαι from sense-perception: in this case *phainomena*, products of the mind, can be specious or even fallacious.

To take another step back, chronologically and conceptually: in Aristotle's predecessor, Plato, *phainomena* straddle the boundary between observable data and philosophical myth. The line between the two meanings is not an impenetrable barrier but a semipermeable membrane across which osmosis can and does take place. Plato sometimes privileges the visible as a means to understanding the world, up to a point, at least the visible as we see it in the form of the heavenly bodies. This is the case in his discussion of the value of astronomy, *Republic* 529c6–d2: ταῦτα μὲν τὰ ἐν τῷ οὐρανῷ ποικίλματα, ἐπείπερ ἐν ὁρατῷ πεποίκιλται, κάλλιστα μὲν ἡγεῖσθαι καὶ ἀκριβέστατα τῶν τοιούτων ἔχειν, τῶν δὲ ἀληθινῶν πολὺ ἐνδεῖν ('The stars that decorate the sky, though we rightly regard them as the finest and most perfect of visible things, are far inferior, just because they are visible, to the true realities,' trans. Lee 2007; all quotations in this book from the Greek text of Plato's *Rep.* are from Slings 2003). The stars are the best evidence there is, but they are not 'true'. The proper astronomer should be wary of falling into the trap of thinking they are the limit of reality (*Rep.* 530a4–b4):

Τῷ ὄντι δὴ ἀστρονομικόν . . . ὄντα οὐκ οἴει ταὐτὸν πείσεσθαι εἰς τὰς τῶν
ἄστρων φορὰς ἀποβλέποντα; νομιεῖν μὲν ὡς οἷόν τε κάλλιστα τὰ τοιαῦτα
ἔργα συστήσασθαι, οὕτω συνεστάναι τῷ τοῦ οὐρανοῦ δημιουργῷ αὐτόν τε
καὶ τὰ ἐν αὐτῷ· τὴν δὲ νυκτὸς πρὸς ἡμέραν συμμετρίαν καὶ τούτων πρὸς
μῆνα καὶ μηνὸς πρὸς ἐνιαυτὸν καὶ τῶν ἄλλων ἄστρων πρός τε ταῦτα καὶ
πρὸς ἄλληλα, οὐκ ἄτοπον, οἴει, ἡγήσεται τὸν νομίζοντα γίγνεσθαί τε
ταῦτα ἀεὶ ὡσαύτως καὶ οὐδαμῇ οὐδὲν παραλλάττειν, σῶμά τε ἔχοντα καὶ
ὁρώμενα, καὶ ζητεῖν παντὶ τρόπῳ τὴν ἀλήθειαν αὐτῶν λαβεῖν;

'Isn't the true astronomer in the same position when he watches the movements of the stars? . . . He will think that the heavens and the heavenly bodies
have been put together by their maker as well as such things can be; but he
will also think it absurd to suppose that there is an always constant and abso-
lutely invariable relation of day to night, or of day and night to month, or
month to year, or, again, of the periods of the other stars to them and to each
other' (trans. Lee 2007).

In Plato, the term *phainomena* normally does *not* signify what is observable.[39]
An important instance is *Republic* 517b7–c1, τὰ δ᾽ οὖν ἐμοὶ φαινόμενα οὕτω
φαίνεται, ἐν τῷ γνωστῷ τελευταία ἡ τοῦ ἀγαθοῦ ἰδέα καὶ μόγις ὁρᾶσθαι ('But
in my opinion, for what it is worth, the final thing to be perceived in the intelligible region, and perceived only with difficulty, is the form of the good'). 'These
phainomena' refer to *imaginative* ones: the term refers to the *myth* of the sun and
the cave, a myth about the deceptiveness of what we think we see. Plato's Socrates
prefaces his statement with a caveat: θεὸς δέ που οἶδεν εἰ ἀληθὴς οὖσα τυγχάνει
(*Rep.* 517b6–7), 'The truth of the matter is, after all, known only to god.' This is
the kind of expression Socrates habitually uses in relation to philosophical myth.
And here indeed we are dealing with the aftermath of one of the key myths of
Plato's *Republic*. So for Plato, *myth* = *phainomena*, and in the event, it is myth, not
appearances, which is 'saved'.[40] At the end of the Myth of Er, Plato's final extrav-
agant revivification of myth in *Republic* Book 10, Socrates comments (*Rep.*
621b8) καὶ οὕτως, ὦ Γλαύκων, μῦθος ἐσώθη, 'and so, my dear Glaucon, his tale
was preserved.'[41]

Plato's salvation of myth was done by turning it into a species of cosmology. The
Myth of Er contains an allegory of the structure of the universe, the 'spindle of
necessity'. This cosmology, although allegorical, reinvents myth as a means by
which it is in fact possible to understand the world.[42] It is this marriage of myth with
cosmology, the *convergence of data and imagination*—both *phainomena*, in ancient
terms—which saves it.

We find the same convergence of data and imagination in Aratus. His world, as
we shall see, is not simply a description of the visible sky, but a vehicle for a certain
understanding of what we think we perceive. This is perhaps clearest in the Myth of
Dike (the constellation Virgo, identified as personified 'Justice', discussed in chapter
1). We shall see this myth as a response to the questions raised by Plato's reinstatement of myth in the *Republic*.

There is a continuous process of renegotiation about the status in the world of the mythical and the 'real' in Aratus and his successors. The Platonic orientation towards the greater reality of what you can *imagine* finds its best expression in Neoplatonism, the systematic reading of Plato and the extraction from his works of a consistent body of dogma. Julian, a 'pagan' philosopher and Roman emperor from 361 to 363 AD, uses *phainomena* in his Neoplatonic *Hymn to King Helios* to mean *not* what is real, but what is 'perceptible' as opposed to the greater reality of the 'intelligible' world of abstract thought or intellection. The 'perceptible' in Neoplatonism is the *reverse* of what is real, although it may be an agent in leading us to what is real, required because of our own imperfections, which include the tendency to rely on our senses. Avienus, the last of Aratus' ancient translators into Latin verse, was an exact contemporary of the Emperor Julian. In effect, he turns Aratus' poem into a Neoplatonic work.[43] The phenomena in it, for the Neoplatonist, are only the observable clues to what is real, and what is real is the opposite of what is perceptible.

So, when approaching Aratus' text we should discard any presuppositions provoked by its title. Depending on the orientation of the reader, the phenomena it describes can be a factual record of the observable universe, or an attractive but ultimately fallacious means through which we approach the truth. We should not privilege one meaning of *phainomena* over the other, or expect Aratus' translators to do so. Aratus' *Phaenomena* is a transparent substance, taking on colour from the context around it. This is one of the keys to its enduring relevance.

Nor should the disjunction between any apparent truth-claims in the poem, and those of our own world view, worry us. For us, the phenomena the *Phaenomena* describes are, quite simply, untrue. Aratus' universe, predicated on the idea of a static earth surrounded by the sphere of the fixed stars, is a conceptual model we no longer believe, and even for Aratus, as he presents it, some of its elements have been superseded.[44] But we should not be too quick to congratulate ourselves on discarding this imaginative scheme, since 'the developed astronomical conception of a universe in which the stars, including our sun, are scattered here and there through an infinite space is less than four centuries old, and it is already out-of-date.'[45] We should listen to Plato's warning about astronomy. The universe we imagine, and therefore see, can be 'more real', but it can never be 'real'. To think otherwise is a great arrogance. The *phainomena* ride a reality which is coy above all, which sometimes allows itself to be anticipated in scientific theory, but in most cases recedes just a little beyond each successive theoretical thrust. To remind ourselves of this is part of the value of reading Aratus.

Debate

Are *phainomena* what you see, or what you imagine? It is scientific theories which fill the space between real and imagined. Aratus' *Phaenomena* does not only record data, but also has its place in a theoretical edifice containing many rooms.

Theories of the world were the subject of as much debate in antiquity, relative to the dissemination of information, as they are now. From Plato's *Timaeus* onwards, contemplation of the celestial order was seen by philosophers with intelligent-design leanings as the best way to arrive at a knowledge of the divine.[46] The view that antiquity inherited from Plato is the one which is characterized in modern writing as 'the ancient world view' or (more idealistically) 'the Greek world view', as though there were only one.[47] You would imagine that we pass directly from Aristotle and Ptolemy (both modalities of a geocentric intelligent design cosmology, with its ultimate origins in Plato) to Copernicus, who was the first to suggest a radically different system.[48]

This is simply not so. There is another side, suppressed in histories of the development of astronomy. The main competitor of the intelligent design model is the Epicurean one ('Epicurean' refers to the philosophical school started by the Athenian Epicurus, 341–270 BC). Epicurean cosmology saw the universe as constructed from atoms. Epicurean philosophy privileged observation, rationalism, religious scepticism, and the demotion of god and man from positions of centrality, no less than do modern rationalizers. This tradition is conveniently obfuscated, in popular science, by those who choose to flaunt their philosophical primacy as rationalists. Even in the history of astronomy it is neglected in favour of presenting ancient science as more monolithic than it was, in order to strengthen the innovations of Copernicus and his successors.

Epicurean cosmology is best, in fact almost exclusively, represented in Lucretius' *De rerum natura* (*On the Nature of the Universe*).[49] I devote a lot of time to this text in a book which is not about it. I study how the *De rerum natura* (henceforward *DRN*) reacts to the universe of Aratus as a paradigm of the opposing model. One by-product of this discussion, a significant one, is the reinstatement of Lucretius, and Epicureanism, in ancient scientific debate. This debate was not arcane, but took place in writings designed to be read by an educated, nonspecialist, Roman audience. It was therefore a public and influential conversation, and we should take more notice of it. More than this, the recognition of the debate can bring much-needed qualification to the idea of a modern prerogative on rationalism and/or religious scepticism. I make no apology for the fact that this foot soldier in modern debate is issued with the full panoply of classical scholarship.

The obfuscation of Lucretius in scientific debate is not merely wilful (although that too), but also a result of historical accidents of several kinds. One of these historical accidents is Cicero. The fact that Epicureanism has been silenced in modern histories of ancient scientific debate should not blind us to the fact that it was, if anything, *dominant* in Cicero's time, if the vehemence of his argument against it at *Tusculan Disputations* 4.6–7 is anything to go by:

> itaque illius verae elegantisque philosophiae, quae ducta a Socrate in Peripateticis adhuc permanit et idem alio modo dicentibus Stoicis, cum Academici eorum controversias disceptarent, nulla fere sunt aut pauca admodum Latina monumenta sive propter magnitudinem rerum occupationemque hominum,

sive etiam quod imperitis ea probari posse non arbitrabantur, cum interim illis silentibus C. Amafinius extitit dicens, cuius libris editis commota multitudo contulit se ad eam potissimum disciplinam, sive quod erat cognitu perfacilis, sive quod invitabantur inlecebris blandis voluptatis, sive etiam, quia nihil erat prolatum melius, illud quod erat tenebant. post Amafinium autem multi eiusdem aemuli rationis multa cum scripsissent, Italiam totam occupaverunt, quodque maxumum argumentum est non dici illa subtiliter, quod et tam facile ediscantur et ab indoctis probentur, id illi firmamentum esse disciplinae putant (text of Pohlenz 1982).

'So there were almost no examples of that true and elegant philosophy which originated with Socrates, and up to that point had been preserved among the followers of Aristotle—the Stoics talked about the same thing in different language, while the Academics picked apart the discrepancies between schools— either because the task was so big and people were otherwise occupied, or because they did not think these things could be palatable to the uninitiated. When everyone else was silent, Amafinius stood up and spoke, and the crowd, moved by his published works, orientated itself predominantly towards that school of thought—whether because it was very easy to understand or because it provided a pretext for the easy attractions of pleasure, or even because they took what there was because nothing better was on offer. After Amafinius, a lot of people emulous of his way of thinking wrote a lot of books, and they invaded the whole of Italy. The greatest proof of the lack of subtlety in their writings is that they are so easily assimilated and that the uneducated enjoy them. They think this is the strong point of their philosophical school' (my trans.).

Amafinius is an Epicurean philosopher mentioned only by Cicero (possibly a straw man invented by him). This argument purports to give the historical context of the development of philosophy in Rome, but clearly Cicero still feels the need to diminish Epicureanism at the time of writing (44 BC). Cicero himself was an academic or sceptic, and so claimed not to argue for one side or another;[50] but in his influential philosophical writings, intelligent-design philosophies consistently get the best arguments (take, for instance, Book 2 of the *De natura deorum*, in which Cicero quotes his own translation of Aratus as ancillary to the Stoic world view).[51]

A greater historical accident was the loss of Lucretius during the Middle Ages. We almost did not have this text at all. Lucretius' poem was lost in the early Middle Ages and not rediscovered until 1417, just over 100 years before the publication of Copernicus' *De revolutionibus*.[52] Greenblatt's recent monograph has tracked the significance of its rediscovery in the Renaissance.[53] Would the survival of Lucretius have made any difference to how the history of astronomy is written, or indeed to astronomy itself? My view is that, had the *DRN* been around in the Middle Ages, it would probably have had a greater impact, and an earlier one, on Western thought. The substance, eloquence, and intellectual cohesion of Lucretius' text makes it difficult to ignore. The loss of Lucretius, a product of the vicissitudes of the medieval transmission of Latin texts, looks like a much bigger problem than we thought. It isn't just the academic philologist's problem, but that of the historian of science as well.[54]

Historians of science underplay the range of views available even before the Copernican 'revolution'. This is evident in Kuhn: 'The great new scientific theories of the sixteenth and seventeenth centuries all originate in rents torn by scholastic critics in the fabric of Aristotelian thought.'[55] Kuhn here attributes the impetus for Copernicus' innovations to the purely medieval phenomenon of scholasticism.[56] He congruently talks down ancient influences on the development of the new cosmology: 'For *most Greek astronomers and philosophers*, from the fourth century on, the earth was a tiny sphere suspended stationary at the geometric centre of a much larger rotating sphere which carried the stars. The sun moved in the vast space between the earth and the sphere of the stars. Outside of the outer sphere there was nothing at all—no space, no matter, nothing. This was not, in antiquity, the only theory of the universe, but it is the one that gained most adherents, and it is a developed version of this theory that the medieval and modern world inherited from the ancients.'[57] Kuhn states that, '. . . after its first establishment, the two sphere framework itself was almost never questioned. For nearly two millennia it guided the imaginations of all astronomers and most philosophers.' It is less the case, however, that the intelligent design universe was 'almost never' questioned, than that its most influential opponent 'almost' did not make it to modernity.

True, Kuhn grudgingly attributes influence to ancient cosmologies other than Aristotelian/Ptolemaic.[58] But while he acknowledges the 'modernity' of ancient cosmologies which did not posit a 'two-sphere' model, he nevertheless insists on referring to them as 'alternate/alternative' or 'significant minority' cosmologies in antiquity.[59] The terminology of alterity and minority marginalizes the Epicurean/Lucretian component of the ancient debate, which was not necessarily at the margins in antiquity, as we have seen, for instance, from Cicero. When did these cosmologies become 'alternative'? Probably not until much later. It was a third historical accident—the adoption of Aristotelian/Ptolemaic cosmology by a powerful political organism (the church)—which established it as the dominant system. In 1616 the church banned all books advocating the reality of the earth's motion (Kuhn 1957: 108). The end-piece of this book, a folio of the first edition of the *De Rev.*, the wax-marks showing where a covering was affixed to Copernicus' famous diagram, either because the reader was offended by it, or because he wanted others to think that he was, is one result.[60] But we should not read into *antiquity* the dominance of one system.

In antiquity, Lucretius contended with other world views on equal terms. His cosmology was not alternative or marginal. At times it looked as though it was winning. In his *DRN* he takes the text of Aratus' map of the intelligent design cosmos, in the form of Cicero's translation of it, fragments it, and places it in the service of his own textual construction of the Epicurean, atomist world.[61] This is a work of deconstruction: he dismantles the rational universe and rebuilds it on his own design, piecemeal and arbitrary. The impact of this strategy is clear from the fact that Cicero felt compelled within a decade to claim his *Aratea* back for the intelligent-design side, as an adjunct to the argument of the second book of the *De natura deorum* (*On the Nature of the Gods*).

If we choose not to obfuscate the ancient debate, we will see that there is nothing new under the sun, although the sun itself may be a ball tossed about in the philosophical argumentation. The militant atheism of some modern rationalists and their arguments against intelligent design find precedent in Lucretius. These modern proselytizers for rationalism represent themselves as original in their attempts to free humanity from the tyranny of religion, in favour of scientific liberation.[62] Their rhetoric ignores the nuance, subtlety, and power of ancient scientific debate. In this debate Aratus plays a part, a quiet but essential role. Aratus' text, as a vehicle for constructive thought about the cosmos and man's place in it, can accommodate many perspectives. Should we be surprised at its afterlife?

An Answer

The preceding section has given us a sort of answer to the question of Aratus' popularity, one which I shall explore further in the coming chapters, namely the role of Aratus' text in ancient debate. But that is not the whole story. I spoke above of the convergence of data and imagination inherent in the term *phainomena*. It is not by chance that the two meanings coexist. Our cosmology—how we imagine the universe— 'demands' number, in the form of the 'raw' data provided by observation. Although not concerned with numbers in the way Manilius (for instance) was, at its most basic level Aratus provides us with a quantifiable list or series of lists: the Northern constellations, the celestial circles, the signs of the zodiac, the weather-signs. There are some omissions, which we shall deal with later, but broadly speaking one can quantify the universe from Aratus. In addition, Aratus' text sets such observations in a wider context provided by windows in the poem such as the Hymn to Zeus and the Myth of *Dike*. These windows open onto the philosophical context of the poem, and tell us to some extent how we should read its lists. Aratus' data exists within an imaginative frame.

Aratus' fusion of data and imagination is not a foregone conclusion, but it looks familiar to us because we are at the other end of the same cultural phenomenon. It is not inherently necessary to have a grasp of astronomical number or mechanics to construct a view of the universe. But our cosmology has developed that way. This was recognized in the 1950s by Kuhn:

> Today we take it for granted that astronomy should affect cosmology. If we want to know the shape of the universe, the earth's position in it, or the relation of the earth to the sun and the sun to the stars, we ask the astronomer or perhaps the physicist. They have made detailed quantitative observations of the heavens and the earth; their knowledge of the universe is guaranteed by

the accuracy with which they predict its behavior. Our everyday conception of the universe, our popular cosmology, is one product of their painstaking researches. But this close association of astronomy and cosmology is both temporally and geographically local. Every civilization and culture of which we have the records has had an answer for the question, 'What is the structure of the universe?' But only the Western civilizations which descend from Hellenistic Greece have paid much attention to the appearance of the heavens in arriving at the answer. The drive to construct cosmologies is far older and more primitive than the urge to make systematic observations of the heavens.[63]

Kuhn's observations are useful in understanding Aratus and his cardinal position in the history of science. Aratus is the first author to make the union between astronomy (data) and cosmology (imagination) in a form accessible to many readers. Aratus accommodates both cosmology and astronomy. He combined technical astronomy with a sense of the larger structures, physical and ethical, of the universe, and he did it in a literary form not just readable but beautiful, illustrative in itself of human ordering capacity. It is the opening Hymn to Zeus of the *Phaenomena* which carries much of the cosmological, as opposed to astronomical, weight. But here is another feature of the *Phaenomena*: the modality of the Hymn, and therefore of the philosophical frame of the poem, varies from translation to translation, era to era. The Hymn provides the cosmological shell in which the astronomical data can nestle, and the hymn changes radically in the course of its life, from Aratus' praise of the Zeus of Stoic philosophy, to the commutation of Zeus into the Roman emperor in Germanicus' first-century translation, to the Neoplatonic Jupiter of Avienus' fourth-century interpretation, and the understated humanist learning and light-touch didacticism of Camerarius in 1535.[64]

Aratus' is a fundamental text in the development of Western science, since it is predicated on a fusion, dynamic and creative, between data (astronomy) and imagination (cosmology). Its most successful survival strategy lies in its simultaneous plasticity and constancy. Cosmologies will 'evolve' as paradigm replaces paradigm in seismic series. The raw astronomical data will not evolve. In all of the translations which follow his original text, the astonomical data are—more or less—a constant, although authors may tweak and update. But the information in the text comes to serve many different ends, in translations—replacing one thought-mode or philosophical frame with another—and in scientific debate. The bipolarity of the *Phaenomena*, which sits so well within the unique history of Western cosmology, is its success.

Programme of the Book

This book spans the period from Aratus' own work (composed c.276 BC[65]) to its translation by Avienus in the second half of the fourth century AD.[66] This exploration, even given the inevitable need to impose limits, reveals a conversation between related texts which lasts more than seven hundred years. In this conversation Aratus plays a leading, but by no means lonely, role. Many texts which have not been considered as part of the repertoire of Aratean studies are also present, with Aratus himself as the harmonizing force between texts and concepts often disparate, even at odds. I begin in chapter 1 with the most accessible part of Aratus' text, the Myth of *Dike*, goddess of Justice, at *Phaenomena* 96–136. It has been rightly recognized time and again that this nearly unique *mythic* episode in the *Phaenomena* is informed by its author's rereading of Hesiod's Myth of the Races.[67] It has not been sufficiently noted, however, that *two* models are present in the *Dike* myth: alongside Hesiod is Empedocles. Further, I argue, Aratus places Hesiod in dialogue with Empedocles as a means of negotiating concepts of time in the myth: historical sequence, in the form of Hesiod's timeline of human degeneration, and cyclical time, in the form of an endlessly repeating cosmic cycle. The pattern of allusion reinforces the narrative in which Aratus commutes Hesiod's sequence into cycle, by converting *Dike* from a goddess, as she is in Hesiod, into a constellation. Further, I shall argue that we are to see Empedocles in Aratus' text as a means of reinstatement of poetry; not poetry-as-myth, but poetry with a claim to cosmic truth, and therefore a good model for Aratus' own undertaking in the *Phaenomena*. I would see *Dike* as an answer to the problem of poetry posed by Plato in *Republic* 10. Poetry, there, was banished because of its flawed plausibility, a plausibility amounting to seductiveness in its worst sense. It has been said that Plato, in the Myth of Er at the end of the *Republic*, 'replaced' poetic myth with prose philosophical myth.[68] Aratus, in his own discussion of Justice, represents the pendulum swing. Aratus in turn replaced Plato's prose myth with poetic myth, but poetic myth with a claim to cosmic truth, something which would not be the case if it drew exclusively on Hesiod. We need his readings of successive texts to create the poetic veracity as well as the chronological strata of his work. His is both a resolution of Plato's problem, and a programme for his own work.

Dike answers, economically and elegantly, the essential question posed by Aratus and the tradition. Why so popular? Because this text is the first accessible coalescence of astronomical data with a cosmology which embraces the world in all its levels, including human morality. In this, she is emblematic of Aratus' undertaking as a whole. Unlike Plato, Aratus does not force us to choose between poetry and philosophy.

If Aratus' debate is enacted in the *Dike* myth predominantly on the theoretical level, history remains of principal concern to his Roman translators, and this is the subject of chapter 2. Here I take three Roman authors—Virgil, Germanicus, and Lucretius—and show how they engage with Aratus. Civil war is uppermost in the Roman tradition of the interpretation of Aratus' *Dike* myth, and this repeating historical quirk of Roman identity obtrudes on Aratus' text. This is equally the case whether the interpretative strategy is allusion to it, as in the case of Virgil, or translation of it, as in Germanicus. One thing which will emerge from this chapter is a new picture of the interaction of sources in Roman approaches to Aratus. It has been rightly recognized that Aratus' Roman translators interpret the *Dike* myth in terms of Roman cultural concerns.[69] What has not been recognized, however, is the continuing dialogue between Aratus and Plato. Plato is used to theorize the Aratean cosmos in the light of human interactions within it, particularly in the form of civil war. Characteristically in the Roman tradition, engagement with Plato is achieved on the level of a sophisticated intertextuality. Plato and Aratus collaborate in the Roman tradition. The effect of this is to provide a theoretical as well as a cosmic framework for Roman discussions of civil war. Further, civil war takes on a cosmic significance, a significance mirrored in a philosophical debate centred around Aratus as a key model, between 'intelligent-design' models of the universe, and atomic randomness. More and more, the universe takes on the characteristics of atomism in the face of civil war, and the textual blueprint for shaping this view of the world is found in the polemical use of Aratus by Lucretius.[70]

By the end of chapter 2 we will have reached a point where the clash between opposing world views, one of which Aratus represents, begins to emerge from our study of the *Dike* myth across cultures. We will have begun to see how Lucretius plays a seminal role in the formation of the debate within the Roman tradition. In chapter 3 we begin to lay bare the anatomy of Lucretius' achievement on the larger scale. The architecture of his work consists—to a much greater degree than people think, as I will argue in depth—of engagement with a key intelligent design model, Cicero's translation of Aratus. Lucretius' rule of engagement, I will argue, is a no-holds-barred approach to Cicero's text, with allusions to it being freely scattered across the *De rerum natura*, to be reused as grist to a peculiarly Lucretian polemical mill. I will argue that Lucretius, in fact, engages almost constantly with Cicero's *Aratea* throughout his *De rerum natura*.

This position is by no means a foregone conclusion, and may seem fanciful or even perverse to some (viz., the scholarly debate detailed in section 3.2.1), so I will argue for it in systematic fashion. I will consider first the external evidence for interest in Aratus in Rome during the 50s BC, when Lucretius was composing the *De rerum natura*, showing how plausible it is that Lucretius had Aratus, and Cicero's translation of Aratus, to hand. Secondly, the internal evidence: allusions to Cicero in Lucretius. In this respect, an essential tool towards the reading of both chapter 3 and chapter 4 is appendix B, which aims to collect every reference to Cicero in the *De rerum natura*. This appendix synthesizes and supersedes the prejudicial list of Merrill (1921) and the more scattered approach in the 'Loci Similes' of Buescu (1941). I begin in chapter 3 by drawing out some of the allusions listed in appendix B, first in the astronomical section of the *De rerum natura*. These are interpreted against the background of Lucretius' attitudes to religion and intelligent design. This proves that Lucretius had Cicero in mind for his astronomy; but the value of this is limited according to subject matter.

In chapter 4, therefore, I expand my study of Ciceronian influence on Lucretius outwards from the astronomical section of *DRN* 5, studied in chapter 3, to many other, *non*-astronomical, passages of the *DRN*. We will see how the influence of the *Aratea* extends well beyond the purely astronomical parts of the *DRN*. Taken together, chapters 3 and 4 paint a picture of 'polemical allusion' in respect of Lucretius' approach to the *Aratea*. Lucretius alludes to Cicero's *Aratea* not only when he is talking about astronomy, but consistently in places where he is at odds with a Stoic or a more generally divinely determined vision of the world. His portrait of Epicurus in the proems to *DRN* 1, 3, and 5, requires careful negotiation of this view of the world and his hero's place within it, and Cicero's *Aratea* has a part in the delicate balancing act which Lucretius undertakes. Not only that, but Lucretius works thematic allusion to the *Aratea* into passages on the divinization of heroes in general (spurious, for the Epicurean); on the tyranny of religion (a fundamental Epicurean tenet), and into his discussion of concepts such as the afterlife (illusory, in Epicurean terms). Cicero's *Aratea* is the bedrock of Lucretius' polemic in all these cases. Allusion to the *Aratea* in Lucretius is thoroughgoing and philsophically pointed. Lucretius evokes a Stoic view of the universe for its language and expression precisely at points where he differs most gravely from its philosophical thrust.

In chapters 3 and 4, then, I show how Aratus, seen predominantly through the refracting prism of Cicero's translation, was an essential element in Roman cosmological debate. By the end of chapter 4, also, we will begin to see how Ciceronian and Lucretian resonances interact in discussions about the *human* sphere, namely the Roman evocation of civil strife. This will form the subject of chapter 5, which both follows on from the philosophical concerns of chapters 3 and 4, and picks up the historical threads of chapter 2, weaving them into a broader canvas. So far, we will have been led to see Aratus as an icon of order. In this chapter, three elements of *disorder* in Aratus come to the fore. These are planetary motion, namelessness, and celestial change. About these forces of potential destabilization, Aratus is either bashful or practically mute. I will take them one by one, and show how they are raised to a position of prominence, and transformed in Roman literature of the first century AD. In early imperial literature, all three elements become part of a system of cosmic symbolism with an *inverse* relation to the orderliness of the Aratean original. In an Aratean universe irrevocably tinged, after the 50s BC, by Lucretius, Roman literature cultivates the germ of disorder. What is more, cosmic forces become emblematic of disorder in the *human* sphere, in the form of civil war. The planets, in particular, come to symbolize the disorderly motion attendant on the human familial and civic failure which results in civil conflict. Oedipus, for instance, is characterized as 'retrograde' in Statius' *Thebaid*; the transgressions of Thyestes make the sun run backwards in Seneca's tragedy. As in chapter 2, I shall again show how useful is the combination of Aratus with Plato in the context, the latter a means of theorizing cosmological material in terms of human values. This chapter will bring us full circle back to chapter 1, *Dike*, as she is transformed by Statius, but here the context will have broadened out considerably to embrace the fundamental questions of the world order and human existence.

In the Roman epic tradition, then, the archetype of order, Aratus, paradoxically contains the seeds of disorder, providing the material towards the cosmic evocation of civil war. Aratus' plasticity comes to the fore once again, in chapter 6, although here we see things in a very different light. If Roman epicists and dramatists of the first century AD 'Lucretianized' Aratus, Aratus' last antique translator, the fourth-century Avienus, 'Platonizes' Aratus, reading the *Phaenomena* through the lens of Neoplatonism.[71] This may at first seem out-of-joint with the text, but we shall see it as drawing out and making explicit currents of thought which we shall have seen as present in Aratus from the beginning. This last, complex, chapter builds in philosophical terms on what has gone before, but in addition sets Avienus like a jewel in his own fourth-century context. Avienus is not just a translator of Aratus: his work represents as well a last vivid and totalizing flowering of Latin literature. It is indicative of Aratus' enduring importance that his should have been among the voices heard at that time.

In chapter 6, we shall see how Aratus' proem becomes imbued with Neoplatonic diction and thought. We shall do this through comparing Avienus' translation of it with the fourth-century astrological writer Firmicus Maternus and with the *Hymn to King Helios* (*Oration* 4) of the Emperor Julian. This will be uncharted territory for Aratean scholars. Not only Neoplatonism: I shall show, further, how Avienus' translation fits into the cultural context of the *Panegyrici Latini*, through detailed comparison with Mamertinus' *Panegyric of the Emperor Julian* (362 AD). Together, these elements, theological and panegyrical, make up the cultural ambience of Avienus' translation. The extraordinary final transformation of the *Phaenomena* in the fourth-century context is testament to the adaptability and durability of Aratus.[72] As we shall see in the Epilogue, another writer of Neoplatonic leanings, Copernicus, was almost certainly still reading the *Phaenomena* more than ten centuries later.

It remains to offer a propitiatory sacrifice to reviewers, in the form of an enumeration of 'chapters I could have written'. These would include a chapter between 5 and 6, on the scholiastic tradition of Aratus in the first three centuries AD; and, following chapter 6, on the medieval tradition of the Aratus Latinus and the renaissance tradition represented by Camerarius' translation. My work on the latter has, in part, already been done (Gee 2008); another book would be needed to disentangle the scholiastic and medieval traditions. The aim of the present work is to show the importance of Aratus' text itself in mainstream cultural contexts.

A final word about translations. All extended passages of Latin and Greek in this book are translated. For translations of Aratus I have used Kidd (1997). All translations of Cicero's *Aratea* are my own, and use the text of Soubiran (1972). Translations of Lucretius' *De rerum natura*, and of Avienus' *Phaenomena*, are also my own. Translations of other works are discretionary and appropriately identified.

1 }

Poetic Justice

Introduction

Aratus' *Phaenomena* is a poem about the universe. It straddles the polarities of *phainomena* as information and imagination. It was seen by at least one of its earliest commentators as designed to impart technical knowledge, therefore open to corrections of a technical kind.[1] But the status of poetry as a vehicle for conveying truth is problematic, and not just because it sometimes gets its facts wrong. On the one hand, poetry carries with it the status of revealed knowledge, from Homer onwards. On the other, disquiet arises about the ability of poetry—an aesthetically seductive and, more often than not, mythic medium—to express rational truth. To deal with the problem, some in antiquity resorted to allegory;[2] others to rejection. Plato famously enacts the latter in Book 10 of his *Republic*. At *Rep.* 607b6[3] Plato reminds us of the 'ancient quarrel' (παλαιά . . . διαφορά) between poetry and philosophy, the latter representing, as much as it may, truth arrived at by objective means (although not, as we moderns are tempted to assume, truth arrived at on the evidence of sense data—rather the reverse). The quarrel may be partly a fiction, designed to lend authenticity to the Platonic debate and proposed banishment of traditional poetry from the ideal city. Whatever the case, Plato does not in the end admit poetry into his own discussion of justice. In *Republic* 10 he substitutes a *prose* philosophical myth, the Myth of Er (*Rep.* 614b1–621b7[4]) for previous *poetic* accounts of justice and its reward, which are to be rejected in the ideal city.[5] In the Myth of Er the account of judgment in the afterlife is set against the backdrop of the Platonic universe, represented by the vision of the 'Spindle of Necessity' (*Rep.* 616c5–617b9), an extended metaphor describing the circular and harmonious orbits of the heavenly bodies. For us, the point is that the Myth of Er used *astronomical* content—a vision of the orbits of the heavenly bodies—in the service of both the ethical and the poetic debate. In performing this manoeuvre Plato adopts a prose medium to express the kind of truth (we might characterize it as eschatological, speculative, mystical) which was hitherto the prerogative of poetry. In so doing he also incorporates a vision of the universe with claims to some kind of truth-status as a model of cosmic functioning.

Conversely, Aratus preserves the status of myth in a 'technical' poem, and deploys it in the poetry-as-truth context. In Aratus' Myth of *Dike* (*Phaenomena* 96–136, of which the text and translation are given in appendix A), the Goddess of Justice who became the constellation Parthenos (= Virgo in the Roman tradition), can be seen as a sequel to the Platonic myth. In Aratus, poetry and philosophy, divorced by Plato, are remarried. Aratus shows in his myth how cosmic truth might *in fact* be expressed in poetic form. He thereby offers a further corrective to the Platonic view, bringing things full circle, as it were.[6]

The Myth of *Dike* has received a lot of attention, more perhaps than any other part of the *Phaenomena*.[7] This is not surprising, since it is the only extended mythic episode in the poem, the archetypal catasterism myth in the tradition, in which *Dike* assumes a role as mediator between Zeus and mankind, reflected in her position among the stars.[8] If I may be forgiven for extreme thin-slicing of the scholarship, the two main approaches to it are represented by, on the one hand, a view of the myth as an ethically-orientated 'moralphilosophische Fabel' (Gatz 1967: 63), or, on the other, a 'moralisch irrelevanter Sternmythos' (Fakas 2001: 175). In my own addition to the debate, I shall show how Aratus uses his poetic models to provide a commentary on the utility of his own mode of discourse, namely his choice of poetry to explain astronomy. I shall examine how two models in Greek poetry, one an early Greek epicist, the forerunner of what we call 'didactic' poetry, Hesiod (eighth to seventh centuries BC), and the other a 'preoscratic philosopher,' Empedocles (fifth century BC), interact in the passage. The interaction of these two known models in the reader's interpretation of Aratus' text raises questions about the nature of time, whether an historical progression, as in Hesiod's Myth of the Races (commonly 'Myth of Ages': gold, silver, bronze, heroic, iron) in his *Works and Days*, or a repeating cycle, as in Empedoclean cosmology, set forth in either one or two works of speculative cosmology written in epic hexameters.[9]

In Hesiod and Empedocles, there coexist different, mutually incompatible, chronological schemata. Hesiod's ages delineate a descending historical spiral, with no backswing; Empedocles' universe is constituted by the cyclically recurring dominance of the cosmological principles of Love and Strife in respect of the elements which make up the universe.[10] Yet both coexist as models in Aratus' Myth of *Dike*. I shall argue that Aratus' text fosters awareness of this inconcinnity, but that it ultimately commutes Hesiodic linear time into Empedoclean cyclical time, with a particular goal in mind, to assimilate the Hesiodic mode of didactic poetry to philosophical notions of the cyclicality of the universe.

In this I shall be giving Aratus' Myth of *Dike* a wider ripple effect than is usual in scholarship. *Dike* becomes a figure of mediation not only between two modalities of poetry, mythic and philosophic broadly speaking, but also between poetry and astronomy. Aratus is to the best of our knowledge the first to fit the myth of the Goddess of Justice (*Dike*) to the constellation Parthenos. In so doing, Aratus makes Hesiod's goddess *Dike* an active participant in the cycles of the cosmos, and a Muse appropriate to the coexistence of poetry and philosophy.

1.1 Aratus and Hesiod

Dike in Aratus represents a version of the Hesiodic myth of races. The relationship between Aratus and Hesiod is self-consciously foregrounded: Aratus' verbal reminiscences are accompanied by intertextual markers. φασιν in *Ph.* 98 is an Alexandrian footnote directing us to Hesiod's passage on Astraeus as father of the stars at *Th.* 378–82. Throughout the passage Aratus points to 'old stuff,' which can be taken, alongside the textual reminiscences we are about to study, to signify the Hesiodic tradition: note ἀρχαῖον in 99 and ἀρχαίων in 103; παλαιῶν in 116.[11] At the same time, Aratus' myth is not just an alternative to Hesiod. She stands in opposition to the Hesiodic model. By turning *Dike* into a star, Aratus makes Hesiod's open-ended narrative of decline into a closed loop in which the notion of cyclicality replaces the Hesiodic timeline.

At first it is not so easy to see how this can happen. In working towards the notion of cyclicality in Aratus' interpretation of Hesiod's Myth of Ages, we can start with synchronicity—a coexistence, rather than sequential juxtaposition, of elements—as a concept intermediate between sequence and cycle. Aratus' account of *Dike* commutes Hesiodic sequence to synchronicity on several levels: by combining in one chronological period elements of several of Hesiod's ages; by combining the Myth of Ages itself with other stories from Hesiod which occur earlier or later in the text of the *Works and Days*;[12] and by combining Hesiod with other models. Aratus both comments on the Hesiodic sequence of tales within and outside the myth of ages, and provides the next stage in the evolution of alternatives. We shall deal with the first two of these types of synchronicity now, the third presently.

> 1. It is often claimed that Aratus changes the Hesiodic landscape by reducing the series of ages from five to three: Hesiod's gold-silver-bronze-heroic-iron progression becomes the more familiar gold-silver-bronze.[13] However, through Aratus' reuse of motifs from the missing ages, we can see through the lattice of the tripartite schema to the five-part schema which lies behind it. He in fact collapses the Hesiodic Ages into one another, a technique followed by his Roman translators (as we shall see in the next chapter). In *Ph.* 125–6, πόλεμοι . . . κακῶν, Aratus draws on the description of the *heroic* age at *WD* 161, πόλεμός τε κακός, although the heroic race is ostensibly elided from Aratus' account.[14] Although Aratus does not explicitly incorporate Hesiod's fourth race in his tripartite schema, nonetheless they are there intertextually, an element of the Hesiodic five-race schema behind the Aratean three races.

In the Hesiodic tradition, the heroic race already shared some of the characteristics of the golden race. In *WD* 112, the golden race ὥστε θεοὶ δ' ἔζωον ἀκηδέα θυμὸν ἔχοντες ('just like gods they spent their lives, with a spirit free from care'; text and all translations of Hesiod in this book are from Most 2006); at *WD* 170, the heroic race after death ναίουσιν ἀκηδέα θυμὸν ἔχοντες /ἐν μακάρων νήσοις ('these dwell with a spirit free from care on the islands of the blessed'). The repeated formula recalls one race (the heroic) in the context of another (the golden). So too, after death, the heroes enjoy the toil-free life of the golden race: compare *WD* 117, καρπὸν δ᾽ ἔφερε ζείδωρος ἄρουρα /αὐτομάτη ('the grain-giving field bore crops of its own accord'), with *WD* 172–3, τοῖσιν μελιηδέα καρπὸν /τρὶς ἔτεος θάλλοντα φέρει ζείδωρος ἄρουρα ('for [them] the grain-giving field bears honey-sweet fruit flourishing three times a year').[15] Nevertheless, the heroes in Hesiod remain separate from the golden race in the narrative sequence. The collapse of the races through allusion to one race in the description of another is a feature adumbrated in Hesiod which comes to fruition in Aratus, and in his Roman successors.

In addition, the way Aratus cuts-and-pastes Hesiod's *Dike* myth ensures that we dwell on the Golden Age and that the Silver and Bronze Ages each take on less significance. Although Aratus' account of the myth of the races is on the face of it a three-phase modification of Hesiod, nonetheless he devotes *exactly half* his text to the Golden Age (*Ph.*100–116) and *exactly half* to the other ages put together (*Ph.* 117–32), providing a precedent for Roman treatments of the myth, in which we move to a bipartite gold and then-everything-else pattern.[16] Aratus reconciles several different chronological patterns in his account of *Dike*: a four- or fivefold one, collapsing Hesiod's larger number of races into his own abridged version; a threefold one, with a straightforward metallic progression gold-silver-bronze; and finally a bipartite one, where gold is contrasted with all the other races.

> 2. Several episodes of Hesiod are visible at one time in this single passage of Aratus. In *Ph.* 111–12, Aratus, unlike Hesiod in the myth of the races, has agriculture exist in the Golden Age.[17] He may have been influenced here by the Hesiodic picture of the just community in his later passage on *Dike* (*WD* 225–37), where, although they share many characteristics of the golden race in that myth which preceded it, the just men ἔργα νέμονται ('do work', *WD* 231).[18] Aratus' innovation comments on the moral convergence of the Golden Age with the just society which follows it in Hesiod.[19] These two passages, sequential in Hesiod, are interwoven, appearing synchronically in Aratus' text.

What is more, Aratus' passage does not just depend on one or two passages of Hesiod, but is a nest of Hesiodic parallels. From the opening of the *Dike* passage Hesiod is both glossed and problematized, with Aratus adverting his own alterity. λόγος . . . ἄλλος ('another story') in *Ph.* 100 has long been seen to evoke Hesiod's ἕτερον λόγον ('alternative story') at the beginning of his account of the races, *WD* 106–7:

> εἰ δ᾽ ἐθέλεις, ἕτερόν τοι ἐγὼ λόγον ἐκκορυφώσω,
> εὖ καὶ ἐπισταμένως . . .

'If you wish, I shall recapitulate another story, correctly and skillfully . . .'

The Aratean phrase seems like an obvious allusion to Hesiod, but there's a mismatch between the load carried by the phrase in Hesiod and in Aratus. In Hesiod, the Myth of Races is 'another explanation' for the existence of evil in the world, and in this context 'another' makes sense. In the *Works and Days* the races followed the myth of Prometheus, to which it also provided an alternative. Hesiod's myth of the races is ἕτερον in two ways:

1. Hesiod's Myth of Races is itself 'alternative' (ἕτερον) to the myth which precedes it, that of Prometheus;
2. Both of these myths are themselves 'alternative' ways of representing Justice to the Myth of *Dike* which comes later in the *WD*.

Aratus signals these Hesiodic alternatives in his own account, in which he simultaneously alludes to all three of these passages. We have already seen how Aratus recalls both Hesiod's Myth of the Races and Hesiod's *Dike*; by embedding in addition a piece from the Prometheus myth in his *Dike* mosaic, he signals the third Hesiodic exploration of the notion of divine justice.[20] The speech of *Dike* is modelled on the speech of Zeus to Prometheus, at *WD* 54–8:[21]

Ἰαπετιονίδη, πάντων πέρι μήδεα εἰδώς,
χαίρεις πῦρ κλέψας καὶ ἐμὰς φρένας ἠπεροπεύσας,
σοί τ' αὐτῷ μέγα πῆμα καὶ ἀνδράσιν ἐσσομένοισιν.
τοῖς δ' ἐγὼ ἀντὶ πυρὸς δώσω κακόν, ᾧ κεν ἅπαντες
τέρπωνται κατὰ θυμόν, ἑὸν κακὸν ἀμφαγαπῶντες.'

"'Son of Iapetus, you who know counsels beyond all others, you are pleased that you have stolen fire and beguiled my mind—a great grief for you yourself and for men to come. To them I shall give in exchange for fire an evil in which they may all take pleasure in their spirit, embracing their own evil'".

Dike's predictive emphasis on evils (κακῶν) at *Ph.* 126 is similar to Zeus' in Hesiod (κακόν . . . κακόν, *WD* 57–8). Further, humans in Hesiod were remote from hardships until Pandora released the contents of the jar, κήδεα λυγρά (*WD* 95), which then wander about among men (*WD* 100–1). Contrast the absence of these things during the Aratean Golden Age, *Ph.* 108–11, especially λευγαλέου (108). Thus far verbal reminiscence. Thematically, Hesiod in the Prometheus myth and Aratus in the *Dike* myth give an aetiology of evil; in both cases one figure—Elpis, *Dike*—is preserved as an incentive to mankind. In contrast to Hesiod, Aratus' myth has a positive outcome: the degeneration of the ages results in a providence-given incentive to mankind, in the still-visible form of *Dike*, to become self-starters. There is also a contrast between Hesiod and Aratus in the endings of their respective myths: Hesiod's Aidos and Nemesis are 'hidden', καλυψαμένω, *WD* 198, in opposition to Aratus' *Dike*, who φαίνεται (*Ph.* 135). As well as being a mythic person (or personification) she is also physically visible. Aratus has chosen to remind us here that what we have is an 'alternative' to the Hesiodic Prometheus myth, as well as to the Hesiodic Myth of Ages itself. He thus collapses Hesiod's alternative myths into his own, single, 'alternative'.[22]

Aratus may interweave passages in his *Dike* episode which were discrete in Hesiod, and this fact may get us part of the way toward interpreting λόγος . . . ἄλλος; but as a reminiscence of Hesiod's ἕτερόν . . . λόγον Aratus' expression is still problematic. If Aratus' Myth of *Dike* is 'another story', what exactly is it 'alternative' to? Unlike in Hesiod's text, Aratus' passage is not one in a series of stories, but a one-off episode.

Aratus starts his myth by presenting two Hesiodic alternatives and apparently rejecting them both. Lines 98–9 read 'whether she is the offspring of Astraeus, who, they say, is the ancient father of the stars, or of some other'. Aratus' phrase τευ ἄλλου (*Ph.* 99) introduces a variant *aition* for the parentage of *Dike*.[23] The father of *Dike* is Zeus, at Hesiod *WD* 256. If the present personage is *Dike*, her Hesiodic father is Zeus (Aratus' τευ ἄλλου, 'some other'). But if she is a star, her Hesiodic father is Astraeus, father of the stars at *Theogony* 378–82:

Ἀστραίῳ δ' Ἠὼς ἀνέμους τέκε καρτεροθύμους,
ἀργεστὴν Ζέφυρον Βορέην τ' αἰψηροκέλευθον
καὶ Νότον, ἐν φιλότητι θεὰ θεῷ εὐνηθεῖσα.
τοὺς δὲ μέτ' ἀστέρα τίκτεν Ἑωσφόρον Ἠριγένεια
ἄστρά τε λαμπετόωντα, τά τ' οὐρανὸς ἐστεφάνωται.

> 'Eos, a goddess bedded in love with a god, bore to Astraeus the strong-spirited winds, clear Zephyrus and swift-pathed Boreas and Notus; and after these the Early-born one bore the star, Dawn-bringer, and the shining stars with which the sky is crowned'.

She can't be both; if she is *Dike* her father must be Zeus, if a star, then Astraeus. Aratus sets up, retroactively as it were, an argument between two Hesiodic source-texts. We must in the end come down against Hesiod's Zeus as parent of *Dike*, if we truly believe her to be a star, and in favour of Hesiod's Astraeus, from a different work, the *Theogony*. Having flagged 'alternatives', both deriving from Hesiodic texts, albeit different Hesiodic texts, Aratus then fails to choose between them, introducing a third alternative, λόγος ἄλλος, which turns out to be a story rather than a genealogy, still leaving open the question of the parentage of *Dike*. Aratus' text is at once inexplicable without reference to Hesiod, and inexplicable *only* in relation to the Hesiodic texts.

In fact, Aratus' *Dike* has her own unique identity, and this identity is a key step in the transition from sequence to cycle in Aratus' recasting of Hesiod. Repetition happens on two levels in Aratus' myth: the reappearance of Hesiod's *Dike* in poetry, and the cyclical reappearance of Parthenos in the sky as a constellation, bringing, as it were, the Hesiodic myth back into view in a regular pattern of looped replay. Cyclicality is already implied by Aratus' permutation of the Hesiodic myth, the most striking innovation of which in respect of Hesiod is to make *Dike* into the constellation Parthenos. This constellation was largely devoid of mythology in the Greek tradition until Aratus' identification of it with Hesiod's personified *Dike* (*WD* 213–85).[24] Aratus was the first to identify the virgin goddess (ἡ δέ τε παρθένος ἐστὶ Δίκη, Διὸς ἐκγεγαυῖα, *WD* 256) with the constellation of the Virgin (Παρθένος).[25]

We have seen how Aratus' *Dike* myth is a clever synthesis of two passages discrete in Hesiod, one of which gives a history of mankind, the other of which examines the consequences of just behaviour in two different contexts in the here-and-now. This is how justice works in both historical and synchronic time. These two types of time are best represented by the stars, which both *progress* across the heaven and *reappear* at fixed intervals, imparting an overall temporal and physical structure to the universe: Aratus unites the two in making his historical figure also celestial.

Dike is not, in Hesiod, part of the star-calendar of the *WD*, although this of course is the main theme which connects the *WD* and the *Ph. largo sensu*. In *Ph.* 112 and 132, however, Aratus makes her so, by alluding, in the context of his *Dike* myth, to the passage on ploughing (*WD* 405–92), which is in the *calendrical* part of Hesiod's work (see appendix A section (iv) for the exact correspondences). Here is the opening of the calendar in which ploughing is situated:

Πληιάδων Ἀτλαγενέων ἐπιτελλομενάων
ἄρχεσθ' ἀμήτου, ἀρότοιο δὲ δυσομενάων. (*WD* 383–4)

'When the Atlas-born Pleiades rise, start the harvest—the plowing, when they set'.

Hesiod's agricultural calendar begins with an astronomical marker which is cyclical as well as sequential: the farmer follows the course of a particular star-group from rising to setting, and he does this every year from its cyclical annual reappearance to its disappearance. With βόες καὶ ἄροτρα (*Ph.* 112) and βοῶν ἀροτήρων (132), Aratus alludes to what follows in *WD* 405, the essential prerequisites for successful agriculture, οἶκον μὲν πρώτιστα γυναῖκά τε βοῦν τ' ἀροτῆρα ('a house first of all, a woman, and an ox for plowing'). Hesiod's passage on ploughing is part of the section in which he expounds agricultural tasks against the background of the sidereal year. The reader is transported by the allusion to this passage in Aratus' *Dike* narrative from the moralizing myths of the early part of the *Works and Days* into the Hesiodic star-calendar. Even before *Dike* is actually herself turned into a constellation, we view her throughout the Aratean passage from the vantage point of the stars.

Aratus also makes *Dike* a 'proleptic star' in ways other than by Hesiodic allusion. Linguistically she behaves as a constellation before she actually becomes one: at *Ph.* 118, she emerges (ἤρχετο, 'rises') at sunset (ὑποδείελος), a time when the stars naturally become visible, appearing to rise on the horizon. The adjective ὑποδείελος occurs only here and in *Ph.* 826, there used explicitly of sunset.[26] Likewise, εἰσωπός in 122 is used elsewhere in the *Phaenomena* (eg. 78–9) of the visibility of stars, and according to Kidd, 'The word is a reminder of the star context of this whole passage, and looks forward to φαίνεται (135).'[27]

There is a spatial progression involved too. In the Silver Age, Aratus' *Dike* comes from the mountains (ὀρέων, *Ph.* 118) to admonish the Silver Age and disappears back into the mountains (ὀρέων, *Ph.* 127) after her speech, mirroring the action of a constellation rising and setting, even before she becomes one. Finally, ὑπουρανίη (*Ph.* 134) marks *Dike*'s final metamorphosis into a constellation. The word is used elsewhere by Aratus of the 'supraheavenly figures', i.e., the constellations (*Ph.* 616–18). In her act of leaping, *Dike* does not just head 'heavenwards' but *becomes* a constellation. *Dike* as Parthenos is now cyclical, a part of the zodiac, whose movements take place in a closed circle; as Aratus himself tells us elsewhere (*Ph.* 497–9), part of the zodiac is always visible above the horizon, part revolves below. She is always there, periodically as well as predictably visible.

1.2 Aratus and Empedocles

Dike as a star, in Aratus' sequel to Hesiod, participates in the cycles of the universe. Thus we have moved from synchronicity to cycle. The coexistence in Aratus of another model—Empedocles—alongside Hesiod makes it doubly so.[28] Aratus invokes Empedocles at two points in the Myth of *Dike*, (i) the absence of conflict in the Golden Age (*Ph.* 108–9),[29] and (ii) the eating of plough-oxen, *Ph.* 132.[30] The two points at which Empedocles intrudes frame the Hesiodic story of decline. Both of these are reminiscences of the same passage of Empedocles, fragment 128 (= Inwood 122/128).1–3:[31]

> οὐδέ τις ἦν κείνοισιν Ἄρης θεὸς οὐδὲ Κυδοιμός,
> οὐδὲ Ζεὺς βασιλεὺς οὐδὲ Κρόνος οὐδὲ Ποσειδῶν,
> ἀλλὰ Κύπρις βασίλεια . . .

'They had no god Ares or Battle-Din,
nor Zeus the king nor Kronos nor Poseidon;
but Kupris the queen . . .' (trans. Inwood 2001).

In Empedocles' cosmology, the world moves through a recurring twofold cosmic cycle created by pendulum swings between the successive actions of Love and Strife upon the elements. In this passage he describes the rule of Love under the designation Kupris (= Aphrodite). It is to this passage that Aratus alludes at *Ph.*108–9,

> οὔπω λευγαλέου τότε νείκεος ἠπίσταντο
> οὐδὲ διακρίσιος περιμεμφέος οὐδὲ κυδοιμοῦ.

'At that time they still had no knowledge of painful strife or quarrelsome conflict or noise of battle' (Kidd).

Κυδοιμοῦ may be the Empedoclean principle of Strife (*Neikos*).[32] Strife is absent from Aratus' Golden Age; the rule of *Dike* is tantamount, on such a reading, to the dominance in the world of Empedoclean Love. A reading of *Dike*-as-Love is supported by Aratus' use of her Empedoclean opposite νείκεος (= Empedocles' Νεῖκος[33]) in the line before, line 108. Traglia at least detected further Empedoclean reminiscence in Aratus' διακρίσιος περιμεμφέος (*Ph.* 109), where διάκρισις is said to be the semantic equivalent of Empedoclean διάλλαξις, the term used in fr.8 (= Inwood 21/8) for elemental 'separation' under the control of Strife, the opposite of μίξις:

ἄλλο δέ τοι ἐρέω· φύσις οὐδενός ἐστιν ἁπάντων
θνητῶν, οὐδέ τις οὐλομένου θανάτοιο τελευτή,
ἀλλὰ μόνον μίξις τε διάλλαξίς τε μιγέντων
ἐστί, φύσις δ' ἐπὶ τοῖς ὀνομάζεται ἀνθρώποισιν.

'I shall tell you something else. There is no growth of any of all mortal things
nor any end in destructive death,
but only mixture and interchange of what is mixed
exist, and growth is the name given to them by men'.

At the same time as Aratus' *Dike* participates in Hesiod's ages, she may also call to mind Empedoclean opposites. Note further ἀναμίξ in *Ph.*104 and ἐπιμίσγετο in *Ph.* 119. Although these terms have usually been taken to denote social 'interaction', given other Empedoclean allusions in this part of Aratus, they might be seen as containing an additional level of meaning, picking up the Empedoclean concept of mixture, the phenomenon of elemental attraction which happens under the dominance of Love. In the Golden Age part of Aratus' *Dike* myth we have inscribed alongside the Hesiodic Golden Age a picture of the Empedoclean dominance of Love at the point where she is directly involved in governing the world. We might see *Dike* as Empedoclean Love, mingled (*Ph.* 104) with everything in the Golden Age; her progressive separation from mankind is analogous to the separation of the elements on the cosmic level, as we see it in Empedoclean cosmology, which leads ultimately to the rule of Strife.[34] Aratus' text, through its bifurcation of models, manages to set up a parallelism between the microcosm (man, represented in Hesiod's Myth of Ages) and the macrocosm (the universe, represented in Empedoclean cosmology).

The argument for a stronger Empedoclean presence in the *Dike* passage than hitherto recognized can be supported by the existence of Empedoclean reminiscence in the *Phaenomena* at large.[35] Empedocles' influence is thoroughgoing and significant. Among Empedocles' surviving fragments, fr.17 (= Inwood 25/17) is of particular relevance for the present discussion. This fragment seems to be Empedocles' main exposition of cyclical change and the roles of Love and Strife. It is therefore significant that Aratus draws on Empedocles' terms in this fragment. Aratus reuses almost exactly the Empedoclean clausula of fr.17.19, νεῖκός τ' οὐλόμενον δίχα τῶν, ἀτάλαντον ἁπάντῃ, 'destructive strife apart from these, alike in every respect,' in his description of the earth's axis:

οἱ μὲν ὁμῶς πολέες τε καὶ ἄλλυδις ἄλλοι ἐόντες
οὐρανῷ ἕλκονται πάντ' ἤματα συνεχὲς αἰεί·
αὐτὰρ ὅ γ' οὐδ' ὀλίγον μετανίσσεται, ἀλλὰ μάλ' αὕτως
ἄξων αἰὲν ἄρηρεν, ἔχει δ' ἀτάλαντον ἁπάντη
μεσσηγὺς γαῖαν, περὶ δ' οὐρανὸν αὐτὸν ἀγινεῖ.   (*Ph.* 19–23)

'The numerous stars, scattered in different directions, sweep all alike across the sky every day continuously forever. The axis, however, does not move even slightly from its place, but just stays forever fixed, holds the earth in the centre evenly balanced, and rotates the sky itself.'

There may be an additional echo of Empedocles in the same passage of Aratus, namely *Ph.* 19–20. Aratus' ἄλλυδις ἄλλοι ἐόντες /οὐρανῷ ἕλκονται πάντ' ἤματα συνεχὲς αἰεί ('. . . scattered in different directions, sweep all alike across the sky every day continuously forever') is a close echo of Empedocles fr. 17 (= Inwood 25/17).34–5:

ἀλλ' αὔτ' ἔστιν ταῦτα, δι' ἀλλήλων δὲ θέοντα
γίγνεται ἄλλοτε ἄλλα καὶ ἠνεκὲς αἰὲν ὁμοῖα.

'But these very things are, and running through each other
    they become different at different times and are always, perpetually alike'
(Inwood).

The allusion to Empedocles in Aratus underlines the contrast between the stars, which are numerous and moving, πολέες τε καὶ ἄλλυδις ἄλλοι ἐόντες, with the stability of the earth. In Empedocles fr. 17, the contrast is between the ever-changing elements and the unchangeability of the principles of their mixture and separation, Love and Strife. In both authors there is a contrast between one and many, the stable and the movable. For Aratus, the stars in their multiplicity take on the role of Empedocles' elements, the axis the role of a separate ordering principle.

Aratus may have these same Empedoclean lines in mind in his description of the alternation of the phases of the moon at *Ph.* 779–81:[36]

Ἄλλοτε γάρ τ' ἄλλῃ μιν ἐπιγράφει ἕσπερος αἴγλη,
ἄλλοτε δ' ἀλλοῖαι μορφαὶ κερόωσι σελήνην
εὐθὺς ἀεξομένην, αἱ μὲν τρίτῃ, αἱ δὲ τετάρτῃ·

'Different evenings paint [the moon] with different light, and different shapes at different times horn the moon as soon as she is waxing, some on the third day, some on the fourth . . .'

Again, the force of the echo lies in its contrast of stability (repetition) with multiplicity (of many phases). In Aratus there is the same set of contrasts as in Empedocles, between unity and mutability, stability and rupture, dynamism and stillness.

Aratus chooses to wheel out Empedocles at signal moments in the *Phaenomena*, where he wants us to think both of the multiplicity of the individual elements of the universe, and the stability of the overall framework which holds it together. This is so in the description of the earth's axis, in the description of the moon's phases, and in the myth of *Dike*, where diachrony (the progressive movement of *Dike* as a star, and the historical progress of the ages) is coextensive with synchronicity (the constant recurrence of the stars; a two-phase repeating vision of the world's history).

To return, then, to the *Dike* passage, armed now with a greater notion of the extent of Empedocles' influence on the *Phaenomena*, we must ask what Empedocles *does* for our reading. Several answers are possible.

1. We have noted the overlay of Hesiod with Empedocles. Embedded in Aratus' text are two models containing different notions of time: the Hesiodic sequence of ages, and the Empedoclean cycle of the universe. Our two models of time in Aratus fulfil different functions. In cosmological terms, *Dike* informs the workings of the universe; in human terms her presence and withdrawal represent the working of the divine plan. To express this on the human scale, Aratus draws on the Hesiodic Myth of Ages; for the cosmic extension, he draws on Empedocles. The coexistence of the two models represents the parallel between microcosm and macrocosm.

2. Because of its use of Empedocles, this story is always going to be slightly edgy, imperfect in both its fusion of models and in its narrative outcome. 'Love' and 'Strife' are morally neutral cosmogonic principles. In Empedocles fr. 35 they can both be described as 'blameless', following a natural order of things, doing what they do. We may be meant to recall their neutrality in Aratus. Aratus' hapax legomenon περιμεμφέος in *Ph.* 109 may be formed on the analogy of Empedocles' ἀμεμφέως and ἀμεμφέος used of the mutually 'blameless' actions of Love and Strife in Empedocles fragment 35 (= Inwood 61/35.9 and 13). Unlike the Golden Age, neither stage of the two-stage cycle can provide a flawless model of polity or a utopian notion of an ideal time-period in history.[37] In the case of Aratus' *Dike* the coexistence of models is part of the story the myth has to tell: a period of harmony is followed by a period of disruption, which is, however, necessary for the development of the world/mankind. We might say that the dominance of Love is a paradox: Love represents stability, but (in Empedoclean terms) Love has to go, in order to restore the world to a state (the rule of Strife) in which each of its components is discernible as a separate entity.[38] Reading Empedocles thus impacts on our interpretation of a positive outcome of the myth of *Dike*: ἔτι φαίνεται (*Ph.* 135), as a sign that, despite Dike's departure, things are as they are meant to be.

3. Aratus' use of Empedocles is significant in itself, independent of its relation with the Hesiodic model. Empedocles' poetry is not epic narrative in the traditional Homeric sense, or (to borrow Plato's word in *Rep.* 607b) 'mimetic'. Empedocles has a lot more to say to us about Aratus' poetic project at large.

Aratus uses a poetic model who is not a poet. This is what Aristotle said in *Poetics* 1447b: οὐδὲν δὲ κοινόν ἐστιν Ὁμήρῳ καὶ Ἐμπεδοκλεῖ πλὴν τὸ μέτρον, διὸ τὸν μὲν ποιητὴν δίκαιον καλεῖν, τὸν δὲ φυσιολόγον μᾶλλον ἢ ποιητήν ('But Homer and Empedocles have nothing in common except the metre: so that it would be proper to call the one a poet and the other not a poet but a scientist', trans. Halliwell 1973). Aristotle strips Empedocles of the status of poet on the grounds that he talked about 'real stuff', or as Halliwell puts it elsewhere, used language for 'affirmative purposes', that is, the expression of truth.[39] It is for this very reason that Aratus is rehabilitating Empedocles as a poet, by the way in which he embeds his Empedoclean reminiscence in a uniquely mythic part of the *Phaenomena*.

He reinstates Empedocles as a poet, furthermore, who enables him to represent cosmic truth in poetic form. In the *Dike* myth, he steps back and meditates on his medium, through his use of models, to show how poetry—*his* kind of poetry—*can* act as the medium of truth. Empedocles in particular becomes a means by which Aratus can construct his new poetry, which at the same time as it flaunts its art, talks about 'truth' (or the reality of the cosmos). Aratus provides an anti-Aristotelian response to the Platonic problem of poetry and truth. You *can* be Empedocles, striving to express cosmological truth, but *still* write poetry.

1.3 *Dike*-as-Muse

In this debate, *Dike* takes on the role of Muse, albeit a new kind: the Muse of astronomical poetry.[40] Aratus casts her as a Muse-figure through reference both to his own invocation of the Muses in the *Phaenomena*, and to the tradition outside his own poem. First, *Dike* in the Silver Age no longer 'associated with anyone using sweet words,' οὐδέ τεῳ ἐπεμίσγετο μειλιχίοισιν (*Ph.* 119), as she had done in the Golden Age. This is one of only two occurrences of the adjective μειλίχιος in the *Ph.*: the other is in the description of the Muses at the beginning of the poem (*Ph.* 16–17, Χαίροιτε δὲ Μοῦσαι, /μειλίχιαι μάλα πᾶσαι). Second, *Dike* is intertextually related to Hesiod's Muses at the beginning of the *Theogony*.[41] She shares a descriptor with the Muses of the *Theogony*, namely ἐννυχίη (*Ph.* 135; *Th.* 10). Aratus' reference to Hesiod's Muses is the more pointed because this is the only place in the *Ph.* where he uses this adjective. There's both an echo of, and a contrast with, Hesiod's Muses: they go about at night, praising Zeus, wreathed in shadows (κεκαλυμμέναι ἠέρι πολλῷ, *Theog.* 9): *Dike* whirls above at night in perfect clarity (φαίνεται, *Ph.* 135). If *Dike* is a Muse, she is a 'transparent' one, unlike Hesiod's Muses, who have the capacity to conceal the truth (*Theog.* 26–8):

'ποιμένες ἄγραυλοι, κάκ' ἐλέγχεα, γαστέρες οἶον,
ἴδμεν ψεύδεα πολλὰ λέγειν ἐτύμοισιν ὁμοῖα,
ἴδμεν δ' εὖτ' ἐθέλωμεν ἀληθέα γηρύσασθαι.'

'Field-dwelling shepherds, ignoble disgraces, mere bellies: we know how to say many things similar to genuine ones, but we know, when we wish, how to proclaim true things.'.

At the departure of Aratus' *Dike*, Hesiod's Muse-figure is translated to the heavens, a symbol of astronomical poetry, the poetry of truth.

There may be another intertextual reference in Aratus' text, one which again throws into relief the debate about the role of poetry. The verb in *Phaenomena* 107, δημοτέρας ἤειδεν ἐπισπέρχουσα θέμιστας, does not sit easily in the *Dike* myth. ἤειδεν means something like 'she *sang/prophesied*'. With its intimations of song and incantation, ἀείδω seems to be an odd expression to use in the context of the otherwise rational, modern, and people-centred judgements of *Dike* (δημοτέρας . . . θέμιστας, *Ph.* 107).

We find a compound of the same verb used by Plato in the same passage of the *Republic* in which he discusses the 'ancient quarrel', namely 607a–608a. Here again it seems odd, although for a different reason. Plato's protagonists argue that there is no place for poetry in the ideal city, unless a poetry which feeds the regime by praise of its great men. If those who love poetry could plead her case in rational *unmetrical* prose (ἄνευ μέτρου λόγον, *Rep.* 607d6–7), then they should be given a fair hearing. But as long as poetry remains undefended, they must keep on trying to drown it out with a prophylactic chanting of the counter-arguments: ἐπᾴδοντες ἡμῖν αὐτοῖς τοῦτον τὸν λόγον, ὃν λέγομεν, καὶ ταύτην τήν ἐπῳδήν, *Rep.* 608a3–4. Plato's recipe for the new city is that poetry should be defended in prose; but paradoxically, such rational prose argumentation is 'sung'; moreover, its singing is a 'charm', ἐπῳδή. Poetry should have its own magic used against it.

In Plato, the prophylactic 'incantation' paradoxically takes the form of prose argument; in Aratus, *Dike* the lawgiver, equally paradoxically, 'sings' her judgements.[42] Aratus' text replaces, as it were, Plato's prose replacement for poetry, with a different kind of poetry, one consonant, perhaps, with the ideal, ungraspable in Plato, of poetry as a vehicle for truth. At the same time, the poetry with which Aratus 'answers' Plato is of a special kind. It is not Plato's 'mimetic' poetry (*Rep.* 607c5) in the Homeric tradition, but technical poetry about the makeup and functioning of the natural world, in the form of Empedoclean epic.

In Aratus and the ensuing tradition, then, the Muse has been translated to the stars; poetically, Hesiodic epos is transmuted with the help of Empedocles into the poetry of the cosmos. Poetry can sing lies, but it can also convey truth, and this is what Aratus' poetry does, in the character of *Dike*. *Dike* is a paradigm for Aratus' work: she unites the two meanings of φαινόμενα. She is both real and mythical, a star and a symbol.

Conclusion

Dike in Aratus acts as a mediating figure in more than one way: she unites, perhaps for the first time, astronomy and cosmology. As a goddess, she is part of an ethical system, a cosmology, in which the world is engineered in such a way as to favour particular conduct, illustrated through a linear model of human development; as a constellation she is part of a cyclical astronomical system. Because of her status as both mythic figure and constellation, a dual status given to her by Aratus himself as the originator of the identification between *Dike* and the constellation Parthenos, she stands as a metaphor for the association between the technical and the mythical central to Aratus' undertaking. *Dike* 'is apparent' φαίνεται (*Ph.* 135) in both senses: she is both observable and symbolic, and is thus able to bridge two worlds, as does the poem.

In giving an explanation for man's fall, *Dike* functions like Plato's Muses in the *Republic* (*Rep.* 545d7–e1 ἢ βούλει, ὥσπερ Ὅμηρος, εὐχώμεθα ταῖς Μούσαις εἰπεῖν ἡμῖν ὅπως δὴ πρῶτον στάσις ἔμπεσε, 'Shall we invoke the Muses, like Homer, and ask them to tell us "how the quarrel first began"?', trans. Lee 2007). In the *Republic* the Muses introduced an alternative model of storytelling, that of philosophical myth, a mode of discourse in which the story is now connected to cosmic truth. Aratus reverses the process, reintroducing poetry into his account of the universe. Through *Dike*, Aratus enacts in verse what Plato had done in prose, claiming for himself a new type of myth, myth used to flag the moral significance of technical verse: a link between astronomical data (the positions of the constellations) and the human understanding of the world as a whole (cosmology).

2 }

Roman Justice

That is how science advances: each new conceptual scheme embraces the
phenomena explained by its predecessors and adds to them.

—Kuhn 1957: 264

Introduction

A text is an organism poised between dynamism and stasis. Aratus' text at its point
of composition is a dynamic act in which sources or ideologies strain against one
another. In the previous chapter I have laid bare the anatomy of this phenomenon.
But when a particular text becomes in its turn a resource (a 'source') for later tradition, the world of that text stops spinning. The text becomes a static artefact which
may be picked up, examined, and placed in its turn in fertile relationship with other
source texts.

A line of ancestry extends, in respect of the myth of ages, from Hesiod to Plato,
and via Aratus to his Roman successors. In the earliest text, that of Hesiod, the
cosmic process evolves organically through the acts of the gods in the creating and
destroying of the races. In Plato, various types of fit between the myth and the cosmos are tried out for size. Aratus is the first to meld together, apparently seamlessly,
the cosmological aspect of the myth with the astronomical data. His Roman successors follow, mapping astronomy onto human society, as an adjunct to the historical
narrative of Rome.

The genealogy is not linear, however. Virgil, for instance, reads Aratus through
Plato, as Aratus himself read Hesiod through Empedocles. Not only is the earlier
text recast in each case by reference to the later, but a later text such as Aratus can
conversely be redefined in relation to an earlier one (Plato) with which its own relationship is only at best implicit. The recombination of textual DNA takes place
through synchrony rather than sequence. The Myth of Ages is a good metaphor for
this process.

Let us begin by looking at Plato's take on it, in the passage referred to at the end
of the previous chapter. There, we saw how *Dike* in Aratus takes a role analogous
to the Muses at *Rep.* 545d8–e1, εὐχώμεθα ταῖς Μούσαις εἰπεῖν ἡμῖν ὅπως δὴ

πρῶτον στάσις ἔμπεσε; ('Shall we invoke the Muses, like Homer, and ask them to tell us "How the quarrel first began"?', trans. Lee 2007). Like Plato's Muses, *Dike* becomes the catalyst for and overseer of the story of how human societies fall apart. There is more to this than a simple functional parallel between *Dike* and the Muses. In fact, the whole passage in Plato is itself a self-conscious reinterpretation of Hesiod's Myth of Ages, a reinterpretation which, before Aratus, yokes the myth to a cosmology informed by an awareness of astronomical cycles. It is this connection which Aratus brought to fruition.

Like Aratus, Plato draws on Hesiod for the mythic framework which will enable him to explain how strife arises in the ideal city. His narrative is glossed by citation of Hesiod's races (τὰ Ἡσιόδου τε καὶ τὰ παρ' ὑμῖν γένη, χρουσοῦν τε καὶ ἀργυροῦν καὶ χαλκοῦν καὶ σιδηροῦν, 'the metals from which the different classes of your citizens, like Hesiod's, are made—gold, silver, bronze, and iron' *Rep.* 547a1–3, trans. Lee 2007).[1] Plato fudges his source a bit: note how the sequence is already modified, with the omission of the heroes who stood between bronze and iron in Hesiod. In the passage which immediately follows at *Rep.* 547a2–5, war is said to result from the *mixing* of these races:[2] ὁμοῦ δὲ μιγέντος σιδηροῦ ἀργυρῷ καὶ χαλκοῦ χρυσῷ ἀνομοιότης ἐγγενήσεται καὶ ἀνωμαλία ἀνάρμοστος, ἃ γενόμενα, οὗ ἂν ἐγγένηται, ἀεὶ τίκτει πόλεμον καὶ ἔχθραν ('And when iron and silver or bronze and gold are mixed, an inconsistent and uneven material is produced, whose irregularities, whenever they occur, must engender war and hatred').[3] Because of the interrelatedness of Plato's races (each representing not just a family tree in the sequence of the metallic ages, but also an aspect of civic function in the ideal state) this war is civil war, the στάσις of 245e1 and 547b2.[4]

Plato's reading of Hesiod's races precipitates two ideas, mixture and civil war. There is a third element: astronomy, albeit a highly schematized and abstract astronomy. In *Rep.* 546a1–6, Plato's Socrates describes the cycles of the *state*, using terminology which could, and elsewhere did, apply to the *celestial* cycles:

> χαλεπὸν μὲν κινηθῆναι πόλιν οὕτω ξυστᾶσαν, ἀλλ' ἐπεὶ γενομένῳ παντὶ φθορά ἐστιν, οὐδ' ἡ τοιαύτη σύστασις τὸν ἅπαντα μενεῖ χρόνον, ἀλλὰ λυθήσεται. λύσις δὲ ἥδε· οὐ μόνον φυτοῖς ἐγγείοις, ἀλλὰ καὶ ἐπιγείοις ζῴοις φορὰ καὶ ἀφορία ψυχῆς τε καὶ σωμάτων γίγνονται, <u>ὅταν περιτροπαὶ ἑκάστοις κύκλων περιφορὰς συνάπτωσι</u> . . .

> 'It will be difficult to bring about any change for the worse in a state so constituted; but since all created things must decay, even a social order of this kind cannot last for all time, but will decline. And its dissolution will be as follows. Not only for plants that grow in the earth, but for animals that live on it, there are seasons of fertility and infertility of both mind and body, seasons which come <u>when their periodic motions come full circle</u> . . .'.

Περιτροπαί and περιφορά are astronomical terms. In astronomical parlance, the τροπαί are the sun's 'turning-points' between the southernmost and the northernmost points on the ecliptic over the course of the seasonal year: the word is thus used already by Hesiod at *WD* 479 and 564, and in Aratus *Ph.* 499. Περιφορά is used by Plato in the *Phaedrus* and elsewhere of the motion of the celestial sphere (e.g., *Phdr.* 247b7–c2, ἔστησαν ἐπὶ τῷ τοῦ οὐρανοῦ νώτῳ, στάσας δὲ αὐτὰς περιάγει ἡ περιφορά; *Phdr.* 247d4–5, ἕως ἂν κύκλῳ ἡ περιφορὰ εἰς ταὐτὸν περιενέγκῃ; cf. περιφορά and similar terms used of the rotation of the Spindle of Necessity, representing the universe, at *Rep.* 616c5, etc.). Plato envisages the phases of human social life in the state in terms of the revolutions of the sphere of the fixed stars.

Plato draws on the same lexicon in the *Politicus* myth. You might call what happens in Plato's myth a 'tropic' model of cosmic change, on the analogy of the sun's pendular motion between the tropics. To model the sun's motion from a geocentric point of view, you must take account of different kinds of motion, linear and cyclical.[5] The sun's is the most basic instance of planetary motion. In geocentric terms, in its diurnal motion the sun moves forward *with* the stars, from East to West. In its diurnal motion also, the sun moves backwards *in respect of* the stars, from West to East, since they 'go faster' around the earth than it does. That is why, in its yearly course, the sun moves through the constellations of the zodiac, as each constellation on the ecliptic (the sun's path) catches it up and overtakes it. In addition there is a linear movement across the horizon between the Northernmost and Southernmost points on the ecliptic, between the tropics. It is on the analogy of the sun's movements, around the earth and between the tropics, I believe, that Plato constructs his model of cosmic change in the *Politicus*.

The universe in Plato's myth periodically reverses its direction of rotation (e.g., *Pol.* 270 b7–8, τὸ τὴν τοῦ παντὸς φορὰν τοτὲ μὲν ἐφ' ἃ νῦν κυκλεῖται φέρεσθαι, τοτὲ δ' ἐπὶ τἀναντία, 'The movement of the universe is now in the direction of its present rotation, now in the opposite direction', trans. Rowe 1995a; text of Burnet 1900). Here we have circular rotation (κυκλεῖται—also κυκλήσεως 271d3) stopping when the divine rope untwists, and resuming the other way. But when the image is repeated, *tropic* movement is also present (*Pol.* 270d4): . . . ὅταν ἡ τῆς νῦν καθεστηκυίας ἐναντία γίγνηται τροπή ('. . . when its turning becomes the opposite of the one that now obtains', Rowe). The meaning of τροπή appears to hover between 'turning-point' and 'rotation'.[6] The ambiguity is resolved if you think of the myth as a mapping onto the *whole* cosmos of the sun's movements. Plato's vision combines rotation with backswing: the universe rotates one way, pauses, and rotates the other way. This combines the notions of circular movement with linear progression, stopping and turning. Plato's myth is constructed on the analogy of these movements as an imaginative extension of them.

In *Pol.* 271, human lives mirror these 'turnings'. Human lives progress in linear fashion, either forwards or backwards. Theirs is a parallel, and in some ways more accurate, analogy for the tropic movements of the sun than that of the universe itself, with its circular motions.

This exemplifies the way astronomy can be used to construct a cosmology, albeit in Plato's case a 'fictive', alternative, or contested one, without the implied truth-status of Aratus'. Moreover, the human world is complicit in cosmic change: when the direction of the universe is changed to its present one, the age of individuals first comes to a stop; then rewinds, as we see at *Pol.* 271b7–8. As well as quantifying cosmological cycles, astronomy also provides the analogy for the alternation described in the myth, of birth to old age/old age back to birth. This observation sets the scene for the arrival of Plato and Aratus as a duo in the Roman tradition.

2.1 Virgil 'Platonizes' Aratus

Plato is an underplayed intermediary between early Greek sources—Hesiod and Empedocles—and Aratus. In the *Politicus*, Plato replaces the Hesiodic sequence of ages with a cyclical two-stage alternation in the cosmos parallel to the human cycle of birth, growth, and death. Like Plato, Roman authors read Hesiodic time as cyclical. In the Roman tradition, the Hesiodic sequence becomes a recurrence, with the predicted *return* of the Golden Age. The idea of golden age recurrence is unique to the Roman tradition, beginning with Virgil.[7] I argue that this new feature stems from a splicing of Plato into the golden age tradition represented by Hesiod and Aratus.

First and most significantly, in the crucial first century BC in Rome, Virgil combines Aratus and Plato: he integrates Platonic myth into the Aratean material he draws on in *Eclogue* 4 and *Georgics* 2.[8] Virgil enacts a poetic trompe l'oeil, in which we see, through the Virgilian works, Plato behind Aratus, and Hesiod and Empedocles behind both. Virgil seems to draw on the *Politicus* myth as a model which collaborates effectively with his Aratean material, alluding to both Plato's myth and Aratus' *Dike* in the same contexts (*Ecl.* 4 and *Geo.* 2). An astute reader, he combines the Aratean picture with a text which accentuates the notion of temporal cyclicality, namely Plato's *Politicus* myth. Virgil brings the Aratean and Platonic myths together in a way which not only provides a sequel to both, but which can constructively inform our reading of the Aratean original. By the way in which he combines his models, Virgil glosses the connection between sequence and cycle latent in the original. Furthermore, in so doing he lays the foundation of Roman interpretations of Aratus' *Dike*, such as that of Germanicus in the first century AD, which emphasize a bipartite cyclicality as a way of explicating the fundamental Roman culture-myth of civil war.

In the passages of Virgil we are about to discuss, there are many points of contact with Aratus.[9] But Virgil also diverges from Aratus in significant ways. The reintegration of Hesiod into the golden age context provides a partial explanation for the differences. However, I am going to argue that these differences are better explained through Virgil's invocation of a model between Hesiod and Aratus, namely Plato's *Politicus*. This intermediate model already adapted Hesiod's races to the idea of cyclical time[10]

To take the fourth *Eclogue* first, in this poem, the so-called 'messianic' *Eclogue*, Virgil celebrates the birth of a boy who will restore the Golden Age.[11] Lines 6–7 allude to Aratus' Myth of *Dike*:[12]

iam redit et Virgo, redeunt Saturnia regna,
iam nova progenies caelo demittitur alto. (*Ecl.* 4.6–7)

'Now also the Virgin returns, the kingdom of Saturn comes back; now a new offspring is sent down from high heaven' (my trans.).

The allusion to Aratus works best if Virgo is envisaged as celestial, like the *nova progenies* to follow, 'sent down from high heaven', *caelo demittitur alto*. Virgo, having gone up to the stars in Aratus, is now returning, thus reversing the direction of the Aratean movement, and rewinding from the decline of justice to its reinstatement. In lines 8–9 what is envisaged is a reverse replay of the Myth of Ages, working from iron back to gold: *tu modo nascenti puero, quo ferrea primum /desinet ac toto surget gens aurea mundo, /casta fave Lucina* ('virtuous Lucina [goddess of childbirth], look well upon this boy at his birth, for whom for the first time the iron race will cease and the golden race spring up in the whole world . . .' –my trans.).

The unravelling of the order of things from iron to gold happens in stages in the body of the poem.[13] At lines 31–3 the vestiges of old imperfections are indexed through various human actions, shipping, warfare, agriculture:

pauca tamen suberunt priscae vestigia fraudis,
quae temptare Thetim ratibus, quae cingere muris
oppida, quae iubeant telluri infindere sulcos.

'But there will still be a few traces of the old imperfection, the kinds of things which induce people to tax the sea with ships, encircle towns with walls and gouge the earth with furrows.' (my trans.)

These lines recall *Ph.* 108–13 (things which were *not*, in the Golden Age):[14]

οὔπω λευγαλέου τότε νείκεος ἠπίσταντο
οὐδὲ διακρίσιος περιμεμφέος οὐδὲ κυδοιμοῦ,
αὔτως δ᾽ ἔζωον· χαλεπὴ δ᾽ ἀπέκειτο θάλασσα,
καὶ βίον οὔπω νῆες ἀπόπροθεν ἠγίνεσκον . . .

'At that time they still had no knowledge of painful strife or quarrelsome conflict or noise of battle, but lived just as they were; the dangerous sea was far from their thoughts, and as yet no ships brought them livelihood from afar . . .'

—combining with these one thing which did exist in Aratus' Golden Age, namely agriculture (*Ph.* 112–13):

ἀλλὰ βόες καὶ ἄροτρα καὶ αὐτὴ πότνια λαῶν
μυρία πάντα παρεῖχε Δίκη, δώτειρα δικαίων.

'. . . but oxen and ploughs and Justice herself, queen of the people and giver of civilized life, provided all their countless needs.'

Virgil accepts the latter's point of view on war and shipping, but banishes agriculture from his Golden Age, although it was admitted by Aratus. Already we begin to
see the extrusion of the bones of an oppositional relationship between Virgil and
Aratus. What is more, the *Saturnia regna* which Virgil prophesies will return in *Ecl.*
4 are non-Aratean: there is no reference to Saturn or Kronos in Aratus' text. The
source here might be Hesiod, *WD* 111, ἐπὶ Κρόνου. The notion of the 'return'
(*redeunt*) of the kingdom of Saturn or Kronos is nowhere in either Aratus or
Hesiod.

The opposition with the Aratean source springs to life again in Virgil's other
'golden age' description, *Georgics* 2.458–542, which is again marked by both reference to Aratus and divergence from him.[15] The point of contact between Aratus
and Virgil comes at *Geo.* 2.473–4:[16]

> . . . extrema per illos [agricolas]
> Iustitia excedens terris vestigia fecit.

> 'As she left the earth, Justice placed her final footsteps amongst farmers' (my
> trans).

Like Aratus' *Dike*, personified *Iustitia* leaves the earth in stages, of which this is
the last (*extrema*); one Virgilian innovation is that her final stage on earth
involved farmers, the last repository of virtue.[17] The Aratean reference may be in
fact more pointed than has been noted. *Vestigia* (*Geo.* 2.474) can mean both
'footsteps' and the 'path' of a heavenly body.[18] Departing Justice is a heavenly
body as well as a goddess, and *vestigia* refer to her upward trajectory (her 'rising')
as well as her 'steps'.

Virgil appears here to follow the Aratean version, identifying *Dike-Iustitia* as the
constellation Virgo. If we identify the farmers with the golden race, as we are prone
to do given their Saturnian associations in the text, then we may also see Virgil as
truncating the Aratean sequence; *Dike*'s departure from earth now takes place at
the end of the golden, rather than the subsequent ages.[19] As in the case of Virgo's
return in *Ecl.* 4, much nuance is gained by our knowledge, only possible since Aratus, that *Iustitia* is a constellation.

The Aratean allusion at *Georgics* 2.473–4 becomes more marked in the light of
the bold gestures towards Aratus which follow. First, a catalogue of subjects for
didactic poetry, beginning and ending with astronomical didactic (*Geo.* 2.475–8):

> me vero primum dulces ante omnia Musae,
> quarum sacra fero ingenti percussus amore,
> accipiant caelique vias et sidera monstrent,
> defectus solis varios lunaeque labores . . .

> 'First let the Muses, sweeter than anything, whose rites I perform, struck with
> tremendous love, receive me and show me the orbits of the stars in the heaven,
> eclipses of the sun and the various phases of the moon' (my trans.).

Virgil's Muses here are astronomical ones, heralded by the presence of *Iustitia* (*Dike*), our Aratean Muse.[20] Virgil's description of the Muses as *dulces ante omnia* reminds us too of Aratus' Muses at the beginning of the *Phaenomena*, who were μειλίχιαι μάλα πᾶσαι ('all of them honey-sweet', line 17).

Here already, Virgil enacts the writing of astronomical didactic by the citation in line 478 of the beginning of Lucretius' astronomical exegesis in the fifth book of the *De rerum natura*, namely *DRN* 5.76–7, *praeterea solis cursus lunaeque meatus /expediam*.[21] This excursus into astronomical didactic develops naturally out of the reference to Aratean Justice which precedes it. *Iustitia* as Virgil's astronomical Muse orchestrates the list of topics which follows her appearance in the text.

Aratus is also present in the description of the Golden Age at *Georgics* 2.536–40:[22]

> ante etiam sceptrum Dictaei regis et ante
> impia quam caesis gens est epulata iuvencis,
> aureus hanc vitam in terris Saturnus agebat;
> necdum etiam audierant inflari classica, necdum
> impositos duris crepitare incudibus ensis.

> 'Before the rule of the Dictaean king [i.e., Jupiter[23]] and before the evil people fed on oxen they'd killed, golden Saturn lived this life upon the earth; they didn't yet dare to blow the war-trumpet or to make the sword ring on resistant anvils' (my trans.).

Late antiquity recognized Aratus: the fourth century commentator Servius says ad *Geo.* 2.537 *Arati est hoc, qui dicit quod maiores bovem comesse nefas putabant* ('this [theme] is that of Aratus, who says that the old-time folk thought it a sin to eat the ox'). Virgil is truer to Aratus in this passage than he was at *Ecl.* 4.31–3. At this point in the *Georgics* he repeats the Aratean topos of the absence of war, but the jury is out at this stage over the inclusion of agriculture.

We saw the combination in Aratus of diachrony with synchrony. In fact the latter gets more emphasis in the Roman models, especially Virgil. In this connection, Virgil gestures towards another model which contains recurring cycles: Plato's *Politicus* myth. It is this model which gives him the new notion of the *return* of the age of Saturn (the *Saturnia regna* of *Ecl.* 4.6) and also the idea of 'cosmic mimesis' in the fourth *Eclogue*, in which the development of a human life tracks the evolution of the universe. Likewise, in the *Georgics* 2 passage, the two-stage opposition between kingdoms, those of Saturn and Jupiter specifically, can *only* be understood in the light of Plato's *Politicus*.[24] Virgil's gestures towards Plato occur, remember, alongside reference to Aratus: Virgil combines Aratus with Plato, using the latter to foreground and annotate a feature latent in Aratus' text, namely the notion of cycles.

To try to understand why Virgil chose to allow the *Politicus* such significant influence in his texts, we need to go back and look at the myth of cosmic alternation in it. In the *Politicus* myth, the functioning of the universe is understood as the alternation of two phases: 'The myth of the *Politicus* relates a cyclical history, the indefinite repetition of identical phases in the history of the world' (El Murr 2010: 295).[25] In one, a god (Kronos = Saturn: cf. Virgil's *Saturnia regna, Ecl.* 4.6) is in control of everything; in the other, the 'kingdom of Zeus (Virgil's *sceptrum Dictaei regis, Geo.* 2.536), divine governance gradually slips and human takes over. It seems to me that the 'Age of Zeus' and the 'Age of Kronos' represent, not control by those particular gods, but use of designations reminiscent of Hesiod's myth of ages (eg. Plato's ἐπὶ Κρόνου, *Pol.* 272b2 = ἐπὶ Κρόνου at *WD* 111) to describe the different phases in the cosmos, which are in fact marked respectively by the presence and absence of the god.[26] In other words, both 'Saturn' and 'Zeus' are powerful metaphors, which represent, by calling to mind the Hesiodic Myth of the Races, a 'golden age' and a period of degeneration from it.

In cosmic actuality these are not periods of rule by one or the other of these gods, but periods of order and the reversal of that order. These periods involved alteration of the direction of the revolutions of the universe. In one period the universe revolves in one direction; in the other, it reverses its revolutions (περίοδοι, *Pol.* 269c6). This reversal is due to its innate tendency to run backward when the divine push is removed (269d2–3). It moves by its own motion, rewinding through many ages (or again 'revolutions', περιόδων, 270a7). During the time of reversal, the growth-pattern of all living creatures is also reversed: from old men, people become babies, until they finally pass into a sort of Roald-Dahl-esque 'minus-land' and disappear (270d6–e9).

This is an adaptation by Plato of the Hesiodic sequence in which the races age exponentially, until the irresponsibility of the Golden Age and the prolonged infantilization of the Silver Age give way to the grey-haired babies of the Iron Age (*WD* 181). This is not the only gesture toward Hesiod. In the age of Kronos, as in the Hesiodic Golden Age, the earth produced food spontaneously, πάντα αὐτόματα γίγνεσθαι τοῖς ἀνθρώποις (271d1). During this period creatures did not eat one another, nor was there war or strife: οὔτε ἀλλήλων ἐδωδαί, πόλεμός τε οὐκ ἐνῆν οὐδὲ στάσις τὸ παράπαν, 271e1–2.[27] This age was a period of agricultural plenty; trees fruited spontaneously (καρποὺς δὲ ἀφθόνους εἶχον ἀπό τε δένδρων καὶ πολλῆς ὕλης ἄλλης, οὐχ ὑπὸ γεωργίας φυομένους, ἀλλ᾽ αὐτομάτης ἀναδιδούσης τῆς γῆς, 272a3–5), and there was plenty of soft grass to lie on (μαλακὰς δὲ εὐνὰς εἶχον ἀναφυομένης ἐκ γῆς πόας ἀφθόνου, 272a7–b1). As in Hesiod (*WD* 174–6), we live in the period of imperfection: τόνδε δ᾽ ὃν λόγος ἐπὶ Διὸς εἶναι, τὸν νυνί, παρὼν αὐτὸς ᾔσθησαι, 272b2–3. Unlike in Hesiod, however, this is not necessarily a bad thing, but contributes to human development.[28]

In the final part of the myth, the cycles of the cosmos are related to the progress of an individual human life ('age', 'time of life', ἡλικίας, 273e7), as they are in the Hesiodic Myth of the Races. At the time of reversal, life is truncated; those born with their hair already grey quickly die and pass beneath the earth again at the change of revolution (273e9–10) so that the life processes may begin again in what we recognize as the 'correct' order in the age of Zeus. All living things change in accordance with the direction of the universe, imitating and following it (ἀπομιμούμενα καὶ συνακολουθοῦντα, 274a1; cf. 274d6–7, καθάπερ ὅλος ὁ κόσμος, ᾧ ξυμμιμούμενοι καὶ συνεπόμενοι τὸν ἀεὶ χρόνον).

We need to answer two questions. Is it really the case that Virgil draws on the *Politicus*? If so, *how* does the interlocution of Plato modify Aratus?

First, the *Saturnia regna* in *Ecl.* 4, Virgil's 'kingdom of Saturn', could be from Hesiod, who uses the specific terminology of rulership: ἐπὶ Κρόνου ἦσαν, ὅτ' οὐρανῷ ἐμβασίλευεν (= *regna*), *WD* 111. At first sight this is a more likely influence on Virgil than Plato's loose ἐπὶ Κρόνου, *Pol.*272b2. But what we get in Plato and not at all in Hesiod, is the notion of the *return* of the *Saturnia regna*. Virgil may have followed Hesiod's cue for the 'kingdom of Saturn', but he has followed Plato's for its cyclical recurrence. His terminology therefore may also be from Plato rather than from Hesiod; or both may be present in the intertextual stratigraphy.

Imitation of the cosmos is the clincher. We have seen this in Plato (*Pol.* 274a1, ἀπομιμούμενα, and 274d6–7, ξυμμιμούμενοι). There, the processes of birth and death had followed the stages of the cosmos, even when those stages run in reverse, as at *Pol.* 271b4–8. More specifically, these phases mimic the passage of the heavenly bodies, since, as we have seen, the terminology used—περίοδοι, *Pol.* 269c4–7, περιόδων, 270a7—resonates, like περιτροπαί and περιφορά at *Rep.* 546a1–7, with the motions of the heavenly bodies which accompany the circular progress of the universe. You don't have to look far for this association. Περίοδος at *Phaedrus* 247d5 (and cf. 248c4) refers to the 'revolution' of the universe around the stable earth (Ἑστία, *Phdr.* 247a1). The gods, probably envisioned as the heavenly bodies at *Phdr.* 246e4–247a4,[29] are carried around by this 'revolution'. In the *Politicus*, too, the phases of human life and the dynamic structure of the universe, envisaged as a spinning sphere containing the heavenly bodies, run in synch.

In the fourth *Eclogue* there is also a process of imitation between the cosmos and human life at stake. *Magnus ab integro saeculorum nascitur ordo* ('a great marshalling of ages begins anew,' *Ecl.* 4.5, my trans.) could allude to cyclical time in the form of 'the astronomical concept of the *magnus annus*, defined by the period between successive occurrences of the same disposition of the heavenly bodies in the sky' (see for instance Cic. *Rep.* 6.24).[30] Here we are in the territory of the two-sphere universe, a system of concentric spheres which aims to reconcile the movements of the sun, moon, planets, and fixed stars. When all of these bodies return to their original positions vis-à-vis one another (an extremely lengthy process), then a 'great year' is completed. The idea is explained by Plato in *Timaeus* 38c; Aratus mentions it at *Ph.* 458–9:

μακροὶ δέ σφεων εἰσὶν ἑλισσομένων ἐνιαυτοί,
μακρὰ δὲ σήματα κεῖται ἀπόπροθεν εἰς ἓν ἰόντων.

'The years of their orbits are long, and at long intervals are their configurations when they come from afar into conjunction.'

The phrasing and line structure in Cicero's translation of this passage of Aratus, written fifty-odd years before Virgil's *Eclogue*, could lie behind *Ecl.* 4.5 (*Aratea* 232–3):

hae [stellae] faciunt <u>magnos</u> longinqui temporis <u>annos</u>,
cum redeunt ad idem caeli sub tegmine signum

'These [heavenly bodies, i.e., the planets, described just before this, at *Aratea* 223–31] create great years of slow-flowing time when they return to the same star-sign under the canopy of heaven' (my trans.).

It seems that the rebirth of the Roman world in *Ecl.* 4 is identified with the beginning of a new 'great year', reflected in a prior translation of Aratus. Note that there are two types of movement involved, prograde and retrograde. The Hesiodic ages in Virgil run in retrograde fashion in counterpoise to the life of the child: as the life of the child moves forward in prograde motion, as it were, they pass backwards from iron through heroic to gold. Likewise, the cosmos returns to the beginning of the cycle, with the new beginning of a great year, which then presumably runs forward in tandem with the life of the child.

The combination of prograde and retrograde movements in the poem may seem odd. But it is explained by their presence in Plato's *Politicus* myth. What is more, such divergent motions are part and parcel of the cosmos, astronomically understood. The planets move backwards (sometimes) while the rest of the universe turns in the opposite way in respect of them. The great year is the main way, in the pre-Copernican universe, in which the irregularity of planetary motions is commuted into predictably returning regularity with respect to the rest of the stars, and the sun and moon.[31] The cameo world of *Ecl.* 4 unites within itself the enormity of the two types of astronomical motion, just as the child contains the seeds of cosmic and historical rebirth.

How then do our sources work in the case of *Ecl.* 4? The sources themselves contain both prograde and retrograde progressions in terms of the history they present. Hesiod's progression in the Myth of Ages is a prograde (historical) one from ideal to degeneration. Plato's take on this in the *Politicus* is to make it into a cycle, in which one phase gives way to another in repeated cycles. Finally, Aratus is the only source which combines the Myth of Ages with the constellation Virgo. A 'new race' is being sent down from heaven; the constellation of *Dike* returns thence. Congruently, the ages repeat themselves and a new great year is inaugurated. These three sources give us all the elements of Virgil's prophecy. For us it shows how Aratus can work in tandem with other texts, which coalesce to form a coherent tradition. In its turn, the synthesis comments on innate tendencies already present in Aratus' text, which make it perfectly adaptable in the context of rebirth and temporal return.

Furthermore, by invoking multiple models, Virgil is able to combine cosmology (Hesiod's, Plato's) with the *astronomical* knowledge Aratus represents. The force of the early allusion to Aratus in the fourth *Eclogue*, through Virgo (understood as Aratus' *Dike*), encourages the reader to see what follows (the moral and historical cosmology) in astronomical terms. Repetition of the cycle of ages is now understood through astronomical conjunction. Astronomy is a powerful analogy for the human state.

We now move to the closing passage of *Georgics* 2. We have already seen how this passage gestures towards Aratus. As with *Ecl.* 4, it is the divergences from Aratus which have the most to tell. Virgil differs from Aratus in respect of his reintroduction of a non-agricultural Golden Age *in combination with* a two-stage cosmic cycle. This particular combination of elements is one which is only found in Plato's *Politicus*.

The status of agriculture in Virgil's Golden Age is ambivalent. For instance, Virgil appears to follow Aratus' admission of agriculture into the Golden Age in *Geo.* 513–14, where the farmers work: *agricola incuruo terram dimouit aratro: /hic anni labor*. This seems not to accord with the appearance a little earlier in the text of *ille deos qui novit agrestis* ('that man who knows the gods of agriculture') at *Geo.* 2.493, who is seen as enjoying a spontaneous Golden Age (*quos rami fructus, quos ipsa volentia rura /sponte tulere sua, carpsit*, 'who picks the fruit that the branches and obliging fields bear of their own accord', 500–1). We have the same image at *Geo.* 2.459–60:

> . . . quibus [agricolis] ipsa procul discordibus armis
> fundit humo facilem victum iustissima tellus.[32]

'For whom [the farmers], far from the strife of weapons, most just earth pours out from the ground an easily gained living.' (my trans.)

The combination of two passages of Hesiod may be sufficient to explain the anomaly. *Geo.* 2.500–501 is a virtual word-for-word translation of *WD* 117–8, . . . καρπὸν δ' ἔφερε ζείδωρος ἄρουρα /αὐτομάτη πολλόν τε καὶ ἄφθονον (*sponte sua* = αὐτομάτη, *WD* 118). This is Hesiod's description of life in the Golden Age. But we remember also that at *WD* the denizens of the just community relive to an extent the life of the golden-age men; the similarity is seen through the repetition of the formula ζείδωρος ἄρουρα at *WD* 117 and 237. In the first case, the word which followed was, we recall, αὐτομάτη, 'of its own accord', 'spontaneously'. Although the just men, on the other hand, have to work, ἔργα νέμονται, 231, we cannot help but recall the spontaneity of the Golden Age through the repetition of the formula ζείδωρος ἄρουρα, and the recall results in a blurring of the picture.[33]

Hesiod might be sufficient to explain the ambivalence between agriculture and spontaneity in Virgil's Golden Age, but what about some of the other features of it, anomalous in respect of Aratus? Saturn (Kronos), for instance, is not in Aratus. In the Stoic picture of the universe which Aratus presents, there is no room for an age of Kronos: for Aratus, everything belongs to an age of Zeus, who arranged things providentially for human progress.[34] It follows that there can be no straightforward opposition between ages of Kronos and Zeus in Aratus. Virgil reintroduced Kronos (= Saturn, *Ecl.* 4.6, *Georgics* 2.538). Virgil may have reintroduced Kronos under the influence of Hesiod. But more likely, given what happens elsewhere in our *Georgics* 2 passage, is the influence of the *Politicus*. In Virgil's two-stage conception of the cosmic cycle in *Georgics* 2, there is a straightforward opposition between the kingdoms of Saturn (*aureus Saturnus, Geo.* 2.538), and of Jupiter (*sceptrum Dictaei regis, Geo.* 2.536). This opposition is found in neither Hesiod nor Aratus, but it is found, as we have already seen, in Plato *Pol.* 272b2 (Κρόνου . . . Διός). In Plato, as in Hesiod, people in the age of Kronos live an αὐτόματος βίος (*Pol.* 271e5). But the combination we find in Virgil, of the self-producing earth with the opposition between Saturn and Jupiter, is Platonic, more than Hesiodic. Plato's ἐπὶ Διός, *Pol.* 272b2, renders more specific the role of Hesiod's Zeus, Ζεὺς Κρονίδης, *WD* 138, *WD* 143 etc.: it is not stated in Hesiod (although it may be implied) that any 'kingdom of Zeus' follows the rule of Kronos.

That the βίος αὐτόματος is reintroduced into the tradition by Virgil under the influence of the *Politicus* is made more likely by other resonances of the *Politicus* in this part of the *Georgics*. The sequence of *topoi* in Virgil tracks the *Politicus* myth in a way too specific to be coincidental. Allusions to Plato's *Politicus* myth in this context are much more pointed than allusions to Hesiod. Take Plato's description of golden-age produce: καρποὺς δὲ ἀφθόνους εἶχον ἀπό τε δένδρων καὶ πολλῆς ὕλης ἄλλης, οὐχ ὑπὸ γεωργίας φυομένους, ἀλλ᾽ αὐτομάτης ἀναδιδούσης τῆς γῆς ('. . . they had an abundance of fruit from trees and many other plants, not growing through cultivation but because the earth sent them up of its own accord', *Pol.* 272a3–5, trans. Rowe). Compare this with *Geo.* 2.516–23:

> nec requies, quin aut pomis exuberet annus
> aut fetu pecorum aut Cerealis mergite culmi,
> proventuque oneret sulcos atque horrea vincat.
> venit hiems: teritur Sicyonia baca trapetis,
> glande sues laete redeunt, dant arbuta silvae;
> et varios ponit fetus autumnus, et alte
> mitis in apricis coquitur vindemia saxis.
> interea dulces pendent circum oscula nati . . .

'Without pause the year blooms with fruit and the offspring of herds and sheaves of grain-stalks, weighs down the furrows with produce and defeats the silos. Winter is coming: olives are crushed on the presses, pigs come home replete with acorns, the woods produce wild strawberries; autumn puts forth various fruits, and the sweet vintage is ripened high up on the warm rocks. In the meantime gentle children hang upon his kisses . . .' (my trans).

Virgil's *nec requies* corresponds to Plato's ἀφθόνους; his list of produce mirrors Plato's picture of various καρποί, more detailed than the καρπός of *WD* 117. At the same time, Virgil seems to be arguing with the Platonic vision in two respects: first, he allows his primitive farmers to have a hand in producing the largesse (sheaves, furrows, and silos in lines 517–18, presumably man-made); secondly, in the fact that family life, unnecessary in Plato, is idealized in Virgil's Saturnian age (contrast κτήσεις γυναικῶν καὶ παίδων, *Pol.* 271e8–272a1, with *Geo.* 2.523). The point is that Virgil here both adopts, and builds on, a series of Platonic motifs.

There is another motif in common between Virgil and Plato, found in *Geo.* 2.527, *ipse [agrestis] dies agitat festos fususque per herbam* . . . A couch of soft grass is a mark of the Saturnian age in Plato, *Pol.* 272a7–b1: μαλακὰς δ᾽ εὐνὰς εἶχον ἀν ἀφυομένης ἐκ γῆς πόας ἀφθόνου. This detail may seem trivial, but it is often the very precise correspondences which are most telling. In fact, this is one of a series of images found in an entire Virgilian sequence imitating the *Politicus*.[35]

At its climax, we have a near-echo of Plato by Virgil. In Plato, the Stranger sums up τὸν δὲ βίον, ὦ Σώκρατες, ἀκούεις μὲν τὸν τῶν ἐπὶ Κρόνου, ('What I describe, then, Socrates, is the life of those who lived in the time of Kronos,' *Pol.* 272b1–2, Rowe). This is echoed in Virgil's peroration at *Geo.* 2.538, *aureus hanc vitam in terris Saturnus agebat* ('Golden Saturn lived this life in the world'), with *vitam* for Plato's βίον.

The important point to emerge from this section is that Virgil deploys the *Politicus* myth *in tandem with* Aratean material in both *Eclogue* 4 and *Georgics* 2. Exploring the possible combinations of these two texts is manifestly important to him. It is parallel to the way Aratus himself combined models; in this case, Aratus himself has become only one of those models. Like Aratus, Virgil sets up an argument between his sources which leads us to reflect, among other things, on the role and nature of agriculture as an index of human progress.

Plato had rewritten Hesiod as a philosophical cosmology. Aratus' *Dike* translates cosmology to the celestial plane, surrounding it with astronomical data. This is what Aratus plus Plato gives Virgil: the connection between astronomy and cosmology. Whilst writing agricultural didactic, Virgil is inscribing that world, and its Roman context, among the stars.

2.2 Germanicus 'Translates' Aratus[36]

The first phenomenon we find in Roman translations of Aratus' Myth of Ages is the further collapse of the sequential structure of the races. The races are never cleanly separated in the Roman tradition: the genetic waters are muddied from the beginning. The theme of mixture leads to the theme of civil war.

At the very beginning of the Roman tradition of translating Aratus, Cicero mixes the races. Here is *Aratea* fr. 18 (Soubiran):[37]

ferrea tum vero proles exorta repentest
ausaque funestum primast fabricarier ensem,
et gustare manu iunctum domitumque iuvencum.

'Suddenly the iron race sprung up, which first dared to forge the death-dealing sword and to taste the ox once yoked and subdued by human hand.'

Cicero's *Iron* Age translates Aratus' *Bronze* Age. Compare the original (*Ph.* 130-2):

χαλκείη γενεὴ προτέρων ὀλοώτεροι ἄνδρες,
οἳ πρῶτοι κακοεργὸν ἐχαλκεύσαντο μάχαιραν
εἰνοδίην, πρῶτοι δὲ βοῶν ἐπάσαντ᾽ ἀροτήρων . . .

'But when these men had died there were born the Bronze Age men, more destructive than their predecessors, who were the first to forge the criminal sword for murder on the highways, and the first to taste the flesh of ploughing-oxen . . .'

Cicero reinstates Hesiod's iron race, omitted by Aratus, who only has χαλκείη in line 130; nevertheless, Cicero applies to the *iron* race the ox-eating motif of the Aratean Bronze Age, mixing bronze and iron. He exceeds the brief presented in Aratus' mildly mixed account.[38]

We don't know whether Cicero's now-incomplete text would have referred, in addition, to civil war. Germanicus for his part combines mixture with civil war, following Cicero's precedent in at least the first respect. The races are mixed at Germanicus *Ph.* 133–6:

> *aerea* sed postquam *proles* terris data, nec iam
> semina virtutis vitiis demersa resistunt
> *ferrique* invento mens est laetata metallo,
> polluit et taurus mensas assuetus aratro . . .

> 'But when the offspring of the bronze age came to the earth, the seeds of virtue were overwhelmed by vice and could no longer resist it; men were delighted by the discovery of the metal iron; the ox, accustomed to the plough, defiled their tables . . .' (text and trans. Gain 1976).

Possanza refers to the 'awkward intrusion of iron into the bronze age' in his catalogue of Germanicus' supposed ineptitudes.[39] But it is better to situate Germanicus' imagery in a tradition of the reception of Hesiod's Myth of Ages, starting from Plato's *Republic* and continuing through Aratus to his Roman reception, in which the races are mixed. If we do this, we can see a chiasmus in the intertextual relationship between Germanicus and Cicero. Cicero has *ferrea proles*, but attributes to them the defining characteristics of Aratus' bronze race (metalwork and ox-eating); Germanicus, on the other hand, begins with the Bronze Age, *aerea proles* (Aratus' χαλκείη γενεή, *Ph.* 130), but goes on to attribute to them the discovery of iron (*ferrique invento . . . metallo*). Germanicus reapplies the Aratean images of metalwork and bulls to the Bronze Age, unlike Cicero, who reinstated the Hesiodic Iron Age; but at the same time Germanicus retains the Ciceronian contamination between iron and bronze.

Furthermore, Germanicus introduces the notion of *civil* war, absent from the Aratean original. In *Ph.* 112–119 he translates Aratus 108–113 (see text and translation of Aratus in appendix A):

> nondum vesanos rabies nudaverat ensis
> nec consanguineis fuerat discordia nota,
> ignotique maris cursus, privataque tellus
> grata satis, neque per dubios avidissima ventos
> spes procul amotas fabricata nave petebat

divitias, fructusque dabat placata colono
sponte sua tellus nec parvi terminus agri
praestabat dominis, sine eo tutissimo, rura.

'Men were not yet so savage as to bare their swords in rage against each other;
<u>discord among blood relations</u> was unknown; no one sailed the seas, men's
own lands being satisfaction enough. Greed for wealth from far away did not
cause them to build ships and entrust them to the hazards of the winds. The
peaceful lands bore fruit unaided for those who dwelt in them. There were no
boundary stones marking off their owners' small domains, for they were
quite safe without them' (Gain).

There is no explicit reference to *civil* war in Aratus, not even to Plato's στάσις; with
consanguineis on the other hand, Germanicus taps into a Roman tradition in which
'war between brothers' means civil war. This is seen, for example, in a passage we
have just looked at, Virgil *Geo.* 2.496, *infidos agitans discordia fratres*, in the context
of other references to Roman politics, picking up the reference to civil war at the
end of Georgics 1 (*paribus . . . telis, Geo.* 1.489).[40] 'Germanicus, unlike Aratus, is not
referring to warfare in an abstract, general way, but is referring specifically to the
great scourge of Roman political life, civil war.'[41]

Germanicus uses a Roman term, *discordia*, in his rendition of Aratus' list of
nouns denoting conflict—νείκεος, διακρίσιος, κυδοιμοῦ, *Ph.* 108–9.[42] Virgil too
used *discordia* at *Geo.* 2.496.[43] This is part of a complex of terms the Roman authors
use to refer to the topos of civil war. *Ensis* ('sword'), usually in a particular metrical
sedes, is another. Virgil, for instance, says of the Golden Age, *necdum /impositos
duris crepitare incudibus ensis* (*Geo.* 2.539–40). This is a reference to Aratus, who
had the same idea, of 'forging' a weapon (ἐχαλκεύσαντο μάχαιραν, what the
bronze-age men did at *Ph.* 131); in the Roman tradition the weapon is not a knife,
as in Aratus, but a sword. The tradition began with Cicero fr.18.2, where 'the iron
race was the first to dare to forge the death-dealing sword,' *ausaque funestum primast fabricarier <u>ensem</u>*. Thus also in Germanicus 112 we have *nondum vesanos rabies
nudaverat ensis*, with *ensis* at the line-end.[44] In the Latin Aratean tradition, *ensis*
becomes a particular symbol, not only of the passing of the Golden Age, but of
civil war. We can see from all this how Germanicus overlays his Roman sources on
the Greek original in his translation of Aratus. What the Roman sources give him,
cumulatively, is an emphasis on civil war as a mark of man's fall from the Golden
Age, which is absent from the text of Aratus.[45]

2.3 Lucretius' Ages (*De Rerum Natura* 5.1241–1349)

There are recurring details in our Roman renditions of Aratus' Myth of Ages
which we have looked at so far. In all cases they are details added to Aratus. In
Cicero, Virgil, and Germanicus we find *ensis* at the line-end, the sword (not Aratus'

knife) as a mark of the advent of civil war. In Germanicus and Virgil we find *discordia* and *sponte sua*. The former is a Roman word for a Roman concept (war which is *civil*, as we see from the added details of *fratres* and *consanguineis* in Virgil and Germanicus respectively). *Sponte sua* is an interpolation into Aratus from either Hesiod or Plato, or the overlay of both, which acts to imbue the Golden Age in the Roman authors with a spontaneity absent from Aratus, whilst at the same time gesturing towards multiple sources. We cannot say whether the last two details would also have been in Cicero. One thing we can say, however, is that *all three* details *are* in Lucretius. Let's look at our three terms again, this time adding in Lucretius:

   (i) *ensis*
       Cicero Arat. fr.18.1–2 *ferrea proles . . . fabricarier ensem*
       Virgil *Geo.* 2.540 *incudibus ensis*
       Germanicus 112 *nudaverat ensis*
       Lucretius 5.1293 *ferreus ensis*,
       all at the line-end.

   (ii) *discordia*
       Virgil *Geo.* 2.496 *discordia fratres*
       Germanicus *Ph.* 113 *discordia nota*
       Lucretius 5.1305 *discordia tristis*,
       all at the line-end.

   (iii) *sponte sua*
       Germanicus *Ph.* 118 *sponte sua*
       Virgil *Geo.* 501 *sponte . . . sua*
       Lucretius 5.938 *sponte sua*
       at the beginning of the line, referring to the earth.

This is strong evidence. *Lucretius* now appears to be the Roman intermediary between Aratus and his Roman translations. This repetition of similar line endings might be a freak of the epic tradition, a mere repetition of formulae, but for the *context* in Lucretius. Lucretius has already combined the idea of the self-producing earth with *ensis* and *discordia* in an extended passage of the *De rerum natura* which reworks the Myth of Ages.[46]

This observation moves the goalposts in our discussion of Roman receptions of Aratus. No longer do we see Aratus coming unmediated to his Roman translators. Our approach to the reception of Aratus must shift up a gear, from model/translation to a much more complex picture. There is a whole raft of ideological and literary historical considerations involved.

First, Lucretius is another Roman interpreter of the Myth of Ages, one who is earlier than all three of our Roman authors except Cicero. Lucretius' *De rerum natura* is a text which inhabits the space between Cicero's *Aratea* and Virgil's *Eclogues*. It will be demonstrated in the next chapter that Lucretius has a wider interest in Aratus. For the moment, let's concentrate only on the 'golden age' sequence in Book 5.

DRN 5 combines sociology and astronomy. In it, the development of the world (lines 91–508) is followed by astronomy (509–770) and human 'evolution' (772–1457).[47] Sedley describes Lucretius' ordering of topics as 'curious'. In his view, the section on astronomy 'interrupts' the two phases of the development of the world, intervening between the growth of the cosmos and the emergence of civilization. He attributes this ordering, not to Lucretius' own design, but to that of his sources.[48] According to Sedley, Lucretius would have transposed the section on astronomy in any final version of the *DRN*, since it belongs 'more naturally' with the cosmic phenomena described in *DRN* 6.[49] Such a transposition 'would have eliminated the unwelcome interruption in Book 5's history of the world, and led to a smooth continuity between the end of 5, on astronomy, and the primary content of 6, the remaining cosmic phenomena.'[50]

I am sceptical of the putative reordering. From what we have already learned about myths of ages, we see that astronomy has an integral place within cosmologies both natural and anthropological, and it serves to situate patterns of human development, which incorporate a moral element, against a view of the world which combines cosmology with 'data'. A cosmology > astronomy > anthropology progression is a natural one in the tradition which includes Aratus.

The Myth of Ages is itself at times clearly visible in *DRN* 5. The point of its clearest emergence is *DRN* 5.1241–1349, on the evolution of the use of metals. Here, Lucretius resumes his account of the origins of the world, 'interrupted' by his astronomy, which culminates, in a passage on its role in the development of religion, with a list of metals (1241–2):

> quod superest, aes atque aurum ferrumque repertumst
> et simul argenti pondus plumbique potestas . . .

> 'To resume: bronze and gold and iron were discovered, and likewise weighty silver and strong lead . . .' (my trans.; all quotations of Lucretius from the text of Bailey 1921).

This is a comprehensive catalogue, as opposed to the selective hierarchical list which composes the Myth of Ages. A rationalist description of the discovery of metals has replaced the Hesiodic analogy between the ages of man and the metals. As it stands we do not have to see this list as related to the Myth of Ages at all. Yet, we shall see, it may at the same time recall the metallic myth, because of context.

In explaining the development of war, Lucretius does subsequently put his metals in a kind of evolutionary sequence (1286–96):

> posterius ferri vis est aerisque reperta.
> et prior aeris erat quam ferri cognitus usus,
> quo facilis magis est natura et copia maior.
> aere solum terrae tractabant, aereque belli

miscebant fluctus et vulnera vasta serebant
et pecus atque agros adimebant; nam facile ollis
omnia cedebant armatis nuda et inerma.
inde minutatim processit ferreus ensis
versaque in opprobrium species est falcis ahenae,
et ferro coepere solum proscindere terrae
exaequataque sunt creperi certamina belli.

'Later strong iron and bronze were discovered. The use of bronze was discovered earlier than that of iron, because bronze is more malleable and more plentiful. With bronze they ploughed the surface of the earth, with bronze they flung together waves of war and sowed massive wounds and took away flocks and fields; for everything naked and unarmed easily gave way to those who were armed. As the iron sword marched ahead on its progress, the form of the bronze sickle fell into disuse, and they began to cleave the levels of the earth with iron and the contests of wavering war became equally matched' (my trans.).[51]

It is in this context in Lucretius that we get *ensis* at the line-end, the mannerism which is found in all of our Latin authors. What is more, Lucretius collapses two lines of Cicero, *ferrea tum vero proles exorta repentest lausaque funestum primast fabricarier ensem* (fr. 18.1–2), into the single expression *ferreus ensis*.[52] Note how Lucretius is drawing on Cicero's translation *of Aratus' Myth of Ages* here. His sequence of metals is put into the familiar myth-of-ages framework through allusion.

Another of the terms in our Roman accounts of the ages pops up at the end of Lucretius' section on the development of war (*DRN* 5.1305–7):

sic alid ex alio peperit discordia tristis,
horribile humanis quod gentibus esset in armis,
inque dies belli terroribus addidit augmen.

'In this way sad Discord gave birth to one thing after another which was terrifying to the human race under arms, and day by day she snowballed the terrors of war' (my trans.).

Discordia is personified as a mother figure, a negative incarnation of the earth-as-mother motif which appears earlier in *DRN* 5 (e.g., 805, 822–3, 925–6). We have already seen how the term is used in Roman authors in the context of civil war in the Bronze or Iron Age. So also in Lucretius *discordia* marks the degeneration from a sort of Golden Age in which the earth acts as mother, to an age of war in which Discordia gives birth. This is a clear instance of the topos of degeneration in Lucretius.

Moreover, *discordia* is part of Lucretius' cosmology. The term as it is used in *DRN* 5 serves to tie the development of humanity with the development of the universe. Let's go back a bit, to the beginning of the world, at *DRN* 5.432–45 (following the order of Bailey's text):

hic neque tum <u>solis rota</u>[53] cerni lumine largo	
altivolans poterat nec magni sidera mundi	
nec mare nec caelum nec denique terra neque aer	
nec similis nostris rebus res ulla videri,	435
sed nova tempestas quaedam molesque coorta	
omne genus de principiis, <u>discordia</u> quorum	[440]
intervalla vias conexus pondera plagas	[441]
concursus motus turbabat proelia miscens,	[442]
propter dissimilis formas variasque figuras	440 [443]
quod non omnia sic poterant coniuncta manere	[444]
nec motus inter sese dare convenientis.	[445]
diffugere inde loci partes coepere paresque	[437]
cum paribus iungi res et discludere mundum	[438]
membraque dividere et magnas disponere partes . . .	445 [439]

'In this period the sun's wheel could not be discerned flying high shedding its light abroad, nor the stars of the great universe, nor sea nor sky, nor even earth or air, nor could anything like what we know be discerned, but some kind of weird ferment and incipient mass, composed of every kind of initial particle, whose warfare (*discordia*) precluded ratios, paths, connections, masses, collisions, comings-together and motions as it mixed them about in battle, on account of their diverging forms and figures, because all these things couldn't remain thus conjoined nor could they find a comfortable reciprocal motion. Then different points in space began to be separated out; like substance began to be joined with like and the world to take shape and to articulate its limbs and distribute its constitutents . . .' (my trans.).

In this prodigious description of the beginning of the universe *Discordia* refers to the war of the elements in cosmogony. *Discordia* is personified as a leader of turbulent atomic armies, *proelia miscens*.[54] Their separation is a kind of Empedoclean Strife (*discordia* = νεῖκος). This is war writ large, on a cosmic scale. At this point in Lucretius we seem to have our earliest Roman meeting of the ideas of Empedoclean Strife and civil conflict, since 'the elements are regarded as the inhabitants of a single state, the *mundus*.'[55] The civil-war nature of cosmogony was even more explicit at 5.380–1:

denique tantopere inter se cum maxima mundi
pugnent membra, <u>pio nequaquam</u> concita <u>bello</u>

'since, then, the giant limbs of the universe fight so much among themselves, roused in a war which in no way follows the law of family relations . . . ' (my trans.).

This describes the war of the elements: *pio nequaquam bello* is without doubt *civil* war ('war between family members—a pointed oxymoron).[56]

Lucretius may be the origin of *discordia* in the Roman authors we saw earlier. *Discordia*, arriving at our later authors via Lucretius, carries more baggage than we thought. But it is baggage which fits: the connection between the Myth of Ages and the cosmos has been with us all along.

Lucretius is the *first* of our texts in which *discordia* is linked with a metallic view of human evolution. Is *Lucretius*, then, responsible for the innovation of civil war in Roman accounts of the Myth of Ages? The affirmative answer is more convincing in the light of the other expression shared between Lucretius 5 and our other Roman authors. The case of *sponte sua* is parallel to that of *discordia*.

From *DRN* 5.925, following the 'war of the atoms' and the development of the cosmos, including the stars, Lucretius plots the development of human culture. At 933–8 we recognize the 'Hesiodic' Golden Age:

nec robustus erat curvi moderator aratri
quisquam, nec scibat ferro molirier arva
nec nova defodere in terram virgulta neque altis
arboribus veteres decidere falcibus ramos.
quod sol atque imbres dederant, quod terra crearat
sponte sua, satis id placabat pectora donum.

'No one took the role of stocky guide of the plough, no one knew how to dig the fields with iron or plant young saplings in the earth, or to prune old branches from the tall trees using pruning-knives. The largesse which the sun and rains gave and which the earth created of her own accord, this pleased their hearts well enough' (my trans.).

Here there is a general similarity to accounts of the Golden Age by Aratus and his Roman followers, for instance in the succession of negatives to describe the life of the Golden Age (compare Aratus 108–11, Virgil *Geo.* 2.495–9 and 501–2; Germanicus 112–17). But the particularity comes with *sponte sua* (*DRN* 5.938). Here is the golden-age formula taken up by both Virgil and Germanicus.

Again Lucretius may be the origin of expressions used across Roman accounts of the Golden Age. Look again at how closely all three Lucretian expressions follow in Germanicus' supposed 'translation' of Aratus (Germanicus *Ph.* 112–18, quoted with translation on pp. 49–50 above):

nondum vesanos rabies nudaverat ensis
nec consanguineis fuerat discordia nota,
ignotique maris cursus, privataque tellus
grata satis, neque per dubios avidissima ventos
spes procul amotas fabricata nave petebat
divitias, fructusque dabat placata colono
sponte sua tellus . . .

The threefold 'Lucretian' sequence begins with a line ending in *ensis* and culminates with *sponte sua*. *Sponte sua* in particular is the expression which reflects the reintegration of Hesiod's Golden Age into the Aratean account. As a Roman innovation in the tradition of Aratus, it may come from Lucretius.

But the Lucretian formula is not wholly innocent. Lucretius employs the same formula in his abnegation of divine agency in creation, earlier in the *DRN*, at 2.1153–64:[57]

> haud, ut opinor, enim mortalia saecla superne
> aurea de caelo demisit funis in arva
> nec mare nec fluctus plangentes saxa crearunt,   1155
> sed genuit tellus eadem quae nunc alit ex se.
> praeterea nitidas fruges vinetaque laeta
> sponte sua primum mortalibus ipsa creavit,
> ipsa dedit dulcis fetus et pabula laeta;
> quae nunc vix nostro grandescunt aucta labore,   1160
> conterimusque boves et viris agricolarum,
> conficimus ferrum vix arvis suppeditati:
> usque adeo parcunt fetus augentque laborem.

'I do not think that a golden rope lowered the race of men into the fields down from heaven from on high, nor did the waves of the sea striking the rocks in lamentation create them. No: that same earth gave birth to them who now nourishes them from herself. What's more, she herself at first created for mortals the glistening crops and flourishing vines, of her own accord; she herself gave gentle offspring and joyous pastures. These nowadays scarcely grow ripe encouraged by our labour. They wear out our oxen and the strength of our ploughmen, we scarcely have enough iron to work the fields: to such an extent are they stingy with produce and profligate of our labour' (my trans.).

Lucretius' Golden Age happens above all in a *rationalist* cosmology, a cosmology at odds, in fact, with the universe of Aratus (designed by Zeus' providence), the cosmologies of Plato, and of the Roman authors who combined them. Lucretius' account is not *prima facie* that of the Myth of Ages, but an account of an arbitrary world in which something so orderly has no place. Yet, we find, the Myth of Ages underlies Lucretius' development of man. It has its uses. *Largo sensu* it tracks the progress of man against the progress of the cosmos. That cosmos can be either divinely informed, or rationalist. The potential for the use of Aratus and the tradition in this very debate, between competing cosmologies, will be the subject of the next chapter.

Wandering Stars

'Ihr messet das Gewicht der Vokale in einem alten Gedicht und setze
Formel zu der einen Planetenbahn in Beziehung. Das ist entzückend, aber es
ist ein Spiel'.

'You measure the weight of the vowels in an old poem and relate the resulting
formula to that of a planet's orbit. That is delightful, but it is a game.'

—Hermann Hesse, *The Glass Bead Game* (1943), trans. Winston (1970): 188

Introduction

How do you live in a world devoid of divine guidance? One answer is that you com-
mute the godless arbitrariness of existence into an illusion of order. This is done
through the establishment and repetition of patterns. Lucretius lays bare the process
of self-deception (*DRN* 5.1430–9):

> ergo hominum genus incassum frustraque laborat
> semper et <in> curis consumit inanibus aevum,
> nimirum quia non cognovit quae sit habendi
> finis et omnino quoad crescat vera voluptas.
> idque minutatim vitam provexit in altum
> et belli magnos commovit funditus aestus.
> at vigiles mundi magnum versatile templum
> sol et luna suo *lustrantes lumine* circum
> perdocuere homines *annorum tempora verti*
> et certa ratione geri rem atque ordine certo.

> 'Therefore mankind always works for nothing and to no purpose, eating up
> the time with pointless concerns, clearly because people don't know the limit
> of possession and the extent of true pleasure. This has, bit by bit, carried life
> out into the deep sea, and has stirred up from the bottom the massive brea-
> kers of war. But those watchful sentinels, the sun and moon, travelling with
> their light around the great revolving vault of heaven, schooled men in the
> notion that the seasons of the year come round, and that everything is done
> to a fixed plan and order.'

Lines 1436–9, I think, should be read ironically. Although the daily grind of human existence is without reason or justification, nevertheless the apparent repetition of the seasons gives the *illusion* that there is an overriding order in things.

For Lucretius, the order of the seasons and the motions of the sun and moon are a spurious form of comfort. We already know this by the time Lucretius gives us the lines just quoted. We know it from the very beginning of Lucretius' exposition of astronomy in *DRN* 5 (lines 76–81):

> praeterea solis cursus lunaeque meatus
> expediam qua vi flectat natura gubernans;
> ne forte haec inter caelum terramque reamur
> libera *sponte sua* cursus lustrare perennis
> morigera ad fruges augendas atque animantis,
> neve aliqua divum volvi ratione putemus.

> 'Moreover, I'll explain the motive principle by which governing nature turns the course of the sun and the wanderings of the moon, in case by chance we assume that they wend their eternal courses between heaven and earth freely and of their own accord, obligingly bent on increasing the crops and livestock, and in case we imagine that their revolutions are the result of some divine plan.'

Despite the ironic use of the 'golden age' tag *sponte sua*, Lucretius' astronomy predicates no Golden Age. Unlike Hesiod's spontaneous earth in the myth-of-ages tradition, the egotistical heavens in Lucretius' universe *don't* make it their business to provide for mankind. The reverse is the premise of Aratus' poem, in which Zeus set up the signs in the sky as evidence of his own providence (*Ph.* 10–13). The purpose of Lucretius' exposition of the stars in *De rerum natura* 5 is to *explode* the myth of divine governance promulgated in the intelligent design tradition Aratus and Roman Aratea represent.

How do you *talk* about how to live in a world devoid of divine guidance? Do you invent a new language fitted only to that purpose, to supersede language already in large part put to use in some naïve assumption of the divine plan? Lucretius does not do this, but rather draws on earlier poetry in constructing his argument; his polemic arises through intertextuality. The text with which he engages most in his polemic is that paragon of celestial order, Aratus, in the form of Cicero's Latin translation.

Consider again *DRN* 5.1430–9. The attentive reader of line 1437 will immediately notice the presence of a Ciceronian formulation in Lucretius' epic language. At *Aratea* 237–8, Cicero describes the celestial circles, the main structural underpinning of the ordered cosmos:[1]

> quattuor, aeterno *lustrantes lumine* mundum,
> orbes stelligeri portantes signa feruntur . . .

> 'Four star-bearing circles, illuminating the world with never-ending light, carrying the star-signs, go on their way . . .'

At *Aratea* 332–3 the parallel is even more striking:

> haec *sol* aeterno convestit *lumine lustrans,*
> *annua* conficiens *vertentia tempora* cursu.

'The shining sun clothes these [zodiacal constellations] with eternal light, completing the seasons of the year with its turning course.'

Compare the whole systactical unit *DRN* 5.1437–9, from the first passage quoted in this chapter:

> *sol* et luna suo *lustrantes lumine* circum
> perdocuere homines *annorum tempora verti*
> et certa ratione geri rem atque ordine certo.

In his construction of the illusion in *DRN* 5.1430–9, Lucretius uses the language of a poem which dealt precisely with the notion of celestial order. The familiar language, like the repeated paths of the heavenly bodies, may lull us into that false sense of security; but a security already undermined, from Lucretius' first devastating exposition of astronomy in *DRN* 5.76–81. These lines establish the thrust of Book 5 in respect of the intelligent designers. Lucretius uses Ciceronian reference here too. Lucretius' expression *lunaeque meatus* in *DRN* 5.76 can be compared with Cicero *Prognostica* fr. 1.1, *ut cum luna means Hyperionis officit orbi.* The expression in Cicero is, as can be judged, the first attestation before Lucretius of the collocation *luna means.*[2] Compare also Lucretius 5.78–9, *caelum . . . /cursus lustrare* with *Arat.* 225 *legitimo cernes caelum lustrantia cursu.* At this point in the *Aratea,* Cicero contrasts the planets to the fixed stars, the latter of which can be understood by *ratio* (*Arat.* 227). Lucretius reuses Cicero's *ratio* in line 81 in a polemical context: it must *not* be thought (unlike in the tradition of Aratus) that divine *ratio* has anything to do with the way the stars function. Likewise the notion of 'governing nature', *natura gubernans DRN* 5.77. The metaphor of government which Lucretius employs is another false lead. We can see how it was used in the Stoic idiom, albeit a decade or so later, by looking at Cicero, *De natura deorum* Book 2. Cicero's Stoic mouthpiece, Balbus, uses just such metaphors of government in reference to the guiding activities of *Natura.*[3] *Natura gubernans* in *DRN* 5.77 may be a sarcastic reference to the intelligent design idea of Nature, which anticipates the debunking of the concept; it is replaced in 107 by *fortuna gubernans* in the same *sedes.*

Lucretius' agenda in setting out the programme of *DRN* 5 is to demolish any notion of 'intelligent design' in the universe. In this he is implicitly arguing against the world-view of the *Aratea,* in which the fixed stars obey predictable laws. For Lucretius, the proposition that they should somehow 'choose' to follow such laws, and in doing so bring benefit to mankind *sponte sua,* is ludicrous. Cicero's *Aratea* is the textual grist to this mill, the verbal substance of the opposing school, ground up, reused, redistributed.

We think here of how Aratus uses Empedocles, a topic explored in chapter 1 above. We saw that Aratus sometimes reuses Empedoclean formulations. Such references to Empedocles are not passive epic gestures merely, but interpretative prompts. The value of such allusions becomes most apparent when they are contextualized in both authors. In addition, Aratus' use of Empedocles in tandem with the earlier Hesiodic model results in a tension, worked through in the *Dike* myth, between sequential and cyclical time. Empedocles gives Aratus a model for synchrony which is very useful to him in converting, as it were, the historic time of Hesiod's Myth of Ages to the cyclical time of the stars. As well as this, Empedocles gives him a special kind of poetic model which answers a problem posed by Plato in his discussion of poetry: how can poetry express truth? Aratus reinstates poetry, but his poetry is cosmological rather than mythical.

Lucretius brief is, paradoxically, in many ways comparable to Aratus', even perhaps a response to it.[4] The *De rerum natura* is in dialogue with Cicero's translation of Aratus throughout. I will demonstrate the extent of his debt to this work in this and the following chapter. The results of such dialogue are both general and specific. Lucretius, like Aratus, reinstates poetry in a philosophy which was, at least on the surface, sceptical of it.[5] Such poetry is represented by the Roman epic tradition, which included Cicero's *Aratea*. As in the case of Empedocles, this is cosmological poetry, and the precise model Lucretius chooses enables him to engage with first century *cosmological* debate. In fact, Lucretius' work uses the materials of earlier epic transgressively in constructing its philosophical argument. Cicero's *Aratea* acts as a fulcrum in his polemical engineering.

3.1 External Evidence in Favour of the Importance of Aratus for Lucretius

So far we have several instances of contact between Lucretius and Cicero, in the Golden Age, and in astronomy. We should pause to examine the assumptions which might colour our recognition of these points of similarity. How likely is it that Lucretius drew on Cicero's *Aratea* in his *De rerum natura*? The thesis which follows is predicated, first, on the notion of Aratus' importance in mid-first-century BC Rome, as a text both recognizable to a reader, and indicative of a certain view of the world; and second, on the congruent importance of Cicero's translation for Lucretius. These two features of the tradition are connected: Cicero's work itself testifying to the importance of Aratus in the first century. We shall start by considering it, among various pieces of evidence in favour of the reading of Aratus in Rome which are external to Lucretius' text. This will show that Aratus was well within the ambit of the first-century literary milieu. Then we shall examine the evidence internal to Lucretius' text of his interest in Cicero's translation as a key intertext. Both types of evidence are compelling.

3.1.1 THE COMPOSITION OF THE *DRN*

First, the composition of the *DRN* took place in the mid-50s BC. We know that it was in more or less complete form by 54 BC when Cicero corresponds with his brother Quintus about reading it: '*Lucreti poemata ut scribis ita sunt, multis lumini-bus ingenii, multae tamen artis . . .*' ('The poem of Lucretius is as you write, shot through with many rays of intelligence and high art . . .').[6] This letter is often coupled with Jerome's reference, under the year 94 BC, the year of Lucretius' birth, to Cicero's supposed emendation of Lucretius: *Titus Lucretius poeta nascitur. Qui postea amatorio poculo in furorem versus, cum aliquot libros per intervalla insaniae conscripsisset, quos postea Cicero emendavit, propria se manu interfecit anno aetatis XLIV* ('The poet Titus Lucretius is born. Later, driven mad by a love-potion, although in the intervals of his insanity he wrote several books, which Cicero later emended, he killed himself at 44 years of age,'–my trans.).[7] This has given rise to debate about whether or not Cicero edited Lucretius, and whether that process is what he is referring to in the letter to Quintus.[8] Even if so, we should be careful about overburdening '*emendo*'. The term may have more to do with lending the reader's authority to a copy from a single exemplar than of 'emending' the text in any scientific sense: 'While the English "emend" conjures up critical editions sparkling with the conjectures of a Bentley, Housman, or Shackleton Bailey, Latin *emendare* refers to the removal of *menda*, "faults," of many different sorts. . . . When applied to correcting manuscripts it could be used of a serious scholarly revision based on philological research, but is far more often applied to the routine process of checking copy against exemplar. . . . No research, no learning, no literary taste even was required. Just a careful comparison of copy and exemplar.'[9] '*Emendavit*' as 'made an authoritative reading of' would be especially appropriate because of Cicero's standing in the literary world of Rome, and as the best proxy for Lucretius if the poet had indeed died by the time his work was circulated.[10] The point for us is that there was probably a process of give-and-take between Cicero and Lucretius, regardless of the form Cicero's 'emendation' took.[11] Cicero and Lucretius may well have read *each other*: we have one side of the equation in Cicero's letter, the other in Lucretius' allusions to the *Aratea*.

3.1.2 CICERO'S *ARATEA*[12]

Cicero's *Aratea* was a key text in the Roman reception of Aratus; it became, too, an exemplum of Roman Stoicism by its quotation in Cicero's later *De natura deorum*. This is evidence of the interest of the author, and by implication his audience, in his own work over a period of more than twenty years, from c.89 to c.44 BC. This spans the period of composition of Lucretius' *DRN*.

It is usually said (following Cicero's citation of his own work in *De natura deorum* 2.104) that Cicero translated Aratus in his youth, as a kind of literary *rite de passage*. This means his first attempt was in 89–85 BC.[13] If this dating is correct,

Cicero's initial translation of Aratus was completed in a time of extraordinary up-
heaval in Rome. The period 91–88 saw the social war between Rome and its Italian
allies over citizenship; from 89–85 (a period comparable to WW I or II) Rome was
at war with Mithridates of Pontus; and in 88 Sulla marched on his own city, starting
a civil war, and providing a precedent for the succession of civil wars which followed
in the first century.

   Yet you would not get a sense of any of this from Cicero's *Aratea*. Is it, then,
mere literary exercise, an *exemplum*, or a retreat into order? Aratus' was a work in
which the forces of disorder—planetary motion, stellar change, namelessness—are
ignored or glossed over.[14] Certainly in Cicero's subsequent works, the *De natura
deorum*, the *De divinatione*, both written much later, in the mid-40s BC, the *Aratea*
becomes a metaphor for the ordered and fully comprehensible universe in the Platonic and Stoic traditions, as opposed to the arbitrary universe of the Epicureans.
It is not, perhaps, by chance that Cicero surrounds his quotation of his own work
in the *De natura deorum* with political metaphors denoting orderly divine government of the universe.[15] We might see political metaphor as wishful thinking (if only
the affairs of men were as orderly!) or as attempted redirection in the light of cosmology (Rome ought to take its cue from the universe). In first-century BC Rome,
man and the universe run contrary to one another. An ideal republic would put this
right, swinging both humanity and the cosmos into the same motion, as it were. In
the *Aratea*, Cicero holds up to Rome a template of cosmic order.

3.1.3 FURTHER EVIDENCE

Cicero's letter to Quintus in 54 is the earliest contemporary mention of Lucretius'
poem. By 54, there is plenty of other evidence of Roman interest in Aratus. What
other Aratean activities were happening in Rome around that time? There are several pieces of evidence for interest in Aratus in this period. This evidence for the 60s
and 50s includes the other works of Cicero during that period, and other instances
of literary engagement with Aratus, including the Cinna epigram at the front of this
book, and the *Ephemeris* of Varro of Atax.

   First, Cicero's works other than his *Aratea* attest sustained engagement with
Aratus. One can set the parameters of Cicero's interest around the period which
spans the first composition of his *Aratea* in c.89 to his redeployment of it in his
philosophical works of 44. There is no drought in between. In 62 BC, for instance,
Cicero wrote his autobiographical/historical poem on his own consulship, the *De
consulatu suo*, which was later to earn him some ridicule. But there are perfectly
sane and interesting parts of what we have left of this poem. It includes an extended
address by the astronomical muse Urania to the poet/protagonist, later quoted by
Cicero himself in his *De divinatione*. This part of the poem is in effect a piece of
astronomical didactic writing, in which the Muse takes on the role of the instructor,
informing the poet and audience about the causes of the celestial portents which
supposedly accompanied the events of Cicero's consulship.[16] In it, Cicero revisits

material from Aratus which he translated at least two decades earlier. In *Ph.* 454–61 Aratus shied away from telling about the planets; at *Aratea* 234 Cicero followed him, with the modest disclaimer *quarum ego nunc nequeo tortos evolvere cursus* ('I am unable to unroll the convoluted courses of these [heavenly bodies]'). This despite the fact that, in the period which intervened between Aratus and Cicero's translation of Aratus, astronomers, including Aratus' commentator Hipparchus, had developed the system of epicycles which was more effective than Eudoxus' homocentric spheres in explaining planetary motion.[17] In his *Aratea* Cicero chose to follow the model at the expense of scientific developments. Not so in the *Cons.*, however. Writing in 62 BC, Cicero acknowledges the debate, and the advances in science:

> et si stellarum motus cursusque vagantis
> nosse velis quae sint signorum in sede locatae,
> quae verbo et falsis Graiorum vocibus *errant*,
> re vera certo lapsu spatioque feruntur,
> omnia iam cernes divina mente notata. (*Cons.* fr. 2.6–10, ed. Soubiran)

> 'And if you want to understand the motion and the wandering courses of those heavenly bodies which are located in the region of the zodiac, which, according to the false etymology of the Greeks 'wander,' but really are carried on a predictable course in space, you will now see it all, clarified by a divine mind' (my trans.).

In this, Cicero highlights the falsehood of an etymology, *errare* for Gk πλανάω, the verb which gives us πλανῆτες, the very etymology he himself propounded in the 'planets' passage of his *Aratea* (*Arat.* 230):

> sic malunt *errare vagae* per nubila caeli
> atque suos vario motu metirier orbes.

> 'Thus they prefer to wander footloose through the clouds of heaven and to measure out their orbits with a variable motion.'

We might see Cicero in the *Cons.* as both responding to Aratus, and updating his own translation of him. The point is that he was somehow motivated to come back to the question, and to his earlier work: one motivation may be the continuing popularity of Aratus in Rome.[18]

Cicero came back to Aratus again in 60 BC. In a letter to his friend and 'publisher' Atticus, dating from June 60[19] (*Att.* 2.1.11), Cicero says, '*Prognostica mea cum oratiunculis propediem expecta*', 'Expect my *Prognostica* forthwith, along with some speechlets' (my trans.). This reference by Cicero to his '*Prognostica*' induced a paroxysm of scholarship, which I do not intend to repeat.[20] The various theories boil down to a couple of plausible alternatives: (i) Cicero wrote a *Prognostica*, i.e., his translation of the second half of Aratus' work, the *Diosemeiai*, alongside his *Aratea* in c.89. Then he revised it and sent it off for publication in 60. (ii) Cicero only translated the first half of Aratus in c.89, and what he was sending to Atticus in 60 was a *new* translation of the *Diosemeiai*. For our purposes it doesn't particularly matter. What the reference to the *Diosemeiai* attests is (a) Cicero maintained enough of an interest in Aratus in 60 to send his poem to Atticus, and (b) that that interest would have been aligned with that of the audience of any 'published' work, and (c) Cicero's composition/revision of his *Prognostica* and the interest in any potential audience coincides with the period in which Lucretius can be presumed to have been writing the *DRN*.

This picture is supported by further Ciceronian evidence, this time from 55 BC. Writing in this year, Cicero affirms that the *docti* all agree that Aratus is the best thing around: *etenim si constat inter doctos, hominem ignarum astrologiae ornatissimis atque optimis versibus Aratum de caelo stellisque dixisse* (*De orat.* 1.69, quoted with trans. above, Introduction, p. 6). 55 BC is a year in which we can be fairly sure that Lucretius was writing the *DRN*.[21]

Also in the 50s BC, though perhaps marginally later than Lucretius, Cicero's *De re publica* attests his interest in Aratus, as well as his audience's putative understanding of astronomical issues. The *Rep.* begins and ends with celestial things, from the discussion of the phenomenon of the double sun in Book 1 to the *Somnium Scipionis* in Book 6. Early on, Aratus is referred to by name (*Rep.* 1.22):

> dicebat enim Galus, sphaerae illius alterius solidae atque plenae vetus esse inventum, et eam a Thalete Milesio primum esse tornatam; post autem ab Eudoxo Cnidio, discipulo ut ferebat Platonis, eandem illam astris quae caelo inhaererent esse descriptam; cuius omnem ornatum et descriptionem, sumptam ab Eudoxo, multis annis post non astrologiae scientia sed poetica quadam facultate versibus Aratum extulisse.

> 'Galus said that the sphere which was solid all the way through was an old invention, and that Thales of Miletus had first made one, which was then taken up by Eudoxus of Cnidus, as pupil, so they say, of Plato, and engraved with the stars which are attached to the heaven. Many years later Aratus took the whole arrangement and order from Eudoxus and set it out in verse, not with any great knowledge of astronomy, but with poetic facility' (my trans.; text of Powell 2006).[22]

It is interesting that Cicero apparently knew the tradition, first attested in Hipparchus, that Aratus versified Eudoxus (see above, Introduction, pp. 7–8). Cicero must have been reading the second-century BC commentator, or a commentary which contained similar material, as well as the text. Lucretius himself may plausibly have been reading Aratus with commentators and translations, including Cicero's, alongside. This became reading practice in respect of Aratus very early on and is reflected in the manuscript tradition, right up to the early printed editions probably read by Copernicus.

In any case, Aratus was a sought-after intellectual commodity in first-century BC Rome. Not only this, but a sought-after material commodity, if Cinna's Epigram is anything to go by. The Epigram accompanies an 'exhibition copy' of Aratus written on mallow bark and brought back from Bithynia (part of modern Turkey), probably in 57–6 BC:[23]

> haec tibi Arateis multum vigilata lucernis
> carmina, quis ignes novimus aerios,
> levis in aridulo malvae descripta libello
>   Prusiaca[24] vexi munera navicula.

> 'I have brought you this poem, which teaches us to recognize the fires in the sky. Aratus kept vigil over it for a long time with his lamp. It is written in a tiny book made of smoothed mallow bark, and I brought it as a gift in a little boat from the land of King Prusias' (my trans.).

Aratus was being copied, and was deemed worth bringing to Rome in the 50s, when Lucretius was composing the *DRN*. Lucretius himself may well have been aware of the genre of the 'Aratean epigram.' *De rerum natura* 1.140–43 might represent a playful instance:

> sed tua me virtus tamen et sperata voluptas
> suavis amicitiae quemvis efferre laborem
> suadet et inducit noctes vigilare serenas
> quaerentem dictis quibus et quo carmine demum
> clara tuae possim praepandere lumina menti.

> 'But your virtue, and the pleasure I hope for from sweet friendship, persuades me to put up with the effort, however, great it may be, and leads me to stay awake through undisturbed nights, seeking the words and the poem with which I might at length be able to offer a clear light to your mind.'

Roman interest in Aratus in the first century BC seems to have been the result of two factors: (i) because he teaches us about the stars, and (ii) because of the excessively careful or learned nature of Aratus' poem (*Arateis multum vigilata lucernis*). The latter is what Cicero also stresses in the *De oratore*.

We should also add the translation of Aratus' weather-signs in the *Ephemeris* of Varro of Atax (b. 82 BC), fr. 13 and 14 Courtney (1993)/120 and 121 Hollis (2007).[25] This work probably dates from sometime after 58 BC.[26] Varro attests interest in Aratus across a period which coincided with Cicero's and Cinna's interest, and may have overlapped with the composition of Lucretius' *DRN*.

Cinna, Varro, and Cicero together represent aspects of the reception of Aratus' work in Rome during the precise period (60s–50s BC) when Lucretius was writing. As external evidence they testify to a sustained and widespread interest in Aratus in Roman intellectual circles in the 60s–50s BC, when Lucretius was writing the *DRN*.

In this literary milieu, it is not in the least surprising that Lucretius is interested in Aratus or that Aratus is coming to him both directly and through Cicero's *Aratea*, which, one may conjecture on the basis of the evidence, was still in circulation and in which there may have been renewed interest at around the same time when Cicero was disseminating his *Prognostica*.

3.2 Lucretius and Cicero: the Internal Evidence

This chapter and the one which follows were initially written in response to a verbal challenge from a friend and distinguished colleague: if you think Cicero influenced Lucretius, prove it. I believe this can be done; not only this, but to do so adds greatly to our idea of the impact of Aratus in Rome, and to our understanding of the nature of Lucretius' *DRN*. I am going to argue here and in the next chapter that Cicero's *Aratea* did influence Lucretius, and it did so not only in isolated cases but in a *thoroughgoing* way. Furthermore, I shall argue that the underlying presence of Cicero's translation of Aratus adds a layer of meaning to Lucretius' text which we ignore at the price of understanding Lucretius' technique of engaging with other philosophical schools. In turn, this will cast light on the philosophical significance of the tradition of Aratus in first-century BC Rome.

3.2.1 DEBATE AND METHODOLOGY

Scholars are strangely reluctant to believe that Lucretius was influenced by Cicero. The debate extends well back into the nineteenth century. The thesis that Lucretius drew on Cicero was first stated by Munro in his edition of Lucretius: 'It is evident Lucretius has studied this translation of Cicero.'[27] Various counter-theses were early proposed. Norden, in his commentary on the sixth book of Virgil's *Aeneid*, was the first and most influential scholar to argue that any similarity between Lucretius and Cicero can be imputed to a shared bank of Ennian expression.[28] Merrill (1921) was the most vehement proponent of the 'no' view. He presented what purports to be a convincing list of parallels between Cicero and Lucretius. But these are reductively assessed as trivial or chance similarities: 'It cannot be denied that there are many instances of similarity, yet, if close examination be directed to them, most of them will prove to be *mere coincidences*' (my emphasis).[29] His ultimate verdict is negative: 'That Lucretius studied and imitated the youthful Cicero's poetry is fundamentally improbable.'[30] This verdict is based on the assumption that Cicero was—simply—not a good enough poet: 'The theory of indebtedness demands that one of the greatest of Roman poets in the maturity of his powers was indebted to the puerile compositions of a *mere versifier*' (again, my emphasis).[31] This view has never been systematically refuted, despite the pendulum-swing implied in the views of Kenney (1971),[32] Costa (1984),[33] and Courtney (1993),[34] and a general if limited rehabilitation of Cicero's poetry.[35]

What is needed is a more nuanced interpretative methodology, but one which is also based on a thorough appraisal of the evidence. This raw evidence is presented in appendix B, where I list all parallels between Lucretius and Cicero's *Aratea*. In assessing them we should first remember Conte's dictum that 'even the most thread-bare poetic residuum, when transferred from one context to another, acquires a varying, stratified connotation.'[36] Second, we must interpret. No re-opening of the debate, nor indeed any study of a relationship between two poets, can be justified unless it adds meaning to the text. If contextual awareness is missing, then discussions of influence of one poet on another are just a *Glasperlenspiel* involving the uncontextualized citation of *loci similes*.

How do we read allusions for meaning? Intertextuality and context. Conte tells us that, when poets allude to other texts, '. . . two different voices are heard within the poem as if they were engaged in dialogue.'[37] Their dialogue may run parallel to wider cultural debate, such as that between opposing schools of philosophy: 'Even when denying the norm . . . [poets] must be aware of the existence of tradition, *often being obliged to use the expressive means of a school they oppose to achieve another end* (my emphasis).'[38] I argue that this is precisely what is involved in the dialogue between Lucretius and Cicero. Further, in reading the poem's intertexts, context is everything. Don Fowler's work on Lucretius, while it does not touch on the *Aratea*, gives a useful direction to our method of interpretation: 'Throughout the purely physical sections of the work, the *De rerum natura* constantly insinuates arguments against its two main targets, the fear of the gods and of death: the wider contexts of the intertexts here assist this process.'[39] Therefore, once an allusion has been identified, my methodology is to look first and foremost at the contexts at both ends of it, the Ciceronian and the Lucretian ends, and see how they rebound off one another.

My argument is both more detailed and more specific than Fowler's. I argue that Aratus' text came to represent what we might call an 'intelligent design' universe, in which all parts are orderly, comprehensible, and divinely guided. Despite differences between them, this was broadly speaking the universe of Plato, Aristotle, and the Stoics, the one which came to predominate in Western culture up to the Copernican revolution. But there is another universe out there, that of the atomists and Epicureans: a vertiginous, limitless world of multiverses formed by the chance collusion of atoms. This is Lucretius' universe, and it is in the context of its exposition that his echoes of Cicero's *Aratea* occur. Lucretius' text is a paradox in that it reuses forms of expression from a text which represented the divinely governed universe to construct the opposing view. Lucetius recomposes Cicero's poem in opposition to itself, and in so doing places himself within a philosophical debate in which the *Aratea* plays an essential part.[40]

Surprisingly, perhaps, there is also considerable opposition to the view that Lucretius' text involves itself in inter-school debate. Sedley, for instance, writes, 'Lucretius appears blissfully unaware of the entire debate raging around him. At no point is his defence of the Epicurean tenet adjusted to resist any known element of the Stoic critique, and he makes no use of the new generation of Epicurean counter-arguments preserved by Philodemus. That would be most surprising either if he had had a serious interest in combating contemporary Stoic cosmology, or if, as often assumed, he had enjoyed significant philosophical interaction with the Epicurean school of Philodemus.[41] Does Lucretius, however, *ever* cite contemporary sources? He may not cite the Stoic Posidonius, but nor does he cite the Epicurean Philodemus, and yet no one doubts that his work is Epicurean. Why should it not contain a critique of the Stoics, similarly uncited? Or, as intertextual criticism would be happier to put it, lay itself open to philosophical interpretation by a readership alive to those concerns?

In fact, many instances of polemical *argumentation*, albeit without direct citation of opponents who hold the opposing views, may be identified in *DRN* Book 5 alone. For example, lines 793–4, *nam neque de caelo cecidisse animalia possunt /nec terrestria de salsis exisse lacunis*, may be taken as 'partly a jeering overstatement of the Stoic theory of the πνεῦμα, anima . . ., which fills the cosmos and also forms the soul of animals and the texture of plants. . . .'[42] Earlier in the book, Lucretius uses a Stoic image (the limbs of world) 5.476–7, in opposition to his specifically Epicurean argument in 5.564–91.[43] The fact that Lucretius does not name contemporary Stoic targets does not seem to me *prima facie* fatal to the view that the *DRN* contains anti-Stoic polemic.

There is a tendency to ignore passages such as these in prescribing which ideas Lucretius *should* have taken on. One of the key pieces of evidence Sedley presents for Lucretius' lack of engagement with contemporary philosophical debate is that he does not take issue with contemporary mechanical devices for demonstrating mathematical astronomy. Epicurus was familiar with such mechanisms and made a point of attacking the observational principles on which they were based.[44] In Book 5 Lucretius chose to omit a critique of such machines, 'A perfectly reasonable decision, no doubt, on aesthetic grounds . . ., but hardly a sign of concern to combat the contemporary Stoic challenge'.[45]

As we'll see in the section below on Lucretius' astronomy, it is my view that Lucretius does in fact engage with the Stoic world model, certainly the conceptual model, possibly even the physical one. Whether or not this is the case, however, engaging with this single idea is not the only index of polemic. It is not only in the sphere of explicit reference to mathematical astronomy that Lucretius can engage with Stoicism.

Similarly reluctant to believe that the *DRN* could be polemical in an inter-school sense, although for a different reason, is Trépanier: 'The desire to find inter-school polemics in Lucretius, notably anti-Stoic arguments, *does not strike me as compatible with an understanding of its status as literature*, defined by broad generic conventions and further shaped by its poetic model.'[46] This attempts to excuse the *DRN* from inter-school debates on the grounds that it is *literature*. But a work does not have to be *either* literary *or* philosophical, and in fact it is to the great benefit of Lucretius' that both readings are encoded within it.[47]

Perhaps because of the 'literary' nature of Lucretius' work, we should not expect him to write an academic paper refuting his opponents, with full citations. Lucretius' favoured argumentative technique is that of oblique polemic. This is achieved primarily through intertextual reference. Lucretius' is a didactic game which both gives pleasure in the recognition, and has the additional benefit of what you might call the 'didactic conspiracy': the art of making the poet and his readers into an inner circle who understand the obliquity of his polemical reference.

3.2.2 LUCRETIUS' ASTRONOMY

In order to understand what Lucretius is arguing against in his appropriation of the *Aratea*, we need first to take a sounding of Lucretius' position on astronomy vis-à-vis that of his Stoic opponents. Lucretius' entire position on astronomy is *inherently anti-Stoic*. All of the astronomy in the *DRN* takes place within this ideological shell. There is no rhyme or reason to Lucretius' stars, nor can they be used as evidence for the divine, as in Stoicism. To get this point across Lucretius uses Ciceronian material, drawing systematically, for instance, on Cicero's passage on the planets from the *Aratea*, but doing so in a context which applies the unreason of the planets to *all* of the stars. In Cicero, the planets are wandering. In Lucretius *all* the stars are wandering, or rather, it doesn't make any real difference whether they are or not.[48]

Lucretius' position on astronomy stems from his position on 'intelligent design'. This position is one which emerges repeatedly across the work, for example in *DRN* 5.156–165:

> dicere porro hominum causa voluisse parare
> praeclaram mundi naturam proptereaque
> allaudabile opus divom laudare decere
> aeternumque putare atque inmortale futurum
> nec fas esse, deum quod sit ratione vetusta
> gentibus humanis fundatum perpetuo aevo,
> sollicitare suis ulla vi ex sedibus umquam
> nec verbis vexare et ab imo evertere summa,
> cetera de genere hoc adfingere et addere, Memmi,
> desiperest.

> 'Furthermore, to say that [the gods] wanted for the sake of humankind to establish the glorious structure of the world, and that therefore it is right to praise it as though it were a work of the gods worthy of praise, and to think that it will last forever and be immortal, and that it is unlawful that a thing which has been established eternally for the races of mankind by the ancient wisdom of the gods should ever be shaken from its foundations by any force, nor besieged by words and destroyed from top to bottom—to fabricate things like this and put them in sequence is to be an idiot, Memmius.'

Lucretius' take on the stars, which follows from this antagonistic position towards the idea of any divine role in the world, is exemplified by the opening of his passage on astronomy (*DRN* 5.76–81, quoted above p. 58). Are the stars put there by providence for the benefit of humans? No, they are not: they are in no way programmed to increase plants and livestock for human benefit. This directly opposes the Stoic position on the stars which can be exemplified by the words of the Stoic speaker in Cicero, *De natura deorum* 2.115: *haec omnis descriptio siderum atque hic tantus caeli ornatus ex corporibus huc et illuc casu et temere cursantibus potuisse effici cuiquam sano videri potest . . .?* 'Can any sane person imagine that this overall pattern of constellations, this massive embellishment of the heavens, can have been the outcome of atoms careering at random in various chance directions?' [Implied answer: Obviously not— the gods made them, and made them for a reason, i.e., for the benefit of humans].

For Lucretius, the stars are fallacious, a chimaera. At the same time, he chooses to talk about them in terms remarkably similar to Stoic texts. The mechanics of this polemical technique can be illustrated from his ironic passage on 'The Wonder of the Stars', *DRN* 2.1030–9:

> principio caeli clarum purumque colorem,
> quaeque in se cohibet, palantia sidera passim,
> lunamque et solis praeclara luce nitorem;
> omnia quae nunc si primum mortalibus essent,
> ex improviso si sint obiecta repente,
> quid magis his rebus poterat mirabile dici
> aut minus ante quod auderent fore credere gentes?
> nil, ut opinor: ita haec species miranda fuisset.
> quam tibi iam nemo, fessus satiate videndi,
> suspicere in caeli dignatur lucida templa!

'First of all, take the fine undiluted colour of the heaven, and those bodies it contains, the stars wandering all over the place, the moon and the brightness of the sun with its pure light: if these were suddenly cast before mortals for the first time all unforeseen, what could be said to be more miraculous than these—or less believable without foreknowledge? Nothing, in my view: so wonderful would the appearance of these things have been. But think how no one, tired with the satiety of gazing, can be bothered to look up into the shining realms of heaven.'

So similar to Lucretius' passage on the stars is the speech of Cicero's Stoic speaker Balbus in *DND* 2.96–7 that we might believe that it, in turn, answers Lucretius:

> quod si hoc idem ex aeternis tenebris contingeret ut subito lucem aspiceremus, quaenam species caeli videretur[?] Sed adsiduitate cotidiana et consuetudine oculorum adsuescunt animi, neque admirantur neque requirunt rationes earum rerum quas semper vident, proinde quasi novitas nos magis quam magnitudo rerum debeat ad exquirendas causas excitare.

'Now supposing after an eternity of darkness we suddenly and similarly beheld the light of day, how would the heavens appear to us? But as things stand, because we routinely see them every day and they are a familiar sight, our minds grow inured to them, so we do not experience wonder, or seek to explain what lies always before our eyes. It is as if novelty rather than the majesty of creation is what must rouse us to investigate the causes of the universe' (trans. Walsh 1997; text of Pease 1955–8).

Note Cicero's *aspiceremus*, with *suspicere in caeli* (Lucretius 2.1039); *species caeli*, with *species* in Lucretius 2.1037; and *admirantur*, with *mirabile* and *miranda* (Lucretius 2.1035 and 1037).

Why would Cicero, a decade after the publication of the *DRN*, have thought it worth while to respond to Lucretius? Perhaps because he has read past the text of the *DRN*, to Lucretius' agenda, which he then seeks to correct in the *DND*. Lucretius prefaces the passage just quoted with an exhortation to truth (*veram rationem*, 2.1023). The celestial phenomena he talks about in this passage are not real. They are tantamount to the shadow-phenomena of Plato's cave (a passage to which both Lucretius and Cicero probably allude here), not the phenomena of the world as it is.[49] Their apparent logic is a myth from which the reader should turn away. But Cicero, who sees through Lucretius' rhetoric, is not happy to turn away. Instead, he writes the stars as evidence of the divine back into the Stoic book of his *DND*, reading the Lucretian passage as anti-Stoic polemic, and claiming it back for the Stoic side. The fact that he felt compelled to reargue the case shows the cut-and-thrust of first-century debate, and demonstrates Lucretius' involvement in it.

Astronomy was the node of the debate, the area in which, according to your philosophical position, you either believed divine intervention was demonstrable, or that it was not. In the case under consideration our two authors strike out on these ideologically divergent routes. Let's look at how the respective passages continue. In this passage of Lucretius 2, the stars are a metaphor for the tendency of the intelligence to be taken in by ceasing to see what is familiar. Lucretius continues that metaphor in lines 1044–7. If the negative side of the metaphor (the inert intelligence) was expressed using the metaphor of wonder at the stars, the positive side is expressed by the limitless universe as a figure for the unshackled mind, *prospicere usque velit mens /atque animi iactus liber quo pervolet ipse* ('where the mind desires to look and where the unfettered trajectory of the intelligence wings itself,' 1046–7).

Almost immediately the metaphor morphs into actuality, when the substance of the teaching gets underway (*DRN* 2.1048–50):

Principio nobis in cunctas undique partis
et latere ex utroque <supra> subterque per omne
nulla est finis . . .

'In the first place, around us in every direction, on both sides and above and below, the universe is infinite . . .'

The open mind is now parallel to the limitless universe of Epicureanism, the true way of seeing the world. Not only is the world limitless, but Epicurean dogma militates for chance in its formation of the universe(s).[50] It is the *semina rerum* (*DRN* 2. 1059)—*not* the stars (contrast *DRN* 5.79)—which act *sponte sua* in the creation of a universe which is nothing like a Golden Age. Note in the surrounding lines (*DRN* 2. 1059–62) the coagulation of words for chance:[51]

sponte sua forte offensando semina rerum
multimodis *temere incassum frustraque* coacta
tandem coluerunt ea quae *coniecta repente*
magnarum rerum fierent exordia semper . . .

'Of their own accord, by knocking together by chance, forced together in many ways without rhyme, reason, or rationale, at length they formed those things which, coming suddenly into contact with one another, could become every time the beginnings of large things . . .'

Cicero's speaker, on the other hand, goes on in *DND* 2.97, after the passage quoted above, to describe the heavenly machinery as evidence for divine providence, in which nothing is left to chance, and to liken it to a wondrous man-made machine (the orrery of Posidonius, which has already been invoked in the same argument, at *DND* 2.88):[52]

quis enim hunc hominem dixerit, qui, cum tam certos caeli motus, tam ratos astrorum ordines, tamque inter se omnia conexa et apta viderit, neget in his ullam inesse rationem eaque casu fieri dicat, quae quanto consilio gerantur nullo consilio adsequi possumus. an, cum machinatione quadam moveri aliquid videmus, ut sphaeram, ut horas, ut alia permulta, non dubitamus quin illa opera sint rationis, cum autem impetum caeli cum admirabili celeritate moveri vertique videamus, constantissime conficientem vicissitudines anniversarias cum summa salute et conservatione rerum omnium, dubitamus quin ea non solum ratione fiant sed etiam excellenti divinaque ratione?

'Who would regard a human being as worthy of the name, if upon observing the fixed movements of heaven, the prescribed dispositions of the stars, and the conjunction and interrelation of all creation he denied the existence of rationality in all these, and claimed that chance was responsible for works created with a degree of wisdom such as our own wisdom fails totally to comprehend? When we observe that some object—an orrery, say, or a clock, or lots of other such things—is moved by some mechanism, we have no doubt that reason lies behind such devices; so when we note the thrust and remarkable speed with which the heavens revolve, completing with absolute regularity their yearly changes, and preserving the whole of creation in perfect safety, do we hesitate to acknowledge that this is achieved not merely by reason, but by reason which is preeminent and divine?' (trans. Walsh 1997)[53]

Cicero is accusing Epicureans in general, and perhaps Lucretius specifically, of being both unworthy of the name of human, because they think the universe came about by chance (*casu*), and arrogant in assuming that they can understand all aspects of the universe. *Casu* carries the weight of polemic in *DND* 2.97. It denotes what Epicureans believe in respect of the world, and it is this belief that makes them sub-human in Stoic eyes. Cicero's Balbus concludes this section by restating the case against chance (*DND* 2.115, quoted on p. 70 above). *DND* 2.115, *casu et temere*, might be answering *DRN* 2.1060 *temere incassum*.[54] There is a further term for chance in *DRN* 2.1060: *frustra*. Behind Lucretius' collocation of *temere* and *frustra* in this line lies Cicero *Aratea* 32–3, *sed frustra, temere a vulgo, ratione sine ulla /septem dicier, ut veteres statuere poetae* ('But in vain, wildly, by the mob, without any rationale, [the Pleiades] are said to be seven, as the ancient poets ordained', my trans.). In Cicero, *frustra* and *temere* express the falsity of the vulgate view of the Pleiades (seven as opposed to six). Lucretius has lifted these expressions from one polemical context and placed them in another.

The pattern of the co-option of these terms in the debate is (i) Cicero *Aratea* (*temere, frustra*); (ii) Lucretius (*temere incassum frustraque*); (iii) Cicero *DND* 2.115 (*casu et temere*). This is a fascinating interchange. In Lucretius, we see the reuse of a Ciceronian formula *against* the tradition in which Cicero himself belongs, i.e., that of Aratus. Lucretian reminiscence of Cicero here is ironic: it helps him express his own view of the random universe. The seeds (so to speak) of the argument may already have been sown in Ciceronian language, but its narrative outcome in Lucretius is the opposite: chance takes on the role of providence. Cicero lived long enough to get his revenge in *DND* 2.97, claiming the terms back for his Stoic speaker, in the context of ridiculing the *Epicureans*.

From this we can see how Lucretius is involved in the cut-and-thrust of first-century cosmological debate. This was a process of adoption and cooption of textual material, not of one-sided allusion or borrowing. Within the framework of polarized debate across texts, I shall now show how Ciceronian reference works in the astronomical passage of Book 5, and how this furthers Lucretius' ideological, polemical, and philosophical ends.

3.2.3 THE STARS AND THE DEVELOPMENT OF RELIGION

According to Lucretius, misleading 'evidence' of the divine is offered to mankind by the heavenly bodies. For the Epicurean, it is only when we don't understand the stars that they appear miraculous (*DRN* 5.1183–93):

> praeterea caeli rationes ordine certo
> et varia annorum cernebant tempora verti
> nec poterant quibus id fieret cognoscere causis.   1185
> ergo perfugium sibi habebant omnia divis
> tradere et illorum nutu facere omnia flecti.

in caeloque deum sedes et templa locarunt,
per caelum volvi quia nox et luna videtur,
luna dies et nox et noctis signa severa   1190
noctivagaeque faces caeli flammaeque volantes,
nubila sol imbres nix venti fulmina grando
et rapidi fremitus et murmura magna minarum . . .

'Moreover, they saw that the logic of heaven was that the different seasons of
the year should come around in a predictable order, but they couldn't identify
the causes of this phenomenon. Because of this, their refuge was to assign
everything to the gods and to make out that all things are guided by their
Diktat. They placed the seat and realm of the gods in the heaven, because
that's where night and the moon seem to revolve—the moon, and day and
night and the pitiless constellations of night, and those night-wandering
torches and flying flamebursts; clouds sun rain snow winds lightning hail and
rapid reports or low threatening rumblings of thunder.'

In this wonderful passage Lucretius moves from thought to thought with increasing
terseness and vehemence. We should not now be surprised to find that *DRN* 5.1193
recalls Cicero, *Arat.* 71, *nec metuunt canos minitanti murmure fluctus*. In *DRN*
5.1184, the collocation *tempora verti* may recall Cicero on the zodiac, *annua conficiens vertentia tempora cursu* (*Arat.* 333). In each case, Lucretius is in angry dialogue
with the Ciceronian view. Cicero's sailors, described in *Arat.* 71, do not fear the
threatening murmurs; it is *because* Lucretius' unenlightened folk fear these very
things that they set off on the misguided and destructive course of religion. In
Cicero, the arrangement of celestial circles, of which the zodiac is most conspicuous, is the best index of the whole celestial plan; in Lucretius, such a plan is only
apparent, and seduces the unwary onto the wrong path.

Here is the passage which follows (*DRN* 5.1204–10):

nam cum suspicimus magni caelestia mundi
templa super stellisque micantibus aethera fixum,   1205
et venit in mentem solis lunaeque viarum,
tunc aliis oppressa malis in pectora cura
illa quoque expergefactum caput erigere infit,
nequae forte deum nobis inmensa potestas
sit, vario motu quae candida sidera verset.   1210

'For when we look up to the celestial regions of the great sky and the ether up
above embossed with shining stars, and we bear in mind the paths of the sun
and moon—then in our hearts, already worn down by other worries, another
concern rears its ugly head: does that immense power of the gods which is
capable of spinning the shining stars in their divergent motions perhaps have
some sway over us?'

After the description of the celestial order ending with *viarum*, we might be led to expect an expression of awe—'How we are taken with wonder!' *vel sim*. Instead, Lucretius characteristically turns the tables with a dark and threatening description of the results of our stargazing, full of terms of worry, care, and anxiety. Beautiful as the stars are, they fill us not with awe but with dread. Lucretius continues a little later (1218–21):

> praeterea cui non animus formidine divum
> contrahitur, cui non correpunt membra pavore,
> fulminis horribili cum plaga torrida tellus
> contremit et magnum percurrunt murmura caelum?

> 'Furthermore, whose mind does not shrink with fear of the gods, whose flesh does not crawl with fear, when the baked earth shakes under the fatal blow of a thunderbolt and rumblings pervade the great sky?'

In the wider context of this passage on the development of religion, Lucretius also chooses to echo expressions from Cicero. For instance, 1205, *stellis micantibus aethera fixum*, recalls *Arat*. fr. 16.3–4 S., . . . *subter praecordia fixa videtur* /*stella micans radiis* . . ., and fr. 20. S., . . . *adfixa videtur* /*stella micans*. Here there is a triple collocation shared between Lucretius and Cicero. Moreover, Ciceronian references act in aggregation in this passage. 1210, *vario motu*, recalls *Aratea* 231, which contains the same collocation. There *vario motu* is also used of the heavenly bodies, but in Cicero's case the *planets*, not, as in Lucretius, all of the stars, because for Cicero the motion of the fixed stars is not variable. In addition, the description of thunder at 1221, *magnum percurrunt murmura caelum*, reminds us of *Arat*. 71, *nec metuunt canos minitanti murmure fluctus*. We remember that Lucretius may already have had this passage in mind at the very outset of his passage on the development of religion, *DRN* 5.1193, *murmura magna minarum*.

The Ciceronian presence in the alliterative onomatopoeic descrption of thunder, furthermore, serves to unite the passage on religion in Book 5 with the famous passage in Book 1 on Epicurus' expurgation of *religio* at *DRN* 1.62–71, which concludes (68–71):

> quem neque fama deum nec fulmina nec minitanti
> murmure compressit caelum, sed eo magis acrem
> irritat animi virtutem, effringere ut arta
> naturae primus portarum claustra cupiret.

> 'Neither fables of the gods, nor thunderbolts, nor the heaven with its threatening rumbling repressed him, but instead these things whetted the drawn steel of his mind all the more to yearn to be the first to break down the narrow approaches to nature's gates.'[55]

In the Book 1 passage, we have an exact replica of Cicero's collocation *minitanti murmure*. In book 5, Lucretius chooses to remind us of it by sketching the same collocation twice in varied form, at the opening and close of his passage on the development of religion. Allusion to Cicero helps bind the two passages into a cohesive discussion of religion, as well as furnishing the material for the attack on it.

3.2.4 LUCRETIUS' ASTRONOMY AND CICERO'S *ARATEA*

So far we have seen in general terms how Lucretius' poem is situated vis-à-vis contemporary debate, and we have begun to note its insidious use of Cicero. Cicero explodes into plain view in the astronomical section of the *DRN*. Lucretius' exposition of astronomy, *DRN* 5.614–704, is a cross-hatching of Ciceronian parallels.[56] This is especially the case in lines 680–95:

crescere itemque dies licet et tabescere noctes,	680
et minui luces, cum sumant augmina noctes,	
aut quia sol idem sub terras atque superne	
imparibus currens anfractibus aetheris oras	
partit et in partis non aequas dividit orbem,	
et quod ab alterutra detraxit parte, reponit	685
eius in adversa tanto plus parte relatus,	
donec ad id signum caeli pervenit, ubi anni	
nodus nocturnas exaequat lucibus umbras.	
nam medio cursu flatus aquilonis et austri	
distinet aequato caelum discrimine metas	690
propter signiferi posituram totius orbis,	
annua sol in quo concludit tempora serpens,	
obliquo terras et caelum lumine lustrans,	
ut ratio declarat eorum qui loca caeli	
omnia dispositis signis ornata notarunt.	695

'Days grow longer and nights diminish, and days grow shorter when nights increase, either because the same sun dissects the regions of the ether, running under and over the earth in unequal semicircles, but doesn't divide the two halves of the circle equally, and gives to whichever half an increase proportional to the amount he subtracts from the other, until he reaches that star-sign where the nub of the year makes equal noctural darkness to light. For the heaven holds his turning-points an equal distance apart between the north and south winds on account of the position of the whole zodiac, in which the spiralling sun brings about the seasons of the year, illuminating earth and heaven with obliquely shed light, as the reasoning of those who have marked out the whole decorative map of heaven with the constellations laid out in order would have it . . .'

'The passage is so full of imitations of Cicero's *Aratea* that it is possible that Lucr[etius] took the explanation from that source.'[57] The apparent rapport between

Lucretius and his source lays a false trail, however. The problem with Cicero vis-à-vis Lucretius' account is that all of Cicero's astronomy is based on three premises, namely that the universe is divinely ordered, capable of definitive explanation, and there for the benefit of mankind. For the Epicurean this is nonsense, as is the idea that there can be a single limiting explanation for the sun's motion. Without pausing to draw breath, Lucretius continues, in the same breath, *aut quia crassior est certis in partibus aer*, '. . . or because the air is thicker in certain parts' (*DRN* 5.696).

What we have in Lucretius' account is a series of alternative explanations for the variation in the length of day and night across the year. The first explanation is attributed not to Lucretius himself, but to *eorum qui loca caeli /omnia dispositis signis ornata notarunt*, those who have *systematized* the heavens. We cannot help but wonder who these people are and whether their explanation is likely to be true, especially when we are subsequently confronted with an alternative, *unmediated* explanation in the following line, one, moreover, which is not reliant on notions of celestial clockwork. On this theory, variation in the length of days and nights is not, as in the astronomy represented by the Aratean texts, a result of the movement of the heavenly bodies around a symmetrical model composed of interlocking circles, but simply because of variations in the thickness of the air.[58]

As we ponder this, a model for the first alternative occurs to us, prompted by Lucretius' own text, which contains many parallels with Cicero's *Aratea*. The picture from Cicero's *Aratea* looks like the sytematized heaven of Lucretius' *eorum qui loca caeli /omnia dispositis signis ornata notarunt* (*Arat.* 237–44):

> quattuor, aeterno lustrantes lumine mundum,
> orbes stelligeri portantes signa feruntur,
> amplexi terras, caeli sub tegmine fulti:
> e quibus annorum volitantia lumina nosces,
> quae densis distincta licebit cernere signis.
> tum magnos orbis magno cum lumine latos,
> vinctos inter se et *nodis* caelestibus aptos,
> atque pari spatio duo cernes esse duobus.

> 'There are borne along, illuminating the sky with constant light, the four star-bearing circles which carry the constellations, girding the earth, fastened beneath the vault of heaven. From these you will recognize the flying luminaries which mark the year, which it will be possible to discern, disposed in close-wrought constellations. Then you will see that the great circles are carried along with great light, mutually tied together and fastened with celestial knots, and that they go two by two at equal intervals.'

In Cicero we have *nodis* for the equinoctial points, like *nodus* (s.) in Lucretius. *Nodus* in an astronomical context occurs before Lucretius only in Cicero's passage on the celestial circles. *Lustrantes lumine mundum* in *Arat.* 237 is recalled by *caelum lumine lustrans* in *DRN* 5.693 (cf. *Arat.* 332, *lumine lustrans*). *Signiferi . . . orbis* in Lucretius 5.691 expresses more deftly Cicero's Romanization of ζῳδιακός, in *orbes stelligeri portantes signa, Arat.* 238. Lucretius 5.688, <u>*nocturnas exaequat lucibus*</u> *umbras* could be taken with *Arat.* 288 <u>*exaequat*</u> *spatium* <u>*lucis*</u> *cum tempore* <u>*noctis,*</u> as a shared triple collocation with *variatio.* Both authors here refer to the sun's intersection with the equator. Compare Lucretius 5.692, *annua sol in . . . tempora,* with Cicero *Arat.* 332–3, *haec* <u>*sol*</u> *aeterno* <u>*convestit lumine lustrans*</u> */*<u>*annua*</u> *conficiens vertentia* <u>*tempora*</u> *cursu.*

This part of Lucretius' argument is figured in Ciceronian language. When, leaving that argument, Lucretius passes on to his non-Stoic argument to account for the varying lengths of day and night in lines 696–700 (the air is thicker), Ciceronian reference peters out also.

Lines 694–5 are crucial, in my view, to understanding the role Ciceronian allusion plays in this passage. These lines characterize the whole passage 680–95 as the part of the argument in which Lucretius engages with 'those who have expounded all the parts of the heaven marked out by the signs in order'. Bailey, perhaps one of Lucretius' most perspicacious critics, noted the incongruity: 'This first explanation is obviously that of orthodox astronomy, as is made clear in 694–5. It has not the true Epicurean ring about it and it is doubtful whether Lucr[etius] fully understood it.'[59] Whether or not he understood it (and I think he probably did), it was not in Lucretius' interest to give an accurate representation of it. Lucretius' phrase is a pointed thrust at those who thought the universe explicable by geometric models, such as Posidonius, whose model sphere is referred to by Cicero in the Stoic book of the *DND* as a paradigm for the order of the universe as understood in Stoicism. Lines 694–5 represent the nearest thing to a direct reference to the other side in the philosophical debate as we get in the *DRN.*

The terms of reference are loaded. Note *ornata* in *DRN* 5.695. This term for artistic activity occurred in the 'craftsman simile' of Cicero *Aratea* 302–6:

> ut nemo, cui sancta manu doctissima Pallas
> sollertem ipsa dedit fabricae <u>rationibus</u> artem,
> tam tornare cate contortos possiet orbis
> quam sunt in caelo divino numine flexi,
> terram cingentes, <u>ornantes</u> lumine mundum . . .

> '. . . so that no one to whom holy Athena herself gave with her most skilled hand the learned art of the craftsman, informed as it is by reason, would be able to bend so skilfully the interlocked circles as they are turned in the sky by divine grace, girding the earth, decking out the sky with light.'

In Cicero's programmatic simile, the artistry of the celestial circles is comparable to its human equivalent, the work of a craftsman. Cicero describes the star-bearing celestial circles as <u>*ornantes*</u> *lumine mundum.*[60] I have elsewhere discussed the Stoic baggage of the craftsman simile, and in particular the use of *ornare* and its cognates.[61] It signifies, as by shorthand, the Stoic conception of the universe. A connected term is *ratio.* In Cicero's craftsman simile *ornare* is coupled with *ratio,* which in Stoicism refers both to the qualities inherent in the divine disposition of the universe, and to the human ability to understand it.[62] *Both* terms are found in Lucretius 5.694–5 (*ut ratio declarat*, 694; *ornata notarunt*, 695). Lucretius' astronomers are here equivalent to the celestial craftsman of Cicero's *Aratea*, marking out the sky *dispositis signis* (695; compare also the work of Aratus' Zeus-as-Providence, ἄστρα διακρίνας, *Ph.* 11). In the Stoic context their activities would mirror the designing intelligence of the Divine Mind, or of Zeus; Lucretius, however, instead of this conclusion, leaves the astronomers hanging, and a different, more arbitrary, argument immediately follows.

Lucretius' dismissal has been anticipated in an earlier echo of Cicero's craftsman simile (*DRN* 5.122–5):

> quae procul usque adeo *divino a numine* distent,
> inque deum numero quae sint indigna videri,
> notitiam potius praebere ut posse putentur
> quid sit vitali motu sensuque remotum.

> 'These [i.e., the natural phenomena itemized a few lines earlier, at *DRN* 5.115] are so far from divine intelligence and so unworthy to be situated among the number of the gods, that instead they should be thought to furnish evidence of what something should be thought to be like if it is divorced from the movement and sense-perception which belongs to life.'

The phrase *divino numine* occurs in Cicero's craftsman simile, describing the perfect disposition of the celestial circles (*Arat.* 304–5): . . . *orbis /quam sunt in caelo divino numine flexi. . . .*[63] With *divino . . . numine*, Lucretius chooses to echo a phrase in which Cicero extols the divine craftsmanship, in order to deny such craftsmanship.

The evidence that Lucretius is engaging with the Stoic argument-from-design, in particular as we find it in Cicero's *Aratea*, is very strong. *DRN* 5.693–5 recall, in addition to the craftsman simile, another programmatic passage of the *Aratea*, the description of the first Namer of Stars (*Arat.* 162–6):

> haec ille astrorum custos *ratione notavit*
> *signaque* dignavit *caelestia* nomine vero;
> has autem quae sunt parvo cum lumine fusae,
> consimili specie stellas parilique nitore,
> non potuit nobis *nota* clarare figura.

> 'For that custodian of the stars recorded in an orderly fashion these star-signs and dignified them with a name true to form; but he was unable to mark out for us with a familiar shape these which are poured out with scant light, stars all similar in appearance and with like magnitude.'

DRN 5.694–5, *ratio . . . /notarunt* is a combination shared with *Arat.* 162, *ratione notavit*; *DRN* 5.694–5 *caelum . . . /signis* is shared with *Arat.* 162, *signaque . . .*

caelestia; and finally (and conclusively) *notarunt* in *DRN* 5.695 picks up *nota* in *Arat.* 166. These details all occur within the same few lines in both Cicero and Lucretius.

Lucretius sets up parallels between the description of the astronomers and the two programmatic passages of the *Aratea* which best represent the Stoic way of looking at astronomy: as evidence of divine craftsmanship,[64] and as the result of the activities of a Namer.[65] Both of these ideas are as far from Epicurean astronomy as it is possible to get. Lucretius' use of these ideas, and of his Ciceronian source-material, are all instances of anti-Stoic, or more generally of anti–intelligent design, polemic.

4 }

Lucretius' *Aratea*

Introduction

I state on p. 60 of chapter 3 that 'The *De rerum natura* is in dialogue with Cicero's translation of Aratus *throughout.*' I have not yet proved this. The discussion in the previous chapter showed how Lucretius draws on Cicero for his *astronomy*, and began to demonstrate the philosophical consequences of the debt. Interesting as this study is in astronomical terms, it proves little about the extent of the relationship between Lucretius and Cicero, and therefore about the importance of the Aratean background. You would *expect* Lucretius to carry some kind of debt to Cicero's astronomy.[1] To demonstrate the influence of Cicero on Lucretius' astronomy is not to demonstrate the thoroughgoing influence of Cicero on Lucretius. The influence of Cicero on Lucretius is only properly significant if it can be shown that it extends beyond the scope of shared information. In this respect, references to Cicero in Lucretius *outside* the astronomical section of *DRN* 5 are a better indicator of debt than references belonging only to the astronomical section.

The raw data for the thesis that Ciceronian reference extends beyond the astronomical parts of the *DRN* is provided in appendix B. The work of this chapter will be to tease out some of the ways in which Lucretius draws on Cicero, and the range of meanings generated by the various types of Ciceronian reference. Lucretius may use Cicero for programmatic reference, a way of thinking about his own task as a poet/philosopher, as in the case of the Lucretian proems; he may choose to make unmistakeable but isolated references, such as *DRN* 3.316; he may concentrate references from different parts of the *Aratea* in a single passage, or obsessively repeat references to a single passage of Cicero across the *DRN*, as in the case of the Dog Star (*Arat.* 107–19).[2]

This discussion is important not only in that it fills the need to redress the damage done by mechanistic reductive readings of scholars such as Merrill, the legacy of which lives on, but, more importantly, in that it rewrites scientific debate in the mid-first century BC, giving Lucretius a bigger share. It also demonstrates the importance of the tradition of Aratus in such debate.

4.1 The Lucretian Proems

'An opening indicates the contextualized norm' (Conte 1986: 82)

There are signficant echoes of Cicero in several of the Lucretian proems. These gestures coincide with the proems which specifically praise Epicurus, namely the proems to books 1, 3, and 5. Ted Kenney argued that Proems 1, 3, and 5 are particularly significant in the structure of the *DRN*, each of these introducing a pair of books in Lucretius' six-book triptych, and that they are linked by repetitions of formulaic leitmotivs.[3] My own argument below will offer a further way of linking Proems 1, 3, and 5, through shared allusion to Cicero's *Aratea*, and in this way also, the importance of Cicero's *Aratea* as a literary model for the *DRN* as a whole, not only the astronomical parts, will emerge. The set of prooemial correspondences will show that Ciceronian reminiscence in the 'Epicurean' proems gives Lucretius a way of defining the character of Epicurus against an opposing philosophical tradition.

4.1.1 LUCRETIUS' FIRST PROEM: *DRN* 1.1–49

There are four points of contact with Cicero in the first ten lines of the *De rerum natura*. These are italicized in the following quotation of *DRN* 1.1–10:

> Aeneadum genetrix, hominum divumque voluptas,
> alma Venus, caeli subter *labentia signa*
> quae mare navigerum, quae terras frugiferentis
> concelebras, per te quoniam genus omne animantum
> concipitur visitque exortum lumina solis:
> te, dea, te fugiunt venti, te *nubila caeli*
> adventumque tuum, tibi suavis daedala tellus
> summittit flores, tibi rident aequora ponti
> placatumque nitet diffuso *lumine caelum*.
> *nam simul ac* species patefactast verna diei . . .

> 'Ancestress of the Aeneid race, pleasure of gods and men, fertile Venus, you who under the sliding signs of heaven fill with your presence the fruitful earth, the ship-enduring sea: since through you the whole tribe of living things is conceived, and, leaping up, sees the light of the sun: the winds and the clouds of heaven part before your coming, the well-wrought earth sends up sweet flowers for you, for you the turbid sea rejoices, and the heaven, soothed, shines with widespread light. For once the veil is flung from day's spring face . . .'

Thereafter there are at least two more Ciceronian references, one of them very strong (line 35): 22–3 . . . *dias in luminis oras /exoritur* ('. . . leaps up to the divine border of light'); 35 *tereti cervice reposta* ('with smooth neck bent back'), followed, at the beginning of the argument of the work, by an initiatory formula with

Ciceronian credentials in line 50, *quod superest*).[4] Cumulatively, Cicero's influence is strong from the very outset of the *DRN*.

DRN 1.2/*Aratea* fr. 3.1–2

Lucretius' first reminiscence of Cicero comes as early as line 2 of the proem, *caeli subter labentia signa* ('under the sliding signs of heaven'). Compare *Arat.* fr. 3.1 *cetera labuntur celeri caelestia motu* ('the remaining heavenly bodies slide along with rapid motion'). *DRN* 1.2 is not cited by Merrill or Buescu in their lists of parallels, even though Munro (1894) had already pointed out that 'Cicero *Arat.* frag. 3 said before Lucretius *cetera labuntur celeri caelestia motu*,' adding, 'Lucretius had attentively studied this translation. . . .'[5] Lucretius gets his terminology from Cicero. It is apparently in the *Aratea* that the verb *labor* as a term for the movement of the heavenly bodies originates, for instance at *Arat.* 226–7 *nam quae per bis sex signorum labier orbem /quinque solent stellae* ('For those five heavenly bodies which are wont to glide through the circle of the zodiac . . .').[6] Typically, Lucretius varies the grammatical elements of the collocation; Cicero's *caelestia* becomes *caeli* in Lucretius, *labuntur* becomes the participle *labentia*.

The allusion is apposite in the light of the dictum of Conte which I quoted at the beginning of section 4.1. The expression comes in each work at a point where the parameters of the discussion which follows are being laid out. Cicero fr. 3 is at the beginning of the mapping of the heavens, incorporating a contrast between the moving stars and the fixed axis (as at Aratus *Ph.* 19–21). Cicero's stars partake of constant motion:

> cetera labuntur celeri caelestia motu,
> cum caeloque simul noctesque diesque feruntur.

> 'The remaining heavenly bodies glide along with rapid motion, and night and day are carried along with the heaven.'

In the Lucretian proem, the reference to the stars might be shorthand for the Aratean/Ciceronian tradition. This tradition is deployed by Lucretius through the collocation *labentia signa*. At this point in the *DRN*, the 'contextualized norm' which emerges is Cicero, and through Cicero, the tradition of Aratus. But the relationship is not necessarily a transparent one. In Cicero the programme is straightforward: in Lucretius it may contain an element of feint, given the contested relationship of the Lucretian proem to the rest of the *DRN*; this modality of relationship between Cicero (for-real) and Lucretius (at-ironic-remove) is characteristic.

DRN 1.6/*Aratea* 230

The Ciceronian expression *labentia signa* is reinforced four lines later, by the Ciceronian mannerism of the hexameter-end *nubila caeli* in line 6. *Nubila caeli* is a Ciceronian signature.[7] Cicero's passage on the planets (in contrast to the preceding reference to the fixed stars) is evoked here.[8] Lucretius' poetic firmament includes both, promiscuously, as we shall see.

The Ciceronian context is *Arat.* 230–1 (from a passage quoted more fully below, with translation):

> sic malunt errare vagae[9] per <u>nubila caeli</u>
> atque suos vario motu metirier orbes.

These lines themselves are distinctively Ciceronian, and are moreover a Ciceronian addition to Aratus. For instance, Cicero's image of the planets' *preference* (*malunt*) is not in Aratus. Lucretius has chosen to draw on a passage where Cicero as 'translator' shows his true colours (i.e., goes beyond 'translation').

Lucretius' interest in Cicero's passage on the planets at *DRN* 1.6 is supported by echo later in the *DRN* of the next line in Cicero's description of them. At *DRN* 2.97 he imitates *Arat.* 231, *vario . . . motu*. This reference also ties in contextually with the proem to Book 1. In both of these cases where Lucretius uses Cicero's passage on the planets, there is a contrast between mobility and stasis, just as in the Ciceronian original there was a contrast between the movement of the fixed stars and the wandering of the planets.[10] In *DRN* 2.92–9 the contrast is one between the summative constancy of the universe, and the dynamic nature of its atomic components:

> . . . quoniam spatium sine fine modoquest
> inmensumque patere in cunctas undique partis
> pluribus ostendi et certa ratione probatumst.
> quod quoniam constat, nimirum nulla quies est
> reddita corporibus primis per inane profundum,
> sed magis adsiduo <u>varioque</u> exercita <u>motu</u>
> partim intervallis magnis confulta resultant,
> pars etiam brevibus spatiis vexantur ab ictu.[11]

'. . . since space is without end or measure, and I have shown by many proofs that it extends illimitable on all sides in every region, and this has been proven by infallible reasoning. Given that we agree on this, there's nothing strange in the assertion that no rest is decreed for atoms throughout the expanse of the void. Rather, some of them, stirred up by ceaseless and varied motion, coming into contact with each other, rebound at great intervals, while others are displaced by the blow for only a short space.'

Here is the context of the original comparison, in Cicero, *Arat.* 223–31:

> haec sunt quae visens nocturno tempore signa
> aeternumque volens mundi pernoscere motum
> legitimo cernes caelum lustrantia cursu.
> nam quae per bis sex signorum labier orbem
> quinque solent stellae, simili ratione notari

non possunt, quia quae faciunt vestigia cursu
non eodem semper spatio protrita teruntur.
sic malunt errare vagae per <u>nubila caeli</u>,
atque suos <u>vario motu</u> metirier orbes.

'These star-signs are the ones which, when you see them at night time and want to know about the ongoing motion of the heaven, you will notice, rake the heaven with a *law-abiding* course. For those five heavenly bodies which usually glide through the circle of the zodiac cannot be identified by similar means, because the tracks they make in their course are not always worn into the same place. They prefer to wander footloose through the clouds of heaven and to measure out their orbits with a variable motion.'[12]

The contrast in Cicero is between the stars, the legitimate movements of which can be discerned, with the planets, which cannot be understood *simili ratione* (*Arat.* 226). We shall see in chapter 5 how important Lucretius' ascription of 'planetary motion' to the elements of the universe becomes. Cicero, in his passage on the *planets*, gives Lucretius the means of talking about the chaos of *atoms*. The relationship with this seminal passage of Cicero is set up from the Lucretian proem onwards.

DRN 1.22–3/*Aratea* 379–80

Ciceronian reference in Lucretius' first proem carries programmatic significance. If we are influenced by the Ciceronian model to see Mars and Venus as heavenly bodies, then they present an appropriate image of celestial *rising* at the beginning of the work. This is first adumbrated in lines 22–3, *nec sine te quicquam dias in <u>luminis</u> oras /exoritur*. When read with *Arat.* 379–80 *repente /**exoritur** pandens inlustria <u>lumina</u> Virgo* ('Virgo rises forthwith, displaying her shining lights'), this line already brings the stars to mind. The gods 'rise' at the beginning of Lucretius poem, just as that important constellation, *Virgo*, rises in Cicero's *Aratea*.

   The imagery which accompanies genesis—of the world, of the poem—is that of rising stars. In due course, this will be contrasted with 'setting' imagery, used consistently of the dying soul in *DRN* 3.[13] The pattern of the poem moves with the stars, and this is another reason why Cicero's *Aratea* is such an important model for the *DRN*.

DRN 1.35/*Aratea* fr. 9.5

Lucretius' expression *tereti cervice reposta*, describing the position of the neck of Mars as he gazes at Venus in the Proem to Book 1, is a strong gesture towards *Arat.* fr. 9.5, *tereti cervice reflexum*. The ancestry of the expression may partly explain its striking nature. As well as containing a lexical echo, the two expressions stand in the same location in the hexameter in each author.

   So, in Lucretius, we see Venus and Mars frozen in embrace at *DRN* 1.35–7:

> atque ita suspiciens tereti cervice reposta
> pascit amore avidos inhians in te, dea, visus,
> eque tuo pendet resupini spiritus ore.

> 'And so, looking up, with smooth neck bent back, he takes nourishment from love, fixing his gaze, full of desire, on you, goddess, and, as he lies back, it's as though he hangs from the rope of your breath.'

In *Aratea* fr. 9.5–6, Cicero describes the relative position of the Bears and Draco in the sky:

> obstipum caput, a tereti cervice reflexum,
> obtutum in cauda Maioris figere dicas.

> 'You might say that [the constellation Draco] turning his head inclined from his shiny neck, fixes his gaze on the tail of Ursa Major.'

As well as the hexameter-end collocation, the idea of gazing is strikingly portrayed in each author. Cicero seems to strive for originality with *obtutum* (the form picking up *obstipum* in the preceding line); Lucretius rings changes on the idea, with *suspiciens* in 35, followed by *avidos inhians in te, dea, visus* in 36.

Just as there is a conjoined relationship between Cicero's constellations, so in Lucretius there is conjunction between the god and goddess. This is appropriate, since Lucretius will go on (shortly after this, in lines 62–79) to ascribe *religio*— veneration of the *gods*—to the *heavens* (*a caeli regionibus . . . /mortalibus instans*, 'from the regions of heaven, lowering over mortals . . .,' 64–5). His use of a *celestial* model for the gods in the proem already rolls the two into one, setting up a tension with the negative view of *religio* which follows, and with Lucretius' own Epicurean view of the detachment of the gods.

In the Lucretian passage, we see the gods in a state of love-fuelled Olympian ataraxia; in Cicero, we perceive the stars in a relation to one another which was established by divine providence.[14] Lucretius' gods have no such role, but paradoxically, they themselves come to look like constellations, frozen in a lover's embrace just as the stars are frozen in their interrelations. Theological debate is implicated in the Lucretian echo of Cicero, right from the start. The success of Lucretius' sleight of hand lies in the fact that the reader, even if only recognizing the Ciceronian echoes instinctually, would nonetheless have his expectations tweaked by them, only to be cheated.

4.1.2 LUCRETIUS' THIRD PROEM: *DRN* 3.1–8

There are two Ciceronian collocations in the first eight lines of *DRN* 3 (I italicize):

> e tenebris tantis tam clarum extollere lumen
> qui primus potuisti inlustrans commoda vitae,
> te sequor, o Graiae gentis decus, inque tuis nunc

ficta *pedum pono* pressis *vestigia* signis,
non ita certandi cupidus quam propter amorem
quod te imitari aveo; quid enim contendat hirundo
cycnis, aut quid nam tremulis facere artubus haedi
consimile in cursu possint et *fortis equi vis*?

'You who first had the ability to conjure bright light out of such darkness, illuminating the best things in life, I follow you, grace of the Greeks, and in your firm tracks I now place the indented imprints of my feet, yearning to emulate you not so much in a spirit of competition, as on account of love. For how can the swallow contend with the swan, or kids use their tremulous limbs in the same career as a strong powerful horse?'[15]

I shall start from *fortis equi vis* in line 8, then return to the less striking, but equally Ciceronian, *pedum pono . . . vestigia* in line 4.

DRN 3.8/*Aratea* 54, 57

Kenney (1984) on *DRN* 3.6–8, remarked on the double comparison these lines contain. He maintained that while the first, between the swallow and the swan, has precedent in the literary tradition, 'the second comparison [between the kids and horse] appears to be an original stroke of invention.'[16] This is not the case. The collocation is a composite of two references to Cicero's *Aratea*, lines 54 and 57:

[. . .] iam vero clinata est ungula vemens
fortis Equi propter pinnati corporis alam.
ipse autem labens mu[l]tis Equus ille tenetur
Piscibus; huic cervix dextra mulcetur Aquari.
serius haec obitus terrai vissit *Equi vis*,
quam gelidum valido de pectore frigus anhelans
corpore semifero magno Capricornus in orbe;
quem cum perpetuo vestivit lumine Titan,
brumali flectens contorquet tempore currum. (*Aratea* 53–61)

'Next, the forceful hoof of the strong horse slopes near the wing of the pinioned figure. The Horse himself, gliding across the sky, is held by the silent Fish, and his neck is stroked by Aquarius's right hand. The powerful horse reaches the horizon later than Capricorn, who breathes out icy cold from his strong breast, with his half-beast body in the great circle [of the zodiac]; when at the winter solstice the Sun has clothed Capricorn with his eternal light, he wheels his chariot and changes direction.'

Lucretius's *fortis equi vis* combines *Equi vis* (*Aratea* 57) with Cicero's earlier phrase *fortis Equi* (*Aratea* 54). It is this threefold collocation, composed of two separate Ciceronian collocations, which produces such a dramatic climax in the praise of Epicurus.

Ostensibly, Lucretius' horse/kids comparison is between animals. But read through Lucretius'allusion to an astronomical model, they are also both constellations, as the Aratean underlay reminds us. Pegasus is a large constellation; the 'Great Square' of Pegasus a prominent feature of the night sky. On the other hand, the Kids are small and faint (Aratus *Ph.* 165–6). Reading with the help of the models, Epicurus is a massive and prominent constellation, his disciple Lucretius a dim, small one. The metaphor is achieved by interplay of ideas of philosophical emulation and poetic emulation. Lucretian allusion to Cicero acts as a powerful metaphor for another process of emulation: Lucretius' philosophical undertaking vis-à-vis Epicurus' achievements.

There are several signals which point us towards the Ciceronian underlay in Lucretius' text, even apart from the verbal allusion itself. The existence of these pointers supports the idea that Lucretius may be consciously playing games of allusion here (in Contean terms, engaging in *aemulatio*). Lucretius's verb *imitari* in *De rerum natura* 3.6 is not only about Lucretius' relationship with his philosophical predecessor, but signals imitation of poetic models, in this case astronomical ones.

Vestigia (*DRN* 3.4) entails a play on the astronomical nature of these models. The term is standard in denoting the paths of the heavenly bodies from Cicero's *Aratea* onwards. Cicero used it of the courses of the planets in *Aratea* 228. As well as describing Lucretius' emulation of Epicurus, *vestigia* might be an intertextual marker, alerting us to look for 'traces' of models.[17] The same sort of play may be involved in *signis*. As Kenney points out, it was not necessary for Lucretius to include all these near-tautological terms for footsteps.[18] Yet *signa* can also mean (and more often does mean) 'heavenly bodies', specifically constellations, and especially the zodiacal constellations. We see this prominently in the passage of Cicero I have just referred to, the passage on the planets, which has *signa* in line 223 of the 'fixed stars' and *signorum* in 226 of the zodiacal constellations through which the planets move. The image of the small constellation Lucretius trailing along in Epicurus' star-dust is reinforced on both the figurative and poetic levels by the use of *vestigia* and *signa*.

Philosophically, Lucretius follows the *vestigia* of the celestial Epicurus. Poetically, however, the *vestigia* which he follows are those of Cicero, whose *Aratea* represents the universe as understood by an opposing philosophical school, that of Stoicism. Philosophical opposition between model and copy generates an important element of meaning in Lucretius' text, one which testifies to the essential but paradoxical importance of the Aratean tradition, as represented by Cicero, in shaping the discourse of the *DRN*.

There is a lack of fit between Epicurus-as-constellation and Epicurean doctrines about deification.[19] Allusion to Cicero's *Aratea* acts as a means of negotiation of this difficult concept in relation to Epicurus. Lucretius implicitly likens Epicurus to a constellation by describing him using the terms of reference of a text at ease with the divine nature and providence of the stars. This assimilation to constellations is not tantamount, but not identical, to making him a god. Through allusion to

Cicero, Lucretius is able to walk the Epicurean tightrope, with its anxieties about deification.

This anxiety can be seen from Cicero's treatment of the topic in the Epicurean book of the *De natura deorum*. At *De natura deorum* 1.37, the Epicurean speaker Velleius attacks the Stoics on the grounds that they attribute divinity to the stars (*divinitatem omnem tribuit astris*). He avows that Epicurus is a true god (*DND* 1.43):[20] *ea qui consideret, quam inconsulte ac temere dicantur, venerari Epicurum et in eorum ipsorum numero, de quibus haec quaestio est, habere debeat. . . . Quoius rationis vim atque utilitatem ex illo caelesti Epicuri de regula et iudicio volumine accepimus* ('If anyone were to contemplate the thoughtless and random nature of all these claims, he would be bound to *revere* Epicurus, and to consign him to the company of those very gods who are the focus of our enquiry . . . We have come to appreciate the force and usefulness of this reasoning as a result of the *divine* treatise of Epicurus entitled "Rule and Judgement,"'—trans. Walsh 1997, with my emphases). In this passage, the lineaments of the same philosophical debate we see in Lucretius are replicated: Velleius hijacks at least one Stoic term in his assertion of the divinity of Epicurus, namely *utilitas*, mentioned for instance by Cicero's Stoic speaker at *DND* 2.60, *quidquid enim magnam utilitatem generi adferret humano, id non sine divina bonitate erga homines fieri arbitrabantur* ('whatever bestows some great service on the human race did not originate without divine beneficence,').[21] Given the complexity of the situation—is Epicurus a god or not, and if so how can this be squared with Epicurean theology?—Lucretius is right to be defensive. He practises deification by allusion. Cicero's *Aratea* gives him the raw materials to refer to Epicurus as god-like (or celestial) without going so far as to specify that he *is* a god.

In his praise of Epicurus in Book 3, Lucretius is using metaphors to describe Epicurus, with which his Roman contemporaries would have been familiar in a context of philosophical debate. Some of the metaphors of divinity and of the stars have their linguistic origin in Cicero's *Aratea*. At the same time, however, we must be aware of the fundamental *differences* between the universes of Epicurus and of Cicero's *Aratea*. The fact is that in the Epicurean system the stars are NOT divine. Two alternative universes are simultaneously present in Lucretius text, in the model (*Aratea*) and copy (*DRN*). Lucretius' praise of Epicurus is about competing philosophical systems rather than just individual philosophers.

The sharp point of the Aratean iceberg extrudes from the surface of Lucretius' text at key moments. By both assimilating his poetic model and opposing himself to it, Lucretius uses Cicero as Aratus uses Empedocles. The *Aratea* acts more broadly in the *DRN* as an alternative universe, the expectations of which, set up in the reader by the use of the Ciceronian model, the Epicurean poet exploits.

DRN 3.4/*Aratea* 451

The Ciceronian collocation *fortis equi vis* in line 8 is supported by another imitation of Cicero in line 4 of Book 3, *pedum pono . . . vestigia*. Discussion of this phrase will show how Ciceronian parallels can reinforce one another. Merrill (1921): 149 cites the parallel *vestigia parva* (*Arat.* 451). But in fact, Lucretius has again given us a synthesis of *two* separate passages of the *Aratea*. The phrase *pedum pono . . . vestigia* finds a closer parallel in *Arat.* fr. 15.4 *vestigia ponit*.[22] *Arat.* fr. 15.4–5, *ille [Ophiuchus] tamen nitens graviter <u>vestigia ponit</u> /atque oculos urget <u>pedibus</u> pectusque Nepai* ('Although he is struggling greatly, [Ophiuchus] nonetheless anchors his path and with his feet presses upon the eyes and breast of Scorpio') supplies all three corners of the triple collocation, although characteristically Lucretius has played fast and loose with syntactical arrangement. The context fits: that of two constellations in spatial relation to one another, pursuing each other across the sky.

However, let us return to Merrill's chosen parallel. Here is the wider context of the Ciceronian passage:

> at caput et totum sese Centaurus opacis
> eripit **e tenebris**, linquens <u>vestigia</u> parva
> ante<u>pedum</u> contecta, simul cum **lumine** pandit
> ipse feram dextra retinens . . . (*Arat.* 450–4)

> 'But the Centaur snatches his head, then all of himself, from the dusky shadows, leaving only the faint tracks of his forefeet in the shade, and at the same time he displays in all its glory the beast he holds in his right hand . . .'[23]

This is the rising of the constellation of the Centaur. Cicero's writing is bold here, with the striking hapax *antepes* ('forefoot'). The passage struck Lucretius too. I have underlined the elements of our pre-existing collocation. We should I think admit as part of the shared collocation the strange compound ante*pedum*, unremarked by Merrill. But there is more. When we look closely at the passage side-by-side with Lucretius' third proem, we find that the rising of the Centaur in Cicero is mirrored in the rising of Epicurus at *DRN* 3.1–4 (translated above, at the beginning of 4.1.2):

> **e tenebris** tantis tam clarum extollere **lumen**
> qui primus potuisti inlustrans commoda vitae,
> te sequor, o Graiae gentis decus, inque tuis nunc
> ficta <u>pedum pono</u> pressis <u>vestigia</u> signis . . .

We can, then, take *DRN* 3.4 with 3.8, as star imagery pertaining to Epicurus. Epicurus 'rises' at the beginning of *DRN* 3, spectacularly assimilated to two significant constellations through the textual foundations on which he stands. Allusion to Cicero has been shown to be much more significant and complex that has been seen before, and this adds much nuance, both poetic and philosophical, to our reading of the praise of Epicurus.

4.1.3 LUCRETIUS' FIFTH PROEM: *DRN* 5.1–54

DRN 5.1/*Prognostica* fr. 4.4–6[24]

Lucretius begins his fifth proem with a question:

quis potis est dignum pollenti *pectore carmen*
condere pro rerum maiestate hisque repertis?

'Who can found in their powerful heart a song fit to express the magnificence
of the universe, and these discoveries?'

Cicero in fr. 4 of his *Prognostica*, lines 4–6, has:

saepe etiam pertriste canit de *pectore carmen*
et matutinis acredula vocibus instat,
vocibus instat . . .

'Often the *acredula*[25] sings from the heart its song shot through with sadness
and persists, persists in its morning call . . .'

The collocation *pectore carmen* apparently occurs only in Lucretius and Cicero.[26] It
is in the same metrical *sedes* in both authors. Lucretius' reference to Cicero is a
'Contean' signature at the outset of Book 5, as at the beginning of both Books 1
and 3. Like the references in the earlier proems, it may carry programmatic value.

Lucretius' appropriation of the Ciceronian *carmen* flags up Lucretius' poetic ancestry in his role as mediator of the song of nature. In Cicero fr. 4, the *acredula* (an uniden-
tified bird, and perhaps one of dubious credibility, *a-credula*, 'the unbelievable bird'?)
vocally insists on signalling the dawn. This is an appropriate image for the (more cred-
ible?) human poet signalling the new dawn by announcing Epicurus' advent.[27]

DRN 5.32–4/*Arat.* 214–15, *Arat.* 116

Coming as it does in line 1 of the fifth proem, the Cicernonian collocation *pectore
carmen* might be expected to trigger other Ciceronian reminiscences. In fact there
are two further gestures towards Cicero in Lucretius' fifth proem, in close proximity
to one another, in a polemical passage about the spurious belief in mythical
monsters. Ciceronian reference occurs in lines 32–4 of *DRN* 5, describing the
serpent-guardian of the golden apples of the Hesperides:

aureaque Hesperidum servans fulgentia mala,
asper, acerba tuens, immani *corpore serpens*
arboris amplexus stirpem . . .

'And the one who guards the shining golden apples of the Hesperides, with
his piercing gaze and his enormous frame, the scaly Serpent embracing the
trunk of the tree . . .'

The first of these Ciceronian reminiscences, *corpore serpens*, recalls the description
of the position of Hydra at *Arat.* 214–15, with the collocation in the same *sedes*:

hic sese infernis e partibus erigit Hydra,
praecipiti lapsu flexo cum *corpore serpens*.

'This Hydra rears itself up from the lower realms writhing in freefalling
curves.'

This is an appropriate image for Lucretius to use. In Lucretius the phrase refers to the Serpent of the Hesperides (*aureaque Hesperidum servans fulgentia mala, DRN* 5.32); in Cicero it refers to the Hydra, identified with the Lernaean hydra.

Corpore serpens in *DRN* 5.33 is followed by another Ciceronian collocation. *Arboris amplexus stirpem* in line 34 recalls *Arat.* 116 *quorum stirpis tellus amplexa prehendit*. The context in the *Aratea* is the ambiguous power of the Dog Star, Sirius (*Arat.* 107–119):

> namque pedes subter rutilo cum lumine claret
> fervidus ille Canis stellarum luce refulgens.
> hunc tegit obscurus subter praecordia vepres,
> nec vero toto *spirans de corpore flammam*[28]
> aestiferos validis erumpit flatibus ignes:[29]
> totus ab ore micans iacitur mortalibus ardor.
> hic ubi[30] se pariter cum sole in lumina caeli
> extulit, haud patitur foliorum tegmine frustra
> suspensos animos arbusta ornata tenere.
> nam quorum stirpis tellus amplexa prehendit,
> haec augens anima vitali flamine mulcet;
> at quorum nequeunt radices findere terras,
> denudat foliis ramos et cortice truncos.

'Beneath the feet [of Orion] that blazing Dog burns with a reddish glow, shining forth with the light of his stars. A dusky thicket covers him below the breast. He does not, indeed, give forth heat-inducing flames in vigorous gusts, breathing fire from his whole body: all his heat is splashed coruscating from his mouth upon mortals. When he thrusts himself into the heavenly limelight at the same time as the sun, he does not suffer saplings decked in their covering of foliage to dither indecisively. The ones whose roots the earth holds fast in her embrace, these he strokes with life-giving breeze, strengthening them in spirit; but as for the ones which are too weak to cleave the earth with their roots, he strips their branches of leaves and their trunks of bark.'

Corpore serpens and *arboris amplexus stirpem* invoke, within two lines of Lucretius, two constellations in the Aratea, the Hydra and Sirius. The shared collocations direct us to the heavens as, in this case, the *spurious* seat of deified figures. This is a context where Lucretius declares the divination of heroes to be impossible. Celestial myth, in which characters are divinized, is an example of what should *not* be believed. In addition, both the constellations carry negative connotations, making them good material for the refutation of ideas about astral divinization. Not everything up there can be good. Later, *DRN* 6.660 reuses one collocation, *corpore serpens*, likewise in the same *sedes*, to describe the symptoms of the Plague.

It is useful to look briefly at the wider argument at stake in this part of Lucretius' text: only then does the full force of the astronomical allusion emerge. We have seen how allusion to Cicero's Hydra and Sirius signals something that Lucretius disagrees with, namely the divinization of heroes in the opposing Stoic tradition.[31] These two allusions give us an aggregation of Ciceronian reference in a context of negative polemic. Lucretius goes further in the refutation of other people's ideas in this passage than anywhere else we have seen so far. The context here is the expressly anti-Stoic argument against the deeds of Hercules, a hero appropriated by the Stoics.[32] This begins at *DRN* 5.22–3:

> Herculis antistare autem si facta putabis,
> longius *a vera* multo *ratione* ferere.

> 'But if you think the deeds of Hercules are superior, you will be carried even further away from true reasoning.'

The language here belongs to standard Lucretian refutation of *myth* in particular: the expression *a vera . . . ratione* is repeated, for instance, at *DRN* 5.405–6, there referring to the myth of Phaethon:

> scilicet ut veteres Graium cecinere poetae.
> quod procul *a vera* nimis est *ratione* repulsum.

> '. . . to be sure, the old Greek poets sang it this way. But that is to depart too far from true reasoning.'

In Lucretius, we are to rank Hercules and his deeds alongside unbelievable myth. But for the Stoics, as exemplified in Cicero's *DND* 2.62, Hercules is first among the benefactors of mankind divinized in Stoic practice:[33]

> utilitatum igitur magnitudine constituti sunt ei di qui utilitates quasque gignebant, atque his quidem nominibus quae paulo ante dicta sunt quae vis sit in quoque declaratur deo. suscepit autem vita hominum consuetudoque communis ut beneficiis excellentis viros in caelum fama ac voluntate tollerent. hinc Hercules, hinc Castor et Pollux, hinc Aesculapius, hinc Liber etiam . . . quorum cum remanerent animi atque aeternitate fruerentur, rite di sunt habiti, cum et optimi essent et aeterni.

> 'So these gods which spawned these several blessings have owed their divine status to the great benefits which they bestowed, and the power residing in each deity is indicated by the names which I cited a moment ago. Our human experience and the common practice have ensured that men who conferred outstanding benefits were translated to heaven through their fame and our gratitude. Examples are Hercules, Castor and Pollux, Aesculapius, and Liber as well . . . These men were duly regarded as gods because their souls survived to enjoy eternal life, for they were both outstandingly good and immortal'.

It is this expressly Stoic view that Lucretius is countering at the end of his fifth proem, by the substitution of Epicurus in the role of god (*DRN* 5.50–1): . . . *nonne decebit/hunc hominem numero divom dignarier esse?* ('Won't it be appropriate that this man be fittingly enrolled in the number of the gods?'). In Lucretius, Stoic opinions about euhemeristic origins of the gods are to be classed as impossible, along with hybrids and myths. Although he does not name the Stoics as his opponents, Lucretius writes Cicero's translation of a Stoic text, the *Aratea*, into his polemic. But this is a dangerous game: Epicurus is intertextually a sort of hybrid himself, his characterization in Lucretius being built upon reference to several different Ciceronian constellations.

4.2 Thematic Allusions

4.2.1 THE STARS AS A MEASURE OF THE IMPOSSIBLE

Let's stop on one of the collocations of the preceding section, *amplexus stirpem* (*DRN* 5.34) and *stirpis . . . amplexa* (*Arat.* 116). This allusion in Lucretius fits into a complex of imagery in Lucretius associated with a particular passage of Cicero, the passage on Sirius. This is also the case in Lucretius 2.700–706:

> nec tamen omnimodis conecti posse putandum est
> omnia: nam volgo fieri portenta videres,
> semiferas hominum species exsistere et altos
> inter dum ramos egigni corpore vivo,
> multaque conecti terrestria membra marinis,
> tum *flammam taetro spirantis ore* Chimaeras
> pascere naturam per terras omniparentis.

'But you mustn't think that there are infinite possibilities for how things combine. Because if that were the case, you would see monstrosities arising quite often. You would see half-man half-beast apparitions jumping out at you, or tall branches forming, with a living body; many cases of land-creature limbs joined with those of sea-creatures, and then again Chimaeras breathing flame from halitose mouth, thriving across the length and breadth of the all-producing earth.'

In the course of denying the possibilies, Lucretius characteristically (you might say exasperatingly) proceeds to sketch those very possibilities. He does this using the language of someone for whom such hybrids were not, at least not in astral form, anathema: Cicero. The imagery here is a *travesty* of the golden-age pleasantry of the all-producing earth. With *pascere naturam per terras omniparentis*, Lucretius takes *omniparentis* too literally: the earth can (literally) produce *anything*. He asserts, on the contrary, that there are fixed laws of atomic combination: things cannot just join on to one another higgledy-piggledy. In so doing, he contemptuously refutes the hybrids of myth.

Cicero is again drawn into the polemic. Compare *DRN* 2.700–6, especially line 705, . . . *flammam* taetro *spirantis ore* Chimaeras, with Cicero's passage on the Dog

Star, quoted above p. 92. In *Arat.* 110 Cicero had <u>*spirans* de *corpore flammam*</u>. The collocation is marked, and the lines are similar in sound. It is explicitly Cicero's Sirius who is invoked by Lucretius, in both sound and sense. We can draw further inferences from the correspondence. What do Cicero's Canis and Lucretius's Chimaeras have in common? One is, after all, a constellation, the other an underworld monster. But this is the point: Lucretius' invective could also be applied to the groupings of the stars within the constellations to make implausible figures. In Book 5, Lucretius' stars are never described in these terms, and the notion of their willing intervention in human affairs is trenchantly denied at 5.76–81. Cicero's Sirius is comparable to Lucretius' equally impossible Chimaeras. The constellation becomes an analogy for the hybrid: both, in Lucretius' world, are *adunata*.

There is a double parallel here (appropriate in an argument involving hybridism). In 2.702 Lucretius has the compound *semiferas*. Cicero has the same compound, of Capricorn, in *Arat.* 57–9:

> serius haec obitus terrai vissit Equi vis,
> quam gelidum valido de pectore frigus anhelans
> corpore *semifero* magno Capricornus in orbe . . .

> 'This powerful Horse reaches the horizon of the earth later than Capricorn with its half-beast body, breathing out frosty cold from its strong chest in its mighty orbit . . .'

The image of exhalation of heat or cold is also shared between the two authors: Lucretius' expression *flammam taetro spirantis ore Chimaeras* is comparable in meaning to Cicero's *gelidum valido de pectore frigus anhelans*.[34] We have a coincidence in both sense and vocabulary. This twofold coincidence strengthens the parallel between Cicero's Capricorn and Lucretius' Chimaeras. What is more, Capricorn, like the mythical Chimaera, is a hybrid. Lucretius uses a compound adjective for a compound being. But the similarity is one of opposition: such hybrids, of which some constellations are also constituted, are impossible in Lucretius. Again, Lucretius denies the plausibility of the sort of world view espoused in the *Aratea*. More than one Ciceronian constellation is involved in the construction of the polemic.

A pattern emerges here. References to Cicero's Sirius in particular have a special function in Lucretius: they generate a particular theme applied to a particular situation. Sirius tends, in the *DRN*, to put in an intertextual appearance when either (a) hybrids, or (b) the underworld is mentioned. These two themes are related. Just as for Lucretius rational belief in hybrids is impossible, so rational belief in the underworld is impossible (as we know already from the polemic at *DRN* 1.112–24).[35] Lucretius, *consistently* across the *DRN* as a whole, employs Ciceronian constellations as part of his polemic, providing the reader with a consistent background against which to measure the implausible.

DRN 1.135/*Arat.* 116

We can see how this 'thematic' use of Cicero's *Aratea* works by looking at other references in the *DRN* to Cicero's Sirius passage. In *DRN* 1.135, *morte obita quorum tellus amplectitur ossa* ('those who have encountered death, whose bones rest in earth's embrace') we have a triple collocation (*quorum/tellus/amplector*) shared with Cicero's Sirius passage, *Aratea* 116.[36] The context of 1.135 is revealing. It is the culmination of a passage where Lucretius gives, as it were, a 'table of contents' for the *DRN*, anticipating how he will 'correct' erroneous views (*DRN* 1.127–35):

> quapropter bene cum superis de rebus habenda
> nobis est ratio, solis lunaeque meatus
> qua fiant ratione, et qua vi quaeque gerantur
> in terris, tunc cum primis ratione sagaci
> unde anima atque animi constet natura videndum,
> et quae res nobis vigilantibus obvia mentes
> terrificet morbo adfectis somnoque sepultis,
> cernere uti videamur eos audireque coram,
> morte obita quorum tellus amplectitur ossa.

> 'For this reason, just as we do well to stick to reason as regards the Things Above—by what rationale the sun and the moon ply their paths, and by what influence everything is brought about on earth—we must also as a matter of primary importance scrutinize by discriminating reason the source from which the soul and the essence of the mind is put together and those hallucinations which accost us and transfix our minds when, awake, we are in the grip of disease, or when we are buried in sleep, so that we think we see and hear those people close at hand who have met their death and whose bones earth holds in her embrace.'

Such correction includes refuting wrong views about the heavenly bodies (*solis lunaeque meatus, DRN* 1.128). This he finally does in Book 5. The beginning of his exposition of astronomy there exactly replicates the phrase he uses here, *solis lunaeque meatus* (*DRN* 5.76). We saw above (Ch. 3 p. 59) that that phrase too is a Ciceronian allusion.

The passage from Book 1 just quoted follows directly from Lucretius' polemic against the existence of the underworld. Lucretius begins his agenda with the heavenly bodies, and ends the same passage with a gesture towards Cicero's own description of one of the constellations, Sirius. Sirius in this context signals the unreality of dreams and visions as evidence of the continuing existence of the dead, in the same way that he signalled the unreality of euhemerist conceptions of the gods (5.34) or of hybrids (2.700–6).

Sirius is attached to the theme of the afterlife, which for Lucretius is not real. We find this device used again and again in the *DRN*. For instance, Cicero's Sirius also appears in Lucretius' polemic against the afterlife and its monsters at 3.1011–12:

Cerberus et Furiae iam vero et lucis egestas,
Tartarus *horriferos eructans faucibus aestus . . .*

'Cerberus also and the Furies and the witholding of light, and Tartarus belching horrible fires from its throat . . .'

The last line is similar in sound, rhythm, and concept to *Aratea* 111, *aestiferos validis erumpit flatibus ignes*. In both cases a compound adjective is used, representing the compound forms of life it describes. This is about the underworld, populated with impossible entities.

Lucretius is also capable of combining the topoi of the underworld and monsters. A reference to Cicero's Sirius passage in *DRN* 4 combines these two Lucretian indices of impossibility. We will already recognize the reference to Cicero in *DRN* 4.734, *quorum morte obita tellus amplectitur ossa* (cf. *DRN* 1.135, *morte obita quorum tellus amplectitur ossa*, discussed above, with *Arat.* 116, *nam quorum stirpis tellus amplexa prehendit*). As well as of the visions of the dead at 1.135, we have also already seen how Lucretius uses the phrase at *DRN* 5.34, of the serpent guarding the golden apples of the Hesperides. The reference in Book 4 combines the ideas of the afterlife, and of monsters. Here is the fuller context (*DRN* 4.732–43):

Centauros itaque et Scyllarum membra videmus
Cerbereasque canum facies simulacraque eorum
quorum morte obita tellus amplectitur ossa;
omne genus quoniam passim simulacra feruntur,
partim sponte sua quae fiunt aëre in ipso,
partim quae variis ab rebus cumque recedunt
et quae confiunt ex horum facta figuris.
nam certe ex vivo Centauri non fit imago,
nulla fuit quoniam talis natura animantis,
verum ubi equi atque hominis casu convenit imago,
haerescit facile extemplo, quod diximus ante,
propter subtilem naturam et tenuia texta.

'So we see centaurs and Scylla's body-parts and Cerberus-like apparitions of dogs, and the images of those who have met their death and whose bones earth holds in her embrace, since images of every kind float about everywhere, some that are spontaneously generated in the air itself, some types that come off various entities, and those that arise from out of these kinds. For it's certain that the image of a centaur does not arise from a living creature, since there never was any living thing like this; but when the image of a horse and a man meet by chance, they easily stick together straight away, as I've said, on account of their wispy and finely woven nature.'

Hybrids (signalled by the now-familiar Ciceronian collocation from the Sirius passage, *quorum . . . tellus amplectitur*) are impossible, but Lucretius provides a rational explanation for them (the coalescence of *simulacra* from different 'species'). As well, intertextuality is at work here, with the use of Cicero as part of the 'weaving' of Lucretius' world.[37]

Sirius, though identified as a dog, is inherently an impossible hybrid: *dog* + *star*. Thus it's appropriate that Sirius is also present in Lucretius' fullest denial yet of the possibility of hybridism. Take the case of *DRN* 5.906, *de corpore flammam*, with *Arat*. 110 *nec vero toto spirans de corpore flammam*. This reference to Cicero occurs in a passage which begins at *DRN* 5.878 (*DRN* 5.878–80):

> Sed neque Centauri fuerunt, nec tempore in ullo
> esse queunt duplici natura et corpore bino
> ex alienigenis membris compacta . . .

> 'But there were never centaurs, nor at any time can there exist beings compacted of mutually incompatible limbs, with a double nature and twofold body . . .'

The reference to Cicero's Sirius follows, in Lucretius' description of another hybrid, the now-familiar Chimaera, at 5.904–6:

> qui fieri potuit, triplici cum corpore ut una,
> prima leo, postrema draco, media ipsa, Chimaera
> ore foras acrem flaret <u>de corpore flammam</u>?

> 'How can it be the case that one being with threefold body—a lion in front, a snake behind, itself [a she-goat] in the middle—should breathe out acrid flame from its body via the mouth?'

When we reach the climax of the series, that Ciceronian reference, in *corpore flammam* (*Arat*. 110, of Sirius), is deployed as a now-familiar device to clinch the hybrids argument.

To conclude my comments on Sirius: Lucretius seems to call on Sirius each time he discusses hybrids, and frequently in his discussions of the aferlife. Sirius represents the impossible, often in combination with reference to other Ciceronian constellations. What is the consequence for reading the dialectic between Lucretius and Cicero? It might be this: for the Epicurean, making sense of the stars through the intelligent design model of the *Aratea* is perhaps like making sense of hybrids or afterlife apparitions: for the Epicurean, *none* of these things add up. However, Lucretius needs to take care here: his evocation of Epicurus in the terms of various Ciceronian constellations is a risky device. The Master can be seen either to supersede the constellations by means of a truer reason, or to partake of their hybridism.

4.2.2 THE SHIPWRECK OF THE UNIVERSE

DRN 2.555/*Aratea* fr. 24

In the case of Sirius, we saw how one passage of Cicero is scattered over many places in the text of Lucretius. The behaviour of Cicero's text, used this way, is a good analogy for the behaviour of the universe in Lucretius. One image which

Lucretius chooses to illustate atomic behaviour is that of a shipwreck (*DRN* 2.547–64):

> quippe etenim sumam hoc quoque uti finita per omne
> corpora iactari unius genitalia rei,
> unde ubi qua vi et quo pacto congressa coibunt
> materiae tanto in pelago turbaque aliena?   550
> non, ut opinor, habent rationem conciliandi
> sed quasi naufragiis magnis multisque coortis
> disiectare solet magnum mare transtra cavernas
> antemnas proram malos tonsasque natantis,
> per terrarum omnis oras *fluitantia aplustra*   555
> ut videantur et indicium *mortalibus edant*,
> infidi maris insidias virisque dolumque
> ut vitare velint, neve ullo tempore credant,
> subdola cum ridet placidi pellacia ponti,
> sic tibi si finita semel primordia quaedam   560
> constitues, aevum debebunt sparsa per omnem
> disiectare aestus diversi materiai,
> numquam in concilium ut possint compulsa coire
> nec remorari in concilio nec crescere adaucta . . .

'Suppose I were to run with the argument that a finite number of bodies gen-erative of one thing were tossed about in the universe: from where, at what point and by what means will the raw materials come together in such a mas-sive sea and alien crowd of stuff? There's no way, in my view, that they can coalesce: but just like when, in the event of a great and copious shipwreck, the mighty sea usually scatters the yardsticks, the prow, masts and oars in the swim, so that from every shore the stern-sculptures can be seen floating about, and serve as a witness to mortals of the deceptive sea, to instil them with a desire to avoid its wiles, and not trust at any time the treacherous seductions of the calm sea: just so, if you decide that for your purposes atoms are of finite number, they will have to be scattered through all eternity and sprinkled about on a tide of indiscriminate matter, so that they can never be forced to come together in concert, nor stay that way, nor grow by increase . . .'

Lucretius' image is this: if matter were not infinite, it would not be able to recom-bine, any more than the parts of wrecked ships can spontaneously reassemble them-selves from the waves. Those (such as the Stoics) who think matter is finite, have not thought through the consequences. This passage of atomic theory contains two Ciceronian references. Compare line 555 with Cicero's image of floating sterns after a shipwreck, *Arat.* fr. 24 *navibus absumptis fluvitantia quaerere aplustria* ('to seek the floating sterns, the ships having been destroyed').[38] Again there is aggregation of Ciceronian parallels; in the ensuing line, *DRN* 2.556, there is another Ciceronian collocation, *mortalibus edant* (with *Arat.* 335 *mortalibus edit*). The first passage brings us into Cicero's description of the rainy constellation of the Kids;[39] the second, into the zodiac, which provides, or should provide, clues for sailors about the viability of sailing.

We might think also of Cicero's description of the zodiacal constellation Capricorn, who at *Aratea* 69–71 is ignored by arrogant sailors, who become the models for Lucretius' mistaken theorists:

> sed tamen anni labuntur tempore toto,
> nec vi signorum cedunt neque flamina vitant,
> nec metuunt canos minitanti murmure fluctos.

> 'But nevertheless they sail along in every season of the year, and they do not bow to the force of the Signs or avoid the winds, and they are not afraid of the white-topped waves with their threatening murmur.'

This hunch is confirmed by further Ciceronian reference a little later, to this very passage, at *DRN* 2.767, in *canos candenti marmore fluctus* ('hoary waves with a white sheen'), with *Arat.* 71, *nec metuunt canos minitanti murmure fluctos.*[40] We remember that the same passage of Cicero, *Arat.* 69–71, influenced the description of *religio* at *DRN* 1.68–9, *minitanti murmure*, and 5.1193, *murmura magna minarum* (see p. 74 above). As in the case of Sirius, Lucretius has spread one Ciceronian passage over various *loci* in the *DRN*. It looks as though the significance of Ciceronian reference in this context is to provide intertextual instances of wrong conduct, which Lucretius applies to his philosophical or religious opponents.

To conclude what I have to say about *DRN* 2.555, then, Lucretius uses Cicero's descriptions of the constellations, particularly as they are inimical to sailors, to create the imagery of an impossible world made of finite amounts of matter. The Lucretian image is a more powerful one given its previous use in a picture of a predictable universe. Lucretius' analogy takes place at the textual as well as figurative level. The 'elements' of the text of Cicero's *Aratea*, scattered like this, could not recombine to make sense of the world: it is atomism which must do this.

4.2.3 NAMELESSNESS

DRN 3.242/*Aratea* 170

Omnino nominis expers in *DRN* 3.242 is a threefold collocation shared with *Aratea* 170, *expertes nominis omnes*. In each author the phrase occurs in the same part of the hexameter. Lucretius varies the syntax in a way we now see is typical of his relationship with Cicero: Cicero's adjective *omnes* becomes Lucretius' adverb *omnino*; Lucretius' *expers* is singular for Cicero's plural; the dependent genitive *nominis* is the stable element within the collocation. Given the strength of the Ciceronian resonance, what meaning does it add to Lucretius' text? To answer that, we must return to the context of the resonance in each author.

The reference occurs in Lucretius' description (at *DRN* 3.237–45) of the fourth element of the soul, too tenuous in its nature for proper identification:

> iam triplex animi est igitur natura reperta;
> nec tamen haec sat sunt ad sensum cuncta creandum,
> nil horum quoniam recipit mens posse creare
> sensiferos motus †quaedamque mente volutat†.[41]
> quarta quoque his igitur quaedam natura necessest
> attribuatur. east *omnino nominis expers*;
> qua neque mobilius quicquam neque tenuius extat,
> nec magis e parvis et levibus ex elementis;
> sensiferos motus quae didit prima per artus.

'Now it's apparent that we've discovered that the nature of the mind is threefold. Yet all of these [elements] are not up to the task of creating perception, because your mind can grasp none of them as the origin of the motion needed for perception, [giving rise to] the sorts of things which in the end it whirls about in the process of thought. A fourth entity must therefore be added to these. That one is totally nameless. There's nothing more mobile and gossamer than this, or made out of elements that are smaller and lighter. This is what first distributes the motions of perception among the body-parts.'

Through his particular variation of Cicero's syntax, Lucretius may be strengthening the wordplay of the phrase: his *omnino* resonates with *nominis*, and the two words are near-anagrams; we can mix up the letters, and have trouble identifying the words, especially in the form an ancient reader would have seen them (*omninonominis*), just as the element of the soul Lucretius is talking about is hard to identify.

How does the expression function in its context in Cicero? Here is the whole passage, *Arat.* 170–182:

> et prope conspicies, *expertis nominis omnis,*
> inter Pistricem et Piscem quem diximus Austri
> stellas, sub pedibus stratas radiantis Aquari.
> propter Aquarius obscurum dextra rigat amnem,
> exiguo qui stellarum candore nitescit.
> e multis tamen is duo late lumina fulgent:
> unum sub magnis pedibus cernetur Aquari;
> quod superest, gelido delapsum flumine fontis,
> spinigeram subter caudam Pistricis adhaesit.
> hae tenues stellae perhibentur nomine Aqua[r]i.
> hic aliae volitant parvo cum lumine clarae
> atque priora pedum subeunt vestigia magni
> Arquitenentis, et obscurae *sine nomine* cedunt.[42]

'But nearby you will see stars without exception nameless, between Pistrix and what we call the Southern Fish, spread out under the feet of shining Aquarius. Close by, Aquarius pours from his right hand a shadowy river, which glows with dimly shining stars. From this mass, two shine with light cast wide: one will be seen under the massive feet of Aquarius; what remains, having fallen from the chilly rill of water, is in a mass beneath the rough tail of Pistrix. These delicate stars are designated "The Water".[43] Here others fly, distinct although their light is dim, and are situated under the front feet of the great Bow-carrier, and make their way obscure and without a name.'

The context in Cicero is the residue of unnamed stars which surround the identifiable constellations. Let's bring the two contexts together. The 'fourth *natura*' is a rogue or unidentifiable element in Lucretius's system, just as the unnamed stars are in Aratus' and Cicero's. Is this necessarily a bad thing? It is instructive to look further at the semantics of namelessness. Note *obscurae sine nomine* in Cicero *Arat.* 182. This is Cicero's translation of *Ph.* 385, πάντα μάλ' ἠερόεντα καὶ οὐκ ὀνομαστὰ φέρονται ('all very hazy and nameless in their courses', Kidd). *Obscurae* (for ἠερόεντα) at the same time carries a resonance absent from the Greek. As well as being 'dim', these stars are 'hard to understand', i.e., in relation to others. This is why they cannnot be classified. In this respect their role is similar to the planets. This is the meaning Lucan later gives to the term in *Pharsalia* 1.663–5, speaking of the desertion of their posts by the constellations in the leadup to civil war:

> . . . cur signa meatus
> deseruere suos mundoque obscura feruntur,
> ensiferi nimium fulget latus Orionis?[44]

Why have the constellations fled from their courses, to move darkling through the sky, while the side of sword-girt Orion shines all too bright? (trans. Duff 1928; text of Housman 1926).

'*Obscura*' here means not 'dark', but 'hard to understand', in the Lucretian sense, as in *Graiorum obscura reperta* (*DRN* 1.136), or *obscura de re tam lucida pango carmina* (4.8). The stars have abandoned their regular movements (*meatus deseruere suos*) and become, like planets, too difficult to classify.

It is appropriate that Lucretius uses Ciceronian reference to the namelessness of elements in the heavens to describe an element of namelessness in the *human* soul: the connection between the sky and humanity is established in the tradition of Aratus, most obviously in the Myth of Δίκη, and Lucretius is able to give us a shorthand reference to it by drawing on a text in the Aratean tradition.

There is, however, a large-scale contrast between namelessness in Cicero and in Lucretius; in the former, namelessness is a mark of disorder; the Epicurean universe, however, glories in such 'rogue' elements, which form an essential part of its makeup.[45] There exists, therefore, an adversarial relationship between Lucretius and his source text in respect of the collocation *omnino nominis expers*.

DRN 3.316/*Aratea* 234

We have just seen that the fourth, tenuous element of the soul is unsusceptable to naming. Likewise, in his exposition of human character shortly afterwards, Lucretius throws up his hands at the possibility of describing its infinite nuance. In doing so, he quotes Cicero, *Arat.* 234 *quarum ego nunc nequeo tortos evolvere cursus* ('I am not now able to unroll the convoluted courses [of the planets]') almost exactly.[46] Again we must ask what Lucretius gains from such a strong resonance. And yet again, context is everything. Here is the Lucretian context (*DRN* 3.314–18):

> inque aliis rebus multis differre necessest
> naturas hominum varias moresque sequaces;
> quorum ego nunc nequeo caecas exponere causas
> nec reperire figurarum tot nomina quot sunt
> principiis, unde haec oritur variantia rerum.

> 'And in many other respects it must be the case that the various characteristics of people, and the personalities contingent on them, differ from one another. I am unable to expound the hidden causes of these or find terms enough to describe all the permutations in origin, from where such a diversity of features arises.'

And here is the Ciceronian context, the description of the Long Year created by planetary egress and return (*Arat.* 232–6):[47]

> Hae faciunt magnos longinqui temporis annos,
> cum redeunt ad idem caeli sub tegmine signum;
> quarum ego nunc nequeo tortos evolvere cursus:
> verum haec, quae semper certo [e]voluuntur in orbe
> fixa, simul magnos edemus gentibus orbes.

> 'These [the planets] bring about the Great Years of long duration, when they return to the same star-sign under the canopy of heaven. I am not now able to unroll their sinuous courses; but I shall proclaim at large the great orbits of those fixed stars which roll round in a predictable course.'

In both cases, the effects of the phenomenon described can be seen; but in each case, the explanation is ineffable. As with Cicero's planets, which make the long year, so with the determinants of character in Lucretius: we see their effects but we cannot set forth their causes.

The connection between Lucretian and Ciceronian disorder is nowhere more apparent than at *DRN* 3.317, the line which follows the almost exact echo by Lucretius of Cicero's formulation of doubt. Following his statement of his inability to express the hidden causes of personality, Lucretius continues, *nec reperire figurarum tot nomina quot sunt /principiis. Figura* seems otherwise an odd word to use of traits of character, if we were not already armed with a knowledge of the connection between the soul and the stars. One way in which we are thus armed is by having been reminded by an equally strong Ciceronian resonance less than 100 lines earlier, with *omnino nominis expers* (3.242) of a Ciceronian passage on the unnamed stars.

In 3.317 we may also be reminded of a seminal passage on unnamed stars, *Arat.* 155–66:[48]

> exinde exiguae tenui cum lumine multae
> inter Pistricem fusae sparsaeque videntur
> atque Gubernaclum stellae, quas contegit omnis
> formidans acrem morsum Lepus: his *neque nomen*
> *nec formam* veteres certam statuisse videntur.
> nam quae sideribus claris natura polivit
> et vario pinxit distinguens lumine formas,
> haec ille astrorum custos ratione notavit
> signaque dignavit caelestia nomine vero;
> has autem quae sunt parvo cum lumine fusae,
> consimili specie stellas parilique nitore,
> non potuit nobis nota clarare *figura.*

'Then there are many small stars with faint light, poured and splashed between Pistrix and the Rudder, all of which the Hare runs up against in his fear of a sharp bite. The people of old do not seem to have conferred a name or a distinct shape on these. For that custodian of the stars recorded in orderly fashion these star-signs and dignified them with a name true to form; but he was unable to mark out for us with a familiar shape these which are poured out with scant light, stars all similar in appearance and with like magnitude.'

These stars cannot be accounted for in terms of groups which form figures, and this makes them unclassifiable. So in Lucretius, the traits of personality similarly cannot be grouped in identifiable 'forms'. The connection between forms and naming determines the abilities both of Lucretius and of the anonymous namer in Cicero.[49]

4.2.4 TOPSY-TURVY LAND: PLANETS AND ATOMS

Cicero's passage on the planets becomes an important programmatic resource in the *DRN*. In Cicero, the universe as a whole is legible, with the exception of a few elements, which include the planets and the unnamed stars.[50] In Lucretius, it is the *universe* on every level which is inexplicable, at least in the terms people usually accept as explanations.

DRN 1.1029–61/*Aratea* 226–36

DRN 1.1029 *et multos etiam magnos servata per annos* ('and this being also preserved through many great cycles of years') echoes *Arat.* 232 *hae faciunt magnos longinqui temporis annos.*[51] The context in Lucretius is one of the preservation of the stability of the world through the behaviour of matter; in Cicero, of the 'great year' created by the conjunctions of the planets with the other heavenly bodies. In Lucretius 1.1029, Cicero's phrasing is transferred from a description of the regular clockwork motion of the heavenly bodies, which create between them the Long Year, to a description of the constancy of *atoms*. In pragmatic Lucretian rationalism, it is the atomic nature of the world, rather than Cicero's celestial clock, which is the measure of constancy.

The force of the allusion may become clearer when we read further into the Lucretian context. We find, at the other end of the passage, 1061, *simili ratione*. This formula is shared with *Arat.* 227, *simili ratione*. That allusion is to Cicero's passage on the planets. *DRN* 1.1061 comes in a passage of polemic where Lucretius criticizes those who think everything tends towards the middle of the universe. Lucretius 1.1061–4 gives an ironic picture of the topsy-turvy land which would result from the logical extension of this principle:

> et *simili ratione* animalia suppa <u>vagari</u>
> contendunt neque posse e terris in loca caeli
> reccidere inferiora magis quam corpora nostra
> sponte sua possint in caeli templa volare . . .

> 'And in similar fashion they argue that creatures wander about head-downwards, but that they can't fall back from the earth into the spaces of heaven below them, any more than our bodies can fly off into the heavenly regions all by themselves . . .'

Given the fact *simile ratione* is a collocation shared with Cicero's passage on the planets, could *vagari* also gesture towards Cicero's planets, using a similar bilingual etymology? We remember that Cicero says of the planets (*Arat.* 230–31, translated on p. 63 above):

> Sic malunt **errare vagae** per *nubila caeli*
> Atque suos *vario motu* metirier orbes.

The argument for Lucretian allusion to Cicero's planets becomes cumulatively stronger and semantically more promising by aggregation. Cicero's planets are extremely useful to Lucretius as an analogy for matter. In his polemic against intelligent design, including the argument against the roundness of the earth at 1.1061, Lucretius makes use of the most irrational thing in the universe of the *Aratea*: the planets. The one inexplicable thing in their system is picked up by Lucretius and made to do all the work in his polemics. Matter—and the world in general—is a random creation: everything in the Epicurean universe is 'planetary' in this sense.

DRN 4.444/*Aratea* 223

DRN 4 is about perception. Quite often, impressions can be false, leading, for instance, to ideas of the gods. Lucretius' aim is to clarify perception according to the principles of Epicurean philosophy. 4.443–6 is a small example:

raraque per caelum cum venti nubila portant
tempore nocturno, tum splendida *signa videntur*
labier adversum nimbos atque ire superne
longe aliam in partem ac vera ratione feruntur.

'When the winds carry wispy clouds across the sky at night-time, then then the bright stars seem to move in contrary motion to the clouds and are said to pass overhead in a very different zone from their true one.'

Night-time clouds can, with their motions, give an illusion of movement to the constellations which does not accord with reality. Ciceronian reference helps Lucretius in his argument. There is a collocation of no fewer than four elements shared with *Aratea* 223, *haec sunt quae visens nocturno tempore signa*. This fourfold collocation is one of the weightiest verbal echoes of Cicero in the *DRN*. Lucretius does not refer to the passage on the planets, but to the lines immediately preceding it, which set up a strong opposition between the fixed stars summarized there and the planets which follow:

haec sunt quae visens nocturno tempore signa	
aeternumque volens mundi pernoscere motum	225
legitimo cernes caelum lustrantia cursu.[52]	224

'These star-signs are the ones which, when you see them at night-time and want to know about the ongoing motion of the heaven, you will notice, rake the heaven with a law-abiding course.'

However, Lucretius shows how the motion of the planets can be imputed to the fixed stars as well. In Lucretius, the stars seem, to our poor perception, due to the influence of the movement of the clouds, to move in a far different direction than true *ratio* indicates. Lucretius is here pulling out the rug of certainty from under our feet. We look at the stars and think they do certain things; if clouds can alter our perception to such a degree, can we be sure we are *ever* right?

Lucretius is describing, not just the ostensibly wandering motions of the planets, but the apparent wandering of all the constellations under certain conditions. But in doing so, he also draws on Cicero's description of the planets. In *Arat.* 227–8, Cicero draws a contrast between the 'fixed stars', which can be understood by the fact that their courses follow certain laws (*legitimo, Arat.* 224), and the planets, which can't be understood *simili ratione* (228). For Cicero, the point is only that the movement of the planets cannot be described *simili ratione* to that of the 'fixed' stars. Lucretius, on the other hand, notes the perception that the stars *all* wander with the clouds at night: this *perception* is what strays *vera ratione*, not the heavenly bodies themselves. In this, he interposes the Epicurean understanding of nature between himself and his model: for Lucretius it makes no difference whether the planets wander, or all the heavenly bodies do. As we learn in Book 5, Epicurean astronomy presupposes no rational system for *any* stars, but gives a series of alternative reasons for their apparent movements.

DRN 5.643–5/*Aratea* 232–3

This is the argumentative thrust of a third reference to Cicero's planets, *DRN* 5.643–5:

> et ratione pari lunam stellasque putandumst,
> quae volvunt magnos in magnis orbibus annos,
> aeribus posse alternis e partibus ire.

> 'And in like manner we must suppose that the moon, and the stars which revolve for vast years in vast orbits, may move driven this way and that by breezes.'

Compare these lines with *Arat.* 232–3 (translated above*),* hae faciunt magnos longin-qui temporis annos, *l*cum redeunt ad idem caeli sub tegmine signum. *Ratione pari* may be a response to Cicero's *simili ratione* in *Arat.* 227: in this case, *all* motions can be understood as arising from the same cause. This cause is not the celestial machine of the Ciceronian universe, but the movement of air pushing the heavenly bodies about.

In this part of *DRN* 5, Lucretius advances various rationalistic theories as to the movements of the heavenly bodies. Ostensibly copying Cicero's, his planets also complete a species of 'great year', but, in opposition to the intelligent design theory of Stoicism, Lucretius advances the happily random explanation that they may be blown about by winds. Cicero does not expound the theories of planetary motion in this passage of the *Aratea*, but leaves their motion in the realm of the mysterious: Lucretius is careful to respond with unremitting rationalist elucidation.

Conclusion: the Significance of Cicero for Lucretius

This chapter has shown that Lucretius is in dialogue with Cicero throughout the *DRN*, not just in the astronomical parts of the poem. It has also shown that there is a *spectrum* of reference to Cicero in Lucretius, ranging from unmistakeable individual references, to thematic agglomeration. In addition (and most importantly) we have seen the *uses* of Ciceronian resonances. These are most often deployed in contexts of anti–intelligent design polemic, and serve as a representation of the alternative universe, a vision to be destroyed in Lucretius' argument.

Far from disengaging from the contemporary debate, Lucretius is in the thick of it, a militant Epicurean answering the tenets of Stoicism (or more generally, of intelligent design philosophies). To single out (for instance) direct reference to the machinery of mathematical astronomy as a benchmark by which to measure Lucretius' engagement with Stoic debate is to set criteria which are too narrow.[53] Within such a restricted ambit it is hardly surprising that a negative answer is returned. But by broadening the approach, we can see that Lucretius engages in debate on both the factual and allusive levels.

Factually, Lucretius *does* sometimes go in for direct argument, even though his opponents remain unnamed, as in the case of the astronomers at *DRN* 5.694–5 (above, ch. 3 pp. 78–80). For the Stoics, as evidenced in the first-century context by Cicero, *DND* 2, the celestial apparatus is the best evidence of the divine. We have seen Lucretius' own engagement with this position in his description of the wonders of the stars at *DRN* 2.1030–9 and his polemic on religion at 5.1183–1221. Lucretius questions astronomical 'fact', in order to displace the model of interlocking celestial circles as a work of divine artistry.[54]

But secondly, more pervasively if more subtly, Lucretius' engagement in the debate takes place at the intertextual level. Lucretius turns the Stoics' own language against them, in the form of Cicero's first-century translation of that archetypal intelligent design poem, Aratus' *Phaenomena*. It is natural, given that this is a first-century Roman debate, that Lucretius should draw his model from the first-century Roman context, rather than (or as well as) reverting to the Hellenistic original. Cicero's text as epic model gives Lucretius a way of integrating Stoic material into his poem. Embedding it in the new context, he manipulates it for non-Stoic or anti-Stoic ends.

Cicero was to reclaim his work a decade later, in the *DND*, which not only incorporates the *Aratea* as an icon of Stoic celestial order, but also contains modes of expression which look like deliberate opposition to Lucretius' account in *DRN* 5, in which Lucretius had appropriated the *Aratea* as both grist to the poetic mill and a stalking horse in the construction of his Epicurean cosmos.

In Lucretius, as we have seen, planetary motion, as we know it from Cicero, is applied to *all* the stars, a destabilizing technique relative to the Aratean tradition, and one in which thematic allusion to Cicero's passage on the planets plays an important part. We remember for instance *DRN* 5.1210, *vario motu quae candida sidera verset*. Lucretius in this passage almost certainly means all the stars,[55] but the formula with which he describes their courses (*vario motu*) is the same one which Cicero used in *Aratea* 231 to distinguish planetary motion from that of the fixed stars.[56] In the chaos of the Epicurean universe, only atomic behaviour is predictable. Atomic behaviour is at bottom an ongoing process of random coalescence and disassociation. Any apparent element of reason to emerge in the superstructures is illusory. In reality it is dog-eat-dog out there, and the atoms exist in a Dawkins-style genetic fundamentalism, the battle for individual survival leaving no room for altruism. Note the imagery Lucretius uses to express this concept (*DRN* 5.380–1):

> denique tantopere inter se cum maxima mundi
> pugnent membra, pio nequaquam concita bello

> 'since, then, the giant limbs of the universe fight so much among themselves, aroused in a war which in no way follows the law of family relations . . .'

Here, *pio nequaquam . . . bello* is *civil* war.[57] The warring elements in Lucretius' universe are described using a Roman cultural paradigm we have already seen operating in chapter 2 above. There (pp. 50–6) I commented on the use of several key terms of Roman civil war, in Virgil and in Germanicus, with the conclusion that Lucretius is a plausible point of origin for the constellation of terms. We recall one of them, *discordia*, in the context of cosmogony (*DRN* 5.437–40, quoted with translation in chapter 2 p. 54):

> . . . discordia quorum
> intervalla vias conexus pondera plagas
> concursus motus turbabat proelia miscens
> propter dissimilis formas variasque figuras . . .

As we have seen in chapter 2, this term is associated with civil war. The elements of Lucretius' universe are mutually hostile entities which claw their way to supremacy in a *civil* war.

Lucretius dissolves the cosmic certainties with which we are familiar from our reading of Aratus. So too, in Lucretius, the sun may describe the motions predicted by the celestial mechanism; or it may be that patches of more cloying air sometimes detain it on its yearly path. In Lucretius, the planets may be explicable using a complicated system of circles; on the other hand they may just be blown about by winds. In the intelligent design universe, the planets wander; in Lucretius, all the stars wander: it makes no difference.

No doubt Lucretius knows as well as we do that some of his explanations are absurd. But what he is doing is giving us a glorious freedom. The stars, planets, and elements after Lucretius are not only evidence for one world view or another, but also a resource in the building and demolition of the world. Freed from the constraints of the clockwork universe, its entities can fight their own battles and become players on the giant field of Roman civil war. Metaphors of namelessness, change, and planetary motion, deriving from the tradition of Aratus but conceptually at odds with it, become in Latin literature tools towards the anaylsis of social, and in particular civil, discord. This process of the cooption of the images of Aratus' universe in the expression of civil war in Roman epic and tragedy will form the subject of the next chapter.

5 }

Planetary Motion

Introduction

This chapter will show how Aratus functions in early imperial constructions of civil war. That Aratus is present within this tradition at all is testimony to his immense importance. That he is an integral part of how civil war is articulated in Roman literature shows the extent to which his text was internalized in the tradition. It is not, however, used, in what would be a straightforward act of imitation, to invoke the orderliness of the universe, but is the requirement for understanding its opposite, the disintegration of order. Such disintegration is pendant to a deficit in human ethics.[1]

The material discussed here follows from what has been studied in chapter 2. There, we established that the Roman tradition injects civil war into the Aratean universe. Although this is most evident in the additions present in Germanicus' 'translation' of Aratus' *Dike* myth, the conceptual seed may well lie in Lucretius' treatment of the intelligent design tradition (as we have seen in chapters 3 and 4). Lucretius is in constant engagement with that tradition, fragmenting an exemplary text and exploding its ideas by means of what I have called 'intertextual polemic.' Aratean material is placed in the service of a universe at war with itself. And things were never the same for the Aratean universe after Lucretius. If Aratus' world is a graphic system representing divine providence, in the Roman tradition the universe becomes a theatre of civil war. Aratus' world has already been changed by the time Germanicus comes to translate the *Phaenomena* into Latin: his rendition of Aratus is achieved under the influence of fundamentally different concerns from those of his Greek original.

It may be that Germanicus was the first explicitly to combine Aratus with the topos of civil war; and it's interesting that he did it in a *translation* of Aratus. But the use of Aratus in this way is a device which occurs across a variety of early imperial works which are *not* translations of the *Phaenomena*. In this chapter, as in chapter 2, we do not just study Aratean texts proper. Here, we shall observe the phenomenon in Lucan, Manilius, Seneca, and Statius.

5.1 Disorder in Aratus

Although Aratus' universe is a representation of celestial order, there are three elements of potential disorder in it. These are: (i) namelessness, (ii) planetary motion or retrogression, and (iii) celestial change. These elements are marginalized by Aratus himself. The Roman tradition, on the other hand, accentuates such elements and, characteristically, yokes them to civil war. This Romanization produces, in the end, a reading of Aratus in opposition to the orderly nature of the original.

Aratus controls his astronomical material to squeeze out notions of disorder or even of excessive complexity. His universe sets out in such a way that the potential for misunderstanding is minimized. In the proem, Zeus distributed the stars so that they should signal fixed (Aratus' word is τετυγμένα, *Ph.* 12), i.e., *predictable* (because recurring), phenomena.

5.1.1 NAMELESSNESS IN ARATUS

Aratus passes over the topic of namelessness in two short passages. The first is *Ph.* 143–6:

> οἷός οἱ πρὸ ποδῶν φέρεται καλός τε μεγάς τε
> εἷς μὲν ὑπωμαίων, εἷς δ' ἰξυόθεν κατιόντων,
> ἄλλος δ' οὐραῖος ὑπὸ γούνασιν· ἀλλ' ἄρα πάντες
> ἁπλόοι ἄλλοθεν ἄλλος ἀνωνυμίῃ φορέονται.

> '. . . such are the stars that in beauty and magnitude move before her feet, one in front of the forelegs, one before the legs that descend from her loins, and another under the hind knees. But all of them, individually in different positions, go on their way without a name.'

In this passage, stars are unnamed because they are one-offs (ἁπλόοι, *Ph.* 145), that is, they do not require a relative taxonomy. In this passage the nameless stars are contrasted with constellations which have both a recognizable form and (unusually for Aratus) a mythology, the Bears, and *Dike*, whose myth they immediately follow.

In Aratus' second passage on namelessness, the nameless stars are both too numerous and too indistinct for taxonomy (*Ph.* 367–85):

> οἱ δ' ὀλίγῳ μέτρῳ ὀλίγῃ δ' ἐγκείμενοι αἴγλῃ
> μεσσόθι πηδαλίου καὶ Κήτεος εἱλίσσονται,
> γλαυκοῦ πεπτηῶτες ὑπὸ πλευρῇσι Λαγωοῦ,
> νώνυμοι· οὐ γὰρ τοί γε τετυγμένου εἰδώλοιο   370
> βεβλέαται μελέεσσιν ἐοικότες, οἷά τε πολλὰ
> ἐξείης στιχόωντα παρέρχεται αὐτὰ κέλευθα
> ἀνομένων ἐτέων, τά τις ἀνδρῶν οὐκέτ' ἐόντων
> ἐφράσατ' ἠδ' ἐνόησεν ἅπαντ' ὀνομαστὶ καλέσσαι
> ἤλιθα μορφώσας· οὐ γάρ κ' ἐδυνήσατο πάντων   375

οἰόθι κεκριμένων ὄνομ' εἰπεῖν οὐδὲ δαῆναι.
πολλοὶ γὰρ πάντη, πολέων δ' ἐπὶ ἶσα πέλονται
μέτρα τε καὶ χροιή, πάντες γε μὲν ἀμφιέλικτοι·
τῷ καὶ ὁμηγερέας οἱ ἐείσατο ποιήσασθαι
ἀστέρας, ὄφρ' ἐπιτὰξ ἄλλῳ παρακείμενος ἄλλος   380
εἴδεα σημαίνοιεν· ἄφαρ δ' ὀνομαστ' ἐγένοντο
ἄστρα, καὶ οὐκέτι νῦν ὑπὸ θαύματι τέλλεται ἀστήρ·
ἀλλ' οἱ μὲν καθαροῖς ἐναρηρότες εἰδώλοισι
φαίνονται, τὰ δ' ἔνερθε διωκομένοιο Λαγωοῦ
πάντα μάλ' ἠερόεντα καὶ οὐκ ὀνομαστὰ φέρονται.   385

'Other stars covering a small area, and inset with slight brilliance, circle between Argo's steering-oar and the Monster, lying below the flanks of the grey Hare, without a name; they are not cast in any resemblance to the body of a well-defined figure, like the many that pass in regular ranks along the same paths as the years complete themselves, the constellations that one of the men who are no more devised and contrived to call by names, grouping them in compact shapes: he could not, of course, have named or identified all the stars taken individually, because there are so many all over the sky, and many alike in magnitude and colour, while all have a circling movement; therefore he decided to make the stars into groups, so that different stars arranged together in order could represent figures; and thereupon the named constellations were created, and no star-rising now takes us by surprise; so that the other stars that shine appear fixed in clear-cut figures, but those beneath the hunted Hare are all very hazy and nameless in their courses.'

Aratus describes these stars as νώνυμοι ('nameless', *Ph.* 370). The stars so described are contrasted with the stars which the unnamed Namer named, and, in so doing, formed, like an artist (*Ph.* 373–5). Aratus' imagery here recalls Plato's discussion of the value of astronomy in the *Republic*. The stars are essentially decorative (τὰ ἐν οὐρανῷ ποικίλματα, ἐπείπερ ἐν ὁρατῷ πεποίκιλται, *Rep.* 529c6–7) and can be used as an aid (only that, in Plato) to the study of reality, just as one would use diagrams drawn by Daedalus or some other craftsman (δημιουργοῦ, *Rep.* 529d).[2] In Aratus, Naming is an important index of the ordered universe: the Namer's activities are an analogue to those of Zeus as demiurge (*Ph.* 10–13), and perhaps also to Zeus as we see him as celestial general in Plato's *Phaedrus* 246e4–247a7, organizing his stars in 'companies' (ὁμηγερέας, *Ph.* 379).[3] But in this organizing process there is a residue.

5.1.2 THE PLANETS IN ARATUS

In a universe constructed as a graphic system of divine morality and beneficent control, the planets are politely passed over (*Ph.* 454–61):

οἱ δ' ἐπιμὶξ ἄλλοι πέντ' ἀστέρες οὐδὲν ὁμοῖοι
πάντοθεν εἰδώλων δυοκαίδεκα δινεύονται.
οὐκ ἂν ἔτ' εἰς ἄλλους ὁρόων ἐπιτεκμήραιο
κείνων ἧχι κέονται, ἐπεὶ πάντες μετανάσται.
μακροὶ δέ σφεων εἰσὶν ἑλισσομένων ἐνιαυτοί,
μακρὰ δὲ σήματα κεῖται ἀπόπροθεν εἰς ἓν ἰόντων,
οὐδ' ἔτι θαρσαλέος κείνων ἐγώ· ἄρκιος εἴην
ἀπλανέων τά τε κύκλα τά τ' αἰθέρι σήματ' ἐνισπεῖν.

'But there are five other stars among [the fixed stars], but quite unlike them,
that circulate all the way through the twelve figures of the zodiac. You cannot
in this case identify where these lie by looking at other stars, for they all
change their positions. The years of their orbits are long, and at long intervals
are their configurations when they come from afar into conjunction. I am not
at all confident in dealing with them: I hope I may be adequate in expounding
the circles of the fixed stars and their guide-constellations in the sky.'

The planets are inexplicable in relation to other stars, i.e., as part of a *system*.
You cannot find them using guide-stars, as you can for instance find the Pole Star.
As he dismissively portrays them, they are simply scattered randomly (ἐπιμίξ)
among the stars. Scholars have hypothesized as to the reason for Aratus' shoulder-
shrug. The consensus seems to be that the planets are inconvenient: 'Put very
loosely, the planets lack cosmos'[4]; 'Aratus does not want them in his description of
the universe.'[5] But things are not so simple. We should note that Aratus is not being
honest in his disavowal of planetary knowledge. Although he chooses to represent
the planets as inexplicable, the regularity of planetary motion was already partly
understood, from Plato onwards.[6] At *Laws* 822a4–8, Plato had already made the
point that, in the case of the planets, what you see is not what you get:

οὐ γάρ ἐστι τοῦτο . . . τὸ δόγμα ὀρθὸν περὶ σελήνης τε καὶ ἡλίου καὶ τῶν
ἄλλων ἄστρων, ὡς ἄρα πλανᾶταί ποτε, πᾶν δὲ τοὐναντίον ἔχει τούτου -
τὴν αὐτὴν γὰρ αὐτῶν ὁδὸν ἕκαστον καὶ οὐ πολλὰς ἀλλὰ μίαν ἀεὶ κύκλῳ
διεξέρχεται, <u>φαίνεται</u> δὲ πολλὰς φερόμενον.

'This doctrine about the moon and the sun and the other heavenly bodies
[ie. the planets] is not correct, that they, as it were, wander. In fact the opposite is the case. Each of them follows its unique path, and this path is not
multiple but a single one which constantly goes in a circle, even though *it
appears* that they follow many paths' (my trans.).[7]

Plato is aware of the disjunction between the term planets and the behaviour of its
referents. Their etymology is from πλανάω, 'to wander.' But in fact, although Plato
still uses the term 'planets', he knew well that they did not 'wander'.[8] His use of the
term, if anything, highlights the 'meaning incommensurability' between the misunderstanding of the planets as wandering, and the understanding, contemporary
with Plato, that their motions were orderly.[9]

In fact, the schizophrenic nature of the planets is reflected in Plato's own ouevre. Despite his recognition of the non-wandering nature of the planets in the *Laws*, Plato refrains from telling of the movement of the outer planets, at least, in a work in which one would think, if anywhere, he would bite the planetary bullet, the *Timaeus*. On the contrary: in this work, Plato not once, but twice puts off explaining the planets. At *Timaeus* 38d6–e3 he seems to profess a degree of aporia, or at least a sense that an explanation of the planets is too weighty for the context:

τὰ δ' ἄλλα οἷ δὴ καὶ δι' ἃς αἰτίας ἱδρύσατο, εἴ τις ἐπεξίοι πάσας, ὁ λόγος πάρεργος ὢν πλέον ἂν ἔργον ὧν ἕνεκα λέγεται παράσχοι. ταῦτα μὲν οὖν ἴσως τάχ' ἂν κατὰ σχολὴν ὕστερον τῆς ἀξίας τύχοι διηγήσεως ...

'As for the remainder, where he enshrined them and for what reasons—if one should explain all these, the account, though only by the way, would be a heavier task than that for the sake of which it was given. Perhaps these things may be duly set forth later at our leisure' (trans. Cornford 1937; text of Burnet 1902).

At 39c5–d7 the ignorance of men as to the motions of the planets is remarked, without further attempt at enlightenment:

τῶν δ' ἄλλων τὰς περιόδους οὐκ ἐννενοηκότες ἄνθρωποι, πλὴν ὀλίγοι τῶν πολλῶν, οὔτε ὀνομάζουσιν οὔτε πρὸς ἄλληλα συμμετροῦνται σκοποῦντες ἀριθμοῖς, ὥστε ὡς ἔπος εἰπεῖν οὐκ ἴσασιν χρόνον ὄντα τὰς τούτων πλάνας, πλήθει μὲν ἀμηχάνῳ χρωμένας, πεποικιλμένας δὲ θαυμαστῶς· ἔστιν δ' ὅμως οὐδὲν ἧττον κατανοῆσαι δυνατὸν ὡς ὅ γε τέλεος ἀριθμὸς χρόνου τὸν τέλεον ἐνιαυτὸν πληροῖ τότε, ὅταν ἁπασῶν τῶν ὀκτὼ περιόδων τὰ πρὸς ἄλληλα συμπερανθέντα τάχη σχῇ κεφαλὴν τῷ τοῦ ταὐτοῦ καὶ ὁμοίως ἰόντος ἀναμετρηθέντα κύκλῳ.

'The periods of the rest have not been observed by men, save for a few; and men have no names for them,[10] nor do they measure one against another by numerical reckoning. They barely know that the wanderings of these others are time at all, bewildering as they are in number and of surprisingly intricate pattern. None the less it is possible to grasp that the perfect number of time fulfils the perfect year at the moment when the relative speeds of all eight revolutions have accomplished their courses together and reached their consummation, as measured by the circle of the Same and uniformly moving'.

Plato's ὅμως at 39d2, 'none the less,' is an 'escape' formula, which appears to resume the argument about time, even though (ὅμως) we have not been told the details.

A more detailed explanation was available to Plato, as to Aratus. According to Cornford, Plato would have known the work of Eudoxus, but 'Plato does not commit himself to Eudoxus' system, which may have been recognised at the time as only giving an approximate picture.'[11] On this line of argument, Plato understood

Eudoxus' system of 'homocentric spheres' but chose to leave matters open.[12] But the explanation half-promised in this section of the *Timaeus* never eventuates, making one wonder whether Plato's aporia is real. This is the problem of the planets from the beginning: how much do you know? how much do you say? In Aratus' case, he chose not to discuss planetary motion, ignoring the development of a workable theory of planetary motion by his technical model, Eudoxus.

Aratus may now be seen to be following tradition: a *praeteritio*-tradition with a Platonic origin. Comparing the passages from the *Timaeus* with *Phaenomena* 460, it turns out that the Aratean shoulder-shrug is a *topos*, inherited, in the tradition surrounding the planets. This is a good strategy if you cannot rid the planets of their baggage of unpredictability or complexity, and further, if such unpredictability or complexity is unwelcome in the world you want to present. But it is a strategy which can backfire if it focuses attention on the failure of explanation.

The planets are amibvalent: although from at least the fourth century efforts, partly successful, were being made to understand their motion in the light of an underlying principle of order, they remain in some sense taboo, not merely in the literary tradition, as in Aratus, but in the cosmology of Plato's *Timaeus*. This is an ambivalence we shall see as both recognized and active in the Roman tradition. Further, we shall see that Aratus' planets are a time bomb in the literary tradition: they contain within their motions the germ of a *universal* disorder. They are the subversive element in the celestial community.

5.1.3 CELESTIAL CHANGE IN ARATUS

Thirdly, celestial change. In the passage on the Namer of stars quoted above, the result of the Namer's activity was complete predictability: οὐκέτι νῦν ὑπὸ θαύματι τέλλεται ἀστήρ, 'no star rising now takes up by surprise' (*Ph.* 382). There can be no more stars other than the ones we know. As with addition to the celestial sum, so with subtraction. The obfuscation or removal of a constellation appears in Aratus only as an assertion of astronomical fact against the force of tradition (*Ph.* 259–61):

> οὐ μέν πως ἀπόλωλεν ἀπευθὴς ἐκ Διὸς ἀστήρ,
> ἐξ οὗ καὶ γενεῆθεν ἀκούομεν, ἀλλὰ μάλ᾽ αὕτως
> εἴρεται.

> 'No star has perished unperceived from Zeus [the sky] in recorded tradition—but all the same, this is what people say' (my trans.).

This is Aratus' position on celestial change: it is impossible that any star has disappeared from the sky. Such a disappearance is outside the order of things as they are disposed by Zeus. And anyway, if it had, someone would have seen it, but as it is, it is ἀπευθής, 'unheard-of'. Furthermore, if anyone had seen it, we would know, but we have never heard, from the beginning of the record, ἐξ οὗ καὶ γενεῆθεν ἀκούομεν. Therefore the present report must be false.

5.2 The Roman Tradition

Let's now see what happens to these three issues, which receive such a light-touch treatment in Aratus, when they meet the Roman tradition.

5.2.1 NAMELESSNESS IN ROME

We have seen above how Aratus describes his unclassifiable stars as νώνυμοι, 'nameless', at *Ph.* 370. This looks morally neutral, but it is not. It is an echo of Hesiod's Myth of Ages, where νώνυμοι occurs in the same emphatic metrical *sedes* at *WD* 154, in the bleak assessment of the fate of the Bronze Age men (*WD* 152–4):

> καὶ τοὶ μὲν χείρεσσιν ὑπὸ σφετέρῃσι δαμέντες
> βῆσαν ἐς εὐρώεντα δόμον κρυεροῦ Ἀΐδαο,
> νώνυμοι . . .

'And these, overpowered by one another's hands, went down nameless into the dank house of chilly Hades' (trans. Most 2006).

It is plausible, given reference to Hesiod's myth in the story of *Dike*, that Aratus intends us to think of it here too. The resonance serves to make a connection between humans and the stars. Aratus' nameless stars become inflected with the hierarchical qualities of the Myth of Ages.

In the Roman tradition these nameless stars are the 'plebs.' Here is Manilius' description of the sky, on the analogy of the state, at *Astronomica* 5.734–45:[13]

> utque per ingentis populus discribitur urbes,
> principiumque patres retinent et proximum equester
> ordo locum, populumque equiti populoque subire
> vulgus iners videas et iam *sine nomine* turbam,
> sic etiam magno quaedam res publica mundo est
> quam natura facit, quae caelo condidit urbem.
> sunt stellae procerum similes, sunt proxima primis
> sidera, suntque gradus atque omnia iusta priorum:
> maximus est populus summo qui culmine fertur;
> cui si pro numero vires natura dedisset,
> ipse suas aether flammas sufferre nequiret,
> totus et accenso mundus flagraret Olympo.

'And as in great cities the inhabitants are divided into classes, whereof the senate enjoys primacy and the equestrian order importance next to this, and one may see the knights followed by the commons, the commons by the idle proletariat, and finally the innominate throng, so too in the mighty heavens there exists a commonwealth wrought by nature, which has founded a city in the sky. There are luminaries of princely rank and stars which come close to this highest eminence; there are all the grades and privileges of superior orders. But outnumbering all these is the populace which revolves about heaven's dome: had nature given it powers consonant with its legions, the very empyrean would be helpless before its fires, and the whole universe would become embroiled in the flames of a blazing sky' (trans. Goold 1977).

As with human society, the stars operate according to hierarchy. Theirs is a hierarchy of stellar magnitude. If the 'people', the myriad nameless stars, were to exert a force relative to their number rather than their magnitude, civil war (the desecration of the *mundus*, in cosmic terms, *ekpyrosis*) would result. But luckily, although they are numerous, their lack of magnitude prevents decisive revolutionary action. As in the case of the planets, order is precariously maintained.

Manilius is writing in the tradition of Aratus, through Aratus' translator Cicero. In his description of the nameless stars Manilius describes them as Cicero does, *sine nomine* (*Arat.* 180–2):

hic aliae volitant parvo cum lumine clarae
atque priora pedum subeunt vestigia magni
Arquitenentis, et obscurae *sine nomine* cedunt.

'These other stars fly along, gleaming with a lesser light, and are found under the forefeet-tracks of great Sagittarius, and they go along unremarked, without a name.'

The phrase, used in the context of the stars, reminds us of the universe of Aratus, as represented by Cicero's *Aratea*. But it is not the only way in which Manilius could have translated νώνυμοι; elsewhere Cicero (imitated by Lucretius) uses *expertes nominis* (*Arat.* 170).[14] Manilius' reference is pointed. *Sine nomine* at *Ast.* 5.737 echoes Cicero's *sine nomine*, *Arat.* 182. Cicero's phrase *sine nomine* (*Arat.* 182) is glossed for us by Manilius as an index of a lack of celestial order by being echoed in a passage where those stars *sine nomine* are recognized as a (potentially) destabilizing force.

Manilius had more than one precedent for the construction of his city in the sky. Greek philosophy as well as Roman politics was concerned with the fusion of the various elements involved. Hesiod created the Myth of Ages, but Plato established the connection between the hierarchy of the Ages and the ideal state. In Plato *Rep.* 415a-b, those fit to rule contain gold in their 'genes' (γένεσι, alluding to Hesiod's 'races'); the second-rankers silver, farmers and craftsmen iron and bronze. The gold rulers must take good note of the admixture of these qualities in their children and demote the bronze and iron throwbacks to their proper place in society. We remember how Plato ascribes the origin of civil war to the mixing of the races: ὁμοῦ δὲ μιγέντος σιδηροῦ ἀργυρῷ καὶ χαλκοῦ χρυσῷ ἀνομοιότης ἐγγενήσεται καὶ ἀνωμαλία ἀναρμόστος, ἃ γενόμενα, οὗ ἂν ἐγγένηται, ἀεὶ τίκτει πόλεμον καὶ ἔχθραν: '. . . and when iron and silver or bronze and gold are mixed, an inconsistent and uneven material is produced, whose irregularities, whenever they occur, must engender war and hatred' (*Rep.* 547a2–5, trans. Lee 2007).[15]

But it was Aratus (in the Myth of Δίκη, on which see chapter 1 above) who translated the Hesiodic/Platonic synthesis to the *celestial* plane, although this move was perhaps suggested by Plato's prior use of astronomical terminology to describe the cycles of human life (as in the phrase we have already remarked, ὅταν περιτροπαὶ ἑκάστοις κύκλων περιφορὰς ξυνάπτωσι, *Rep.* 546a5–6). Aratus, rendering the connection explicit, retells the Myth of Ages presided over by a star, the constellation Parthenos. Hesiod's myth is given astronomical 'spin', and this in turn achieves the seminal Aratean synthesis between moral cosmology (man in the universe) and astronomy (the data required to understand the universe).

Manilius' socio-astronomical edifice is immediately comprehensible within the tradition, but also complex in that it contains many textual strata in its construction: Hesiod, Plato, Aratus, and Cicero's translation of Aratus. All of these together give him his celestial metropolis. Above all, this metropolis is a Roman one, composed as the Roman social pyramid of *populus, equester ordo, patres*. Manilius' *patres* ('senators') are the equivalent of Plato's gold race in the Republic; the *equites* of his silver, and so on. Aratus is here too, since he first interpreted Hesiod's Myth of the Races in an astronomical context; but in Manilius, the stars are an explicit analogy for the *Roman* state. Although Manilius uses *ordo* in the quoted passage in the political sense, it is difficult to believe that he would have been unaware of its usage in Stoic philosophy in particular, to denote the order of the cosmos, particularly the stars, as at Cicero *DND* 2.97, *ratos astrorum ordines*. But in Manilius, the *ordines*, celestial *and* political, veer towards revolution.

5.2.2 THE PLANETS IN ROME

My thesis here is that, although the regularity of planetary cycles was recognized at least from Plato onwards, vestiges of the old meaning still adhere throughout the tradition up to late antiquity: we can call this *'the paradox of the planets'*.[16] The planets retain their disorderly nature even after it has been seen that they can be reduced to order, and it is this which makes them alive as a metaphor for the Roman poets.

We saw how the phenomenon of meaning incommensurability works in the previous section. It is worth fine-tuning this concept here: the phenomenon is perhaps better called 'incomplete meaning incommensurability' since the irrationality of the planets stubbornly subsists in the tradition. They never fully detach themselves from their etymology but stand as a grey area at the least; at the most, a symbol of disorder.

How much is the reality of them as phenomena important in informing their symbolic significance? Less than you would think. The planets detach themselves for the reality of the phenomena and become metaphor. In the Latin literary tradition, the planets become a way of mapping astronomy onto human society, as an adjunct to the historical narrative of Rome. More than that, planetary *motion* itself, once detached from those bodies to which it pertains and made into an abstract concept, can fulfil the same metaphorical function.

(i) Cicero's Planets

The Romans understood the orderliness of the planets just as well as did the Greeks. To the passage from Plato's *Laws* quoted above, compare Cicero, *De natura deorum* 2.51:

> maxume vero sunt admirabiles motus earum quinque stellarum quae falso vocantur errantes; nihil enim errat quod in omni aeternitate conservat progressus et regressus reliquosque motus constantis et ratos.

> 'Most remarkable, too, are the movements of the five planets, mistakenly labelled "those that stray"; mistakenly, because nothing can be said to "go astray" which through all eternity maintains in a steady, predetermined pattern its various movements forward, backward, and in other directions' (Walsh).

Note also Cicero, *Rep.* 1.21–2 *stellarum quae errantes et quasi vagae nominaretur.* Compare Cicero's *quasi*, 'so to speak', with Plato's ὡς ἔπος, 'so to speak,' at *Tim.* 39c7. Both of these inflections carry the weight of the meaning incommensurability in the term 'planets'.

In fact, Cicero's output perfectly exemplifies in the Roman context the schizophrenic nature of the planets. In his early *Aratea*, Cicero follows his source to the letter in shying away from them (*Arat.* 223–35):

haec sunt quae visens nocturno tempore signa	
aeternumque volens mundi pernoscere motum	225
legitimo cernes caelum lustrantia cursu.	224
nam quae per bis sex signorum labier orbem	
quinque solent stellae, simili ratione notari	
non possunt, quia quae faciunt vestigia cursu	
non eodem semper spatio protrita teruntur.	
sic malunt errare vagae per nubila caeli	230
atque suos vario motu metirier orbes.	
hae faciunt magnos longinqui temporis annos,	
cum redeunt ad idem caeli sub tegmine signum;	
quarum ego nunc nequeo tortos evolvere cursus:	
verum haec, quae semper certo [e]voluuntur in orbe	235
fixa, simul magnos edemus gentibus orbes.	

'These star-signs are the ones which, when you see them at night-time and want to know about the ongoing motion of the heaven, you will notice, rake the heaven with a *law-abiding* course. But those five heavenly bodies which usually glide through the circle of the zodiac cannot be identified by similar means, because the tracks they make in their course are not always worn into the same place. They prefer to wander footloose through the clouds of heaven and to measure out their orbits with a variable motion. These bring about the

Great Years of long duration when they return to the same star-sign under the canopy of heaven. I am not now able to unroll their sinuous courses; but I shall proclaim at large the great orbits of those fixed stars which roll round in a predictable course.'

Like his model, Cicero claims not to be equipped to tell of the planets. But he also, characteristically, *adds* to Aratus. Cicero's planets in the *Aratea* have a mind of their own (*malunt*). Cicero used *legalistic* terminology to distinguish them from the stars. The planets are opposed to the fixed stars, which *legitimo cernes caelum lustrantia cursu* (*Arat.* 224), and which he will present in his work. *Legitimo* is a Latin term which Cicero adds to his source to describe the course of the fixed stars. There is no equivalent for it in Aratus. The stars, like good citizens, follow *leges*, while (by implication) the planets are anarchic. Here we have the beginning of a moralizing use of astronomical fact. This is what Cicero as a Roman poet has *added* to Aratus' planets. The latter were cold, lacking in personality: Cicero animates them and situates them in relation to the institutions (*leges*) of the Roman state. In this context, there is no doubt that they are a subversive element. We won't talk about *them*!

Although he emphasized their 'wandering' nature in his translation of Aratus in c.89 BC (with the double etymology *errare vagae*), two decades later he was prepared to acknowledge the falsity of this etymology in his autobiographical poem, the *De consulatu suo* (*Cons.* fr. 2.6–10, on which see also above, with translation, chapter 3 p. 63). In the *Cons.* he emphasizes the falsity of the appellation 'wanderers' to the planets, drawing attention, as did Plato in the *Laws*, to the meaning incommensurability:

et si stellarum motus cursusque vagantis
nosse velis quae sint signorum in sede locatae,
quae verbo et falsis Graiorum vocibus *errant*,
re vera certo lapsu spatioque feruntur,
omnia iam cernes divina mente notata.

Why did Cicero treat the planets differently in two different poems? The answer that the poems were more than two decades apart in Cicero's career will not do. Even as early as 89, Cicero did not have to follow Aratus in professing bafflement about the planets. The same theoretical arsenal was available to him in 89 and in 62 BC. Cicero's knowledge was (in theory) better than Aratus'. It would have incorporated not only the homocentric spheres of Eudoxus, but also of the epicycles and deferants of Hipparchus, who, in the period which intervened between Aratus and Cicero's translation of Aratus, had developed a system which was more effective in explaining planetary motion than Eudoxus' homocentric spheres.[17] You might have expected Cicero to flag the fact in his earlier work as much as his later one. It is not that planetary theory had radically changed in the interim.

Alternatively, you might argue that Cicero's own knowledge could have changed in the interim between his two works. In theory it is possible that Cicero was reading an introductory work on Aratus along the lines of our existing scholia, and that he was influenced by it to give a fuller explanation of the planets in 62 than in 89. The falsity of the idea of 'wandering' when applied to the planets is already recognized in the earliest introductory works which accompanied the text of Aratus, such as the 'Prolegomena' to Aratus, Par. Suppl. Gr. 607a (*saec.* X, Martin, *Scholia in Aratum vetera*, p. 26.17–24):

περὶ ἀπλανῶν καὶ πλανητῶν· ὅσα τῶν ἄστρων ἐκ τῶν αὐτῶν ἀεὶ τόπων τὰς ἀνατολὰς ποιεῖται καὶ εἰς τοὺς αὐτοὺς καταδύσεις, ταυτὶ δὴ ἀπλανῆ καλεῖται, ὅσα δὲ ἀμείβει τάς τε ἀνατολὰς καὶ τὰς δύσεις ἐξ ἄλλων τόπων εἰς ἄλλους, ταυτὶ δὴ πλανώμενα ἐπίκλην, οὐχ ὅτι πλανᾶται (τεταγμένως γὰρ φέρονται), ἀλλ᾽ οἱ ἀρχαῖοι μὴ συνιέντες αὐτῶν τῆς τάξεως ἐκείνως ἐκάλησαν, ἡμεῖς δὲ τῇ συνηθείᾳ ἑπόμενοι οὕτως καλοῦμεν . . .

'Concerning fixed and wandering [stars]: those stars which rise and set in the same location are called 'not-wandering' [ἀπλανῆ], but those which change their risings and settings from one location to another are called 'wandering' [πλανώμενα]. This is not because they wander (in fact they move in orderly fashion), but because the ancients, not understanding their order, called them this, as do we, following their usage . . .' (my trans.).

This later accession to Cicero's knowledge is possible, but it seems to me just as likely that Cicero was aware of the contradictions in the Platonic tradition. The planets in Cicero are horses for courses. In the *Aratea*, he is 'being Aratus', and expressing the hesitation of the didactic author. In this, Aratus follows Plato in the *Timaeus*, who appears to run out of puff when he comes to the outer planets. But there are two sides to the tradition even in Plato, as we've seen. Cicero in the *Cons.* both responds to Aratus and updates his own translation of him. When he does this, however, he does it in the light of the Platonic tradition of the *Laws* passage, with its impetus towards a fuller, if abstract, systematization of the planets. This suits the context, since the speaker in the *De Cons.* is the Muse Urania, who might be supposed to know everything there is to know about the planets. In addition, the certainty is needed in the context: Cicero the statesman against the forces of disorder (the Catilinarian conspirators). Fuller knowledge is more useful than uncertainty.

(ii) Manilius' Planets

From the beginning of their Roman life, the planets are schizophrenic. They can be a subversive element, or they can be tamed. Roman authors had some investment in the idea of the planets as disorderly. Despite the recognition that they could, in fact, be made part of a system, the notion of planetary or cosmic anarchy becomes *more* explicit as we track the tradition. Writing under Tiberius (14–37 AD), Manilius makes the planets 'at war' with the fixed stars, deploying, as Cicero does, Roman political terminology:

omnia concordi tractu veniuntque caduntque,
qua semel incubuit caelum versumque resurgit.
sunt alia adversa pugnantia sidera mundo,
quae terram caelumque inter volitantia pendent,
Saturni, Iovis et Martis Solisque, sub illis
Mercurius Venerem inter agit Lunam volatus. (*Ast.* 1.537–8, 805–8; text
  of Goold 1977)[18]

'[The fixed stars] all move on a consistent course, coming into view and setting where heaven ever sinks and, turning, reappears. There exist other stars,
which strive against the contrary motion of the sky and in their swift orbits
are poised between heaven and earth: Saturn, Jupiter, Mars, and the Sun, and
beneath them Mercury performing its flight between Venus and the Moon'
(trans. Goold 1977).

Here we have the idea that the planets are different from the fixed stars: they are *alia*
sidera. But violence on a Lucretian scale is now part of their portrayal. They do not
just move backwards periodically, but fight their way back against the onslaught of
celestial motion. In Manilius the planets have become perpetrators of war, *adverso*
pugnantia sidera mundo, a civil war between the heaven and the celestial bodies
which are part of it. So also at *Ast.* 2.119, Manilius personifies the planets as waging
war against the fixed stars, *aeternum et stellis adversus sidera bellum* ('and the planets'
everlasting war against the stars', trans. Goold 1977). This might remind us of the
political terminology Lucretius applied to the warring elements at *DRN* 5.380–1:

denique tantopere inter se cum maxima mundi
pugnent membra, pio nequaquam concita bello

'Since, then, the giant limbs of the universe fight so much among themselves,
aroused in a war which in no way follows the law of family relations . . .'

—and *DRN* 5.437–40:

         . . . discordia quorum
intervalla vias conexus pondera plagas
concursus motus turbabat proelia miscens
propter dissimilis formas variasque figuras . . .

'. . . [first bodies] whose warfare (*discordia*) shook up ratios, paths, connections, masses, collisions, comings-together and motions, as it mixed them
about in battle, because of their diverging forms and figures . . .'[19]

Manilius' planets enact the opposite of the *concordia* (peaceful civic interrelation)
of his fixed stars, which move *concordi tractu*: the *modus operandi* of the planets, it
is implied, is the *discordia* of the Lucretian elements. Here we see an extension of
the Ciceronian application of political terminology to the planets. Manilius' take
on it would have looked comprehensible in civil-war terms to a Roman audience.

(iii) Lucan's Planets

Lucan, writing his civil war epic under the Emperor Nero (54–68 AD) about the civil war of 49–45 BC between Caesar and Pompey, directly recalls Cicero's use of legalistic terminology, as the astrologer Nigidius Figulus sums up the Roman outcome of the planetary configuration he observes, at *Pharsalia* 1.642–68:

'aut hic errat' ait '*nulla cum lege* per aevum
mundus et incerto discurrunt sidera motu,
aut, si fata movent, urbi generique paratur
humano matura lues. terraene dehiscent   645
subsidentque urbes, an tollet feruidus aer
temperiem? segetes tellus infida negabit,
omnis an infusis miscebitur unda uenenis?
quod cladis genus, o superi, qua peste paratis
saeuitiam? extremi multorum tempus in unum   650
conuenere dies. summo si frigida caelo
stella nocens nigros Saturni accenderet ignis,
Deucalioneos fudisset Aquarius imbres
totaque diffuso latuisset in aequore tellus.
si saeuum radiis Nemeaeum, Phoebe, Leonem   655
nunc premeres, toto fluerent incendia mundo
succensusque tuis flagrasset curribus aether.
hi cessant ignes. tu, qui flagrante minacem
Scorpion incendis cauda chelasque peruris,
quid tantum, Gradiue, paras? nam mitis in alto   660
Iuppiter occasu premitur, Venerisque salubre
sidus hebet, motuque celer Cyllenius haeret,
et caelum Mars solus habet. cur signa meatus
deseruere suos mundoque obscura feruntur,
ensiferi nimium fulget latus Orionis?   665
inminet armorum rabies, ferrique potestas
confundet *ius omne* manu, scelerique nefando
nomen erit uirtus . . .

"'Either," he said, "this universe strays forever *governed by no law*, and the stars move to and fro with courses unfixed; or else, if they are guided by Fate, speedy destruction is being prepared for Rome and for mankind. Will the earth gape and cities be swallowed up? Or will burning heat destroy our temperate climate? Will the soil break faith and deny its produce? Or will water everywhere be tainted with streams of poison? What kind of disaster are the gods preparing? What form of ruin will their anger assume? The lives of multitudes are doomed to end together. If Saturn, that cold baleful planet, were now kindling his black fires in the zenith, then Aquarius would have poured down such rains as Deucalion saw, and the whole earth would have been hidden under the waste of waters. Or if the sun's rays were now passing over the fierce Lion of Nemea, then fire would stream over all the world, and the upper air would be kindled and consumed by the sun's chariot. These heavenly bodies are not active now. But Mars—what dreadful purpose has he, when he kindles the Scorpion menacing with fiery tail, and scorches its claws? For the benign star of Jupiter is hidden deep in the West, the healthful planet Venus is dim, and Mercury's swift motion is stayed; Mars alone lords it in the heaven. Why have the constellations fled from their courses, to move darkling through the sky, while the side of sword-girt Orion shines all too bright? The madness of war is upon us, when the power of the sword shall violently upset *all legality*, and atrocious crime shall be called heroism'" (trans. Duff 1928; text of Housman 1926).

Lucan draws on the established terminology of the debate about celestial motion. Furthermore, he does this in order to construct a parallel between the anarchy of the *mundus* and anarchy and earth (666–8). Like Cicero, Lucan deploys legalistic terminology: the phrases *nulla cum lege* (641) and *ius omne* (667), frame the passage, invoking both the Roman context and the Ciceronian literary antecedent. The application of legalistic concepts to the stars (the *mundus*) recalls Cicero. But as well as that, Lucan's **errat** . . . *mundus* (*Phars.* 1.641–2), brings to mind, perhaps, Cicero's etymology for the planets *malunt errare vagae* (*Aratea* 230). Lucan has applied the concept of 'wandering' not just to the 'wanderers,' but to the *mundus*, the whole of which wanders under the influence of civil war. There are thus two levels of allusion in Lucan's portrayal of the civil-war universe: Cicero, and Lucretius' take on Cicero, seen in the way that the concept of wandering, applied in Cicero only to the planets, is extended to the universe as a whole.[20]

Similarly, in 642, all of Lucan's stars, like the *mundus*, move *incerto motu*. They are in *opposition* to Cicero's fixed stars, which *certo [e]volvuntur in orbe*, 'describe a predictable orbit' (*Arat.* 235). Again, planetary motion is applied to the whole. Lucan's collocation *incerto motu* might also recall Cicero's *vario motu*, of the planets in *Aratea* 231, now reapplied by Lucan to all of the stars, the *mundus* in general. Again the technique is Lucretian.

In this passage, Lucan presents two alternatives. One of these alternatives is that the whole sky wanders, like Cicero's planets. The other is that the mechanism is moved by the hand of Fate. The alternatives might be those of an Epicurean or Stoic. But the Stoic alternative is also celestially inflected. Disaster is impending (*Phars.* 1.649–51):

quod cladis genus, o superi, qua peste paratis
saeuitiam? extremi multorum tempus in unum
conuenere dies.

We can compare this alternative to Seneca's contemporary description of the end of the world, at *Quaestiones Naturales* 3.28–29:

> aqua et ignis terrenis dominantur; ex his ortus, ex his interitus est. ergo quandoque placuere res nouae mundo, sic in nos mare inmittitur desuper, ut feruor ignisque, cum aliud genus exitii placuit. . . . Berosos, qui Belum interpretatus est, ait ista cursu siderum fieri. adeo enim adfirmat ut conflagrationi atque diluuio aeque tempus adsignet. arsura enim terrena contendit quandoque omnia sidera quae nunc diuersos agunt cursus in Cancrum conuenerint, sic sub eodem posita uestigio ut recta linea exire per orbes omnium possit; inundationem futuram cum eadem siderum turba in Capricornum conuenerit. illic solstitium, hic bruma conficitur, magnae potentiae signa, quando maxima in ipsa mutatione anni momenta sunt.

> 'Water and fire lord it over terrestrial things; they bring about creation, they bring about destruction. So whenever the world has decided on revolution, the sea is sent crashing down over us, just as heat and fire are when another form of extinction is approved. . . . Berosus, who translated Belus, says that the movement of the stars is the cause of all this. He is so confident in his assertion that he gives a date for both the conflagration and the flood. He maintains that the earth will burn whenever all the stars that now have different courses converge in Cancer and are positioned beneath the same point, so that a vertical line can pass through all their spheres; a flood will occur when the same group of stars converges in Capricorn. The summer solstice occurs in the former constellation, the winter solstice in the latter; these are very powerful zodiac signs, since they are the most important turning points in the annual cycle' (trans. Hine 2010; text Hine 1996).

In this passage, Seneca combines solstitial and planetary motion. He has the periodic destructions of the world aligned with the clustering of the planets in the solstitial signs. Seneca notably expresses the idea of world destruction in Roman political terms (*res novae*). Both of these features are relevant for our interpretation of Lucan 1.649–51. For Seneca, the periodicity of the universe is determined by planetary conjunction in the zodiacal sign of the summer solstice (Cancer). One might say that the lives of the planets all come together at their final point.[21] Compare Lucan's *extremi multorum tempus in unum /conuenere dies*. A celestial interpretation of this would not be out-of-step with the surrounding context as we have seen it. Lucan's description of the catastrophe which awaits, with the advent of civil war, is redolent of planetary period as an analogy for human life. When the planets conjoin at the end of a Great Year, in either the sign of flood or fire, it is a return of many to one: likewise, in Lucan, the ends of many will converge at one point in time. Planetary motion is an analogy which enables Nigidius to predict human history.

So, the link in Nigidius' speech, between the downfall of Rome and the over-throw of the world order, is achieved through the imagery of planetary motion. Planetary motion and its involvement with the theme of Fate frames Book 1 of the *Pharsalia*. We have seen a passage from near the end of the book; now consider one proximate to its beginning, *Pharsalia* 1.70–80:

> invida fatorum series summisque negatum
> stare diu nimioque graves sub pondere lapsus
> nec se Roma ferens. sic, cum conpage soluta
> saecula tot mundi suprema coegerit hora
> antiquum repetens iterum chaos, [omnia mixtis
> sidera sideribus concurrent,] ignea pontum
> astra petent, tellus extendere litora nolet
> excutietque fretum, fratri contraria Phoebe
> ibit et obliquum bigas agitare per orbem
> indignata diem poscet sibi, totaque discors
> machina diuolsi turbabit foedera mundi.

'It was the chain of jealous fate, and the speedy fall which no eminence can escape; it was the grievous collapse of excessive weight, and Rome unable to support her own greatness. Even so, when the framework of the world is dis-solved and the final hour, closing so many ages, reverts to primeval chaos, then all the constellations will clash in confusion, the fiery stars will drop into the sea, and earth, refusing to spread her shores out flat, will shake off the ocean; the moon will move in opposition to her brother, and claim to rule the day, disdaining to drive her chariot along her slanting orbit; and the whole distracted fabric of the shattered universe will overthrow its laws' (Duff).

In Lucan's analysis of the causes of civil war there is a direct link—within the half-line in fact—between Rome and the cyclical perishing of the universe. It can be theorized through Plato, *Rep.* 546a1–b4, describing the dissolution of the ideal state:

> χαλεπὸν μὲν κινηθῆναι πόλιν οὕτω συστᾶσαν· ἀλλ' ἐπεὶ γενομένῳ παντὶ
> φθορά ἐστιν, οὐδ' ἡ τοιαύτη σύστασις τὸν ἅπαντα μενεῖ χρόνον, ἀλλὰ
> λυθήσεται. λύσις δὲ ἥδε· οὐ μόνον φυτοῖς ἐγγείοις, ἀλλὰ καὶ ἐν ἐπιγείοις
> ζῴοις φορὰ καὶ ἀφορία ψυχῆς τε καὶ σωμάτων γίγνονται, ὅταν περιτροπαὶ
> ἑκάστοις κύκλων περιφορὰς συνάπτωσι, βραχυβίοις μὲν βραχυπόρους,
> ἐναντίοις δὲ ἐναντίας. γένους δὲ ὑμετέρου εὐγονίας τε καὶ ἀφορίας, καίπερ
> ὄντες σοφοί, οὓς ἡγεμόνας πόλεως ἐπαιδεύσασθε, οὐδὲν μᾶλλον λογισμῷ
> μετ' αἰσθήσεως τεύξονται, ἀλλὰ πάρεισιν αὐτοὺς καὶ γεννήσουσι παῖδάς
> ποτε οὐ δέον.

'It will be difficult to bring out any change for the worse in a state so consti-tuted; but since all created things must decay, even a social order of this kind cannot last for all time, but will decline. And its dissolution will be as follows: not only for plants that grow in the earth, but for animals that live on it, there are seasons of fertility and infertility of both mind and body, seasons which come when their periodic motions come full circle, a period of longer duration for the long-lived, shorter for the short-lived. And though the rulers you have trained for your city are wise, reason and observation will not always allow them to hit on the right and wrong times for breeding; some time they will miss them and then children will be begotten amiss' (trans. Lee 2007).

There may thus be a Platonic substructure to Lucan's ideology; but it is a feature we begin to see as characteristic of the Roman tradition that Lucan should also evoke Lucretius in this context. *Machina mundi* (*Phars.* 1.80)—the world mechanism—brings to mind at the point of cataclysm in Lucan Lucretius' description of the end of the world (*DRN* 5.92–6):

principio maria ac terras caelumque tuere;
quorum naturam triplicem, tria corpora, Memmi,
tris species tam dissimilis, tria talia texta,
una dies dabit exitio, multosque per annos
sustentata ruet moles et machina mundi.

'First consider sea, earth and sky. A single day will destroy the triple identity of these three bodies, Memmius, although they are all so apparently different from one another, three massive entities woven together in threefold way, and although the bulky mechanism of the cosmos has stood for so long, it will perish.'

Plato may provide the politico-cosmic frame, Lucretius the idea of dissolution, but it is the tradition of *Aratus* which allows for the insertion of an *astronomical* concept into the theoretical template. Lucan's link between the downfall of Rome and the overthrow of the world order is achieved not least through the imagery of celestial imbalance, in the form of *planetary* motion. *Pharsalia* 1.74–5 *omnia mixtis / sidera sideribus concurrent* makes explicit the fact that *all* the stars become planetary.[22] With Lucan's *mixtis*, compare Aratus' ἐπιμίξ. In Aratus the planets cannot be discretely grouped and are therefore an instrument of disorder. In Lucan all the stars are mixed up and therefore an element, in this case, reflective of disorder already present in the human sphere.

The Aratean tradition is even closer at hand here. There may be allusion to Germinicus' translation of Aratus. Note how the moon, in Lucan 1.77, runs counter to her brother (the sun), *fratri* <u>contraria</u> *Phoebe. She* behaves as a planet does in the tradition of Aratus. Here is Germanicus' translation of Aratus' passage on planets (Germanicus *Ph.* 437–9):

quinque aliae stellae diversa lege feruntur
et proprio motu mundo *contraria* volvunt
curricula exceduntque loco et vestigia mutant.

'There are five other celestial bodies, which travel under a different law: they have their own movements and in their courses they sweep around in a circle in the opposite direction to the sphere of the fixed stars; they wander from the constellations they are in and change their positions' (Gain).

The moon, by being like a planet (*contraria*) ruptures sibling relations among the stars. We understand the implications through Germanicus' translation of Aratus, with its own grafting of civil-war terminology onto the Aratean original.

(iv) Planetary Motion in Statius

The use of planetary motion in the context of civil war continues in the Roman tradition of the first century. Statius wrote under the Emperor Domitian (ruled 81–96 AD), who had fought his way to power alongside his father Vespasian through the chaos of the 'year of four emperors'.[23] In the *Thebaid*, Statius employs ideas of celestial motion as metaphor for human malfunction. In *Theb.* 1, Oedipus, the founding father of the Theban war, is described as living his life in a retrograde motion reminiscent of the planets (*Theb.* 1.233–5):

scandere quin etiam thalamos hic impius heres
patris et immeritae gremium incestare parentis
appetiit, proprios—monstrum!—revolutus in ortus.

'. . . In fact, this heir, unsuited to family relations, has even made so bold as to climb into his father's marriage-bed and commit incest in the lap of his innocent mother, regressing outrageously to his own life's point of origin' (my trans.; text of Klotz 1973).

In his incestuous marriage Oedipus *proprios . . . revolutus in ortus* (*Theb.* 1.235), he goes 'backwards towards his rising.' *Ortus* is the standard astronomical term for 'rising', the counterpart of *obitus*, 'setting'.[24] Likewise, *volvere* and its compounds refer to the circular orbits of heavenly bodies as we have seen in Cicero's passage on the planets at *Arat.* 234–5: he cannot follow them (*evolvere*) in their courses; instead, he will talk about the fixed stars which circle (*[e]voluuntur*) predictably. Oedipus is *revolutus in ortus*: his orbit takes him backwards. The reader should draw a parallel between the planetary behaviour of Oedipus and the 'illegitimate' planets in Cicero's translation of Aratus. Again, as in Lucan, this may be conceptually combined with the theoretical background of Plato, *Rep.* 546a5–6: 'When all things come full circle', ὅταν περιτροπαὶ ἑκάστοις κύκλων περιφορὰς συνάπτωσι . . ., then that is the origin of civil war.

This brings *us* full circle, as it were, to the material covered in chapter 2. We saw in the *Politicus* also the tendency to relate human lifespan and celestial motion. Plato's *Politicus* myth introduced the idea of cosmic mimesis, the 'imitation' in human lives of the states of the universe (ἀπομιμούμενα, *Pol.* 274a1; μίμημα, *Pol.* 274a2). Virgil, we saw, takes up this theme in the fourth *Eclogue*, where the cosmic cycles reverse themselves, then come into line with the life of the salvific 'boy'. Statius' is the negative spin on this idea, rather than a positive alignment.

(v) Cosmic Reversal in Seneca

This theme has more to offer in the interpretation of later Roman literature. We have not yet drained the *Politicus* in particular of its potential to shed light on the Latin tradition. I shall now show how Seneca, like Virgil, Lucan, and Statius, combines Platonic cosmology with Aratean 'data', within the political sphere of civil war.

We remember Plato's myth in the *Politicus* starts as the rationalization of a portent (*Pol.* 268e8–10): Ἦν τοίνυν καὶ ἔτι ἔσται τῶν πάλαι λεχθέντων πολλά τε ἄλλα καὶ δὴ καὶ τὸ περὶ τὴν Ἀτρέως τε καὶ Θυέστου λεχθεῖσαν ἔριν φάσμα. 'There have occurred in the past, and will occur in the future, many of the things that have been told throughout the ages; one is the portent relating to the quarrel between Atreus and Thyestes' (Rowe). Plato's myth in the *Politicus* brands itself at the outset as a rationalization of a portent in the myth of Atreus and Thyestes. This portent was the reversal of the sun's daily cycle at the point of greatest atrocity (the eating by Thyestes of his own children, served up to him in a grotesque extremity of rivalry by his brother Atreus). This is what Plato uses to kick off his theory of *cosmic* reversal, expounded in the *Politicus*-myth. In other words, the reversal of its course by the sun is extended into a myth about the reversal of the cosmos as a *whole*: the sun's movements are mapped onto the universe.

We can see traces of Plato's allegorization, I think, in Seneca's treatment of the myth in his *Thyestes*, written, like Lucan's *Pharsalia*, under the emperor Nero. It is unlikely that Seneca would have been unaware of the previous re-setting of the myth of Plato. Three of its elements would have served him well: (i) the *Politicus* myth is a myth of *kingship*; (ii) the myth Plato allegorizes is a feud *between brothers*;[25] (iii) in addition, a *cosmic* aspect is present in the *Politicus*, with its cycle of universal destructions (φθοραί, *Pol.* 270c11).[26]

All of these elements are present in the *Thyestes*. The *Thyestes* is itself an allegory: a political one, of civil war and the will to power of the individual. But it also contains a cosmic allegory in the reversal of the universe as a symptom of familial and social discord. As well as adopting the myth of Atreus and Thyestes, Seneca, reading it through Plato, adopts the idea of cosmic reversal as an index of human degeneracy. Like his predecessors and contemporaries in the Roman tradition, he combines the theme of 'Platonic' retrogression with Aratean astronomical 'data'. Although Seneca may be thinking about the cosmic reversal in Plato's *Politicus* for the framework of his myth, in its detail he draws on Aratus.

First, retrograde motion in Seneca's *Thyestes*. Atreus emphasizes the initial portent—the eclipse—in his address to the Sun at *Thy.* 776–8:

> O Phoebe patiens, fugeris retro licet
> medioque raptum merseris caelo diem,
> sero occidisti!

'Enduring Sun, even though you have run backwards, snatched the day from the middle of heaven and immersed it, you have set too late' (my trans.; text of Tarrant 1985).

Seneca's destruction of the cosmos begins with the failure of the sun: a solar eclipse if we want to use rationalizing language. This is Plato's 'portent'. It is a double failure: the eclipse is a failure of the sun, a failure which itself fails because it does not succeed in cloaking the atrocity completely.

Atreus continues, in almost identical terms, in the address to Thyestes which follows (*Thy.* 784–8):

> verterit currus licet
> sibi ipse Titan obuium ducens iter
> tenebrisque facinus obruat taetrum nouis
> nox missa ab ortu tempore alieno grauis,
> tamen uidendum est.

'Although the Sun has turned his chariot, performing a journey counter to himself, and though portentous night, released from the point of rising at a time foreign to her, engulfs the disgusting crime with unforeseen shadows—all the same, it must be seen' (my trans.).

The 'portent' gives the starting point for the chorus which follows. The chorus mesmerically repeats Atreus' language, *ortus* (790), *noctis* (791), *vertis* (792). The last repeated term (*verterit* 784 > *vertis* 792) is salient. This is *tropic* language (*verto* = Gk. τρέπω > τροπή—recall the use of the term at *Pol.* 270d4). The sun does not here simply turn at the tropic points, but turns unnaturally back on itself in retrograde motion, signalling a state of extreme disorder. We are inside the parameters of Plato's myth. This is how we understand that the world in the *Thyestes* is entering its period of reversal.

While Plato's cycles occur naturally, as a result of the composition of the universe, Seneca's are human-induced. Seneca's portent is familiar to the Romans in the civil war context. Cicero, in his *De consulatu suo*, already had eclipses as the celestial signposting of the Catilinarian conspiracy (*Cons.* fr. 2.18–22):

> cum claram speciem concreto lumine luna
> abdidit et subito stellanti nocte perempta est.
> quid vero Phoebi fax, tristis nuntia belli,
> quae magnum ad columen flammato ardore volabat,
> praecipitis caeli partis obitusque petessens?

'. . . when the moon hid her shining aspect, her light tamped down, and was subsumed by starry night. Or what about the sun's torch, harbinger of grim war, which, gathering itself in a great column, flew with red-hot passion to seek its setting in the steepest part of heaven?' (my trans.)

Here at the beginning of the tradition, as in Seneca at its culmination, the sun's eclipse is described as his precipitate haste to get away-from human atrocities. In Cicero it also mirrors, perhaps, the impetuosity of the conspiracy's protagonists.

In Virgil, an eclipse accompanies the assassination of Caesar (*Geo.* 1.463–8):[27]

> sol tibi signa dabit. solem quis dicere falsum
> audeat? ille etiam caecos instare tumultus
> saepe monet fraudemque et operta tumescere bella;
> ille etiam exstincto miseratus Caesare Romam,
> cum caput obscura nitidum ferrugine texit
> impiaque aeternam timuerunt saecula noctem.

> 'The sun will give you the signs. Who would dare to call the sun false? He often warns that unforeseen upheavals are imminent, or conspiracy or open war coming to a head; he pitied Rome when Caesar died and hid his shining head under a darkening patina, and the guilty generation was terrified that the night would go on forever' (my trans.).

Let us recall here what we said in chapter 2 about the conjunction of Aratus and Plato in the Roman tradition of the Golden Age. Plato was useful for the cosmological framework he provides, primarily in the *Politicus*; Aratus for the astronomical detail. In this passage of Virgil, just as Plato is present in the tradition of man's participation in cycles of cosmic destruction, Aratus is present in this tradition of portents. Virgil's predictive sun follows directly from his translation of Aratus' weather-signs in the preceding lines: there is no seam between them. *Sol tibi signa dabit* looks back to the weather-signs and forward to the portents of civil war: the sun acts as the hinge. What the sun becomes in Virgil—an index of cosmic change and accomplice to human catastrophe—is utterly foreign to the universe of Aratus.

Seneca, too, utilizes Aratus in a context foreign to the world of the *Ph.*, and in so doing, he also collapses sequential and cyclical time in a way prompted by the Aratean text, but very different from the positive outcome of the original. The 'zodiac' chorus in the *Thy.* is the moment where Aratean 'data' takes over from Platonic theory. It is also the moment where we move from the possible (eclipses do happen), to the impossible (the stars *never* go out). We remember here *Ph.* 382: no star has ever perished from the sky in living memory. The 'zodiac' chorus takes us, in the one work, from the theme of planetary motion to that of celestial change.

The unworking of the universe of Aratus is most clearly signalled at *Thy.* 813–14:

> solitae mundi periere uices.
> nihil occasus, nihil ortus erit.

> 'The usual cycles of the world have perished: there will be no setting, no rising' (my trans.).

The play's conflict resonates in the universe: the whole zodiac participates in it. At the point of crisis, the infanticide and anthropophagy of the myth, the sun and the zodiac, including the familiar constellation of Virgo (= *Dike*), *disappear* in series.[28] Rather than the enumeration of the constellations on the celestial map, in Seneca we get an enumeration of their disappearance. Here is the climactic passage (*Thy.* 842–68):[29]

> ibit in unum
> congesta sinum turba deorum.
> hic qui sacris peruius astris
> secat obliquo tramite zonas,
> flectens longos signifer annos,
> lapsa uidebit sidera labens;
> hic qui nondum uere benigno
> reddit Zephyro uela tepenti,
> Aries praeceps ibit in undas,
> per quas pauidam uexerat Hellen;
> hic qui nitido Taurus cornu
> praefert Hyadas, secum Geminos
> trahet et curvi bracchia Cancri;
> Leo flammiferis aestibus ardens
> iterum e caelo cadet Herculeus;
> cadet in terras Virgo relictas,
> iustaeque cadent pondera Librae,
> secumque trahent Scorpion acrem;
> et qui neruo tenet Haemonio
> pinnata senex spicula Chiron
> rupto perdet spicula neruo;
> pigram referens hiemem gelidus
> cadet Aegoceros frangetque tuam,
> quisquis es, urnam; tecum excedent
> ultima caeli sidera Pisces.
> monstraque numquam perfusa mari
> merget condens omnia gurges.

'The throng of gods will tumble in a heap into a single abyss. This zodiac, which, forming a road through the sacred stars, cuts the zones with its oblique path, turning the lengthy years in a curve, will catch sight of the fallen stars as it itself falls. This Ram who, before kindly spring has arrived, restores sails to the breeze as it grows warm, will go headfirst into the sea over which it carried Helle in her fear; this Bull who with shining horn carries the Hyades on his forehead, will drag down the Twins and the claws of the flexible Crab; the Herculean Lion, burning with fiery heat, will fall again from the sky; Virgo will fall back to the earth she once left, and Libra's scales of justice will drag the spiky Scorpion down with them. Venerable Chiron, who holds his pinioned arrows against the Haemonian bowstring, will drop his arrows from the ruptured string; frosty Capricorn, who usually brings back chill winter, will fall and break your urn, whoever you are; and with you will pass away Pisces, the final stars of the sky. The billows will engulf and hide all these forms which are never normally submerged' (my trans.).

The notion of mixture at the beginning of the passage might remind us of Aratus' planets, which are indiscriminately 'mixed in' with the zodiac (*Ph.* 454–5):

οἱ δ᾽ ἐπιμὶξ ἄλλοι πέντ᾽ ἀστέρες οὐδὲν ὁμοῖοι
πάντοθεν εἰδώλων δυοκαίδεκα δινεύονται.

'But there are five other stars among [the fixed stars], but quite unlike them, that circulate all the way through the twelve figures of the zodiac.'

In Seneca's case the zodiac itself is 'mixed', and its constellations themselves behave promiscuously, taking on the characteristics of the planets: *ibit in unum / congesta sinum turba deorum* (*Thy.* 842–3). We might also be led, in these lines, to think of planetary conjunction and the destruction of the world, as we have seen it in Seneca's natural philosophical work, and in Lucan's civil war epic: compare Lucan *Phars.* 1.650–1, *extremi multorum tempus in unum /conuenere dies*, and Seneca, *Quaestiones Naturales* 3.29, *quandoque omnia sidera, quae nunc diuersos agunt cursus, in Cancrum conuenerint.* Here we are in the territory of world-cycles, most closely related to Plato's *Politicus* myth. Seneca's eclipse may be predicated on the Platonic 'portent model', but, true to the Roman tradition, it drags down *Aratus'* universe with it.

For Seneca's list is constructed on the analogy of a standard zodiac list in the Aratean tradition, as we find it in Aratus, *Ph.* 544–52, Cicero *Aratea* 320–31, and the 'Quintus Cicero' fragment.[30] As well as being a traditional zodiac list in all but its notion of celestial decay, the passage is written in the idiom of the Aratean tradition of 'synchronic risings and settings'. These were set forth by Aratus in *Ph.* 559–732 for the purpose of still being able to tell the time of night if cloud happens to obscure the constellation you are looking for. If you know which constellations are adjunct to each other, you can estimate the position of the one you want, even if obfuscated, by looking at the surrounding stars. In the Aratean tradition of synchronic risings and settings, heavenly bodies 'drag' each other along, as at Cicero *Arat.* 343, *nam semper signum exoriens Titan trahit unum* ('For always when he rises the Sun drags one constellation along with him'), or *Arat.* 362–3, *[Arctophylax] quattuor hic obiens secum deducere signa / signifero solet ex orbi . . .* ('Arctophylax is accustomed to drag down four signs of the zodiac with him when he sets'). Thus at *Thy.* 852–4 *Taurus . . . /secum Geminos /trahet*, and at 858–9 *iustaeque cadent pondera Librae /secumque trahent Scorpion acrem.* But in Seneca the stars don't *set* together, they *fall* together, a group suicide.

In his anti-*Phaenomena*, Seneca follows his zodiac with the Northern constellations (*Thy.* 869–74 = Aratus, *Ph.* 45–54):

> et qui medias diuidit Ursas,
> fluminis instar lubricus Anguis
> magnoque minor iuncta Draconi
> frigida duro Cynosura gelu,
> custosque sui tardus plaustri
> iam non stabilis ruet Arctophylax.

'. . . and the slimy Serpent, who, like a river, divides the Bears down the middle, and the lesser Bear, Cynosura, frosted with solid ice, adjunct to massive Draco, and sluggish Arctophylax, custodian of his wagon—now destabilized, shall rush down'.

Again, Seneca gestures towards Aratus and the Roman tradition of Aratus. The description of Draco as 'like a river,' *fluminis instar* (870), is, like the Virgin, a signature Aratean image, corresponding to οἴη ποταμοῖο in *Ph.* 45. Here Aratus is invoked through his previous Roman translator Germanicus—*fluminis instar* is Germanicus' description of Draco in *Ph.* 48. In fact, the stars in Seneca are redolent of Germanicus' description of them as *vaga sidera* in *Ph.* 17. Note that Germanicus is already describing *all* the stars, not just the planets as *vaga*. Likewise, you could see Cicero's translation of Aratus peeking through Seneca's *sidera labens* (*Thy.* 847; cf. *labentia . . . signa, Aratea* 336–7 and elsewhere). In Seneca, though, the imagery of the *moving* stars becomes their *falling*. With all these gestures to the tradition, Seneca knits himself into the Aratean universe, paradoxically unravelling the universe of Aratus as he does so.[31]

What will fill the blank canvas of the sky is anyone's guess. Atreus thinks he knows, in the gross arrogance of the lines which directly follow (*Thy.* 885–8):

> aequalis astris gradior et cunctas super
> altum superbo uertice attingens polum.
> nunc decora regni teneo, nunc solium patris.
> dimitto superos; summa uotorum attigi.

'Equal to the stars I strut above all things, striking the high-ceilinged sky with my lofty head. Now I have the trappings of rulership, now my father's throne. I dismiss the gods: I have attained the apex of my prayers' (my trans.).

He thinks he is a Platonic hero, head above the glass ceiling which mortal souls (figured as chariot teams) struggle to break out of in Plato's *Phaedrus* (248a1–b1):

> καὶ οὗτος μὲν θεῶν βίος· αἱ δὲ ἄλλαι ψυχαί, ἡ μὲν ἄριστα θεῷ ἑπομένη καὶ εἰκασμένη ὑπερῆρεν εἰς τὸν ἔξω τόπον τὴν τοῦ ἡνιόχου κεφαλήν, καὶ συμπεριηνέχθη τὴν περιφοράν, θορυβουμένη ὑπὸ τῶν ἵππων καὶ μόγις καθορῶσα τὰ ὄντα· ἡ δὲ τοτὲ μὲν ἦρεν, τοτὲ δ' ἔδυ, βιαζομένων δὲ τῶν ἵππων τὰ μὲν εἶδεν, τὰ δ' οὔ. αἱ δὲ δὴ ἄλλαι γλιχόμεναι μὲν ἅπασαι τοῦ ἄνω ἕπονται, ἀδυνατοῦσαι δέ, ὑποβρύχιαι συμπεριφέρονται, πατοῦσαι ἀλλήλας καὶ ἐπιβάλλουσαι, ἑτέρα πρὸ τῆς ἑτέρας πειρωμένη γενέσθαι.

'This is the life of the gods: of the other souls the one which follows a god best and has come to resemble him most raises the head of its charioteer into the region outside, and is carried round with the revolution, disturbed by its horses and scarcely catching sight of the things that are: while another now rises, now sinks, and because of the force exerted by its horses sees some things but not others. The remaining souls follow after them, all of them eager to rise up, but unable to do so, and are carried round together under the surface, trampling and jostling one another, each trying to overtake the next' (Rowe).

Atreus thinks he has made it to the top: this is the life of the gods! But really his is a *Lucretian* arrogance—he thinks he has got rid of the gods, like Epicurus himself at *DRN* 1.62–79. In Lucretius' paean of Epicurus, the result of the Sage's efforts was the triumph of rationalism (*DRN* 1.78–9):

quare religio pedibus subiecta vicissim
obteritur, nos exaequat victoria caelo.

'. . . therefore religion, trampled bit by bit under our feet, is ground down, and our victory makes us equals of heaven.'

Like all rationalists, Atreus puts himself in the place of the gods: heaven, he proclaims, is a meritocracy. This approach to rulership on earth is doomed. Unlike Epicurus he has not won a victory equalling him to the heavens, but is more like *religio*, the tyrannical oppressor looming down from the sky at *DRN* 1.62–5:

humana ante oculos foede cum vita iaceret
in terris oppressa gravi sub religione
quae caput a caeli regionibus ostendebat
horribili super aspectu mortalibus instans . . .

'When human life lay bedraggled before our eyes upon the earth oppressed under the weight of religion, which reared its head from the regions of the sky, standing over mortals with terrifying appearance . . .'

Too well, Atreus resembles a god. This is the arrogance of the rationalist, of thinking you understand the universe, that you can live in it immune from the reach of consequence.

This state of affairs has been forecast by the Fury at the beginning of the play (*Thy.* 47–51):

et fas et fides
iusque omne pereat. non sit a uestris malis
immune caelum; cur micant stellae polo
flammaeque servant debitum mundo decus?
nox alta fiat, excidat caelo dies.

'Let covenant and trust and every law perish! Let not even the heaven be immune from your crimes—why do the stars shine in the sky and their fires pay homage to the proper order of the universe? Let there be deep night, let day fall from heaven'.

The agenda of Seneca's Fury, brilliantly representative of human perversion, is to unmake the ordered universe. She is supremely antisocial, and this translates into cosmic terms, predicting the celestial fall of the 'zodiac' chorus. The idea that the stars might 'owe' something to the world is anathema to her. She is a *Lucretian* Fury. We remember Lucretius' trenchant rejection of the idea that the stars might harbour altruistic impulses, positioned at very the beginning of his exegesis of astronomy, *DRN* 5.76–81. Only a fool would think the cosmos owes us anything. This is where Seneca's Fury is coming from: she too is a misanthropic debunker of the order of the universe. Lucretius represents the juncture in Roman literature between the cosmos and civil war. Combined with both Aratean astronomy, and with the unravelling of the universe in the Platonic cycles, the idea is a powerful one. It leads us from the theme of planetary motion to that of celestial change.

5.2.3 CELESTIAL CHANGE IN ROME

Seneca's treatment of the myth of Atreus and Thyestes moved from cycle (the movements of the sun) to open-ended sequence (the falling of the stars). This movement was a consequence of civil war, in this case, war between brothers. Like Seneca, Statius in the *Thebaid* displaces Roman anxieties about civil war from the immediate political context, onto the myth of the sons of Oedipus. Here too we find the theme of celestial change as an index of civil war. This theme is a reworking of the Aratean tradition. It will bring us full circle, to the story of *Dike* we have seen in chapters 1 and 2. *Dike* will figure in the second of the two passages of Statius I propose to examine here.

(i) The Descent of Amphiaraus in *Thebaid* 8

In the midst of his epic aristeia, the prophet Amphiaraus falls headlong into the world of the dead. Amphiaraus' is no epic Descent to the Underworld, *katabasis*, as we have seen it in the *Odyssey* or *Aeneid*, nor is it achieved by the usual stealthy means. It is seismic (*Theb.* 7.809–17):

sive laborantes concepto flamine terrae
ventorum rabiem et clusum eiecere furorem,
exedit seu putre solum carpsitque terendo
unda latens, sive hac volventis machina caeli
incubuit, sive omne fretum Neptunia movit
cuspis et extremas gravius mare torsit in oras,
seu vati datus ille fragor, seu terra minata est

fratribus: ecce alte praeceps humus ore profundo
dissilit, inque vicem timuerunt sidera et umbrae.

'Whether the lands, struggling with wind they had conceived, expelled the madness of the blasts and their pent-up fury, or concealed water ate away the rotten soil and broke it up it by erosion, or the structure of the whirling universe leant on it, or Neptune's prong stirred up the whole deep, and twisted the sea too heavily onto the edges of the coast, or whether it was a crash of applause for the seer, or the earth threatened the brothers: see how the earth leapt up headlong from a vast gulf, and the stars and ghosts shuddered in counterpoint' (my trans.).

Lucretius is perhaps the most visible element in the mix at this point. In a self-indulgent excursus on the causes of earthquakes not directly connected to the narrative, Statius uses a didactic technique we have seen already in Lucretius, that of multiple causation for phenomena.[32] The phrasing too is Lucretian: in *machina caeli* (*Theb.* 7.812) we may recognize Lucretius' *machina mundi* from a passage quoted above, p. 127 (*DRN* 5.92–6). Statius points to a place in Lucretius describing the projected collapse of the integrity of the three parts of the universe, in palingenesis, or the unmaking of the atomic universe.

Given the 'scientific' phenomena attached to Amphiaraus' disappearance, it is appropriate that the *effect* of this disappearance should be described in similar terms, through the simile of a disappearing constellation, at *Theb.* 8.368–77:

> minor ille per alas
> septimus extat apex. liquido velut aethere nubes
> invida Parhasiis unum si detrahat astris,
> truncus honor Plaustri, nec idem riget igne reciso
> axis, et incerti numerant sua sidera nautae.
> sed iam bella vocant: alias nova suggere vires,
> Calliope, maiorque chelyn mihi tendat Apollo.
> fatalem populis ultro poscentibus horam
> admovet atra dies, Stygiisque emissa tenebris
> Mors fruitur caelo . . .

'That seventh crest stands up along the battleline in diminished state. It's as though an envious cloud were to remove one of the Arcadian star-group: the Wagon's glory would be cut down, the axis would not be as sturdy with one of its fires excised, and sailors would hesitate as they counted their stars. But now, war calls. Novel Calliope, imbue me with different powers, and let a more eminent Apollo offer me the lyre. A black day brings the final hour to peoples who ask for it of their own accord, and, released from the Stygian dark, Death romps in heaven' (my trans.).

At this point, Aratus comes to the fore. Statius' readers are well aware of the significance of the Bears: they are the first and most important constellation in Aratus

(*Ph.* 27–39), the one by which we orient ourselves on the star-map (and hence the opposite of the planets, which are devoid of guide-stars). Being the closest of any constellation to the North celestial pole, they never pass below the horizon for an observer in the Northern Hemisphere, and are always visible at night, the most reliable guide to sailors. The significance of Statius' simile is this: for the Argive army, it is as though the first of Aratus' constellations has vanished with the disappearance of Amphiaraus; as Aratus' sailors would be if bereft of the Bears, so the Argives are rudderless without the prophet's direction.

The reference to the counting of stars by sailors, *Theb.* 8.372, is important because it shows us Statius' technique of multilayered reference, and in so doing again brings us from Aratus himself into the tradition of his Roman translators. *Aratus'* sailors do not enumerate the stars of the Bears. But Virgil, translating Aratus in *Georgics* 1.137–8, has sailors, introduced to work by a provident Zeus, first learning to 'count' the stars, including the Bear:

> navita tum stellis numeros et nomina fecit
> Pleiadas, Hyadas, claramque Lycaonis Arcton.

> 'The sailor then counted the stars and named them: the Pleiades, the Hyades, and the conspicuous Bear, the daughter of Lycaon' (my trans.).

Sailors enumerate the stars in the Great Bear: so how many *are* there? We would not know the number of stars in the constellation from reading Aratus or Virgil; to know this, we need to move to Germanicus' translation of Aratus. In characteristic fashion, Germanicus meticulously adds to his Greek model the number as well as the position of the stars in each of the Bears (*Ph.* 24–7):[33]

> axem Cretaeae dextra laevaque tuentur
> sive Arctoe seu Romani cognominis Ursae
> Plaustrave, quae facies stellarum proxima verae:
> tres temone rotisque micant, sublime quaternae.

> 'The Bears of Crete, called Arctoe, or, in Latin, Ursae, guard [the celestial axis] on the right hand and on the left. They are also called Ploughs, and the shape of a plough is the closest to the real shape formed by their stars: each has three stars at the pole and the wheels, four in the upper part' (Gain).

In the Amphiaraus simile, Statius shows his hand as a follower of the Roman astronomical tradition. There are *seven* stars in the Bear. We know this from Germanicus. Statius' simile is particularly appropriate, armed with this knowledge. It describes the disappearance of one of the *Seven* Against Thebes. The parallel is flagged in Statius by *septimus* in *Theb.* 8.368. He exploits the theme of number in the Roman astronomical tradition to give his simile point.

Moreover, he exploits the mythical tradition, interweaving different versions of myth to create resonance. Both Aratus and Germanicus, as quoted, give two versions of the myth: that the Bears were bears, or that they were wagons. Statius refers to the latter in line 371 (*plaustrum*), choosing one of the Aratean alternatives. But there are anomalies in Statius' description. Why should the cloud covering the constellation in Statius be 'envious' (*invida, Theb.* 8.370)? And why are the stars in Statius Parrhasian (Arcadian) rather than Cretan, as in Aratus' description of the Bears at *Ph.* 31? Because, in a third mythical version of the Bear, the constellation was identified as the Arcadian (Parrhasian) nymph Callisto. This is the identification Virgil alluded to at *Georgics* 1.138 (*Lycaonis*). This story is told not by Aratus or Germanicus, in this case, but by Ovid in the *Fasti* and the *Metamorphoses*.[34] Callisto was loved by Jupiter, making Juno jealous: hence *invida* in Statius, the cloud acting as an externalization of Juno's envy. Juno caused her to be changed into a Bear and to be hunted by her son Arcas, who was about to kill her when Jupiter averted disaster by making her a constellation. In further revenge for this unmerited catasterism, Juno decreed that Callisto should never be allowed to bathe. This is a mythological aetion for the astronomical fact that the Bears do not set. This is why they are such a good guide for sailors.

And this is also why Statius' simile of the loss of a star from this constellation has such force: the point is that, under normal conditions, the Bears are always visible: mythology tells us so, as well as celestial geography. The disappearance of Amphiaraus in the course of an unnatural war gives rise to a simile the force of which hangs on an astronomical impossibility.

Stars do not—cannot—disappear or go backward in Aratus. When Statius uses the topos of the disappearance of a star, he is adumbrating something impossible. The impossible becomes possible in the Theban war. This is because it is a war between brothers, so already cheats natural law; moreover, those brothers are the sons of the 'planetary' king Oedipus. Doubt about the providential order of things has replaced Aratean certainty: in the Statian universe we cannot be sure that the same constellations will always be there; nor can we be sure that they will always move as we predict.

As with celestial subtraction, so with addition. The most prominent of Aratus' constellations is replaced in the sky by personified *Mors*—Death, who at *Theb.* 8.377, just after the simile of Amphiaraus' disappearance, now *fruitur caelo*, revels in the heavens.[35] *Mors* is described as though a constellation. The phrase used of its occupation of the heavens is lifted straight out of a description of a constellation by another of the Roman followers of Aratus, Ovid, who at *Fasti* 3.457 uses the expression *nunc fruitur caelo* of the constellation Pegasus. By lifting this phrase from a context in which it is used to describe a constellation (a large conspicuous one), Statius is conferring on *Mors* the status of a constellation: the *katasterism* (enstarment) of Death. Amphiaraus plunges into the abyss: his epic *katasterism* is twisted into a *katabasis*. His disappearance is likened to the disappearance of a constellation. As in the case of the zodiac in Seneca, it is replaced in the sky by something more sinister. Here we look up and we see, not the ordered circling of the constellations, but the ascended Death.

If the heaven is now the lot of Death, the correct partition of the regions of the world are upended, just as the partitioning of the kingdom of Thebes has failed. The 'takeover' of the heavens by the underworld is a metaphor for this human failure. No longer do humans contemplate the celestial motions as evidence of the divine hand, but their own actions obtrude before our sight of the heavens, changing their configuration.

(ii) The Descent of Justice in *Thebaid* 11

The Amphiaraus simile is not the only place in Statius where the possibility of a disappearing constellation is adumbrated. Another constellation in Statius which threatens to vanish is Virgo, Aratus' Δίκη, the celestial icon of Justice. This of course brings us back to the most prominent episode of Aratus, discussed in chapters 1 and 2. In chapter 2 we saw how *Dike* can be Romanized: in Statius, the episode of *Dike* is both Romanized and metamorphosed into an episode of celestial change, a thing impossible in Aratus (she is *always* there).

The departure of Statius' version of *Dike* is anticipated by Jupiter's injunction to the clouds to obscure the stars (*Theb.* 11.130–5):

'nunc etiam turbanda dies: mala nubila, tellus,
accipe, secedantque poli: stat parcere mundo
caelitibusque meis; saltem ne Virginis almae
sidera, Ledaei videant neu talia fratres.'
sic pater omnipotens, visusque nocentibus arvis
abstulit . . .

'"Now again day must be upended: earth, receive evil clouds, and let the poles fall away: I decree that the sky and my celestial relatives be spared; at least let not the stars of the kind Virgin or the Ledaean brothers see such things." Thus the Almighty Father spoke, and averted his gaze from the offending regions' (my trans.).

The 'constellation of the kindly virgin' (132f) is Aratus' Δίκη, *Parthenos*, *Virgo* in Latin. The theme of the withdrawal of gaze from human atrocity is one which we could track, from the withdrawal of Aratus' Δίκη to the perverse insistence in Seneca's *Thyestes* that Atreus' crimes must be seen (*cur, Phoebe, tuos rapis aspectus?*, 'Why do you snatch away your gaze,' *Thy.* 793).[36] In Statius, the 'Ledaean brothers' in 133 are Castor and Pollux, the constellation Gemini, a celestial monument to *harmonious* brothers, in antithesis to the warring brothers of Thebes. Statius' obfuscated constellations are those which have clear symbolic importance in the civil war context.

Their significance comes through the reader's knowledge of Aratus and the tradition. The link between the stars and the withdrawal of the divine presence is an Aratean one. Aratus was the first to give a constellation (Δίκη, Virgo) the role of Hesiod's Aidos and Nemesis. We have seen in chapter 1 how Aratus commutes the pessimistic ending of Hesiod's Myth of Ages to a providential outcome. In Aratus, Δίκη is still visible to men (ἔτι φαίνεται ἀνθρώποισι, *Ph.* 135) as she presumably looks reciprocally down on them, part of the scheme of divine providence. The link between humanity and the stars, that index of divine care, has not been severed.

In Germanicus' translation of Aratus, on the other hand, *Iustitia* goes about in her disillusioned state looking like Aidos and Nemesis, with her face covered, *ore velato*, reawakening the Hesiodic theme, seen at *WD* 197–201, of goddesses hiding their faces from the evils of mankind:

> at postquam argenti crevit deformior aetas,
> rarius invisit maculatas fraudibus urbis
> seraque ab excelsis descendit montibus ore
> velato tristisque genas abscondita rica,
> nulliusque larem, nullos adit illa penatis.
> tantum, cum trepidum vulgus coetusque notavit,
> increpat 'o patrum suboles oblita priorum,
> degeneres semper semperque habitura minoris,
> quid me, cuius abit usus, per vota vocatis?
> quaerenda est sedes nobis nova; saecula vestra
> artibus indomitis tradam scelerique cruento.'
> haec effata super montis abit alite cursu,
> attonitos linquens populos graviora paventis.   (Germanicus, *Ph.* 120–32)

'However, when the age of silver, less attractive than before, arose, Justice rarely visited the cities, tainted with crooked dealing, but came down from the high mountains only late in the day, her face veiled and her sorrow-filled eyes hidden. She accepted the hospitality of no one's hearth and home. She merely chided the frightened crowds when she saw them: "Offspring forgetful of the fathers that have gone before you, destined to have a progeny that is becoming ever more degenerate, why do you call upon me with your vows now that you have ceased to follow me? I must go elsewhere; I will leave this generation of yours to its own devices and to bloody crime." When she had finished speaking, she flew away over the mountains, leaving the people thunderstruck and expecting an even worse fate than their present one' (Gain).

In Germanicus, *ore velato*, 'with veiled face' = καλυψαμένα χρόα 'with hidden faces,' of the goddesses Aidos and Nemesis at *WD* 198. This is the inverse of Aratus' φαίνεται. In Statius, Jupiter predicts a similar sequel (*Theb.* 11.133–4). Statius reverts to the pessimism of Hesiod, while acknowledging the Aratean model: Virgo is a constellation, as in Aratus, but she is an Aratean paradox: a star you can't see.

In Statius, Aratus' Δίκη comes to have a civil war identity. This is seen at *Thebaid* 11.457–73:

> iamdudum terris coetuque offensa deorum
> aversa caeli Pietas in parte sedebat,

non habitu, quo nota prius, non ore sereno,
sed vittis exuta comam, fraternaque bella,
ceu soror infelix pugnantum aut anxia mater,
deflebat, saevumque Iovem Parcasque nocentes
vociferans, seseque polis et luce relicta
descensuram Erebo et Stygios iam malle Penates.
'quid me', ait, 'ut saevis animantum aut saepe deorum
obstaturam animis, princeps Natura, creabas?
nil iam ego per populos, nusquam reverentia nostri.
o furor, o homines diraeque Prometheos artes!
quam bene post Pyrrham tellus pontusque vacabant!
en mortale genus!' dixit, speculataque tempus
auxilio, 'temptemus', ait, 'licet inrita coner.'
desiluitque polo, niveus sub nubibus atris
quamquam maesta deae sequitur vestigia limes.

'Long since offended by earth and the community of gods, Pietas was sitting in an out-of-the-way part of heaven, without her characteristic attire and calm demeanour, but with her hair straggling from its bands, she was lamenting the war between brothers just like the unhappy sister or anxious mother of the combatants, rebuking cruel Jupiter and the vindictive Fates, saying that she would presently leave the light and descend to Erebus, and that she preferred the Stygian household gods. "Why," she said, "did you create me, ruling Nature, to stand in the way of the unbridled intentions of living things and often of the gods? I'm nothing in the eyes of the peoples, there's no reverence for me. O outrage, o men versed in the terrible arts of Prometheus! How good it was when earth and sea lay empty after the time of Pyrrha! Now look at the race of mortals!" She spoke, and, looking for an opportunity to help, she said, "Let me try, even though my attempt may be pointless." She jumped down from the sky, and even though she was sad, a snowy wake followed the footsteps of the goddess' (my trans.).

Statius' *Pietas* has 'long since' (*iamdudum*) been a wallflower in the celestial dance, offended with the gods, tucked away in her own little corner of the sky (*aversa caeli . . . in parte*). She's let herself go—*vittis exuta comam*—as a sign of mourning over the war. She goes so far as to threaten that she will desert the heaven altogether and take up residence in the house of Hades (*seseque polis et luce relicta / decensuram Erebo et Stygios iam malle Penates*, 463–4). In her monologue she berates *Natura, furor, homines* and—in a reference to the cycle of myths which opens Hesiod's *Works and Days*, the *diraeque Prometheos artes*, the terrible skills of Prometheus, that is, the perverse ability of humans to live without divine aid.[37] Nonetheless she resolves to help mankind, and leaps down from the sky like a shooting star, leaving a snowy trail (*desiluitque polo, niveus sub nubibus atris /quamquam maesta deae sequitur vestigia limes*).

Pietas here is Statius' version of Aratus' Δίκη. Statius provides a sequel to or commentary on Aratus' Myth of Δίκη, adapted to the civil war context.[38] When Roman authors imitated Aratus' *Dike* they more usually translated *Dike* as *Iustitia* or *Virgo*. But Statius' *Pietas* is a particularly appropriate rendition of *Dike* in a context of civil war, since *pietas* is a politically inflected term in Rome, with connotations of the extension of right behaviour toward one's family and to society at large.

Nota prius ('known before,' *Theb.* 11.459) is an intertextual marker, a signal that we should look for previous literary tradition. *Where* does the reader recognize her from? We have seen *Pietas* before. *Pietas* is already a part of the Roman cosmos. We recall Lucretius' *pio nequaquam . . . bello* (*DRN* 5.381), of the contending elements.[39] The elemental war was in no way reflective of *pietas*, right social relations. It was, however, fully within the Roman cultural mindset, in which civil conflict loomed constantly large.

As a *constellation* we recognize *Pietas* from the Roman tradition of Aratus. The *constellation* of *Pietas* would, you'd think, act as the antithesis of Lucretius' civil war, a reflection in the natural order of good relations. But Statius brings her down, and not in any good way, as Virgil had brought her back in *Eclogue* 4, at the return of the Roman Golden Age.[40] Statius develops the motif, seen in Aratus, of *Dike*'s progressive translocation as an index of man's degeneracy. Just as Aratus' *Dike* moves from the earth to the hills to the stars, so Statius' *Pietas*, beginning in an already remote area of the heavens, threatens in lines 463–4 (like Aratus' *Dike* in *Ph.* 122) to depart, but her predicted move is much more extreme, not to say perverse: she intends to migrate, not to the heavens, but to the underworld. In the event she carries out the threat, but only in part: she leaps down from heaven to earth. *Pietas* has been assimilated to an Aratean constellation, only to be banished from the sky in a Statian cosmic reversal.

Her banishment is achieved with the help of Aratus' Roman translators. We remember that, in Aratus, *Dike* remains conspicuous in order to remind men of a better age. We've already seen how Germanicus has his *Iustitia* going about *ore velato*, and how Statius also veils her in Jupiter's speech. Moreover, in Statius, *Pietas* has 'long since' (*iamdudum*) occupied a distant part of the heaven (*aversa caeli in parte Pietas sedebat*). *Iamdudum* is a response to Germanicus' *quaerenda est sedes nobis nova* (*Ph.* 117): in Statius, she's been in a more secluded location 'for some time', having done what she threatened to do in Germanicus. Furthermore in the *Thebaid*, the goddess *Pietas* already sits in an *inconspicuous* part of the sky (*aversa caeli in parte*, 11.458). This is because she is now as disillusioned with the gods (*coetu offensa deorum*, 457) as with men: in Statius she's removed herself from both. Statius' *aversa caeli in parte* is a development of Cicero, *Aratea* fr. 19 ed. Soubiran, [*Iustitia*] *et Iovis in regno caelique in parte resedit*. Both formulae are of the same constellation—Aratus' Δίκη-represented in Cicero's case, by *Iustitia*, in Statius', by *Pietas*. But in Statius, *Pietas* is not just *caeli in parte*, as she is in Cicero, but *aversa caeli in parte*, because of the failure of the gods as well as of men. She has shifted her position on the star-map to one less conspicuous, even perhaps one in the Southern Hemisphere, the side of the celestial sphere facing away (*aversa*), the part you can't see. This anticipates her intention of further removal to the 'antipodes' of the Underworld (lines 463–4).

Virgil's *Georgics* also help Statius in his reversal. In the *Gerogics*, the goddess *Iustitia*, passing on up to heaven, leaves her footprints (*vestigia*) last among virtuous farmers (*Georgics* 2.473–4), *extrema per illos /Iustitia excedens terris* <u>vestigia</u> *fecit* ('Justice, departing the earth, placed her last footsteps among them'). Virgil and Statius both refer to *Iustitia*'s (*Pietas*') *vestigia*, a word which can mean both 'footsteps' and the 'path' of a heavenly body.[41] In Virgil *Iustitia* places her footsteps on an upward trajectory; Statius uses the word, in the same metrical position, of the *descent* of *Pietas* at *Theb.* 11.472–3, *desiluitque polo, niveus sub nubibus atris /quamquam maesta deae sequitur* <u>vestigia</u> *limes*. Here, a white trail follows the despairing footsteps/path of the goddess, who is described like a falling star. By using *vestigia* of *Pietas*' descent, Statius alludes to Virgil's *Iustitia*; at the same time he reverses the direction of her movement.

Given the downward moral spiral of the *Thebaid*, it is fitting that Statius should invert the direction of the Aratean goddess. In Statius, as in Aratus, we have a two-stage movement of Justice. In Aratus, she flees first to the mountains (*Ph.* 117–8), then up to the sky (134), separating herself from men but remaining up there as a beacon of hope. Statius' *Pietas* moves in the opposite direction from Aratus' *Dike*: first down from the sky (*desiluitque polo*, 472), then (potentially) to the Underworld (463–4). In Statius, the stars will be folded into the Underworld in a counterpart to the superimposition of *Mors* on the sky in Book 8: a reversal of the realms of the universe.

Finally, an endnote on the relationship between *Dike* and the Emperor Domitian, whose reign is the political context of the *Thebaid*. Celestial change can come from addition as well as subtraction. Additions to the celestial map remain a sticking point at least up to the time of the adoption of the Copernican universe in the Western tradition. This is because such change entails a breakdown of difference between earth and the supralunar region, collapsing the Aristotelian distinction between the heavens, which are unchangeable, and the mutable earth.[42] In Statius, the emperor is invoked near the beginning of the poem as a potential *star* (*Theb.* 1.24–31):

> licet artior omnis
> limes agat stellas et te plaga lucida caeli,
> Pleiadum Boreaeque et hiulci fulminis expers,
> sollicitet, licet ignipedum frenator equorum
> ipse tuis alte radiantem crinibus arcum
> imprimat aut magni cedat tibi Iuppiter aequa
> parte poli, maneas hominum contentus habenis,
> undarum terraeque potens, et sidera dones.

'Even though a more circumscribed path confine the stars, and a shining area of heaven which does not contain the Pleiades, the North Wind or the cleaving thunderbolt tempt you, even though the driver of the flame-footed horses should himself set the high-shining diadem upon your locks or Jupiter grant you an equal share of heaven, remain satisfied with the governance of men, sovereign over sea and earth, and give stars to the sky' (my trans.).

Domitian is already lord of earth and sea (*undarum terraeque potens*): there only remains for him the celestial choice, but he is offered the still-vacant Southern Hemisphere rather than the prepopulated North, since Octavian, who opens Virgil's *Georgics*, with his predicted apotheosis, has already bagged a spot in that hemisphere, among the Northern constellations (*Geo.* 1.32–5):[43]

anne novum tardis sidus te mensibus addas,
qua locus Erigonen inter Chelasque sequentis
panditur (ipse tibi iam bracchia contrahit ardens
Scorpius et caeli iusta plus parte reliquit) . . .

'Or whether you add yourself to the slow-moving months as a star, where a place is made available between Erigone and the Claws which follow (now burning Scorpio draws in his arms and leaves you more than your fair share of the heaven) . . .' (my trans.).

Once we have read Statius' epic, we know also that *Pietas* inhabits the inverse hemisphere. Is this a good thing for Domitian? How do we insert the emperor into a universe in which celestial change is, at best, destabilizing vis-à-vis the tradition of Aratus, and, at worst, the upending of the cosmos under the influence of civil war?

Conclusion

This chapter has brought us back to the material of chapters 1 and 2. There we saw the moral construction of Aratus' universe, most clearly in the Myth of *Dike*. We saw what Roman translators of Aratus made of the myth. This chapter has taken that theme and activated it in the sphere of Roman epic. In a sense, *all* the passages of Roman epic and tragedy we have seen might be read through Aratean *Dike*. Aratus gave us *Dike* as a constellation; in so doing he first 'ethicized' the sky. This makes the Roman 'epicization' of the sky also possible. What results, though, is a universe at odds with the Aratean one, ethically and cosmologically defective under the pressure of civil war, the salient cultural myth of Rome, brought out in various forms, both mythical and contemporary, by the Roman poets we have seen.

Aratus gives us the blueprint for the recognition of cosmic reversal in the Roman tradition. If we did not understand the orderly universe, its dissolution would not be so powerful. This leads to a paradox in relation to the Aratean model: the archetype of order contains the seeds of disorder. These seeds germinate when cross-fertilized. Roman authors impose on Aratus the flux of Lucretius or the cyclicality of Plato, or, as we have seen, sometimes both. This mixture is not as incongruous as it may at first seem in the light of philosophical differences between the intelligent design model of Plato and the randomness of Lucretius' atomism.

Plato is a useful tool in that his philosophy is more edgy, and therefore more realistic, than Aratus'. Though uncompromising in his insistent return to a reality which can't be seen, Plato also recognizes, most clearly in the myths, that human existence is an uneasy compromise between contrary drives toward perfection and imperfection, an attempt, often failed, at the reconciliation of two movements to produce an harmonious whole.

This is perhaps clearest in the myth of the *Politicus*. The will to disorder is innate in the world. When in the *Politicus* myth the universe begins to go off the rails during its period of self-governance without the divine hand, Plato has his speaker say something extraordinary (*Pol.* 273b2–c2):

κατ᾽ ἀρχὰς μὲν οὖν ἀκριβέστερον ἀπετέλει, τελευτῶν δὲ ἀμβλύτερον·
τούτων δὲ αὐτῷ τὸ σωματοειδὲς τῆς συγκράσεως αἴτιον, τὸ τῆς πάλαι
ποτὲ φύσεως σύντροφον, ὅτι πολλῆς ἦν μετέχον ἀταξίας πρὶν εἰς τὸν νῦν
κόσμον ἀφικέσθαι. παρὰ μὲν γὰρ τοῦ συνθέντος πάντα καλὰ κέκτηται·
παρὰ δὲ τῆς ἔμπροσθεν ἕξεως, ὅσα χαλεπὰ καὶ ἄδικα ἐν οὐρανῷ γίγνεται,
ταῦτα ἐξ ἐκείνης αὐτός τε ἔχει καὶ τοῖς ζῴοις ἐναπεργάζεται.

'At the beginning [the universe] fulfilled [the demiurge's instruction] more accurately, but in the end more dimly; the cause of this was the bodily element in its mixture, its accompaniment since its origins long in the past, because this element was marked by great disorder before entering into the present world-order. For from the one who put it together the world possesses all fine things; but from its previous condition, everything that is bad and unjust in the heavens—this it both has itself from that source, and produces in its turn in living creatures' (Rowe).

The default condition of the universe is *dis*harmony, and the world sees a gradual growth towards *dis*order, the 'awkward and unjust things' (χαλεπὰ καὶ ἄδικα) with their origins, surprisingly, 'in the heaven'. What are we to make of this mind-boggling assertion? The explanation is an astronomical one. Just as the pull-back is inherent in celestial motions—the sun, the planets—so a retrograde or disorderly, body-like (σωματοειδές) element is inherent in the makeup of the universe. The Roman tradition selects from the Aratean and Platonic options. Choosing the Aratean universe at its ground zero, at the same time it works the Platonic antipathy, strips bare the bones of failure and dwells on the unreconcilable nature of the two kinds of motion in human civic life, as in the geocentric universe.

Coda: the Taming of the Planets

It was centuries on before the planets were finally incorporated in a system of order. The fifth century Neoplatonist Proclus 'tamed' the planets by placing them in an orderly universe as 'cosmocrators', guardians of time (Proclus on *Timaeus* 39d-e 271C): ὁ κόσμος τελειότερος γέγονε διὰ τῆς τοῦ χρόνου γενέσεως τὸ παντελὲς ζῷον μιμησάμενος κατὰ τὸ αἰώνιον καὶ ἡ γένεσις ὑπέστη διὰ τὴν ἑπτὰ κοσμοκρατόρων φοράν (ἀπὸ γὰρ ταύτης ἡ ποικιλία κατὰ τὴν γένεσιν ἀνεφάνη . . . ('The world became more perfect through the generation of time, imitating the perfect living thing according to eternity, and genesis was established by the trajectory of the seven Cosmocrators, because from this the variety pertaining to generation was made manifest . . .', my trans.; text of Diehl 1903–6). For the Neoplatonist, they represent the essential plurality-from-unity impulse of creation. The incorporation of the planets into the universe as an element of order grew in part from the recognition that there is a larger 'wobble' in the movement of the sphere of fixed stars: they do in fact move, due to the phenomenon known as precession of the equinoxes. This irregularity was the final irregularity which overrode the superficial irregularity of the planets.[44]

My concluding nod to Neoplatonism here is not a chance one. The next chapter will take us into the Neoplatonic universe and show how Aratus was incorporated within it by the last of his ancient translators, Avienus.

6 }

Late Antique Aratus

Introduction: Aratus in the Fourth-Century Context

The *Phaenomena* of Avienus is a strange work, ostensibly a product of mainstream culture, yet weirdly off-centre. Avienus was a member of the Roman (more precisely Etrurian—his family were probably from Volsinii) aristocratic establishment. He wrote various works on the subjects of astronomy and geography, including his translation of Aratus.[1]

The work can be dated with certainty between 310 and 386. The ancient literary witnesses for Avienus' *Phaenomena* give a *terminus post quem* of 310 (Avienus' translation is not mentioned among the translations of Aratus available at this date by Lactantius at *Inst.* 1.21.38; 165–8; 5.5.4, 112–13; 5.5.5) and a *terminus ante quem* of 386 (Avienus is cited by Jerome among the translators of Aratus, his translation characterized as '*nuper*', 'recent', *Comm. Epist. ad Tit.* 1.12, composed in 386–7). The time within which Avienus' *Phaenomena* could have been composed spans this period, even though within it the dating of the *Phaenomena* is difficult to establish with precision.[2] In terms of the relative chronology of Avienus' works, the *Phaenomena* was probably composed after his translation of Dionysius the Periegete, the *Descriptio orbis terrae*.[3] Weber (1986): iii dates the composition of Avienus' *Phaenomena* not long before Jerome's reference to it. Some take the date earlier in the fourth century; for instance Zehnacker (1989): 325 situates the *Phaenomena* around 350; Bellandi, Berti, and Ciappi follow Soubiran in dating it to around 360.[4] There is no small investment in the question of date, as we shall see in section 6.2.4 below.

For now, let's just emphasize that the *Phaenomena* is a work of the fourth century AD, and a *product* of that particular cultural environment.[5] I do not agree with Alan Cameron, who has characterized Avienus' works as limited to purely literary interest, with no contemporary relevance: '[Avienus'] translations are of purely antiquarian inspiration, quite uninfluenced by contemporary issues.'[6] I shall set out to prove that this is not the case. This view does not, in my view, make sense if you examine Avienus' translation of the *Phaenomena*, taking Aratus' original as a starting point. The differences are too stark. The work raises too many questions as to why there *are* differences between original and translation, and why *these* differences. In this chapter, I will give an answer by comparing Avienus' Aratus with various contemporary works. Avienus' poem can be shown to have affiliations to a

148

variety of contexts, theological and panegyrical, which carry contemporary relevance for the fourth century. It becomes a question of which fourth-century interpretative switch it is most fruitful to activate in the interpretation of Avienus' *Phaenomena*: we are spoiled for choice.

So, I am going to argue here that, above all, Avienus' *oeuvre* is at home in the fourth-century context. Yet where *is* 'home' in the fourth century? After Constantine, Rome was no longer the cultural centre:[7] a Volsinian aristocratic poet, who might seem at first sight 'mainstream' to a scholar of Republican and early Imperial literature, is now the representative of a *displaced* centre. Avienus is close to 'home'; but home is no longer Rome. And Avienus' work is in itself not what we expect: it engenders a weird sense of displacement in the reader. Avienus' *Phaenomena* is a *Neoplatonic* reinterpretation of Aratus. In it, two modalities of 'monotheism' meet head on: the Stoic monotheism of the Aratean Zeus is transformed into the Neoplatonic monotheism of the syncretistic Zeus figure who combines in himself demiurge, prime mover, Stoic deity, sun-god, even emperor-figure.

In one fell swoop, Avienus brings us into highly contested areas of the religious history of late antiquity: monotheism and syncretism.[8] I do not intend here to get involved in that essentially modern debate, or in the related, equally thorny, question of 'Christian or Pagan', which, in any case, is a conversation, often overheated, about different modalities of monothesim.[9] However, we cannot avoid making at least a passing observation that, with Avienus' *Phaenomena*, we are in the very centre of the Christian-pagan nexus. In purely chronological terms, it is worth pointing out that Augustine's conversion to Christianity took place in 386, and that this date coincides with the latest date for the composition of Avienus' *Phaenomena*, the *terminus ante quem* provided by Jerome *Comm. Epist. ad Tit.* 1.12. Ideologically too, some have seen Christian sympathies in Avienus.[10] The characterization of Avienus' work as either 'pagan' or 'Christian' is, I think, tangentially relevant at best, even aside from the fact that the dichotomy involved in it is a dubious one. Avienus' is a translation of a Greek original. His translation draws freely, one might say indiscriminately, on the various intellectual, religious, and cultural materials available to the fourth-century *literati*. To draw on one or other of these is not necessarily to profess it as ideology.[11]

6.1 Avienus' Proem

Aratus' proem is bold, simple, and accessible without mediation.[12] But reading its 'translation' by Avienus, we are immediately confronted with an entity different from anything else we have seen in the Aratean tradition, and baffling. Avienus' proem seems hugely prolix and in many parts inexplicable with reference to the Aratean model alone. What gives Avienus the raw materials for the expansion of Aratus' 18 lines into 76? The vast disproportion between Aratus' proem and Avienus' 'translation' of it can be seen by a glance at appendix C to this volume.

I am going to argue that the raw materials can be found primarily in Avienus' own literary environment. I will show this through close comparison with contemporary fourth-century works—the *Mathesis* of Firmicus Maternus,[13] the *Hymn to King Helios* of the Emperor Julian,[14] the panegyrics of the later *Panegyrici Latini*.[15] His is a fourth-century 'foreignizing' of the Aratean tradition.[16]

In this section (6.1), I intend to discuss some of the more striking and extraordinary expressions in Avienus' proem vis-à-vis the Aratean model. In subsequent sections I shall offer explanations of these in relation to particular works, in the first instance Plato, then fourth-century works which can be shown to share Avienus' key concerns.

The first thing which strikes any reader of Avienus who is expecting translation, is how very light the Aratean fingerprint is: the brush of a fingertip only. Although Avienus 1–98 corresponds to Aratus 1–26, the points of contact are few and Avienus tends towards repetition and expansion of just a few motifs.[17] At the same time, there is a wealth in Avienus of expressions which seem very odd indeed, not to say baffling, for the reader of Aratus. A morass of increasing strangeness envelopes the reader confronted by Avienus' descriptions of the Aratean Jupiter. First, Avienus describes his innumerable identities, characteristically stringing together threefold expressions composed of adjective + abstract noun + genitive, as in the following:

> 8 *perpes substantia lucis* ('never-ending material of light')
>
> 10 *materiaeque gravis concretio* ('weighty coagulation of matter')
>
> 30 *pigra inclinatio nodi* (?) ('gentle incline of the ecliptic')
>
> 31 *insociabilium discretio iusta deorum* ('just mediator between irreconcilable gods')

Avienus's lexicon is often prosaic, post-classical or unusual, and this in itself imparts a quality to his text radically different from the accessibility and light touch of Aratus himself. *Perpes* and *substantia* are post-classical;[18] *concretio* belongs in Ciceronian philosophical prose, imitated in later, Christian writers (Tertullian, Firmicus Maternus[19]); *inclinatio* is a term used in astronomy.[20] The addition of *pigra* and *nodi* here makes for an expression of the utmost obscurity, especially when the reader remembers that this expression denotes an entity, namely the Aratean Zeus. '*Discretio*' is both rare and post-classical;[21] as for its coupling with *iusta* and *insociabilium deorum*, although it is possible to say, on the analogy of earlier Roman philosophy, that some kind of political analogy is invoked (note *iustus, societas*[22]), it is impossible on first reading to derive much sense from the expression.

When Avienus moves from the titles of the entity praised, to his activities in the world,[23] the obscurity does not lift, although the modality of the syntax used to describe it may change, using verbs and participles rather than abstract nouns, as appropriate to a description of dynamic activity rather than static identity. Note the following instances of Avienus' peculiar impenetrability:

> (i) 12–14 *qui discurrente meatu /molis primigenae penetralia dura resolvens / implevit largo venas operatus amore* ('dissolving the solid inner parts of

the primeval mass by running through it on his path, he filled its interstices, acting upon them with widespread love')

(ii) 26–8 *sexuque immixtus utroque /atque aevi pariter gemini simul omnia lustrans, /sufficit alterno res semine* ('containing an admixture of the two sexes and encompassing all matters of double generation equally at the one time, he was capable of creating the universe from the seeds of both')

(iii) 44–5 *tenebris*[24] *hic interlabitur aethrae /viscera* ('he interweaves his shadowy form into the innards of the ether')

Well may interpretation of Avienus' Jupiter require initiation into the mysteries (for the image, see below on *vox secreta canit,* Avienus *Ph.* 18).

6.2 Comparative Readings of Avienus *Phaenomena* 1–98

6.2.1 PLATO, *PHAEDRUS*

In this chapter I contend that Avienus' reading of Aratus is influenced by the dominant current of religious thought in the fourth century, namely Neoplatonism. At the outset, however, it will be as well to distinguish between Neoplatonism, and the reception of Plato, whose influence in any given text may be both direct and mediated. We have seen this phenomenon in action in the case of some Roman versions of the *Dike* myth. There lies behind Avienus' proem the 'celestial parade' of Plato, *Phdr.* 246e4–247a7, a passage whose influence on this part of the *Ph.*, direct and/or indirect, is strong.[25] It is a seminal passage for the interpretation of the idea of Zeus/ Jupiter in Avienus, as arguably also in the interpretation of Aratus' own proem.[26] Therefore we shall begin by examining it in its own right.

In the myth of the *Phaedrus*, Zeus leads the other gods in their journey to the region beyond the heavens (*Phdr.* 246e4–247a7):

ὁ μὲν δὴ μέγας ἡγεμὼν ἐν οὐρανῷ Ζεύς, ἐλαύνων πτηνὸν ἅρμα, πρῶτος πορεύεται, διακοσμῶν πάντα καὶ ἐπιμελούμενος· τῷ δ᾽ ἕπεται στρατιὰ θεῶν τε καὶ δαιμόνων, κατὰ ἕνδεκα μέρη κεκοσμημένη· μένει γὰρ Ἑστία ἐν θεῶν οἴκῳ μόνη. τῶν δ᾽ ἄλλων ὅσοι ἐν τῷ τῶν δώδεκα ἀριθμῷ τεταγμένοι θεοὶ ἄρχοντες ἡγοῦνται κατὰ τάξιν ἣν ἕκαστος ἐτάχθη. πολλαὶ μὲν οὖν καὶ μακάριαι θέαι τε καὶ διέξοδοι ἐντὸς οὐρανοῦ, ἃς θεῶν γένος εὐδαιμόνων ἐπιστρέφεται πράττων ἕκαστος αὐτῶν τὸ αὑτοῦ, ἕπεται δὲ ὁ ἀεὶ ἐθέλων τε καὶ δυνάμενος· φθόνος γὰρ ἔξω θείου χοροῦ ἵσταται.

'First in the heavens travels Zeus, the great leader, driving a winged chariot, putting all things in order and caring for all; after him there follows an army of gods and divinities, ordered in eleven companies. For Hestia remains in the house of the gods alone; of the rest, all those who have their place among the number of the twelve take the lead as commanders in the station given to each. Many, then, and blessed are the paths to be seen along which the happy race of gods turn within the heavens, each of them performing what belongs to him; and after them follows anyone who wishes and is able to do so, for jealousy is excluded from the divine chorus' (trans. Rowe 1986).

Note Plato's use of military terminology: ἡγεμών ('leader' or 'general'), στρατιὰ θεῶν ('an army of gods'), ὅσοι ἐν τῷ τῶν δώδεκα ἀριθμῷ τεταγμένοι θεοὶ ἄρχοντες ἡγοῦνται κατὰ τάξιν ἣν ἕκαστος ἐτάχθη ('all those who have their place among the number of the twelve take the lead as commanders in the station given to each', the repeated notion of τάξις, 'military position' being the salient one). Likewise, Avienus uses military or imperial terminology from the outset when he commutes the Aratean Zeus to the Roman Jupiter: note *imperator* (2, 4), *dux* (2, 41). This military terminology is without parallel in Aratus.

It is appropriate that Avienus should invoke this particular passage of Plato in the proem to his astronomical poem. Zeus is also leader of the heavenly bodies, according to Hermeias, the Neoplatonic commentator on this passage, who remarks 'some take Zeus as the sun'. There is some evidence that this passage was read astrologically, if we buy Hermeias' version of events:

εἰσὶ δὲ οἳ οὕτως ἐξηγοῦνται· Δία μὲν τὸν ἥλιον λαμβάνουσι, τὸν δὲ ὅλον κόσμον φασὶ πρὸς αὐτὸν συντετάχθαι· καὶ Ἑστίαν μέν φασι τὸ δωδεκατημόριον ἐν ᾧ ἐστιν ὁ ἥλιος, ἐπειδὴ ἐν αὐτῷ μένει, τὰ δὲ ἕνδεκα τὰ λοιπὰ ζῴδια συνδημιουργεῖν αὐτῷ.

'There are those who think in this way: they identify Zeus as the sun, and they say that the whole cosmos is disposed around him. And they say that Hestia is the zodiacal sign in which the sun is, and when he remains in it, the other eleven signs combine their effect with it' (my trans.).[27]

This is not the full extent of the presence of this passage of Plato in Avienus' reinterpretation of Aratus' proem. At *Ph.* 17–18, Avienus characteristically trumps Aratus. Instead of the 'first and last' motif of Aratus 14, τῷ μιν ἀεὶ πρῶτόν τε καὶ ὕστατον ἱλάσκονται ('That is why men always pay homage to him first and last', Kidd), we have: *rite hunc primum, medium atque secundum /vox secreta canit* ('It is right that the awed voice sings him first, middle and following'). Not only does Avienus give us three for two in terms of praise, but also Aratus' communal act of praise (ἱλάσκονται, 14) is replaced in Avienus by something shady, almost underhand: the *vox secreta* of line 18. Surely it is not appropriate that Aratean Zeus should be hymned 'in secret'? But what then is the meaning of *secreta*? Unlike Aratus' democratic hymning of Zeus, in Avienus, the singer (we shall see) is an *initiate* participating in the activity of the mysteries, in one sense a ritual which is public and shared, in another, confined to the elect. This change of emphasis from the Aratean model is partly explicable by Plato's use of the terminology of the mysteries in the

Phaedrus myth; partly by the fourth-century context. We note the former in the first instance.

At *Phdr.* 250b6–c4, Plato describes the culmination of the celestial procession:

> ὅτε σὺν εὐδαίμονι χορῷ μακαρίαν ὄψιν τε καὶ θέαν, ἑπόμενοι μετὰ μὲν
> Διὸς ἡμεῖς, ἄλλοι δὲ μετ' ἄλλου θεῶν, εἶδόν τε καὶ ἐτελοῦντο τῶν τελετῶν
> ἣν θέμις λέγειν μακαριωτάτην, ἣν ὠργιάζομεν ὁλόκληροι μὲν αὐτοὶ ὄντες
> καὶ ἀπαθεῖς κακῶν ὅσα ἡμᾶς ἐν ὑστέρῳ χρόνῳ ὑπέμενεν, ὁλόκληρα δὲ καὶ
> ἁπλᾶ καὶ ἀτρεμῆ καὶ εὐδαίμονα φάσματα μυούμενοί τε καὶ ἐποπτεύοντες
> ἐν αὐγῇ καθαρᾷ . . .

'. . . where with a happy company they saw a blessed sight before them - ourselves following with Zeus, others with different gods—and were initiated into what it is right to call the most blessed of mysteries, which we celebrated, whole in ourselves, and untouched by the evils which awaited us in a later time, with our gaze turned in our final initiation towards whole, simple, unchanging and blissful revelations, in a pure light . . .' (Rowe).

Here, Plato uses the metaphor of initiation to denote the soul's progress towards true sight of the Forms. Μυούμενοί is said to refer to the basic stage of Eleusinian initiation, ἐποπτεύοντες to the later stage.[28] Avienus' *secreta vox* amounts to a Latin calque of Plato's μυούμενοί (from the verb μύω, 'to keep one's mouth shut', i.e., 'be an initiate into the mysteries'). Thus in Avienus the *vox secreta* is the voice of the initiate, hymning Zeus in the context of the mysteries. As well as leading directly to back Plato, Avienus' expression also carries Neoplatonic overtones, which will be seen below.[29] Avienus' importation of the terminology of the mysteries differentiates his *Phaenomena* sharply from its source-text. His is a particularly good way of describing the process of didactic enlightenment into the 'mysteries' of the heavens. *'Phainomena'* now becomes the process of mystic 'sight' or understanding, Aratus the vehicle for these concerns.

Finally, we have in line 37 the expression *anni pulcher chorus*. The image of the dance of the year may evoke the image of the celestial dance at *Phdr.* 247a7 θείου χοροῦ ('the divine chorus'). In Avienus, the 'beautiful chorus of the year' invokes Jupiter as the chorus-leader. If Jupiter 'is' the sun, he is of course the leader of the seasons as well as of the stars. We shall see below that Plato's influence here may be direct and/or mediated: the Emperor Julian in his Neoplatonic *Hymn to King Helios* has χορὸς ἀστέρων ('chorus' or 'dance' of the stars', *HH* 135a).[30]

6.2.2 FIRMICUS MATERNUS' *MATHESIS*

We saw above that Avienus' expression *vox secreta* in line 18, which jars when read against Aratus, takes on meaning when read against Plato. But it is Firmicus Maternus who provides the *fourth-century* link. More than once, Firmicus uses *secreta* in the sense of 'mysteries.' In *Math.* 5. pr. 6, Firmicus uses the neuter plural to refer to the mysteries of the supreme god: *da veniam quod gracilis sermo ad numinis tui secreta pervenit* ('Give grace that my elegant prose penetrates to the mysteries of your divinity'[31]). Also, in the transition from *Math.* 6 to *Math.* 7, Firmicus distinguishes between what he has already taught and what is to come: *nunc qui primis caerimoniis initiati ad ipsum secretorum limen accessimus* ('Now we who have passed the first stage of initiation have arrived at the very threshold of the mysteries,' *Math.* 6.40.3). The reader has now reached a higher stage of 'initiation' into the *secreta* of the gods. At stake here is the status of astrological learning as mystery, a trope ultimately sanctioned by the terminology of the mysteries in Plato's *Phaedrus* myth, at the point where the soul achieves sight of the 'things above the heavens' (*Phdr.* 250b7–c4). We have already seen how this passage may impact on Avienus' proem. It is equally appropriate that Firmicus should use *secreta*, the Latin equivalent of μυστέρια, from the same verb as denotes the first stage of the Eleusinian mysteries, i.e., μύω, to refer to the transition from the astrological preliminaries to more advanced material.

Avienus' similarities with Firmicus do not stop with his use of *secreta*. The prologue to *Math.* 5, for instance, is important not only because it sheds immediate light on Avienus' expression *vox secreta*, but also because it is evidence of a slippage, both in the immediate context of Firmicus, and in the tradition surrounding Avienus, between the supreme god and the sun god. Firmicus, who began the prologue to *Math.* 5 by addressing the supreme god as '*quicumque es*' (5 pr. 3). is by 5 pr. 6 addressing the sun. This is not merely a traditional currying of favour with the god whose powers are explicated, but an apology to the sun for Firmicus' actual revelation of his 'mysteries' (i.e., his astrological conjunctions, etc.) in the body of the *Mathesis*. An identification between the supreme god and the sun, is, as we shall see, key to understanding certain features of Avienus' proem. At bottom the identification could be characterized as a Neoplatonic one, and this will emerge more clearly when we come to look at Julian's *Hymn to King Helios*.

Firmicus' prayer at *Math.* 5 pr. 3 further demonstrates his closeness to Avienus. This is clearly shown in a blow-by-blow analysis. Both authors address the god in the anaphoric style of hymnody; in both the theme of absolute power is illustrated in various ways. Firmicus' prayer begins astronomically:

> quicumque es deus, qui, per dies singulos, caeli cursum celeri festinatione continuas, qui maris fluctus mobili agitatione perpetuas, qui terrae soliditatem immoto fundamentorum robore roborasti, qui laborem terrenorum corporum nocturnis soporibus recreasti, qui, refectis viribus, rursus gratiam dulcissimi luminis reddis, qui fragilitatem corporis divina mentis inspiratione sustentas, qui omnem operis tui substantiam salutaribus ventorum flatibus vegetas, qui fontium ac fluviorum undas infatigabili necessitate profundis, qui varietatem temporum certis dierum cursibus reddis, solus omnium gubernator et princeps, solus imperator ac dominus, cui tota potestas numinum servit, cuius voluntas perfecti operis substantia est, cuius incorruptis legibus conventa natura cuncta substantia perpetuitatis ornavit, tu, omnium pater pariter ac mater . . .

'God, whoever you are, you who from day to day sustain the course of the heaven in all its rapidity, who maintain the waves of the sea in their supple motion, you who continually shore up with strength the earth's bulk on its immobile foundations, you who continually make the bodies of beings on earth fit once again for work through nightly rest, you who, with their powers restored, imbue them with the renewed gift of sweetest light; you who sustain the fallible body by the infusion of divine Mind; you who make strong all the material of your creation by health-giving gusts of wind, who pour forth with tireless destiny the waters of springs and rivers; you who bring back the change of seasons by the predictable march of days: you alone are the guiding principle and ruler, alone the general and master, to whom the whole potentiary of the gods bows down, whose will is the raw material of finished creation. By your incorruptible laws, in which nature acquiesces, she embellished everything with the raw material of immortality: you, at once father and mother of everything . . .' (my trans.).

The similarity with Avienus, both conceptually and in expression, is striking. Note Firmicus' threefold use of his favoured term *substantia* here, in the last instance juxtaposed with *perpetuitatis*, and compare the collocation in Avienus line 8, <u>*perpes substantia*</u> *lucis*. Note also that the god's *voluntas* ('will') is the *substantia perfecti operis* ('the raw material of finished creation'). Reading Avienus' unusual collocation *perpes substantia lucis* through Firmicus, in it we seem to have a conjunction, as it were, of two ideas, namely will = eternity = creation (Firmicus), and light = eternity = creation (Avienus), with *substantia* being the underlying substance of what is permanently established in creation.[32]

We also see the same kind of political terminology deployed by Firmicus to describe the supreme god as in Avienus. Compare Avienus lines 2–4 (*dux . . . imperio*) with Firmicus' *solus omnium gubernator et princeps, solus imperator ac dominus* ('you alone are the guiding principle and ruler, alone the general and master'). In Firmicus, there is a conjunction in political terminology between the supreme god of *Math.* 5 pr. 3 and the sun, invoked at 5. pr. 5. At 5 pr. 3, the god is addressed as *qui fragilitatem corporis divina mentis inspiratione sustentas* ('you who sustain the fallible body by the infusion of divine Mind'); he is *solus omnium gubernator et princeps*. At 5 pr. 5, the sun, whose naming is deferred, is addressed in almost identical terms:

et tu, o omnium siderum princeps, qui menstruis Lunae cursibus lumen adimis pariter et reddis, Sol optime maxime, qui omnia super omnia per dies singulos maiestatis tuae moderatione componis, per quem cunctis animantibus immortalis anima divina dispositione[33] dividitur, qui solus ianuas aperis sedis supernae, ad cuius arbitrium fatorum ordo disponitur . . .

'. . . and you, o *princeps* of all the stars, who in the monthly courses of the moon deprive her of light and likewise restore it, Sun Best and Greatest, you who pile one thing upon another day after day by the mediating power of your might; you through whom the immortal soul is partitioned between all living things by divine dispensation, you who alone open the gates of the heavenly realm; on whose judgement the sequence of Fate is decided . . .'(my trans.).

If Firmicus' god was at the outset interpretable as or at least compatible with the Christian god, he has to share his place with the sun god, who has in addition inherited the title of Jupiter, *optimus maximus*. There is a syncretism between the supreme god and the sun which is also present in Avienus (see further below).[34]

Firmicus' prayer, like Avienus' invocation, culminates with the asking of indulgence for the literary work at hand. Firmicus' final petition includes a signature reference to tradition (5 pr. 6):[35] *sed animus divina inspiratione formatus totum conatus est quod didicerat explicare, ut quicquid divini veteres ex Aegyptiis adytis protulerunt, ad Tarpeiae rupis templa perferret* ('But my mind, shaped by divine inspiration, has tried to set forth all it has learned, so that it will bring to the temples of the Tarpeian rock whatever our god-filled predecessors have carried away from Egyptian shrines'). In his spin on the topos in the peroration to his invocation, Avienus uses *adyta*, not of the shrines of Egyptian astrology, as in Firmicus, but of his source of literary inspiration, namely the 'grottoes' of the Muses: *o mihi nota adyti iam numina Parnasei!* (*Ph.* 71). Again, the idea may be redolent of the mysteries, *adyta* denoting the inmost shrines.

The same complex of ideas appears in the prologue to *Math.* 7, which again is worth studying for its striking similarities to Avienus. In the proem, Firmicus speaks of the characteristics of the god whose devotees he and his patron Marvortius are (7.1.2):

> . . . per fabricatorem mundi deum, qui omnia necessitate perpetuitatis excol<u>it, qui Solem formavit et Lunam, qui omnium siderum cursus ordinesque disposuit,[36] qui maris fluctus intra certos terrae terminos coartavit, qui ignem ad sempiternam substantiam divinae perpetuitatis inflammat, qui terram in medio collocatam aequata moderatione sustentat, qui omnes homines, feras, alites et omnia animantium genera divina artificii maiestate composuit, qui terram perennibus rigat fontibus, qui ventorum flatus cum quadam facit necessitatis moderatione variari, qui ad fabricationem omnium quattuor elementorum diversitate composita, ex contrariis et repugnantibus cuncta perfecit . . .

> '. . . By the god who made the world, who took care of everything with an eye to eternity, who formed the sun and moon, who put the courses of all the stars in order, who contained the floods of the sea within fixed boundaries of land, who kindles the fire with the purpose of maintaining in perpetuity the substance of divine immortality, who maintains the earth located in its middle position with balancing force, who made all men, beasts, birds, and every kind of living thing by the divine power of the demiurge, who waters the earth with never-ending springs, who with whatever necessary modulation makes varied the blasts of the

winds, who, for the purpose of manufacturing everything, settled the differences between all of the four elements, and made everything out of entities which were at loggerheads and contrary to one another . . .'(my trans.).

The fullness of Firmicus' verbiage rings a bell for the reader of Avienus. The piling up of titles and achievements looks familiar. The progression of ideas as well as their expression is similar, the order of activities very close. Note, for instance, Firmicus' *fabricatorem mundi deum*: cf. Avienus *Ph.* 28–9, *rerum opifex hic, /hic altor rerum, rex mundi* . . . ('he is the craftsman of the universe, the one who brings it to fruition, king of the heaven . . .'). Firmicus' is a god *qui Solem formavit et Lunam*: cf. Avienus 32–3, *ignea cuius /lumina sunt late, sol et soror* . . . ('his are the fiery lights cast far and wide, the sun and his sister'), Once he has disposed the rest of the universe, Firmicus' god *terram in mediam aequata moderatione sustentat* ('maintains the earth in its middle position with balancing force'); in Avienus *Ph.* 32, the earth is his final achievement: *cuius et extremum tellus opus*. Like Avienus' Jupiter, Firmicus' is a god of the elements in creation, *qui ad fabricationem omnium quattuor elementorum diversitate composita . . . perfecit* ('for the purpose of manufacturing everything, settled the differences between all of the four elements, and made everything . . .'; cf. Avienus *Ph.* 7, *vita elementorum*).

That Avienus is working in the tradition of Firmicus' revelation of the astrological mysteries of the deity might explain some of his verbal profligacy in comparison with his Aratean model. Moreover, Firmicus might help to elucidate obscure points of detail in Avienus as well, such as *vox secreta* (*Ph.* 18) or *mundani ortus* (*Ph.* 47). The comparison is thus fruitful on the level of close reading, but has more far-reaching implications too in the study of Avienus.

Avienus has traditionally been seen as the guardian of a cultural treasure ruined by Christianity and barbarism, who transmitted for the last time the knowledge of a secular civilization.[37] But it is not useful to characterize Avienus as a pagan if it leads us to look only for resonances in overtly pagan texts: this is to limit the possibilities of exegesis. Study of Firmicus as a parallel has already shown what can be done outside the constraints imposed by such a view. It is notable that, although the *Mathesis* was (a) written under Constantine, and (b) by an author who was or became a Christian,[38] nevertheless, Avienus shares the concerns and the language of this work. The religious mix in Firmicus is also very close to that of Avienus. Like Avienus, Firmicus displays a 'goût de syncrétisme';[39] he is influenced by Stoicism and Neoplatonism, among other currents of fourth-century thought.[40] Clearly the work of both Avienus and Firmicus needs to be set in the wider context of the fourth century, embracing in common thought and language earlier and later, Christian and pagan, currents. The question is not whether Avienus was a Neoplatonist, a Christian, or anything else for that matter.[41] We might potentially compare Avienus' proem to a variety of 'theological' texts, spanning the fourth century, written in both a Christian and a pagan context. We have begun with Firmicus Maternus, who may have been a Christian, and we will come in a moment to a pagan text, the *Hymn to King Helios* of the Emperor Julian, which is also a Neoplatonic text. There is a marked Neoplatonist element in the literature of the fourth century which is a rich seam to be mined in the interpretation of Avienus.[42] Let us prepare the ground by looking first at the merging of identities in Avienus' proem, between Zeus and Helios.

6.2.3 ZEUS AS HELIOS: INTERTEXTUAL OBSERVATIONS

Let us proceed with a discussion of two further problematic expressions in Avienus. In *Ph*. 31–2 Jupiter is described as *pigra inclinatio nodi, /insociabilium discretio iusta deorum* ('the gentle incline of the ecliptic, the just mediator between irreconcilable gods,' as I have translated the lines in appendix C). Nothing in Aratus points the way to the meaning of these baffling expressions. I am going to argue that both expressions assume an identity between Jupiter and the sun, an identity which would have been perfectly familiar to Avienus' fourth-century readers.

The expression *pigra inclinatio nodi* has foxed commentators. Soubiran, for instance, provides no fewer than five alternative explanations for it, of which 'La plus banale, la plus familière aux lecteurs anciens, celle qui a le plus de chances d'être reconnue' would have been the obliquity of the ecliptic (Soubiran 1981 ad loc.). On this reading, *nodus* designates the intersection between the ecliptic and the equator, and *inclinatio* the obliquity of the ecliptic.[43] Against this interpretation, Soubiran comments, 'L'expression demeure cependant maladroite (ce n'est pas le noeud lui-même qui est oblique), et le sens de *pigra* curieuse aussi . . .' Nor, we might add, does it obviously explain what follows, *insociabilium discretio iusta deorum*. In what follows I propose to take the two expressions closely together.

First note that the astronomical use of *nodus* might be paralleled by Lucretius *DRN* 5.682–93:

> . . . sol idem sub terras atque superne
> imparibus currens anfractibus aetheris oras
> partit et in partis non aequas dividit orbem,
> et quod ab alterutra detraxit parte, reponit   685
> eius in adversa tanto plus parte relatus,
> donec ad id signum caeli pervenit, ubi anni
> *nodus* nocturnas exaequat lucibus umbras.
> nam medio cursu flatus aquilonis et austri
> distinet aequato caelum discrimine metas   690
> propter signiferi posituram totius orbis,
> annua sol in quo concludit tempora serpens,
> obliquo terras et caelum lumine lustrans . . .[44]

'. . . the same sun dissects the regions of the ether, running under and over the earth in unequal semicircles, but doesn't divide the two halves of the circle equally, and gives to whichever half an increase proportional to the amount he subtracts from the other, until he reaches that star-sign where the nub of the year makes noctural darkness equal to light. For the heaven holds his turning-points an equal distance apart in a middle course between the north and south winds, on account of the position of the whole zodiac, in which the spiralling sun brings about the seasons of the year, illuminating earth and heaven with obliquely shed light . . .'

In Lucretius 5.687–8, *anni /nodus* is 'the point, or rather the two points, at which the ecliptic cuts the equator, known as "the knots"'.[45] Here Lucretius is offering alternative explanations of the differing lengths of the days and nights across the year, of which the first, generally accepted one, is that the sun does not describe an exact half-circle around the earth except at the equinoxes. We remember that this is one of the most Aratean passages of Lucretius, heavily reliant on Cicero, *Aratea* 237–43, the passage describing the celestial circles, in which *nodis caelestibus* refers to the points of inter-section between the celestial circles, including the sun's intersection with the equator.[46]

Manilius apparently uses *nodi* to refer to the tropics, the points which mark the ligatures between the seasons (*Ast.* 3.618–22):[47]

sed tamen in primis memori sunt mente notanda
partibus adversis quae surgunt condita signa
divisumque tenent aequo discrimine caelum;
quae tropica appellant, quod in illis quattuor anni
tempora vertuntur signis *nodosque* resolvunt . . .

'But above all one must mark with a retentive mind the signs which rise from their places in opposite parts of the sky and mark its division into equal por-tions. They are called tropic signs, since in them turn the four seasons of the year and untie the *bonds* which fasten them together' (Goold).

With these passages of Lucretius, Cicero, and Manilius in mind, it is possible to say that *nodus* in Avienus' expression *pigra inclinatio nodi* may refer, first, to the point of intersection between one celestial circle and another; secondly, that the point of intersection to which it refers is the point of intersection between the eclip-tic and the equator, thirdly, that the point is envisaged as being specifically at the tropics, where in the eye of the observer on earth the sun turns back from one tropic sign (Cancer or Capricorn) towards its opposite number, which respectively mark the limits of progress of the seasonal year.

In fact Avienus seems to be thinking of these passages of Lucretius and/or Cicero throughout this passage. He used *omnia lustrans* of Jupiter at the end of line 27: com-pare the line-end of Lucretius 5.693, *lumine lustrans* and Cicero *Ph.* 332 *haec [the zodiacal constellations] sol aeterno convestit lumine lustrans*. Note that in both the astronomical writers it is *sol* which is the subject of *lustrans*. In Cicero, the thing on which the sun sheds light is the ecliptic, alternatively designated the zodiac because it contains all the zodiacal constellations. This is also the *signifer orbis* of Lucretius 5.691. In Avienus, although it is Jupiter 'gazing (shedding light) on all things to do with twofold generation', through his use of the astronomical didactic lexicon Avienus may be tapping into an expression with a precise frame of reference to the sun.[48]

So far, then, we have the idea of *nodus* as a point of intersection, specifically in astronomy the point of intersection between the ecliptic, the celestial circle representing the annual path of the sun, and the equator. Avienus uses this term to describe Jupiter. Jupiter is also described a few lines earlier by Avienus as *lustrans*, a participle used of the sun in the astronomical tradition Avienus is following in his translation of Aratus. It looks as though Jupiter, conceived by Avienus under the influence of Neoplatonism as *sol*, is being described using the metaphor of his annual path, the ecliptic. If I am right, *pigra inclinatio nodi* refers to the ecliptic.

The ecliptic is in itself an 'intersection' (*nodus*), and is thus defined by Kuhn: 'A great circle is the simplest of all curves that can be drawn on the surface of a sphere—the intersection of the sphere's surface with that of a plane through the sphere's centre—and the new simplicity of the sun's motion results from the fact that on a celestial sphere the ecliptic, too, is just a great circle, dividing the sphere into two equal halves. . . . The ecliptic is a slanted circle, intersecting the celestial equator in two diametrically opposite points at an angle of 23½°. . . .'[49] On this reading, *pigra* is not as much of a problem as Soubiran thinks: it can refer to the 'gentle' or 'lazy' angle (*inclinatio*) of the ecliptic relative to the equator: the angle of 23½° is not steep. We might then translate *pigra inclinatio nodi* as 'the gentle incline of the ecliptic'. We should remember that this expression designates the Aratean Zeus, who is now the *nodus*, or connecting belt which girds the celestial sphere, also the path of the sun, and simultaneously the sun on this path. If the identification of Juipiter as the ecliptic is right, it may shed light on Avienus *Ph.* 18–19 *sibi nam permixtus utrimque /et fultus sese geminum latus, unus et idem.* The ecliptic divides the celestial sphere into two interlocking, mutually connected, hemispheres.

This may seem strange, and the reader may require more convincing. Next, therefore, we can introduce the idea of the sun as a unifying force. This will in turn help us to interpret the other part of Avienus' sequence, *insociabilium discretio iusta deorum.*

The conception of the supreme god as the sun is paralleled in Tiberianus' Neoplatonic hymn, dating from the third or fourth century, lines 15–25:[50]

> tu, siquidem fas est in temet tendere sensum
> et speciem temptare sacram, qua sidera cingis
> immensus longamque simul complecteris aethram,
> fulmineis forsan rapida sub imagine membris[51]
> flammifluum quoddam iubar es, quo cuncta coruscans
> ipse vides nostrumque premis solemque diemque.
> tu genus omne deum, tu rerum causa vigorque,
> tu natura omnis, deus innumerabilis unus,
> tu sexu plenus toto, tibi nascitur olim
> hic deus, hic mundus, domus haec hominumque deumque,
> lucens . . .

'If it is right to turn our gaze upon you and speculate as to your sacred form, by which, immeasurable, you gird the stars, and embrace in your fastness the whole extent of the ether at once: you are, as it were, the beam, flowing with flame, with its fast-moving form like the extremities of a thunderbolt, by which, pulsating, you yourself see everything and come into relation with our sun and our day. You are the whole race of the gods, you the cause and sustaining force of the universe, you are all of nature, god many-in-one, you incorporate both sexes, to you is born at one time this god, this world, this shining habitation of men and gods . . .' (my trans.).

In this poem, the supreme god has a solar identity (the force of *iubar, coruscans*). He is a metaphysical sun in the noetic world, duplicated in the world of perception by our own sun (*nostrumque premis solemque diemque*), a concept explicable through Neoplatonism and articulated more fully in Julian's *HH*.[52] Tiberianus' god girds the stars and embraces the extensive ether (*sidera cingis /immensus longamque simul complecteris aethram*). We are here to visualize the sun as a belt, girding the aether, i.e., *as the ecliptic*. This is a nice parallel for the concept of the *pigra inclinatio nodi*—god as a connective belt—in Avienus.

This shows us the god/sun as a unifying force. The *nodus* is the linking point between the two celestial circles, the point at which the equator and the ecliptic coincide and at which, therefore, day and night are of equal length. The expression which follows in Avienus, *insociabilium discretio iusta deorum*, appears to show us the opposite: the god as a dividing force (*discretio*). This can be taken closely with what just precedes it, as the other side of the coin, as it were. By nature, the ecliptic is both a *nodus* (link) and a *discretio* (something which holds things apart). This chimes well with the idea of Jupiter as containing opposites within himself: just as he embraces both sexes, and acts as both *neikos* and *philia* in cosmogony, so, as the ecliptic, he acts as both a unifying and a differentiating force in the structure of the universe. To illustrate this, we can return for a moment to Lucretius 5.689–91:

nam medio cursu flatus aquilonis et austri
distinet aequato caelum discrimine metas
propter signiferi posituram totius orbis . . .

'For the heaven holds his turning-points an equal distance apart in a middle course between the north and south winds on account of the position of the whole zodiac . . .'

Costa (1984) ad loc. gives the meaning of lines 689–91 as follows: 'For half-way through the course of the blast of the north wind and of the south wind the sky *holds apart the tropics* equally distant (from where the sun then is) owing to the position of the whole zodiac.' More precisely, it is not the sky which 'holds apart' the tropics, but the ecliptic. Its circle is marked out into four parts: two points (opposite one another) at which it intersects the equator (the vernal and autumnal equinoxes, when the sun is in Aries and Libra, respectively); two points (also opposite one another) on which are the summer and winter solstices (the tropics of Cancer and Capricorn).[53] The sun turns back in its lateral yearly path along the horizon (from the observer's point of view) when it is in either of these constellations. Thus Jupiter-as-ecliptic is both a *nodus* (intersection) and *discretio* (separation). Admittedly, this is not the only possible meaning of *discretio*: commentators adduce a variety of meanings,[54] and I myself will introduce another possibility below. But it is a reading which does justice to the astronomical context, and which is satisfying given the character of the solar Zeus elsewhere attested, as a link and a reconciler of opposites.

My idea is that, if *inclinatio* equals the path of the sun (the ecliptic—above), then the *insociabiles dei* referred to may be Capricorn and Cancer. The constellations are sometimes referred to as 'gods' or by similar periphrasis.[55] These particular 'gods', Capricorn and Cancer, might well be considered inimical to one another.[56] Seen as a band through the heavens, the ecliptic holds them apart. I therefore take the two expressions *pigra inclinatio nodi* and *discretio iusta deorum* closely together, as jointly referring to Jupiter's role as the sun. The sun/ecliptic is the *nodus* that ties the whole celestial structure together; the sun both holds apart the inimical constellations which mark the summer and winter solstices, and links them together as points on a great circle, the ecliptic or the zodiac, inclined at a slight angle to the equator. The important thing is that there appears in both expressions to be an identification between Jupiter and the sun, referred to by its path, the ecliptic, as though that belt were a solid, tangible thing continuous with the sun upon it, as in fact would be the case on an armillary sphere, representing Jupiter-as-Helios in visual form.

The syncretism between Zeus and Helios seems to be a product of late antiquity reflected in Avienus, albeit uniquely, obscurely, and idiosyncratically expressed in poetic form. The remarkable thing is that Aratus' Zeus is activated to carry all this baggage. What we have in Avienus is a fourth-century Platonizing interpretation of Aratus. Perhaps Avienus followed a prompt in the exegetical tradition, or the Platonic commentaries. But there is also much contemporary material available which could have given him the connection. We have already seen Firmicus in particular. We shall now examine a specifically Neoplatonic text which is, to the best of our knowledge, exactly contemporary with Avienus.[57]

6.2.4 THE EMPEROR JULIAN'S *HYMN TO KING HELIOS*

There is no little investment in the questions of date discussed in the introduction to this chapter. In particular, Zehnacker's agenda is to align the composition of the *Phaenomena* with the 'pagan conversion' of the Emperor Julian, which took place in 351.[58] In such a view, Avienus' *Phaenomena* reflects a growing pagan presence in the political and literary culture, which culminated in Julian's manifesto, the *Hymn to King Helios*. Further, Julian became Augustus in 360 and sole Augustus in 361: a date of c. 360 for Avienus' *Phaenomena* might fit with a determined and now more powerful promulgation of 'pagan' theology as a response to Christian monotheism.

Although not essential to a Neoplatonic reading of the work, the idea of parity in date between Avienus' *Phaenomena* and the *HH* of Julian opens up a very fruitful area of thought. Not only does the *HH* show us ways toward reading some of Avienus' most difficult expressions, but once we begin to draw systematically on the *HH* as a comparadum, we find it an extremely rich source of ideas which help us to understand not only aspects of Avienus' *Phaenomena* itself, but the poet's motivation in writing the work. This is a new departure in the history of Aratean scholarship and opens up an interesting vista of Aratus against the fourth-century backdrop.

The *HH* is a politico-theological document.[59] The similarities between the god invoked in Julian's *Hymn*, and Avienus' Jupiter, are both striking and, to my mind at least, conclusive. One important point to emerge from this discussion is that, if the *HH* is a source for Avienus, then panegyric as well as theology is implied in Avienus' proem, in which Aratus' Zeus has become both Neoplatonic deity and a model for the fourth-century Roman emperor.[60] Avienus combines two takes on the Aratean proem which have hitherto been relatively separate: the theological current in the Stoic hymn of the original text, and the panegyrical current, evident in Germanicus' substitution of the emperor for the god. The *HH* helps us to develop a panegyrical strand in the interpretation of Avienus' *Ph.*; one which will be further developed in our study of fourth-century panegyric itself in section 6.2.5 below.

The study of Julian's *Hymn* assists, then, at every level in the interpretation of Avienus' proem. We shall study both the microcosm, at the level of individual expressions, and the macrocosm, the overriding motivation of the poet in choosing Aratus' text to translate in the fourth-century context.

There are many points of immediate contact between the two texts. Let us begin our analysis of Avienus' relationship to the *Hymn* with the expression which most recently caused us difficulty, Avienus' *insociabilium discretio iusta deorum*. Above, I conjectured an astronomical explanation, that Jupiter as the ecliptic, a trope for the sun itself, at the one time separates and mediates between the opposing constellations of the tropics, Cancer and Capricorn. We noted the problem of the meaning of *deorum*. One of the hypotheses I advanced was that the *insociabiles dei* were the 'tropic' constellations of Cancer and Capricorn. In Julian, Helios is in charge of the tropics (*HH* 147d). What's more (*HH* 148c), he is in charge of the whole zodiac. Note how its constellations are described: . . . τοὺς τρεῖς γὰρ τετραχῇ τέμνων διὰ τῆς τοῦ ζωοφόρου κύκλον πρὸς ἕκαστον αὐτῶν κοινωνίας τοῦτον αὖθις τὸν ζωφόρον εἰς δώδεκα θεῶν δυνάμεις διαιρεῖ . . .' ('For as he divides the three spheres by four through the zodiac, which is associated with every one of the three, so he divides the zodiac also into twelve divine powers . . .'). It is the division of the zodiac by four which gives the seasons, which in turn make the 'turnings' (τὰς τροπὰς) of time. And it is Helios who holds it all together. Furthermore, we are told that Zeus and Helios are identical (ὑπὸ Διὸς . . . ὅσπερ ἐστὶν ὁ αὐτὸς Ἡλίῳ, *HH* 149c).

Alternatively, Zeus' powers of reconciliation may exist in a different sphere. Julian asserts that Helios' 'middleness' consists in his position between the visible pericosmic gods (ἐμφανῶν καὶ περικοσμίων θεῶν) and the immaterial and intelligible gods who surround the Good (138d–139a).[61] Helios mediates between these two sets of gods, though he himself is distinct from both (ἀμιγὴς ἀφ᾽ ὅλων τῶν θεῶν ἐμφανῶν τε καὶ ἀφανῶν καὶ αἰσθητῶν καὶ νοητῶν, 'distinct from the whole number of the gods, visible and invisible, both those perceptible by sense and those which are intelligible only', *HH* 139a[62]). This role of mediation may help us gloss the strange expression *insociabilium discretio iusta deorum* in Avienus *Ph.* 32. On the analogy of Helios, identified with Jupiter, we might read Avienus' Jupiter as the 'boundary' (*discretio*) between the intelligible and perceptible gods. Thus we might interpret Avienus' phrase as meaning, not (as above) 'Just separation between inimical gods (/constellations)', but 'just line of distinction between incompatible gods' (i.e., between θεῶν ἐμφανῶν τε καὶ ἀφανῶν, the sensible and intelligible ones). It is remarkable, if so, that Avienus is expressing Neoplatonic concepts using the vehicle of Aratus' Zeus.

This is not the only place where Julian makes us think further about particular expressions in Avienus. For instance, take *amore* in Avienus line 14 (cf. *amoris*, 20). Here, some commentators adduce Empedocles' principle of Love. Avienus could conceivably have got *amor* direct from Empedocles, or from Empedocles via some mediator such as Aristotle;[63] but it is more likely, in the fourth-century context, that he shared the concept with Julian. At the beginning of his definition of Helios' middleness, discussing Helios' unifying role at *HH* 138d, Julian glosses Empedoclean 'Love' as ἁρμονία ('harmony'):

> μεσότητα μὲν δή φαμεν οὐ τὴν ἐν τοῖς ἐναντίοις θεωρουμένην ἴσον ἀφεστῶσαν τῶν ἄκρων, . . . ἀλλὰ τὴν ἑνωτικὴν καὶ συνάγουσαν τὰ διεστῶτα, ὁποίαν τινά φησιν Ἐμπεδοκλῆς τὴν ἁρμονίαν ἐξορίζων αὐτῆς παντελῶς τὸ νεῖκος.

> 'Now "middleness" we define not as that mean which in opposites is seen to be equally remote from the extremes, . . . but that which unifies and links together what is separate; for instance the sort of thing that Empedocles means by Harmony when from it he altogether eliminates Strife.'

This is a passage which seems to have thoroughgoing similarities with Avienus' proem. Jupiter's role, like that of Helios, is as a harmonizing influence. This idea seems to me to unite the two concepts we have studied above in relation to Avienus: Jupiter as *nodus* or connecting force (note Julian's τὴν ἑνωτικὴν καὶ συνάγουσαν τὰ διεστῶτα, 'that which unifies and links together what is separate'), and Jupiter as *discretio*, i.e., differentiating force.[64] This would further support the argument above, concerning the continuity in the Avienian sequence *pigra inclinatio nodi, / insociabilium discretio iusta deorum* in lines 31–2.

We might also note Avienus 19–20, *unus et idem est /auctor agendorum* ('one and the same, he is the instigator of things to be done.') This description looks like Julian's description of Helios as ἕν ('one'), and as μονοειδὴς τῶν ὅλων αἰτία, 'this uncompounded cause of the whole,' 132d. Julian identifies him with Helios, but at the same time assimilates him to Zeus in *HH* 143d and 144b.

In fact, Avienus' sequence in lines 1–45 may follow a familiar pattern of Neoplatonic theological exegesis. The characteristic mode of exposition of Julian's source Iamblichus was to describe (i) essence (οὐσία), (ii) powers (δυνάμεις), (iii) activities (ἔργα);[65] this is also Julian's scheme at *HH* 132b. In Avienus we may find a similar progression from titles and identities (lines 1–12) to spheres of influence (lines 12–21), to activities, beginning with cosmogony (21–45). At 135c Julian discourses on the three actions of Helios, creative, perfective, cohesive; here we might think of Avienus' description of Jupiter at lines 21–45, running from cosmogony (*chaos altum /lumine perrupit . . .*) to perfection (*extremum . . . opus*, 32), to his penetrative interweaving of the cosmos in 44–5, *tenebris hic interlabitur aethrae /viscera et aeternos animat genitalibus artus* ('he interweaves his shadowy form into the innards of the ether and vivifies its everlasting limbs as a creative force'). A broad adherence to this pattern of exposition might explain Avienus' fulsomeness in relation to Aratus.

Individual images in Avienus, too, bring us into close contact with Julian. We have already noted *anni pulcher chorus* in Avienus line 37, likening it to Plato, *Phdr.* 247a7 θείου χοροῦ. But now we see that the image is also in Julian *HH* 135a, in a specifically astronomical context: χορὸς ἀστέρων. At *HH* 135a–b the whole 'chorus of the stars' follows the sun:

> ᾧ (the Sun) πᾶς μὲν ὑπείκει χορὸς ἀστέρων, ἕπεται δὲ ἡ γένεσις ὑπὸ τῆς τούτου κυβερνωμένη προμηθείας· οἱ μὲν γὰρ πλάνητες ὅτι περὶ αὐτὸν ὥσπερ βασιλέα χορεύοντες ἔν τισιν ὡρισμένοις πρὸς αὐτὸν διαστήμασιν ἁρμοδιώτατα φέρονται κύκλῳ . . .
>
> '. . . to whom the whole band of the heavenly bodies yields place, and whom all generated things follow, piloted by his providence? For the planets dance about him as their king, in certain intervals, fixed in relation to him, and revolve in a circle with perfect accord . . .'[66]

Note here now Julian paraphrases the passage of Plato we have already studied above: ᾧ . . . ἕπεται picks up Plato's τῷ (i.e., Zeus) δ' ἕπεται στρατιὰ θεῶν ('after him there follows an army of gods') at *Phdr.* 246e6. In Julian, the Platonic Zeus has become Zeus-Helios, actualizing the astrological symbolism latent in Plato *Phdr.* 247a7 and identified by commentators such as Hermeias (see above, section 6.2.1).[67] This is why, in Avienus 37, *istius ille anni pulcher chorus*, 'his is the beautiful dance of the year', because the stars mark out the seasons, as the body of the poem will tell us, and Jupiter, as we've seen, is the leader of the stars. In Avienus, Plato may be mediated through Julian, or the poet could be referring cleverly both to his near Neoplatonic neighbour and to that neighbour's Platonic source.

If we are still in doubt as to the parallels between Avienus and Julian, it is the small details, as we saw in the case of Virgil and the *Politicus* in chapter 2, pp. 39–48 above, that may help to close the loop. In Avienus' proem, we have two specific metaphors, namely *flos* (12) and *fons* (49). In 46–9, Jupiter's reasons for instructing Eudoxus in astronomy are 'so that our faint hearts should not languish for a long time, and so that the mind should not, forgetful of its celestial origin, bit by bit[68] conceive base thoughts and should fail to raise itself to the principles of the eternal source (*fontis . . . aeterni*)'. In terms of the tradition we have already seen, of the supreme god/Zeus/Helios as the celestial source of the soul, the *fons* here is presumably Jupiter. Indeed, he is addressed as such in line 12, where among his titles is *flos et flamma animae* ('flower and flame of the soul').[69] We find *both* of these images in Julian's description of the supreme god. At *HH* 134a Julian speaks of the demiurgic activity of the sun's rays, which are the 'flower' of divine light: αὐτοῦ δὲ τοῦ φωτὸς ὄντος ἀσωμάτου ἀκρότης ἂν εἴη τις καὶ ὥσπερ ἄνθος ἀκτῖνες ('And of light, itself incorporeal, the culmination and <u>flower</u>, so to speak, is the sun's rays'). The accepted theory is that they emanate from the activity of Mind (*HH* 134b): οὐκ ἀπᾴδει δὲ οὐδὲ ὁ λόγος, εἴπερ αὐτὸ τὸ φῶς ἀσώματον, εἴ τις αὐτοῦ μηδὲ τὴν <u>πηγὴν</u> ὑπολάβοι σῶμα, νοῦ δὲ ἐνέργειαν ἄχραντον εἰς τὴν οἰκείαν ἕδραν ἐλλαμπομένην . . ., ('And in harmony with this is our theory, seeing that light itself is incorporeal, if one should regard its <u>fountainhead</u>, not as corporeal, but as the undefiled activity of mind, pouring light into its own abode . . .').[70]

Not only do we have in this passage of Julian two images shared with Avienus, making the likelihood of the relationship between the two texts in my view much stronger, but we can use Julian's exposition at this point of the *HH* to explain many of the elements of Avienus' overall progression in *Ph.* 5–12:

> iste paterni   5
> principium motus, vis fulminis iste corusci,
> vita elementorum, mundi calor, aetheris ignis
> astrorumque vigor, perpes substantia lucis
> et numerus celsi modulaminis. hic tener aer
> materiaeque gravis concretio, sucus ab alto   10
> corporibus caelo, cunctarum alimonia rerum,
> flos et flamma animae . . .

'He is the beginning of generative motion, he the power of the scintillating lightning bolt, the life-force of the elements, warmth of the world, strength of the ethereal fire and of the stars, the never-ending material of light, and the number of celestial harmony. He is the gauzy air and the weighty coagulation of matter, he is moisture from the high heaven for bodily creatures, nutriment of all things, flower and flame of the soul.'

At the point in the *HH* just referred to, Julian is discussing the visible sun, the 'third in rank' (τρίτος, 133c) in the Neoplatonic *kosmoi*. The sun's rays are the manifestation in the visible cosmos of the intelligible light, which is itself, though transparent (διαφανές, 133d), the basis of all the elements (πᾶσι . . . συνυποκείμενον τοῖς στοιχείοις, 133d). This gives a theoretical basis for Avienus' *vita elementorum* (*Ph.* 7): Jupiter as the sun is the demiurgic manifestation of the elemental blueprint in the intelligible world. What is more, Julian, like Avienus, may single out the heavenly bodies as visible manifestations of the transparent underlying demiurgic light-substance, of which the principle is the sun (*HH* 134a): τὸ δὲ φῶς εἶδός ἐστι ταύτης οἷον ὕλης ὑπεστρωμένης καὶ παρεκτεινομένης τοῖς σώμασιν ('And light is a form of this substance, so to speak, which is the substratum of, and coextensive with, the heavenly bodies'). Likewise, Avienus' Jupiter is *aetheris ignis lastrorumque vigor*. Jupiter is therefore, on the Neoplatonic model, both the light itself and its underlying substance: the *perpes substantia lucis* (line 8).

The progression in Julian *HH* 133d–134b elucidates, so to speak, Avienus' progression: in Julian, (i) light is demiurgic (= Avienus' *principium*, line 6?); (ii) intelligible light is the underlying basis of the elements (= Avienus' *vita elementorum*, line 7); (iii) it is visibly manifest in the 'bodies' [of the stars] (= Avienus 7–8); (iv) the sun's light is the 'flower' (*flos*, Avienus 12) and the fountain (*fons*, Avienus 49) of incorporeal light.

Julian draws on Plato, *Rep.* 508a5–9 and 509b1–5 for the role of the sun in his *Hymn*. In the former passage, it is the sun which allows us to see best the visible world; in Julian this becomes the quasi-demiurgic role of the sun's light in *HH* 133–4. In the latter passage of Plato, the sun is the adjunct to generation, prefacing his generative role in Julian, who assigns him the craftsman-role,[71] and in Avienus: note Plato's γένεσιν καὶ αὔξιν καὶ τροφήν ('origin and growth and nourishment,' *Rep.* 509b2-3), alongside Avienus' *principium/alimonia/auctor* in *Ph.* 6, 11, and 20. Here again, the links between Avienus and Julian help to bring out an identification between Jupiter and the sun latent in the Platonic background, but not explicit in Aratus.

So far we have seen several points of contact between the *HH* and Avienus' proem. These signal the validity of our study of Julian as a source or parallel for the *Ph*. Let us now work back and essay a broader analysis of the *HH*, since many points in it elucidate Avienus. Early in the *HH*, Julian proclaims the universal paternity of Helios, who 'sows the earth with souls' (ψυχὰς . . . σπείρων εἰς γῆν, *HH* 131c). This is the concept behind Avienus *Ph*. 12, *flos et flamma animae*. Julian then goes on to set out his programme, the sequence of which we have seen Avienus following: he is going to talk about the god's substance and origin (περὶ τῆς οὐσίας αὐτοῦ καὶ ὅθεν προῆλθε, *HH* 132b); his powers (τῶν δυνάμεων καὶ τῶν ἐνεργειῶν διελθόντες, ὁπόσαι φανεραὶ ὅσαι τ᾽ἀφανεῖς, *HH* 132b), and finally the blessings he bestows (his activities, on the Iamblichean scheme): περὶ τῆς τῶν ἀγαθῶν δόσεως, ἣν κατὰ πάντας ποιεῖται τοὺς κόσμους, *HH* 132b). This schema corresponds to Avienus 1–21 (substance and origin); 21–35 (powers); and 36–42 (activities in the world).

At *HH* 136a Julian is explicit about the joint nature of Zeus and Helios: κοινὴν ὑπολάβωμεν μᾶλλον δὲ μίαν Ἡλίου καὶ Διὸς ἐν τοῖς νοεροῖς θεοῖς δυναστείαν . . . ('let us then assume that, among the intellectual gods, Zeus and Helios have a joint or rather a single sovereignty'). Further, Julian adds Hades, whom he identifies with Serapis. This implied trifold identity of Zeus helps us to understand the non-Aratean references to Erebus which intrude in Avienus *Ph*. 30 and 95; it could also help to explain one of his most obscure expressions, *tenebris hic interlabitur aethrae /viscera et aeternos animat genitabilis artus* (44–5). The case and/or usage of *tenebris* has puzzled commentators.[72] Reading through Julian's identification of Zeus-Helios-Hades, we might simply take it as an ablative, 'interweaves the innards of the aether with shadows,' or as I have put it in in my translation in appendix C, 'interweaves his shadowy form into the innards of the ether', understanding that the identity of the 'hidden' god, Hades (ἀιδῆ, Julian 136a, playing on the etymology) is implicit in the sudden 'shadowy' identity of Jupiter.

The darkness of Zeus here is in contrast to Avienus' earlier emphasis on *aether* at the outset of his proem (*aethram*, 2; *aethera*, 4). *Aether* in Julian is the cohesive force of the universe (*HH* 139c–d):

οὐχὶ καὶ περὶ τὸν οὐρανὸν φαίνεται κύκλῳ πορευομένη τοῦ πέμπου σώματος οὐσία, ἣ πάντα συνέχει τὰ μέρη καὶ σφίγγει πρὸς αὐτὰ συνέχουσα τὸ φύσει σκεδαστὸν αὐτῶν καὶ ἀπορρέον ἀπ' ἀλλήλων;

'Again is there not visible in the heavens also, travelling in its orbit, the nature of the fifth substance, which links and compresses together all the parts, holding together things that by nature are prone to scatter and to fall away from one another?'

This is the equivalent, visible in the sensory world through the motion of the heavens, to the ordering force in the intelligible world (139c). Helios binds these two ordering or cohesive forces into one (*HH* 139d): δύο δὴ ταύτας τὰς οὐσίας συνοχῆς αἰτίας, τὴν μὲν ἐν τοῖς νοητοῖς, τὴν δὲ ἐν τοῖς αἰσθητοῖς φαινομένην ὁ βασιλεὺς Ἥλιος εἰς ταὐτὸ συνάπτει . . . ('These existences, therefore, which are two causes of connection, one in the intelligible world, while the other appears in the world of sense-perception, King Helios combines into one . . .'). Thus Jupiter-Helios in Avienus 'reveals' (*reserat*, line 2) the *aether* to men, and through his agency Avienus is able to expound it (line 4).[73] Thus also in line 10–11 he is *materiaeque gravis concretio* and *sucus ab alto corporibus caelo*. The latter can be explained by Julian 140a, where the rays descend to all things in the visible world from the primary creative substance: ἀφ' ἧς κάτεισιν οὐσίας πρωτουργοῦ εἰς τὸν ἐμφανῆ κόσμον ἡ περιλάμπουσα τὰ σύμπαντα αὐγή; ('. . . from that primary creative substance do not the rays of his light, illuminating all things, descend to the visible world?'). Perhaps, then, Avienus' *perpes substantia lucis* is not so much 'the eternal substance of light', but 'the eternal substance *in the form of light*'.

Again, much of Avienus' excess verbiage makes sense when read through Julian. Consider the concepts discussed above, Jupiter as *nodus* and Jupiter as *discretio*, both a linking and a dividing force. We find these concepts in close proximity in Julian *HH* 141a: οὐχ οὗτός ἐστι τῆς διακρίσεως τῶν εἰδῶν καὶ συγκρίσεως τῆς ὕλης αἴτιος; ('Is not he the cause of the *separation* of the forms, and of the *combination* of matter?'). Like Avienus' Jupiter, who is *rerum opifex* (line 28), so through his unifying powers Julian's Helios is τὴν δημιουργικὴν . . . διάκρισιν τῆς ποιήσεως, 'the master workman . . . who gives an individual existence to everything that is created' (*HH* 141a). One manifestation of Helios' unifying power in Julian is that he binds together extremes, especially the elements (*HH* 143c–d), as in Avienus line 24, *hic dispersa locis statuit primordia iustis*. Julian explicitly states that this coincides with the creative power of Zeus (συντρέχει δὲ αὐτῷ καὶ ἡ τοῦ Διὸς δημιουργικὴ δύναμις, *HH* 143d), and Zeus and Helios have equal sway over that intellectual creation which preceded the visible creation (τῆς φανερᾶς . . . δημιουργίας, *HH* 144b).

We noted above the Platonic/Neoplatonic background to Avienus' expression *anni pulcher chorus* in line 37. In *HH* 146c–d, the metaphor continues, of the 'dance' of the planets around Helios: οἵ τε γὰρ πλάνητες εὔδηλον ὅτι περὶ αὐτὸν χορεύοντες μέτρον ἔχουσι τῆς κινήσεως τὴν πρὸς τὸν θεὸν τόνδε τοιάνδε περὶ τὰ σχήματα συμφωνίαν . . . ('For it is evident that the planets, as they dance in a circle about him, preserve as the measure of their motion a harmony between this god and their own movements . . .'). Likewise in Avienus line 9, Jupiter is the *numerus caelesti modulaminis*, the measure of the celestial harmony. Moreover, Helios in Julian causes the seasons (*HH* 147d): τὰς τροπὰς ἐργαζόμενος . . . πατὴρ ὡρῶν ἐστιν ('Since he causes the winter and summer solstice . . . Helios is the father of the seasons'). The theme of the seasons is developed by Avienus in the *anni pulcher chorus* passage, *Ph.* 36–40.[74]

At *HH* 152b–c, Julian cites Plato to justify the study of astronomy:

> οὐρανόν φησι Πλάτων ἡμῖν γενέσθαι σοφίας διδάσκαλον. ἐνθένδε γὰρ ἀριθμοῦ[75] κατενοήσαμεν φύσιν, ἧς τὸ διαφέρον οὐκ ἄλλως ἢ διὰ τῆς ἡλίου περιόδου κατενοήσαμεν. φησί τοι καὶ αὐτὸς Πλάτων ἡμέραν καὶ νύκτα πρότερον.[76] εἶτα ἐκ τοῦ φωτὸς τῆς σελήνης, ὃ δὴ δίδοται τῇ θεῷ ταύτῃ παρ᾽ ἡλίου, μετὰ τοῦτο προήλθομεν ἐπὶ πλέον τῆς τοιαύτης συνέσεως, ἁπανταχοῦ τῆς πρὸς τὸν θεὸν τοῦτον στοχαζόμενοι συμφωνίας.

'Plato says that the sky is our instructor in wisdom. For from its contemplation we have learned to know the nature of number, whose distinguishing characteristics we know only from the course of the sun. Plato himself says that day and night were created first [*Tim.* 39b, 47a]. And next, from observing the moon's light, which was bestowed on the goddess by Helios, we later progressed still further in the understanding of these matters: in every case conjecturing the harmony of all things with this god.'

Julian probably has *Republic* 7 in mind (see above, Introduction pp. 10–11 for the passage). Julian uses the same term, συμφωνία, in *HH* 148b, where he discusses the role of astronomers as οἱ . . . ὑποτίθενται τὸ πιθανὸν ἐκ τῆς πρὸς τὰ φαινόμενα συμφωνίας ('[Astronomers] make plausible hypotheses from the harmony that they observe in the visible spheres'). Plato provides a clear starting point for this idea at *Rep.* 529a1–2: [ἀστρονομία] ἀναγκάζει ψυχὴν εἰς τὸ ἄνω ὁρᾶν καὶ ἀπὸ τῶν ἐνθένδε ἐκεῖσε ἄγει ('[astronomy] compels the mind to look upwards and leads it from the earth to the heavens,' trans. Lee 2007). Plato then goes on to reposition astronomy, i.e., the study of visible things, as a way into the study of the abstract: we must regard the stars, which are essentially decorative, as the best and most accurate of material things, although they fall short of the abstract truth (*Rep.* 529c7–d2: for the passage, see above, Introduction p. 10). We must therefore use these patterns as an adjunct to the study of invisible reality, just as one would diagrams drawn by Daedalus or some other craftsman (δημιουργοῦ, *Rep.* 529d9). The heavenly craftsman (τῷ τοῦ οὐρανοῦ δημιουργῷ, *Rep.* 530a7) made these things in the best way given the limitations of the material, but we cannot assume that phenomena such as the proportion of day and night (τὴν δὲ νύκτος πρὸς ἡμέραν ξυμμετρίαν, *Rep.* 530a8) remain constant in the material world.

If this is indeed the passage of Plato which Julian is referencing at *HH* 152c, then it reinforces his message. In the wider context of Plato's *Republic*, the sun was the first instructor in the true astronomy, leading us to look at the heavenly bodies, as the most prominent among them, which in turn leads to the study of true astronomy. In Julian too, there are two parallel universes, one perceptible, one intelligible only; for Julian, the sun becomes the mediator between the two. The sun in Neoplatonism allows men to intuit intelligible ideas by seeing their visible manifestation ('*phainomena*') on earth.[77]

Behind this must lie also Plato *Rep.* 517b, the conclusion to the Myth of the Cave: we must liken the perceptible world (τὴν μὲν δι᾽ ὄψεως <u>φαινομένην</u> ἕδραν, 'the realm revealed by sight,' *Rep.* 517b1–2, trans. Lee) to the prison and the light of the fire in it to the sun. The ascent from the prison in the myth represents the soul's ascent from the perceptible to the intelligible worlds. We have discussed in the Introduction the meaning of *Rep.* 517b7–c1, τὰ δ᾽ οὖν ἐμοὶ <u>φαινόμενα</u> οὕτω <u>φαίνεται</u>, ἐν τῷ γνωστῷ τελευταία ἡ τοῦ ἀγαθοῦ ἰδέα καὶ μόγις ὁρᾶσθαι ('But in my opinion, for what it is worth, the final thing to be perceived in the intelligible region, and perceived only with difficulty, is the form of the good' trans. Lee). *Phainomena* here, as we've seen, refers to *myth*; it cannot be by chance, however, that the myth is one which deals with what is 'perceptible' or apparent (*phainomena*) as a way into the intelligible.

Julian uses the theme of '*phainomena*' throughout his *Hymn*, ringing changes on the verb φαίνομαι and its parts.[78] But it is clear that there is a shift in the meaning of '*phainomena*' involved here, and exploration of the importance of the theme to Julian can tell us why Aratus was important in the fourth century and why Avienus chose this text. The salient passage is *HH* 140b, where Julian speaks of the generative powers in the intelligible and perceptible worlds, and of Helios' position between them: πρόδηλον οὖν ὅτι καὶ τὸ γόνιμον τοῦ βασιλέως Ἡλίου τῆς ζωῆς μέσον ἐστὶν ἀμφοῖν, ἐπεὶ τούτῳ μαρτυρεῖ καὶ τὰ φαινόμενα ('It is therefore evident that the life-generating power of King Helios also is midway between both the worlds: and the phenomena of our world also bear witness to this').

This is the importance of *phainomena*: that they *'bear witness to'* (μαρτυρεῖ) the whole cosmic superstructure. If we read Avienus' proem against the backdrop of this Neoplatonic text, then Avienus' motivation for translating the *Phaenomena* of Aratus in the fourth century is immediately clear. This text provides the ideal vehicle for the study of the visible world, in the form of the most perfect part of it (according to Plato, above), the *'phainomena'* themselves, the heavenly bodies, as Julian himself describes them, τοῖς κατ' οὐρανὸν φαινομένοις, at *HH* 139d. Only once we have perfected this can we as potential initiates 'see' the truth and get an inkling of the intelligible world which is our final goal in understanding. Aratus has become an essential tool in this process, and has been coopted into this fourth-century pattern of thought. Aratus' *Phaenomena*, which emphasizes the underlying principles of order in the celestial realm, is a prime candidate for annexation in the Neoplatonic argument for *phainomena* as sensory evidence for the intelligible world.

The essential thing which has emerged from the foregoing analysis is that Avienus' proem can be read as a *Neoplatonic* reinterpretation of Aratus. Aratus' Zeus is now Zeus-Helios, sharing characteristics with the sun. The reader realizes, studying Avienus and the *HH* side-by-side, that the former even tracks the latter in the sequence of ideas. The influence of Neoplatonic modes of thought and expression, as manifest in the *HH*—even perhaps the direct influence of the *HH*, although the priority of the *HH* over the *Ph.* is unprovable in purely chronological terms— helps to explain the striking differences between Avienus' *Phaenomena* and its source-text.

6.2.5 PANEGYRIC

The chameleon nature of Avienus' *Phaenomena*, manifest most directly in the extraordinary proliferation of Jupiter's titles, fits its identity as a product of the fourth century. While it partakes of the multiplicity of tradition available to that century, it cunningly evades its crises. Avienus does not explicitly follow Germanicus into the quicksands of imperial panegyric: he does not go down Germanicus' road of the substitution of the Roman emperor for Jupiter in his translation of Aratus' proem.[79] If imperial panegyric exists in his proem, it is, as we shall see, substrate. Although Avienus does not shun politically inflected terms such as *dux, augur,* and *imperium* in his description of Zeus, he nowhere explicitly links these with Rome. Instead of situating power within the Roman Empire and in the person of its emperor, as Germanicus had done, he ostensibly returns more closely to the original context of Aratus, with its opening praise of the providential deity. Avienus' evasiveness about the identity of power is astute, and ensures the literary validity and survival of his work in all fourth-century contexts.

Yet, there is, inevitably, a level of 'intertextual panegyric'[80] involved already, in Avienus' proximity to Julian. Julian describes his *Hymn to King Helios* as a 'panegyric', ἐγκώμια, *HH* 132b. On the primary level, of course, it is a panegyric of a god. But he is a god with characteristics in common with an ideal earthly ruler. In Julian, Helios enjoys a military-style leadership over the intelligible gods (*HH* 133c): ἄρχειν καὶ βασιλεύειν αὐτῶν ὑπὸ τἀγαθοῦ τεταγμένος ('he has been appointed by the Good to rule and govern them'). In Avienus *Ph.* 2–4, military terminology is likewise prominent. The praise of the god in these terms comes in a self-confessed 'panegyric'; it is a theme shared with panegyric of Roman emperors, not least with Julian's own panegyrics. Here we have the crossover point between theology and encomium, a way of reading along the fault line between divine and human kingship. The identification between the Flavian rulers and Zeus-Helios helps.[81]

The Emperor Julian performed in both genres, as he quips at *Or.* 2.69c, his panegyric of Constantius: ἐπαίνους ἅμα καὶ δόγματα ᾄδειν ('In the same breath [to] utter panegyric and philosophical theories,' trans. Wright 1980).[82] If his *HH* has a self-confessed touch of panegyric, his imperial panegyrics are heavily theological, assimilating the role of the emperor to the god of fourth-century Neoplatonism.[83] For instance, in his panegyric of Constantius (*Or.* 2.69d–70d, especially 70c) there is an emphasis on the special recognition by a king of the human affinity with god. In fact, at *Or* 2.90a there is already an analogy between the king and Zeus as δημιουργός. It is a short step from here to the assimilation of the emperor *with* god, as seen in the *Panegyrici Latini*.[84]

The *Panegyrici Latini* also negotiate around the concept of *deus*, as much as any theology of the period does, but they do it specifically in connection with the emperor, giving a fuller, political, syncretism. In Julian's *HH* we had the equation Zeus = Helios. In the *PanLat*, we now have the further equation Zeus = Helios = Emperor. The connection between Zeus (Jupiter) and the emperor was already established in the Augustan period; but also by now the emperors of the 'second Flavian dynasty' saw themselves as proxies of Helios, who was identified, as we have seen, with Zeus, in the syncretistic theology of the fourth century.[85]

Avienus can be situated within this political-theological nexus. He opens his proem with a complex of Roman imperial terminology: *imperator* (2, 4), *dux* (2, 41), *auctor* (20). From the outset he is extolling Jupiter in the language of imperial panegyric. There is nothing in Aratus to parallel the expropriation of political terminology to describe Zeus, who is addressed only as πάτερ, line 15.[86] The Aratean scholia give us a clue to a panegyrical interpretation of Aratus' proem, adding the language of kingship to the Aratean Zeus, who is βασιλεὺς δὲ τῶν ὅλων ὁ Ζεὺς καὶ πατήρ.[87] The analogy here between Zeus and the king links the human and divine spheres.[88] But there are more specific instances of commonality between Avienus and the *panegyric* genre, and here the similarity extends to correspondences in terminology. Consider, for example, Avienus' description of Zeus in *Ph.* 12–21 alongside *PanLat* 11.3.2–4, a passage from the 'Genethliacus' (Birthday Oration) for Maximian, delivered in 290–1 AD (shared terminology is underlined):

> qui discurrente meatu
> molis primigenae penetralia dura resolvens
> implevit largo venas operatus amore,
> ordinis ut proprii foedus daret. iste calorem
> quo digesta capax solidaret semina mundus

inseruit. rite hunc primum, medium atque secundum
vox secreta canit: sibi nam permixtus utrimque
et fultus sese geminum latus, unus et idem est
<u>auctor agendorum</u> propriique patrator amoris
et mundi vere sanctus <u>pater</u>.

'Dissolving the solid inner parts of the primeval mass by running through it on his path, he filled its interstices, acting upon them with widespread love, to confer the treaty of foreordained order. He himself instilled the heat by means of which the world, full of potential, might amass the disjunct seeds of things. It is right that the awed voice sings him first, middle, and following. For combining with himself on one side and the other, and supporting himself on both flanks, one and the same he is the instigator of things to be done, and the accomplisher of his own love, indeed the holy father of the universe.'

profecto enim non patitur hoc caelestis ille vestri generis conditor vel <u>parens</u>.[89] nam primum omnium, quidquid immortale est stare nescit, sempiternoque motu se servat aeternitas. deinde praecipue vestri illi parentes, qui vobis et nomina et imperia tribuerunt, perpetuis maximorum operum <u>actionibus</u> occupantur. ille siquidem Diocletiani <u>auctor</u>[90] deus praeter depulsos quondam caeli possessione Titanas et mox biformium bella monstrorum perpeti[91] cura quamvis compositum gubernat imperium,[92] atque hanc tantam <u>molem</u> infatigabili manu volvit, omniumque rerum ordines ac vices pervigil servat.

'He assuredly would not allow it: I mean that heavenly founder, or parent, of your family. Now first of all, what is immortal does not know how to stand still, and eternity preserves itself by ceaseless motion. Second, those parents of yours, who have given you both name and empire, are chiefly employed in the perpetual performance of tasks of the highest importance. Indeed that god, Diocletian's ancestor, besides having expelled the Titans once from their occupation of heaven and having engaged in war soon afterward against the two-formed monsters, governs with uninterrupted care his realm, peaceful though it is, and revolves this enormous mass with tireless hand, and ever watchful preserves the arrangement and succession of all things.'[93]

The *caelestis ille vestri generis conditor vel parens* is Jupiter.[94] Note how the author of the panegyric paraphrases Plato here. With *nam primum omnium, quidquid immortale est stare nescit, sempiternoque motu se servat aeternitas,* the author of the *Panegyric of Maximian* is translating Plato *Phdr.* 245c5, τὸ γὰρ ἀεικίνητον ἀθάνατον ('that which is ever-moving is immortal'), as Cicero had already done in the *Somnium Scipionis,* the blueprint for the idea of Roman cosmic statesmanship, at *SS* 27: *nam quod semper movetur, aeternum est.* His Jupiter is both the inheritance of Maximian's *gens,* and the god of the *Phaedrus,* nicely collapsing the boundaries of the imperial and universal.

Avienus refers to the god in line 23 as *ipse parens rerum*. The author of the *Genethliacus* draws an immediate parallel between Maximian's *parentes* and the god (*parens*): the latter does not remain still, nor do the former cease from *actiones*. Jupiter is described as *ille siquidem Diocletiani auctor deus*. *Actionibus* and *auctor* are parallel to Avienus' *auctor agendorum*, 'the instigator of things to be done,' line 20. Jupiter performs in the cosmic sphere what the imperial dynasty performs in the earthly sphere. Indeed, Jupiter himself acts in the panegyric, as in Avienus, within the terminology of Roman power (*imperium*). His 'imperial' role is to set the world (*molem*) spinning on its axis; likewise in line 13 Avienus' Jupiter loosens the strictures of the *moles primigena* ('primeval mass'). Jupiter-Helios is the mediator between the celestial (*caelestis*) and earthly spheres, the latter in his manifestation as emperor. These parallels help us to see how Avienus' imperial terminology is integrated into his theology.

Our example here, the *Genethliacus* of Maximian, comes about 100 years before Avienus; one might, therefore, be sceptical of the relationship. But the *PanLat* are consistent in terms of their discourse; the earlier works set the tone for the fourth century, and Avienus could well have been aware of this idiom. Closer to Avienus in date, the supreme god in *Panegyric* 12 (written in 312 AD, the year of Constantine's conversion) is *quisnam deus* (12.2.4), the *divina mens* (12.2.5; 16.2; 26.1), the *divinum numen* (12.4.1), *deus ille mundi creator et dominus* (12.13.2), and *summus rerum sator* (12.26.1).[95] Constantine mirrors the characteristics of the god. Compare to the passage of the *Genethliacus* we have just looked at, the following passage of *PanLat* 12 (22.1–2): *quae divinitas perpetuo vigens motu? omnium rerum intervalla sunt: cessat terra novalibus, dicuntur interdum flumina resistere, sol ipse noctibus adquiescit. tu, Constantine, solus infatigabilis bellis bella continuas . . .* ('What is this divinity thriving on perpetual motion? All things have interruptions: the earth rests in fallow lands, rivers are said to stand still now and then, the sun itself reposes at night. You alone, Constantine, tirelessly follow one war with another. . .'). Here the emperor is referred to as *divinitas* and compared with a triad of examples from nature, culminating with *sol*. His level of activity as a *divinitas* is greater even than that of his patron deity. He is constantly in motion. Compare Avienus' designation of Jupiter in lines 5–6 as *iste paterni /principium motus*.

Constantine has a privileged position in respect of divinity: that of direct mediator of its 'mysteries' (*PanLat* 12.2.5): *habes profecto aliquod cum illa mente divina, Constantine, secretum, quae delegata nostri diis minoribus cura uni se tibi dignatur ostendere* ('You must share some secret with that divine mind, Constantine, which has delegated care of us to lesser gods and deigns to reveal itself to you alone'). In Neoplatonic terms, Constantine takes on the role of the sun in the hierarchy of the universe. Note here the discourse of the mysteries, used in the description of the supreme power by both Firmicus and Avienus. At 12.5.5 Constantine himself is a present divinity (*tuo praesenti numini*).[96] At 12.13.2 he is actively compared, as the bringer of a sort of divine judgement, with Jupiter as controller of signs from heaven: *ut deus ille mundi creator et dominus eodem fulmine*[97] *suo nunc tristes nunc*

*laetos nuntios mittit, ita eadem sub numine tuo tela inimicos aut supplices tuos perni-
cie aut conservatione discernunt* ('As that god, creator and master of the world,
sends messages now sad, now glad, with his same thunderbolt, so the same shafts
under your divine power distinguish between your enemies or petitioners by destruction or preservation').[98]

The panegyrist ends with a prayer to the supreme deity to preserve his lookalike,
Constantine (*PanLat* 12.26.1):

> quamobrem te, summe rerum sator, cuius tot nomina sunt quot gentium lin-
> guas esse voluisti (quem enim te ipse dici velis, scire non possumus), sive tute
> quaedam vis mensque divina es, quae toto infusa mundo omnibus miscearis
> elementis, et sine ullo extrinsecus accedente vigoris impulsu per te ipse move-
> aris, sive aliqua supra omne caelum potestas es quae hoc opus tuum ex altiore
> Naturae arce despicias . . .

> 'For this reason, you, supreme creator of things, whose names you wished to
> be as many as the tongues of the nations (for what you yourself wish to be
> called we cannot know), whether you are some kind of force and divine mind
> spread over the whole world and mingled with all the elements and move of
> your own accord without the influence of any outside force acting upon you,
> or whether you are some power above all heaven which look down upon this
> work of yours from a higher pinnacle of Nature . . .'

This can be compared both to Firmicus' fifth prologue, studied in section 6.2.2
above, and to Avienus. In particular, the system of self-consciously piling up names
and titles (*tot nomina sunt quot gentium lingua*), often as alternatives, helps us to
explain the myriad titles given to Jupiter by Avienus. Avienus' *ipse parens rerum* (line
23) and his agricultural imagery following line 36, *nec defit genitis pater ullo in tempore rebus*, evoke Jupiter as the *summe rerum sator* of the panegyric; Avienus uses
vis in line 6 and *potestas* in line 29. *hoc opus tuum* in the panegyric must refer to the
earth, the *extremum opus* of Jupiter in Avienus 32. The concept of the god as running through everything (*mensque divina es, quae toto infusa mundo omnibus mis-
cearis elementis*) is found in Avienus 12 (*discurrente meatu*) and 44–5, *tenebris hic
interlabitur aethrae /viscera et aeternos animat genitalibus artus.*

Praise of the universal god has a place in imperial panegyric of the fourth century because of the likeness between emperor and god. Avienus speaks the same
language. In his translation of the *Ph.*, Aratus' proem is shot through with imperial
panegyric. Panegyric and theology meet in Avienus precisely because the Aratean
tradition is a perfect vehicle for both.

Mamertinus' Panegyric of Julian[99]

Julian's apparent concern to integrate panegyric with theology, which we have seen
above, perhaps has some bearing on the fact that his own appearance as an addressee in the corpus of *Panegyrici Latini* (no. 3) is signalled by a literary equipage

different from that of the other emperors in the corpus, containing explicitly theological, not to say 'Aratean', material. Expressly, the golden-age imagery in Mamertinus' panegyric of Julian stands out, and also ties back into the Aratean tradition itself.

The panegyric is a *gratiarum actio* to Julian delivered in 362. It may therefore be exactly contemporary with Avienus' *Phaenomena*, and with the *HH*.[100] It contains material specific to Julian's role as restorer of pagan philosophy: 'Mamertinus' remark that Julian has restored philosophy to its proper position in the state counts not only as a commonplace element of the *laus principis* but as an oblique announcement of a pagan programme.'[101] Importantly for us, given what we have seen in chapters 1 and 2, is that the imagery of the *Golden Age*, with its Aratean associations, is here coupled with (a) imperial praise and (b) the projected restitution of a pagan monotheism consonant with the Neoplatonism we have seen in Julian's own *Hymn*. For us, it is both a sequel to the Aratean material studied in earlier chapters, and a justification of the place of the Aratean tradition among the key concerns— panegyrical, theological, antiquarian—of the fourth century, and therefore of Avienus' choice to work with Aratus' text.

The section on Julian's restoration of (pagan) philosophy is of greatest interest for us. Mamertinus begins the lead-in with an agricultural analogy, *ecquis deus uno in anno multiplices fructus agro uni dedit*? ('Has any god in one year given multiple harvests to one meadow?' *PanLat* 3.22.1). Julian here is assimilated to Jupiter as bringer of seasons (compare Jupiter in Avienus 36–40).[102]

In 23.1, we have a golden-age tableau beginning with a reference to the Isles of the Blest:

> habitari ab iustis viris in Oceano terras ferunt quas Fortunatorum insulas vocant, quod per eos non arato solo frumenta nascuntur, fortuitis vitibus iuga collium vestiuntur, sponte pomis arbor gravatur, ad herbarum vicem olus vulgo est. quantula ista sunt, si deum auctorem consideres, munera!

> 'They say that just men inhabit lands in the Ocean which they call the Isles of the Blest, because throughout them grain grows from unplowed soil, mountain ridges are covered with vines growing by chance, of their own [accord] trees are laden with fruits, instead of grass there are vegetables all over. How paltry these gifts are, if you consider that god is their author!'

Ferunt is a signifier of the literary tradition, in this case again the tradition of the Myth of the Races in Hesiod, *Works and Days*.[103] The reference comes in the description of the afterlife of the heroic race, at *WD* 167–73:

τοῖς δὲ δίχ' ἀνθρώπων βίοτον καὶ ἤθε' ὀπάσσας
Ζεὺς Κρονίδης κατένασσε πατὴρ ἐς πείρατα γαίης,
καὶ τοὶ μὲν ναίουσιν ἀκηδέα θυμὸν ἔχοντες
ἐν μακάρων νήσοισι παρ' Ὠκεανὸν βαθυδίνην·

ὄλβιοι ἥρωες, τοῖσιν μελιηδέα καρπὸν
τρὶς ἔτεος θάλλοντα φέρει ζείδωρος ἄρουρα.

'. . . but upon others Zeus the father, Cronus' son, bestowed life and habita-
tions far from human beings and settled them at the limits of the earth; and
these dwell with a spirit free of care on the Islands of the Blessed beside deep-
eddying Ocean—happy heroes, for whom the grain-giving field bears honey-
sweet fruit flourishing three times a year' (Most).

We recall also how this is linked to the *Dike* passage a little later in Hesiod, in which
the earth identically bears fruit for just men in line 237, . . . καρπὸν δὲ φέρει
ζείδωρος ἄρουρα.[104]

This reference in the panegyric of Julian is not, possibly, the only explicit reference in the *PanLat* to the Myth of Ages and its associated tradition.[105] But it may
well be significant that this reference is attached to Julian, in the context of his resurrection of philosophy. I contend that, in the context, we are supposed to think
both of Hesiod and of the Aratean sequel to the Hesiodic myth, the Myth of *Dike*
in the *Phaenomena*.[106] There is an implied comparison between Jupiter, who in Hesiod established the Isles of the Blessed as the postmortem habitation of the heroes
(*WD* 168), and the Emperor Julian. In Hesiod, the Isles of the Blessed were connected with both the Heroic Age and the Golden Age (see above, chapter 1, p. 24–5);
thus Mamertinus can justly say at 23.2, *quantula ista sunt, si deum auctorem consid-
eres, munera!* It is quite clear what age his audience is now in. Julian has introduced
a new Golden Age.

This is a Golden Age in which the study of astronomy in particular is restored.
Enthroned among the 'fruits' of Julian's reign is philosophy (23.4–5):

> tu extincta iam litterarum studia flammasti, tu Philosophiam paulo ante sus-
> pectam ac non solum spoliatam honoribus sed accusatam ac ream non modo
> iudicio liberasti, sed amictam purpura, auro gemmisque redimitam in regali
> solio conlocasti. suspicere iam in caelum licet et securis contemplari astra
> luminibus, qui paulo ante pronorum atque quadrupedum animantium ritu in
> humum uisus trepidos figebamus. quis enim spectare auderet ortum sideris,
> quis occasum? ne agricolae quidem, quorum opera ad motum signorum cae-
> lestium temperanda sunt, tempestatum praesagia rimabantur. ipsi nauitae,
> qui nocturnos cursus ad astra moderantur, stellarum nominibus abstinebant.
> prorsus terra marique non ratione caelesti, sed casu ac temere uiuebatur.

> 'You have rekindled the already extinguished study of letters, you have not
> only freed Philosophy from condemnation, which not long ago was suspect
> and not only despoiled of honors but accused and arraigned, but you have
> clothed it in purple and placed it, crowned with gold and gems, on the royal
> throne. Now we are permitted to look up to heaven and gaze upon the stars
> with untroubled eyes, we who not long ago fixed our trembling sights upon

the ground in the manner of stooping, four-legged beasts. For who dared to watch a constellation's rising, who dared to watch its setting? Not even farmers, whose works must be managed in accordance with the movement of heavenly signs, were examining presages of the seasons. Even sailors, who regulate their nocturnal courses by the constellations, refrained from naming the stars. In short, people lived on land and at sea not in accordance with heavenly science but haphazardly and at random.'

The chosen illustration of the reinstatement of philosophy is astronomy: *suspicere iam in caelum licet et securis contemplari astra luminibus*. . . . We remember Julian's own enthusiasm for the study of astronomy in the *HH*, and its Platonic hinterland. What the panegyrist says here accords with the emperor's own concerns. The panegyrist's phrasing may be taken from Germanicus' translation of Aratus, which celebrates the resurrection of astronomy under the *Pax Augusta* after the Roman civil wars (Germ. *Ph.* 11–14):

nunc vacat audacis ad caelum tollere vultus
sideraque et mundi varios cognoscere motus,
navita quid caveat, quid scitus vitet arator,
quando ratem ventis aut credat semina terris.

'At last there is an opportunity to lift one's gaze boldly to the sky and learn of the celestial bodies and their different movements in the heavens and discover what the sailor and the canny ploughman should avoid, when the sailor should entrust his ship to the winds and the ploughman his seed to the soil' (Gain).

What is more, Mamertinus takes us right into the tradition at stake in the study of astronomy. Consider the expression with which he ends his excursus on astronomy, *casu ac temere uiuebatur*: in the days before astronomy, 'people lived haphazardly and at random'. We recognize the expression from chapter 3 above. We remember that Cicero wrote *casu et temere* in *DND* 2.115. We recall also, as I argued in chapter 3, pp. 70–3, that this appeared to answer Lucretius 2.1060, *temere incassum frustraque*. Lucretius had just been discussing the stars in deceptively 'Stoic' terms (*DRN* 2.1030–9); he then goes on to describe the creation of the world, including the heavens (*caeli, DRN* 2.1059–62), as the work of chance, the interaction of particles which were 'feckless, vacant and without intent'. In this passage of the *DND*, as we've seen, Cicero answers Lucretius' *incassum* ('vacant') with *casu* ('by chance'); his assertion in the *DND* is that it is impossible to believe that the celestial artwork (*haec omnis descriptio siderum atque hic tantus caeli ornatus*) came about *casu ac temere*.

Involved in this exchange is a debate about the degree to which chance operates in the world. Mamertinus configures his astronomical passage to accord with the *Ciceronian* side of the debate, the operation of rationality in the universe. In Mamertinus, it is precisely the rediscovery of astronomy under Julian which means that men do not now live *casu ac temere*: they live in a Ciceronian/Aratean, rather than a Lucretian, universe.

We can now conjecture with reasonable certainty about Avienus' motivation in translating Aratus. The Golden Age of *PanLat* 3 is an age of astronomy: not only Hesiod, but also Aratus, is implicated. Aratus is the only text which contains both the Golden Age and astronomy. Aratus' is a text permeable to the key influences on fourth-century thought and literature, namely theology and panegyric. Strands which manifest themselves independently in the two different genres of theology and encomium are potentially united in this single text, Avienus' *Phaenomena*—a study of the stars as an adjunct to true understanding and an act of praise for the supreme ruler, both of heaven (Jupiter) and of earth (Julian).

Conclusion

We have reached a striking conclusion in our study of Avienus. Avienus' *Phaenomena* is less a translation of Aratus than we are led to think. Aratus is merely the starting point for an astronomical exegesis which was in tune with the times. Avienus' translation of Aratus reflected the emperor's own concerns, and was equally, though more subtly, a manifestation of praise for Julian, not a scholastic exercise but the rendering actual and contemporary for the fourth century of a fundametal text in the study of astronomy. Theology and panegyric are the two interpretative buttresses which support Avienus' reworking of Aratus. Together, they motivate Avienus' choice of source-text. But the choice of that text also has wider implications: Aratus' was a text which, over and over again, was coopted on the side of intelligent design. The emperor-as-god, through Aratus' text, also becomes the underpinning of the rational universe.

Epilogue

suspicere iam in caelum licet et securis contemplari astra luminibus

—(*Panegyrici Latini* 3.23.4)

Finally, consider the following passage, in the light of all we have seen so far:

> in medio uero omnium residet Sol. quis enim in hoc pulcherimo templo lampadem hanc in alio uel meliori loco poneret, quam unde totum simul possit illuminare? siquidem non inepte quidam lucernam mundi, alii mentem, alii rectorem uocant. Trimegistus uisibilem Deum, Sophoclis Electra intuentem omnia. ita profecto tanquam in solio regali Sol residens circumagentem gubernat Astrorum familiam. tellus quoque minime fraudatur lunari ministerio, sed ut Aristoteles de animalibus ait, maximam luna cum terra cognationem habet. concipit interea a sole terra, et impregnatur annuo partu. inuenimus igitur sub hac ordinatione admirandam mundi symmetriam, ac certum harmoniae nexum motus et magnitudinis orbium: qualis alio modo reperiri non potest.

> 'At rest, however, in the middle of everything is the sun. For in this most beautiful temple, who would place this lamp in another or better position than that from which it can light up the whole thing at the same time? For, the sun is not inappropriately called by some people the lantern of the universe, its mind by others, and its ruler by still others. [Hermes] the Thrice Greatest labels it a visible god, and Sophocles' Electra, the all-seeing. Thus indeed, as though seated on a royal throne, the sun governs the family of planets revolving around it. Moreover, the earth is not deprived of the moon's attendance. On the contrary, as Aristotle says in a work on animals, the moon has the closest kinship with the earth. Meanwhile the earth has intercourse with the sun, and is impregnated for its yearly parturition. In this arrangement, therefore, we discover a marvelous symmetry of the universe, and an established harmonious linkage between the motion of the spheres and their size, such as can be found in no other way' (trans. Rosen and Dobrzycki 1978).

For the moment I am going to tease the reader as to the identity of the author. While you are waiting, you will immediately see that the passage finds a close parallel in a text explored in the final chapter of this book, the Emperor Julian's *Hymn to King Helios* (*HH* 135a-b):

… ᾧ [Ἡλίῳ] πᾶς μὲν ὑπείκει χορὸς ἀστέρων, ἕπεται δὲ ἡ γένεσις ὑπὸ τῆς τούτου κυβερνωμένη προμηθείας; οἱ μὲν γὰρ πλάνητες ὅτι περὶ αὐτὸν ὥσπερ βασιλέα χορεύοντες ἔν τισιν ὡρισμένοις πρὸς αὐτὸν διαστήμασιν ἁρμοδιώτατα φέρονται κύκλῳ, στηριγμούς τινας ποιούμενοι καὶ πρόσω καὶ ὀπίσω πορείαν, ὡς οἱ τῆς σφαιρικῆς ἐπιστήμονες θεωρίας ὀνομάζουσι τὰ περὶ αὐτοὺς φαινόμενα, καὶ ὡς τὸ τῆς σελήνης αὔξεται καὶ λήγει φῶς, πρὸς τὴν ἀπόστασιν ἡλίου πάσχον, πᾶσί που δῆλον.

'… to [the sun] the whole band of the heavenly bodies yields place, and [him] all generated things follow, piloted by his providence? For that the planets dance about him as their king, in certain intervals, fixed in relation to him, and revolve in a circle with perfect accord, making certain halts, and pursuing to and fro their orbit, as those who are learned in the study of the spheres call their visible motions; and that the light of the moon waxes and wanes varying in proportion to its distance from the sun is, I think, clear to all.'

The reader might also be familiar with the technique of exposition seen in the first passage, namely the agglomeration of ancient parallels. We find it in the Aratean scholia, exemplified by the following:

οἱ δὲ Δία τὸν ἥλιον νοήσαντες λέγουσιν ὅτι καὶ Σοφοκλῆς Δία τὸν ἥλιον καλεῖ λέγων (fr. 752 Pearson) "ἠέλιος οἰκτείρειέ με, / <ὃν> οἱ σοφοὶ λέγουσι γεννητὴν θεῶν / πατέρα <τε> πάντων", καὶ ἔννοιαν τῆς δόξης ταύτης φασὶν ἔχειν τὸν ποιητὴν ὅταν λέγῃ. (N 837) "ἠχὴ δ' ἀμφοτέρων ἵκετ' αἰθέρα καὶ Διὸς αὐγάς", καὶ τὸ "ἠέλιός θ', ὃς πάντ' ἐφορᾷς καὶ πάντ' ἐπακούεις" (Γ 277), παρό ἐστι "πάντα ἰδὼν Διὸς ὀφθαλμὸς καὶ πάντα νοήσας" (Hesiod Opp. 267).[1]

'Those who think that Zeus is the sun say that Sophocles also called Zeus the sun when he said "Let the sun pity me, whom learned men say is the father and begetter of all the gods", and they say that The Poet [i.e., Homer] was aware of this view when he said "And the sound on both sides reached the ether and the beams of Zeus", and likewise "Sun, you who see everything and hear everything" and moreover "The eye of Zeus which sees and perceives everything"' (my trans., omitting Martin's references to the ancient works).

Indeed, the listing of the identities of the sun in the first passage—*lucernam mundi, mentem, rectorem, uisibilem Deum intuentem omnia*—reminds us of the many identities of Jupiter (the Neoplatonic permutation of Aratus' Zeus) at the opening of Avienus' all-inclusive translation of Aratus, which was itself influenced by the Aratean scholia (*Ph.* 5–9):

> iste paterni
> principium motus, vis fulminis iste corusci,
> vita elementorum, mundi calor, aetheris ignis
> astrorumque vigor, perpes substantia lucis
> et numerus celsi modulaminis.

'He is the beginning of generative motion, he the power of the scintillating lightning bolt, the life-force of the elements, warmth of the world, strength of the ethereal fire and of the stars, the never-ending material of light, and the number of celestial harmony.'

Would you now be surprised to learn that our first passage is from Copernicus?[2] It is Copernicus' justification for the position of the sun in his new cosmology. This is where Avienus' Neoplatonic Aratus catches up with Copernicus' 'new' world view.[3] Aratus comes full circle. Copernicus writes in the idiom of the Neoplatonist hymn, which he shares with Julian and Avienus; and in the idiom of the Aratean scholia, which, like his contemporary Camerarius, he was probably reading in a composite edition such as the Aldus of 1499, and which contained Aratus' text, translations (including Avienus), and scholia.

These parallels may strike the reader as inapposite. We are accustomed, after all, to handle Copernicus with more reverence than our customary exegesis of classical texts would accord him. These parallels show him not as a great modernizer of science, but as the successor of Aratus and his interpreters. This line of descent far transcends the issue of 'translation'.

But, shared idiom aside, what about the break between Copernicus and 'ancient astronomy'? Perhaps, given all we have seen, it has been overstated, or read in reverse. Should we see antiquity as (sometimes) anticipating Copernicus, or Copernicus as following the lead given by antiquity? For instance, we might say that Julian, in the passage quoted, appears to *anticipate* Copernicus' heliocentric system. Of course there is a difference. In Julian, Helios is the middle *planet*, ἐν τοῖς πλαν ωμένοις μέσης 135c; in Copernicus, he is the middle of the *solar system*. But the difference may not be as great as it seems. In *HH* 148a he is not only the middle of the planets, but the middle of the 'three *kosmoi*' (τριῶν . . . τῶν κόσμων) or worlds of Neoplatonism. The sun in Julian is not just middle in location, but mediates between perceptible (illusory) and intelligible (true) worlds. I have argued that Avienus' translation of Aratus, exactly contemporary with Julian's Hymn, commutes Aratus' Zeus into the Zeus-Helios of Neoplatonism, and that, in Avienus as in Julian, the god performs a mediating role.

In fact, the physical location of the sun is immaterial to the Neoplatonist. It is the mediation between the perceptible and the abstract which is important, *not* whether the sun goes around the earth or the earth around the sun. For Julian, for Avienus—and for Lucretius, albeit coming from a different philosophical perspective—the geocentric universe was already irrelevant. Neoplatonism ultimately militates against any conception of a unitary and finite universe as much as Epicureanism did. Copernicus' closeness to these sources suggests the flexibility of the ancient systems.

This flexibility is best demonstrated, before Copernicus, in Aratus, whose text was receptive to all these different modalities of seeing the world. The shifting meanings of '*phainomena*' also give us a history of the text. Aratus' *Phaenomena* takes on different meanings throughout its history: it could be a vehicle for the intelligent design universe (in Cicero); a straw man in the argument against intelligent design (in Lucretius); or a gateway (in Avienus) for a greater journey into the abstraction of truth. The plasticity of Aratus' poem—its adaptability and receptivity to other elements—is its evolutionary survival strategy. The poem became a means of referring to a certain view of the world, but the world itself is evasive of capture.

APPENDIX } A

Text of Aratus' Δίκη Myth, and references to Hesiod

Ἀμφοτέροισι δὲ ποσσὶν ὕπο σκέπτοιο Βοώτεω
Παρθένον, ἥ ῥ᾽ ἐν χειρὶ φέρει Στάχυν αἰγλήεντα.
εἴτ᾽ οὖν Ἀστραίου κείνη γένος, ὅν ῥά τέ φασιν
ἄστρων ἀρχαῖον πατέρ᾽ ἔμμεναι, εἴτε τευ ἄλλου,
εὔκηλος φορέοιτο. λόγος γε μὲν ἐντρέχει ἄλλος   100
ἀνθρώποις, ὡς δῆθεν ἐπιχθονίη πάρος ἦεν,
ἤρχετο δ᾽ ἀνθρώπων κατεναντίη, οὐδέ ποτ᾽ ἀνδρῶν
οὐδέ ποτ᾽ ἀρχαίων ἠνήνατο φῦλα γυναικῶν,
ἀλλ᾽ ἀναμὶξ ἐκάθητο καὶ ἀθανάτη περ ἐοῦσα.
καί ἑ Δίκην καλέεσκον· ἀγειρομένη δὲ γέροντας   105
ἠέ που εἰν ἀγορῇ ἢ εὐρυχόρῳ ἐν ἀγυιῇ,
δημοτέρας ἤειδεν ἐπισπέρχουσα θέμιστας.
οὔπω λευγαλέου τότε νείκεος ἠπίσταντο
οὐδὲ διακρίσιος περιμεμφέος οὐδὲ κυδοιμοῦ,
αὔτως δ᾽ ἔζωον· χαλεπὴ δ᾽ ἀπέκειτο θάλασσα,   110
καὶ βίον οὔπω νῆες ἀπόπροθεν ἠγίνεσκον,
ἀλλὰ βόες καὶ ἄροτρα καὶ αὐτὴ πότνια λαῶν
μυρία πάντα παρεῖχε Δίκη, δώτειρα δικαίων.
τόφρ᾽ ἦν ὄφρ᾽ ἔτι γαῖα γένος χρύσειον ἔφερβεν.
ἀργυρέῳ δ᾽ ὀλίγη τε καὶ οὐκέτι πάμπαν ἑτοίμη   115
ὡμίλει, ποθέουσα παλαιῶν ἤθεα λαῶν.
ἀλλ᾽ ἔμπης ἔτι κεῖνο κατ᾽ ἀργύρεον γένος ἦεν,
ἤρχετο δ᾽ ἐξ ὀρέων ὑποδείελος ἠχηέντων
μουνάξ, οὐδέ τεῳ ἐπεμίσγετο μειλιχίοισιν,
ἀλλ᾽ ὁπότ᾽ ἀνθρώπων μεγάλας πλήσαιτο κολώνας,   120
ἠπείλει δήπειτα καθαπτομένη κακότητος,

185

οὐδ' ἔτ' ἔφη εἰσωπὸς ἐλεύσεσθαι καλέουσιν·
Ὀίην χρύσειοι πατέρες γενεὴν ἐλίποντο
χειροτέρην· ὑμεῖς δὲ κακώτερα τεξείεσθε.
καὶ δή που πόλεμοι, καὶ δὴ καὶ ἀνάρσιον αἷμα   125
ἔσσεται ἀνθρώποισι, κακῶν δ' ἐπικείσεται ἄλγος.'
ὣς εἰποῦσ' ὀρέων ἐπεμαίετο, τοὺς δ' ἄρα λαοὺς
εἰς αὐτὴν ἔτι πάντας ἐλίμπανε παπταίνοντας.
ἀλλ' ὅτε δὴ κἀκεῖνοι ἐτέθνασαν, οἱ δ' ἐγένοντο
χαλκείη γενεὴ προτέρων ὀλοώτεροι ἄνδρες,   130
οἳ πρῶτοι κακοεργὸν ἐχαλκεύσαντο μάχαιραν
εἰνοδίην, πρῶτοι δὲ βοῶν ἐπάσαντ' ἀροτήρων,
καὶ τότε μισήσασα Δίκη κείνων γένος ἀνδρῶν
ἔπταθ' ὑπουρανίη, ταύτην δ' ἄρα νάσσατο χώρην,
ᾗχί περ ἐννυχίη ἔτι φαίνεται ἀνθρώποισι   135
Παρθένος ἐγγὺς ἐοῦσα πολυσκέπτοιο Βοώτεω.

'Beneath the two feet of Bootes you can observe the Maiden, who carries in her hand the radiant Spica [Ear of Corn]. Whether she is the daughter of Astraeus, who, they say, was the original father of the stars, or of some other, [100] may her way be peaceful! There is, however, another tale current among men, that once she actually lived on earth, and came face to face with men, and did not ever spurn the tribes of ancient men and women, but sat in their midst although she was immortal. [105] And they called her Justice: gathering together the elders, either in the market-place on the broad highway, she urged them in prophetic tones to judgements for the good of the people. At that time they still had no knowledge of painful strife or quarrelsome conflict or noise of battle, [110] but lived just as they were; the dangerous sea was far from their thoughts, and as yet no ships brought them livelihood from afar, but oxen and ploughs and Justice herself, queen of the people and giver of civilized life, provided all their countless needs. That was as long as the earth still nurtured the golden age. [115] But with the silver she associated little, and now not at all willingly, as she longed for the ways of the earlier folk. But nevertheless she was still with this Silver Age too. She would emerge from the sounding mountains towards evening all alone, and not engage anyone in friendly conversation. [120] But filling the broad hillsides with people, she would then speak menacingly, rebuking them for their wickedness, and say she would never more come face to face with them, even if they called her: 'What an inferior generation your golden fathers have left! And you are likely to beget a still more evil progeny. [125] There will surely be wars, yes, and unnatural bloodshed among men, and suffering from their troubles will come upon them.' So saying she made for the mountains, and left the people all staring after her. But when these men also had died and there were born [130] the Bronze Age men, more destructive than their predecessors, who were the first to forge the criminal sword for murder on the highways, and the first to taste the flesh of ploughing oxen, then Justice, conceiving a hatred for the generation of these men, flew up to the sky and took up her abode in that place, [135] where she is still visible to men by night as the Maiden by conspicuous Bootes.' (Kidd)

(i) The Myth of Ages

Ph. 100 λόγος . . . ἄλλος *WD* 106 ἕτερόν . . . λόγον[1]

Ph. 101 ἐπιχθονίη *WD* 123 ἐπιχθόνιοι[2]

Ph. 110 ἔζωον = *WD* 112[3]

?*Ph.* 110 χαλεπὴ δ' ἀπέκειτο θάλασσα *WD* 151 μέλας δ' ἀπέκειτο σίδηρος[4]

Ph. 113 μυρία πάντα *WD* 116 ἐσθλὰ δὲ πάντα[5]

Ph. 114 γένος χρύσειον *WD* 109 χρύσεον . . . γένος[6]

Ph. 115 ἀργυρέῳ *WD* 128 ἀργύρεον, in the same *sedes*[7]

Ph. 117 ἀλλ' ἔμπης, with *WD* 179 ἀλλ' ἔμπης καὶ τοῖσι μεμείξεται ἐσθλὰ κακοῖσιν[8]

Ph. 123–4 γενεήν / . . . χειροτέρην *WD* 127 γένος . . . χειρότερον[9]

Ph. 125–6 πόλεμοι . . . κακῶν *WD* 161 πόλεμός τε κακός[10]

Ph. 126 κακῶν . . . ἄλγος, with *WD* 200, ἄλγεα λυγρά, and *WD* 201, κακοῦ . . . ἀλκή[11]

Ph. 129 ἀλλ' ὅτε δὴ κἀκεῖνοι ἐτέθνασαν *WD* 140 αὐτὰρ ἐπεὶ καὶ τοῦτο γένος κατὰ γαῖα κάλυψεν[12]

Ph. 130 χαλκείη γενεή *WD* 143–4 γένος . . . /χάλκειον[13]

Ph. 133 καὶ τότε = *WD* 197[14]

Ph. 135 φαίνεται ἀνθρώποισι, contrasted with *WD* 199, προλιπόντ' ἀ νθρώπους[15]

*Ph.*135–6 ἀνθροπώσι | Παρθένος *WD* 199–200 ἀνθρώπους | Αἰδὼς καὶ Νέμεσις

(ii) Dike

Ph. 97, Παρθένον, *WD* 256 ἥ δέ τε παρθένος ἐστὶ Δίκη[16]

Ph. 101 ἐπιχθονίη, *WD* 252 ἐπὶ χθονί

Ph. 104 ἀναμὶξ ἐκάθητο *WD* 259 πὰρ Διὶ πατρὶ καθεζομένη Κρονίωνι[17]

Ph. 108–9 οὔπω λευγαλέου τότε νείκεος ἠπίσταντο *WD* 228–9 οὐδέ ποτ' αὐτοῖς /ἀργαλέον πόλεμον[18]

Ph. 111 βίον = *WD* 232

Ph. 111 οὔπω νῆες . . . ἠγίνεσκον *WD* 236–7 οὐδ' ἐπὶ νηῶν /νίσονται[19]

Ph. 116 ἤθεα λαῶν = *WD* 222[20]

(iii) Prometheus

Ph. 101 ἐπιχθονίη *WD* 90 ἐπὶ χθονί

Ph. 113 δώτειρα δικαίων *WD* 57 δώσω κακόν

Ph. 126 κακῶν δ' ἐπικείσεται ἄλγος *WD* 57 δώσω κακόν (and *WD* 58, κακὸν ἀνφαγαπῶντες)[21]

(iv) Ploughing

Ph. 112 βόες ... ἄροτρα, *Ph.* 132 βοῶν ... ἀροτήρων *WD* 405 βοῦν τ᾽ ἀροτῆρα[22]

(v) *Theogony* proem

Ph. 107 θέμιστας *Th.* 85, in the same metrical *sedes*

Ph. 135 ἐννυχίη *Th.* 10 ἐννύχιαι of the Muses hymning Zeus[23]

Parallels Between Lucretius' *DRN*, and Cicero's *Aratea*

	Lucretius	Cicero, *Aratea*
DRN 1	**1.2** *caeli subter labentia signa*	*Arat.* fr. 3¹ *cetera labuntur celeri caelestia motu,* *cum caeloque simul noctesque diesque feruntur.* Cf. 226 *nam quae per bis sex signorum labier orbem*
	Note: On the Proem to *DRN* 1, see above, Ch. 4 pp. 82–6. For *labor* of celestial motion, see also *Arat.* 329 and 390; *DRN* 1.1003–4 *fulmina . . . llabentia*; 1.1034, *labentes aetheris ignes*; 5.712, *labitur ex alia signorum parte per orbem*, and 5.766, *perlabier orbem*; 6.334, *celeri volat impete labens.*	
	1.6 *nubila caeli* Cf. 1.278 *nubila caeli*; 5.466 *nubila caelum*; 6.214, *nubila caeli*	230 *nubila caeli*
	Note: There is an aggregation of parallels between Lucretius and this passage of the *Aratea*: L. also echoes *Arat.* 231, *vario motu*, at *DRN* 2.97.	
	1.9 *lumine caelum* Cf. 4.208 *lumina caelum* and 5.976, *lumina caelo*	113, 405, *Prog.* fr. 4.10 *lumina caeli*

(continued)

Lucretius	Cicero, Aratea
1.10 *nam simul ac*; cf. *DRN* 3.14	350 *nam simul ac*
1.22–3 *nec sine te quicquam dias in luminis oras* *exoritur*	379–80 *repente* *exoritur pandens inlustria lumina Virgo*
Note: *Exoritur* is enjambed and in the same *sedes* in both authors, and is followed by a strong caesura.	
1.35 *tereti cervice reposta*	*Arat.* fr. 9.5 *tereti cervice reflexam*
1.39 *suavis ex ore loquelas/funde*	*Prog.* fr. 3.9 *fundens e gutture cantus* *Prog.* fr. 4.2 *fundere voces* *Prog.* fr. 4.6 *ore querelas*
1.50 *quod superest*	177 *quod superest*
Note: The formula occurs in the same *sedes* in both authors. Note also *DRN* 5.261 *quod superest . . . flumina fontes* with *Arat.* 177 *quod superest . . . flumine fontes*. In this case the formula occurs in a four-fold collocation shared between Cicero and Lucretius. That L. has used this formula again there, in conjunction with another Ciceronian collocation from the same line, makes its presence at *DRN* 1.50 more likely.	
1.64 *caeli regionibus*	193 *caeli regione* 472 *caeli in regione*
1.68–9 *minitanti /murmure*	71 *minitanti murmure*
Note: Cf. Lucr. 1.276 *minaci murmure ventus*, with the line-end at *Arat.* 71; and 5.1193 *murmura magna minarum*.	

1.94 *donarat nomine regem* **1.95** *ad aras* **1.95** *tremebundus* **1.99** *mactatu maesta parentis*	212 *donavit nomine Graium* 213 *ad Aram* 88 *tremebundis aethera pinnis* 122 *tremebundus* *Arat.* fr. 31 *aspectum maesta parentis*
Note: there is an aggregation of Ciceronian reference in these lines of Lucretius. Is this significant for the mythical Iphigenia, being described at this point in the *DRN*?	
1.128 *solis lunaeque meatus* Cf. 5.76, 5.774	*Prog.* fr. 1.1 *luna means*
1.135 *morte obita quorum tellus amplectitur ossa* Cf. 4.734 (with note below) *quorum morte obita tellus amplectitur ossa* 5.34 *arboris amplexus stirpem*	116 *quorum stirpis tellus amplexa prehendit*
Note: See above, Ch. 4 pp. 96–8. Reference in Lucretius to Cicero's passage on the Dog Star, Sirius, seems consistently associated with (false) matters such as the afterlife. The phrase is used here of visions of the dead. Cf. 1.724, 3.1012 and 4.734 for a similar connection, also 5.34 *arboris amplexus stirpem*, of the serpent guarding the golden apples of the Hesperides (myth is also tantamount to impossibility in the Lucretian diatribe of Bk 5).	
1.142 *noctes . . . serenas*	104 *nocte serena*
1.144 *praepandere lumina* Cf. 5.657 *lumina pandit*	*Arat.* fr. 21 *lumina pandit* 380 *pandens . . . lumina* 452 *lumine pandit*

(*continued*)

Lucretius	Cicero, Aratea
1.154 *divino numine* 6.91 (=1.154) 4.1233 *divina . . . numina* (irony) 5.122 *divino a numine* (polemic)	305 *divino numine*
Note: philosophical opposition between C. and L.: *DRN* 1.154 is in a passage of anti-intelligent design polemic; the Ciceronian passage represents the apex of intelligent design, the layout of the celestial circles.	
1.170 *oras in luminis exit* Cf. 1.179 *effert in luminis ora*	113–4 *in lumina caeli lextulit*
1.187 *exorta repente*	*Arat.* fr. 18.1 *ferrea tum proles exorta repentest* 379–80 *repente lexoritur pandens inlustria lumina Virgo*
Note: For another parallel with Cicero's 'iron age' fragment (fr. 18), see *DRN* 5.1293. For an additional parallel with Cicero's Virgo, see 1.22–3 above.	
1.191 *grandescere* Cf. 2.1122, 1160 Cf. 2.296 *adaugescit*	*Prog.* fr. 5 *grandescere fetu* *Prog.* fr. 3.6 *adaugescit*
Note: *grandescere* is in the same *sedes* in L. and C. The parallel is further supported by the fact that, before the time of Columella, only Cicero and Lucretius use *grandescere* (*BTL*). For further Lucretian allusion to *Prog.* fr. 5, see below, 1.252–3.	
1.199–200 *natura . . . lnon potuit* **1.200** *pontum per vada* Cf. 6.716 *etesiae*	160–66 *natura . . . lnon potuit* *Arat.* fr. 23 *hoc modo radiantis etesiae in vada ponti*

Note: *DRN* 1.199–200 and *Arat.* 160–6 are both passages about demiurgic activity. For L.'s response to C.'s craftsman simile elsewhere, see *DRN* 5.76–81, and discussion in Ch. 3, pp. 70 and 78–80. *DRN* 1.200 may contain double allusion, in one case to a line L. can be shown to have followed elsewhere. The second allusion to C. by L. in line 200, *pontum per vada*, imitates the same passage, *Arat.* fr.23, which later gives rise to one of the most indisputable Ciceronian references anywhere in the *DRN*, namely *etesiae* (6.716), which only occurs in Cicero and Lucretius (*BTL*). Lucretius thus has *Arat.* fr. 23 in mind in both Book 1 and Book 6.	
1.252–3 *at nitidae surgunt fruges ramique virescunt arboribus, crescunt ipsae fetuque gravantur* Cf. 2.1122 *grandescere*	*Prog.* fr. 5 *iam vero semper viridis semperque gravata* *lentiscus, triplici solita grandescere fetu,* *ter fruges fundens tria tempora monstrat arandi.*
1.287 *validis cum viribus amnis* ?cf. 1.899, *validis . . . austris*	146 *magnis cum viribus amnem*
Note: Lucretius may well have had Cicero's passage on Eridanus in mind here. He has *magno* in the line preceding this, and so varies the Ciceronian expression *magnis cum viribus* to *validis cum viribus*, whilst nevertheless retaining a form of *magnus* in the same context. *validis . . . viribus* may be an Ennian collocation; cf. *Annales* 298 (ed. Skutsch 1985), . . . *viri validis . . . viribus luctant*. But cf. *Arat.* 67, *at validis aequor pulsabit viribus Auster*, with Lucr. 1.899, *validis . . . cogentibus Austris*. Although the collocation *validis . . . viribus* may be Ennian, the yoking of this with *Auster* is apparently Ciceronian: see also *Arat.* 195 *tum validis fugito devitans viribus Austrum*. This illustrates the potential problems of teasing out the Ennian from the Ciceronian in Lucretius' epic language.	
1.290 *venti . . . flamina*	198 *flamine ventus*
Note: Although this collocation looks too general to act as an index of debt, we might take it in aggregation with 1.287 (see note above).	

(*continued*)

Lucretius	Cicero, *Aratea*
1.351–3 *crescunt arbusta et fetus in tempore fundunt,* *quod cibus in totas usque ab radicibus imis* *per truncos ac per ramos diffunditur omnis.*	113–9 *hic ubi se pariter cum sole in lumina caeli* *extulit, haud patitur foliorum tegmine frustra* *suspensos animos arbusta ornata tenere.* *nam quorum stirpis tellus amplexa prehendit,* *haec augens anima vitali flamine mulcet;* *at quorum nequeunt radices findere terras,* *denudat foliis ramos et cortice truncos.*

Note: *DRN* 1.351–3 describes the dissemination of nourishment in trees as evidence for void; *Arat.* 113–9 the rising of Sirius, a passage L. demonstrably has in mind elsewhere. See discussion in Ch. 4 above.

Lucretius	Cicero, *Aratea*
1.357 *haud ulla . . . ratione*	32 *ratione sine ulla*
1.366 *at contra* cf. 1.570 and passim	475 *at contra*
1.388 *tempore totum*	69 *tempore toto*

Note: While it may seem too general to be promising, the collocation occurs in the same *sedes* in each author. The context may also be apt: in L. the expression is used of the gradual filling up of void, in C. of sailors setting out. It is typical of L. to speak of the primary particles in anthropomorphic terms.

Lucretius	Cicero, *Aratea*
1.402 *vestigia parva*	451 *vestigia parva*

Note: In C. the expression comes in a description of the disappearance of the constellation of the Centaur; in L. of the 'tiny traces', which alert us to the existence of void. The understanding of atoms is the proper alternative to star-gazing: L. borrows the terminology of the latter in his description of the former.

1.413 *de pectore fundet*	*Prog.* fr. 4.2–4 *cum clamore paratis inanis fundere voces* *absurdoque sono fontis et stagna cietis.* *saepe etiam pertriste canit de pectore carmen . . .*
1.432 *quod quasi*	*Arat.* fr. 16.2, *quod quasi*
1.663 *aestifer ignis . . . iacit* cf. *DRN* 1.724, 6.721.	111 *aestiferos validis erumpit flatibus ignes* (Sirius)
1.722–3 *minantur /murmura*	71 *minitanti murmure*
Note: See note on 1.68 above for further parallels with *Arat.* 71.	
1.724 *faucibus eruptos iterum vis ut vomat ignis*	111 *aestiferos validis erumpit flatibus ignes*
Note: The Ciceronian reference here is supported by the context: Lucretius has invoked Cicero just before this, with *minantur . . . murmura* at 1.722–3. For the shape of line 724, with its compound adjective, and its similitude to *Arat.* 111, cf. 3.1012, *Tartarus horriferos eructans faucibus aestus.* In both of these cases, reference to Cicero's Sirius coincides with the idea of the underworld. In Lucretius Sirius becomes an emblem of the impossible (for instance the underworld, nonexistent for the Epicurean).	
1.794 *quae . . . diximus ante*	120 *quos diximus ante*
Note: Merrill (1921) lists nine examples of similar expressions in L. (there are probably more) and four in Lucilius. This looks like a relatively rare instance of a shared hexameter-end filler. Buescu (1941, '*Loci Similes*', ad *Arat.* 120) comments '*Enniana, ut vid.*'	
1.818 *cum quibus*	447 *cum quibus*, in the same *sedes*
Note: A hexameter-opening formula? Merrill (1921) lists three other instances in L., at 2.761, 1008 and 1014.	

(continued)

Lucretius	Cicero, *Aratea*
1.833 *sed tamen*	69 *sed tamen*, in the same *sedes*
Note: Merrill (1921) lists nine Lucretian examples, plus one from Lucilius. This is a rare instance of an 'epic formula'.	
1.879 *et magis . . . in fronte locata* cf. *DRN* 3.296, 5.629, 1171, and 1344, 6.773 (*et magis*) and cf. *DRN* 4.71 and 97 (*fronte locata*)	*Arat.* 13 and 80 *et magis* *Arat.* 93 *in fronte locatas*
1.992 *sub caeli tegmine* cf. 2.663, sub tegmine caeli; 5.1016, *caeli sub tegmine*	47 *sub tegmine caeli* 233 *caeli sub tegmine*
1.1015–6 *nec mortale genus nec divum corpora sancta* <u>*exiguum possent horai sistere tempus*</u>	185 <u>*exiguo superum quae lumen tempore tranat*</u>
Note: The collocation might seem common, but context may be revealing: the expression *exiguo . . . tempore* in Cicero refers to the brief flight across the sky of the constellation Ara, in Lucretius *exiguum . . . tempus* refers to the brief life-span of both humans and gods (the latter including, one might think, the heavenly bodies, considered divine since Plato's *Timaeus*).	
1.1029 *et multos etiam <u>magnos</u> servata per <u>annos</u>*	232–3 *hae faciunt <u>magnos</u> longinqui temporis <u>annos</u>* *cum redeunt ad idem caeli sub tegmine signum*
Note: Lucretius already had this passage of Cicero in mind with the expression *sub caeli tegmine* at 1.992 (see above). Now in 1.1029 we see him deploy a collocation, *magnos . . . annos*, from the preceding line of the *Aratea*. In Cicero, the planets make the 'Long Year'. The passage of Cicero in question, on the planets, is one which is particularly important to Lucretius (cf. 1.1061 *simili ratione*; 4.444; 5.644 and 648). Lucretius tends to use Cicero's 'planets' passage in polemics against intelligent design (see above, Ch. 4).	

1.1034 *labentes aetheris ignes*	*Arat.* fr. 3.1 *cetera labuntur celeri caelestia motu*

Note: For *labor* as a term for the movement of the stars in Cicero see above on 1.2. 1.1034 should be taken with the complex of Ciceronian allusion noted at 1.1029. The whole context at this point in L. is a celestial one.

1.1061 *simili ratione*	227 *simili ratione*

Note: L. reuses the collocation *simili ratione* at *DRN* 2.299, 377, 857, 1073, 1084; 3.572; 4.163, 751, 754; 5.910. I treat elsewhere (Gee 2013) Lucretius' possible *variation* of the Ciceronian collocation in his expression *nulla ratione* at *DRN* 4.445 (and cf. 1.153 = 6.90; see Buescu 1941 'Loci Similes,' ad *Arat.* 227). 1.1061 comes in a passage of polemic (1.1061–4) where L. criticizes those who think everything tends toward the middle (as Aristotle, for instance, argues in *De caelo* Book 2). In so doing he appears to utilize Cicero's terminology for one of the few elements of disorder in the Aratean universe, the planets, of which Cicero says (*Arat.* 226–31):

nam quae per bis sex signorum labier orbem
quinque solent stellae, simili ratione notari
non possunt, quia quae faciunt vestigia cursu
non eadem semper spatio protrita teruntur.
sic malunt errare vagae per nubila caeli
atque suos vario motu metirier orbes.

As well as *simili ratione*, Lucretius' *vagari* in 1.1061 may reference this passage (see above, Ch. 4 p. 105). Lucretius thus makes multiple reference to this passage of Cicero. For Lucretian borrowing elsewhere of two other collocations from this passage, *nubila caeli* and *vario motu*, see on 1.6 and 2.97.

1.1062 *loca caeli*	130 *caeli . . . per loca*

Note: Although this collocation may not look promising in itself, it is made stronger by aggregation (the preceding line) and context. Cicero's 'upside-down' ship Argo is a good model for L.'s 'topsy-turvy' animals and implausible mixtures between heaven and earth.

(continued)

	Lucretius	Cicero, *Aratea*
DRN 2	**2.1** *turbantibus aequora ventis*	90 *perturbans aequora signum*
	2.25 *retinentia dextris*	369 *dextra retinens* Cf. 453, *dextra retinens*
	Note: See also below on 3.4. In *DRN* 2.25 it is ostentatious statues which grasp something in their right hand; in C. it is the statuesque constellation Orion. L. favoured the dramatic picture of Orion presented in Cicero: see also 2.1114; 4.368; 5.1333–6; 6.311, 8.819–20.	
	2.69 *longinquo . . . aevo*	232 *magnos longinqui temporis annos*
	Note: Lucretius' passage is about the ebb and flow of matter within the sum of things, Cicero's about the 'Long Year'. In support of his possible use of the passage here, L. also used Cicero's 'long year' passage at 1.1029. See n. below on 2.147–8.	
	2.97 *vario . . . motu*	231 *atque suos vario motu metirier orbes*
	Note: Cf. n. on 1.1061–4 in this appendix, and see the discussion of these passages in Ch. 3 p. 63 and Ch. 4 pp. 104–5 above.	
	2.130 *retroque repulsa reverti*	152 *retro ad Pistricis terga reverti*
	2.144 *[spargit] lumine terras*	473 *[vestivit] lumine terras*
	Note: L.'s description is of dawn, C.'s of starlight (that of Aquarius). This could be an allusion, but it also seems to be a standard hexameter-end formula (see Buescu 1941: '*Loci Sim.*' ad loc.). It's true to say, however, that L. and C. are the earliest examples he cites.	

2.147–8	332–3
quam subito subeat sol ortus tempore tali *convestire sua perfundens omnia luce* Cf. 5.619, 692, etc.	*haec sol aeterno convestit lumine lustrans* *annua conficiens vertentia tempora cursu* cf. 60–1 *quem cum perpetuo vestivit lumine Titan,* *brumali flectens contorquet tempore currum.*

Note: This continues the description of dawn in which we have already identified a Ciceronian reference (2.144 above). Lucretius is now drawing on a different passage of Cicero, Cicero's passage on the Long Year (cf. n. on 2.69 above), one he draws on frequently (eg. 5.635, 644, 687; 6.748; see below on 5.692–3). Here two distinctively Ciceronian verbs are used, namely *lustrare* and *convestire*. For *convestire* and *lustrare* see on 5.692–3 below (and cf. 5.79, 575, 693, 1437; 6.737 etc.). Munro (1894) ad 2.148 notes that Cicero in the *Aratea* uses *convestire* or *vestire* of light five times and that: 'Lucretius has probably borrowed this, as many other expressions, from him.' It is characteristic that L. may combine references to several passages of C. Thus the present passage might also refer to *Arat.* 60–1. For Lucretius' use of another collocation from this latter passage, see also 5.616 *brumalis adeat flexus*, with *Arat.* 61 *brumali flectens*, and 640 *brumalis usque ad flexus*, with *Arat.* 61 *brumali flectens*.

2.210 *caeli de vertice*	297 *caeli de vertice*

Note: In both cases the expression is used of a stabilizing element in the universe, Cicero's axis, Lucretius' sun. In the first case the stabilizing element is real; in the second illusory. The linguistic echo may help emphasize the disjuncture between the two philosophies.

2.216 *cognoscere avemus*	341 *aves . . . cognoscere*
2.273 *viribus . . . magnis*—see on 1.287 cf. 5.819 *magnis viribus*, 6.559 *magnis . . . viribus*	146 . . . *funestum magnis cum viribus amnem*

(continued)

Lucretius	Cicero, Aratea
2.296 nam neque adaugescit quicquam nec deperit inde.	*Prog.* fr. 3.5–6 aut densus stridor cum celso e vertice montis ortus adaugescit, scopulorum saepe repulsus.
Note: *Adaugesco* occurs *only* here and in *Prog.* fr. 3.6, in the same *sedes* (*BTL*). This is not the only place in which L. appears to refer to the *Prognostica*: see also 5.298–9 *ignibus instant* / *instant* with *Prog.* fr. 4.5–6, *vocibus instant* / *vocibus instant instat*. Astonishingly, Merrill (1921: 148) omits both of these parallels, choosing instead to note the seemingly innocuous *et post* at 2.299, citing *Arat.* 40 and 389 (see below).	
2.299 *et post*	40 *et post* (cf.389)
Note: The usefulness of this as a specific parallel may look unlikely. But the wider passage in which *DRN* 2.299 occurs may, unnoticed by scholars, allude to a different part of the *Aratea* prominent in L., the passage on planets. See next entry.	
2.296–9: nam neque adaugescit quicquam nec deperit inde. quapropter quo nunc in motu principiorum corpora sunt, in eodem ante acta aetate fuere *et posthac semper simili ratione feruntur* . . .	**226–8** nam quae bis sex signorum labier orbem quinque solent stellae, *simili ratione notari* non possunt . . .
Note: Taking this passage as a whole, there are allusions in it to three passages of Cicero, *Prog.* fr. 3, *Arat.* 40 (*et post*), and *Arat.* 226–8 above. The motion of L's *principiorum corpora* looks a bit like the motion of the heavenly bodies (note also *feruntur* in 2.299 with *feruntur*, seen shortly after Cicero's passage on the planets, at *Arat.* 238).	
2.321 *omnia quae . . . confusa videntur*	371 *omnia quae* and 99 . . *fusa videntur* cf. 156 *fusae sparsaeque videntur* [*stellae*]

Note: An example of the conflation of two formulae which are also found in Cicero: a self-illustrating 'confusion' by Lucretius of the Ciceronian source, to exemplify the confusion of separate things caused by the illusion of distance (the context of the Lucretian passage)? Cicero's unnamed stars (*Arat.* 156) is a particularly apt image for this, since they are a potential source of confusion in the heavenly system (see above, Ch. 5).

2.336 *simili* sint *praedita forma*	**6 *simili forma***
cf. 2.723, 758, 895 etc. *praedita forma*	*Arat.* fr. 26 *verum haec est magno atque illustri praedita signo* contra *Haedi exiguam iaciunt mortalibus ignem*

Note: At 2.336 L. may again combine two passages of C. The second passage (fr. 26) is elsewhere in evidence in the *DRN*: with Cicero's *iaciunt . . . ignem*, see *DRN* 6.389, *iaciunt ignem* (see note on 2.675 below).

2.367 *tremulis cum vocibus*	*Prog.* fr. 3.9
	haud modicos tremulo fundens e gutture voces cantus . . .

Note: For reference to the *Prognostica* (specifically fr. 3) see above on 2.296.

2.379 *certam formam*	159 *formam . . . certam*

Note: In L. the formula is used of the fixed model of an atom; in C., of the nameless stars in the craftsman simile. See above, Ch. 4 p. 104 and n.49.

2.555 *fluvitantia aplustra*	*Arat.* fr. 24
	navibus absumptis fluvitantia quaerere aplustra
	(See Soubiran 1975: 75).

Note: An indisputable parallel. The collocation occurs only in Cicero and Lucretius. The context fits too: both are storm scenes. The passage in L. (2.552–6) works out an analogy between matter and a shipwreck (see above, Ch. 4 pp. 98–100). For further reference to Cicero in the following line, see next entry below.

(*continued*)

Lucretius	Cicero, Aratea
2.556 *mortalibus edant*	**335** *mortalibus edit*
Note: Cicero reference here also fits the shipwreck context in the preceding line. *Arat.* 335 comes from Cicero's zodiac list, essential for sailing. Those sailors who don't heed it are described at *Arat.* 69–71.	
2.600 *docti cecinere poetae*	**33** *veteres statuere poetae*
Note: In Cicero the phrase is used about false tales of the Pleiades; in L. of the Magna Mater as allegory for the Earth, a theory debunked shortly after, at 2.645, *longe sunt tamen a vera ratione repulsa*. L. makes use of formulae similar to that used by Cicero of the Pleiades in other places where he aims to question received wisdom, as at 5.405, . . . *veteres Graium docti cecinere poetae*, of the myth of Phaethon, debunked in 5.406 by *quod procul a vera nimis est rationed repulsum*. Cf. 6.754 *Graium ut cecinere poetae* (the story of Cecrops, a *mythic* tale). Cicero is the beginning of this way of distinguishing truth from received falsehood. Also compare *Cons.* fr. 2.8, of the planets: *[stellae] quae verbo et falsis Graiorum vocibus errant*. On the topos of naming in Lucretius, see 6.908.	
2.609 *horrifice*	**121–2** *ictus /horrificos metuens rostri tremebundus acuti*
Cf. 3.906, *horrifico . . . busto.*	
Note: Cicero invokes the gravity of the supposed situation (the Hare about to be snapped up by the Dog's sharp muzzle, *rostri*) by the use of two weighty adjectives, *horrificos* and *tremebundus*. *BTL* gives the *Arat.* as the earliest occurrence of the *horrific*-compound. Cf. *DRN* 3.906 *horrifico . . . busto*. Both contexts in L. are instances of things which create needless emotion (the panoply of the Magna Mater in *DRN* 2.609; mourning beside the pyre at 3.906). The Ciceronian compound enhances the impression of bathos in Lucretius.	
2.629 *Curetas nomine Grai /quos memorant*	*Arat.* fr. 14
Cf. 6.908 *quam magneta vocant patrio de nomine Grai*	*quem claro perhibent Ophicum nomine Grai*
	212
	quam nemo certo dignavit nomine Graium
	222
	Ante Canem Graio Procyon qui nomine fertur

Note: It is important to remember that Cicero's *Aratea* is the earliest attempt to Romanize Greek terms (in this case star-names) and that it does so with self-consciousness (viz., the expressions above, which distinguish Greek from Roman naming). L. consistently imitates Ciceronian expressions of 'translation', at the same time exploiting a sense of scepticism as to the truth of what is claimed.

2.662 *sub tegmine caeli*
cf. 1.988 with note above; 5.1016.

47 *sub tegmine caeli*
cf. 346 *caeli de tegmine*

2.675 *unde ignem iacere*
Cf. 6.389 *iaciunt ignem*

Arat. fr. 26.2 *contra Haedi*
exiguum iaciunt mortalibus ignem
331 *et Gemini clarum iactantes lucibus ignem*

Note: See above on 2.336.

2.702 *semiferas hominum species*

59 *corpore semifero . . . Capricornus*

Note: Capricorn is a hybrid. Lucretius, invoking the Ciceronian context, is describing the impossibility of such conjunctions between disparate parts.
The whole passage 2.700–6 is about the impossible conjunction of things:
nec tamen omnimodis conecti posse putandum est
omnia. nam vulgo fieri portenta videres,
semiferas hominum species existere et altos
interdum ramos egigni corpore vivo,
multaque conecti terrestria membra marinis,
tum flammam taetro spirantis ore Chimaeras
pascere naturam per terras omniparentis.
See following note, on 2.705, and below 4.587.

(*continued*)

Lucretius	Cicero, Aratea
2.705	110–12
...flammam taetro spirantis ore Chimaeras	*nec vero toto spirans de corpore flammam*
cf. 5.905–6 *Chimaera*	*aestiferos validis erumpit flatibus ignes*
ore foras acrem flaret de corpore flammam	
Note: In both of his references to the mythical Chimaera, Lucretius has evoked Cicero's passage on the Dog Star. Taken with 2.702 (previous n.), L.'s invective could be applied to the groupings of the constellations, which are equally spurious in Epicurean astronomy. L. has used an image of something impossible to represent the impossible. See also below on 5.1099. For fuller discussion, see above, Ch. 4 pp. 94–5.	
2.719 *disterminat*	94 *disterminat*, in the same *sedes*
Note: *Disterminat* is rare. According to the *OLD* (*distermino* I) and the *BTL* database, only Cicero *Arat.* 94 uses it before Lucretius (thereafter Lucan, Pomponius Mela, Pliny).	
2.767	71
vertitur in canos candenti marmore fluctus	*nec metuant canos minitanti murmure fluctos*
Cf. 1.68–9 *minitanti murmure*; 5.1193 *murmura magna minarum.*	
Note: Buescu comments (1941, 'Loc. Sim.' ad *Arat.* 71) '*fluctus canos et minitanti murmure Ennio deb. ut vid.*' I see little evidence of debt to Ennius. L. and C. are the earliest attested examples of the collocations *fluctus canos* and *minitanti murmure* (*BTL*); debt to Ennius is an *argumentum ex silentio*.	
2.800 *luce refulget*	108 *luce refulgens*
	cf. 154

Note: The collocation occurs in the same *sedes* in both authors. L.'s passage is about colour-perception; C.'s about Sirius. Buescu (1941, 'Loc. Sim.' ad *Arat.* 108) cites *Aen.* 1.588 *luce refulsit* (cf. *Aen.* 2.590), and comments (on the principle of shared ancestry) 'Enniana, ut vid.' It seems more likely on the direct evidence that Lucretius is imitating Cicero, Virgil one or both.

2.806 *larga cum luce*	394 *larga*/*larga cum luce*
2.1039 *suspicere in caeli . . . templa*	104 *suspiciens in caelum* *Prog.* fr. 4.10 *spectantes lumina caeli*

Note: This Lucretian passage is a programmatic excursus about the wonder of the stars (see Ch. 3, 3.2.2, above). Reference to Cicero is therefore both probable and appropriate. For other significant Lucretian references to the *Prog.*, see on 2.296, 5.298–9 and for fr. 4, on 4.992 and 6.504.

2.1060 *temere . . . frustra*	32 *sed frustra, temere a vulgo . . .*

Note: We may see L. as responding to the Ciceronian tradition of scepticism by applying it to the created universe (see above, Ch. 3, 3.2.2). L. reuses the formula *temere incassum frustra* at 5.1002.

2.1099 *tempore praesto*	74 *tempore praesto est*
2.1114 *corpore terra*	433 *corpore terras* cf. 435, 438

Note: In both L. and C. the description is of violence, in C. of the death of Orion, in L. of the 'blows' which distribute and redistribute bodies (2.1112–5). For the collocation, see also below, 6.857. L. favoured the dramatic picture of Orion presented in Cicero: see also 2.25; 4.368; 5.1333–6; 6.311.

2.1122 *grandescere adactu* See on 1.191	*Prog.* fr. 5 *grandescere fetu*

(continued)

	Lucretius	Cicero, Aratea
	2.1126 *late dispersa* (OQ; *dispessa*, Munro)	105 *late dispersum*
DRN 3	**3.4** *pedum . . . vestigia* Cf. 3.389–90, *pedum vestigia . . . lponunt.*	451 *vestigia parva* *Arat.* fr. 15.4 *vestigia ponit*
	Note: In this instance there is a collocation of three elements shared between L. and both passages of the *Aratea* cited. *DRN* 3.4, . . . *pedum pono pressis vestigia signis* can be compared with *Arat.* fr. 15.4–5, *ille [Ophiuchus] tamen nitens graviter vestigia ponit latque oculos urget pedibus pectusque Nepai,* and the whole of Lucretius 3.1–4 with *Arat.* 450–3, the rising of the Centaur (see my discussion in Ch. 4 above), a passage which Lucretius may also have in mind in Proem 2 (note on *DRN* 2.25 above).	
	3.8 *fortis equi vis* Cf. *DRN* 2.264; 3.764; 4.987; 5.397	54 *fortis equi*, and 57, *Equi vis*
	Note: For discussion of the third Proem see Ch. 4 pp. 86–90 above.	
	3.81 *maerenti pectore letum*	148 *letum maerenti voce canentes*
	Note: There is a potential analogy here between the story of the sisters of Phaethon weeping over the death of their brother (in Cicero), and those who bring death upon themselves (in Lucretius) by striving against the fear of death. L. may have the passage in mind elsewhere: he also uses *lacrimis spargunt* (from *Arat.* 147–8, the same passage) at 2.977.	
	3.99 *in parte locatum*	27 *ex parte locatas*; 145 *in parte locatum*, etc.
	3.102 *dicitur esse*	*Arat.* frr. 4.2; 6.2
	3.109 *corpore toto* Many other parallels in the *DRN*: see Merrill (1921) 149; Buescu (1941) 'Loc. Sim.' ad *Arat.* 289.	289 *corpore toto*
	3.124 *non aequas partes*	359 *non aequa parte secatur*

3.140 *situm media regione*	193 *sub media caeli regione locatam* cf. 481 *mediis regionibus*
3.143 *cetera pars*	95 *cetera pars*
3.146 *cum neque*	246 *cum neque*, in the same *sedes*
3.172 *at tamen insequitur*	355 *quam tamen insequitur*
3.175 *esse necessest.* Cf. 3.216, 4.674, etc.	312 *esse necessest*
3.201 *cum pondere magno*	132 *magno cum pondere*
colspan note	Note: References from 3.99 to 3.201 are together illustrative of 'shared epic discourse' or 'shared formulae'. We may not be able to single each one out as significant in itself, nor should every element of diction shared between Cicero and Lucretius necessarily have a pendant interpretation. But we should remember the dictum of Conte quoted in Ch. 3 above, that 'even the most threadbare poetic residuum, when transferred from one context to another, acquires a varying, stratified connotation.'[2] Cumulatively these small debts illustrate the formation of Lucretius' epic language (particularly interesting are expressions thought to be characteristically Lucretian, such as *necessest*, which turn out to have Ciceronian precedent). For an instance of how Conte's dictum might be put into practice, see below on 3.413.
3.218 *toto iam corpore cessit*	462 *toto cum corpore cedit* cf. *Arat.* 356; 391
colspan note	Note: The expression in the *Arat.* is about the setting of Canis; in Lucretius, the evanescence of the soul. The comparison between death and the setting of a star is apt to the poignancy of the Lucretian context (perhaps also see below, 3.309, there *animus* rather than *anima*; and on 3.529). One might argue for a consistent thematic connection between the human personality and Cicero's stars in this passage of Lucretius. Human identity is thematized intertextually through the stars. See below on 3.529, 557, 657–9, 829, 849.

(continued)

Lucretius	Cicero, *Aratea*
3.242 *omnino nominis expers*	170 *expertes nominis omnes*
Note: Threefold shared collocation, discussed in Ch. 4 pp. 100–2 above.	
3.296 *vis . . . leonum* cf. 3.8, and discussion in Ch. 4 pp. 86–9.	321 *vis torva leonis* and 370 *vis . . . leonis*
3.304 *caecae caliginis* cf. 4.456 *caligine caeca*	345 *aut adiment lucem caeca caligine nubes* *Prog.* fr. 1.2 *stinguuntur radii caeca caligine tecti*
Note: In L., it is the 'torch of anger', '*irai fax . . . lfumida*', *DRN* 3.303–4, which, paradoxically, suffuses things not with light but with shadow (*umbra*).[3] The paradox may be partly explained by L.'s recollection of Cicero's more conventional image in *Arat.* 344–5, where mountains or clouds obscure the stars: *sin autem officiens signis mons obstruet altus* *aut adiment lucem caeca caligine nubes . . .* L. may have these lines of C. in mind elsewhere. For the mountains, see 6.448–9 below.	
3.309 *animi vestigia prima*	378 *Canis vestigia prima*
Note: See above on 3.218 and below on 3.529.	
3.316 *quorum ego nunc nequeo caecas exponere causas*	234 *quarum ego nunc nequeo tortos evolvere cursus*
Note: One of the most unmistakeable Ciceronian references in Lucretius: see Merrill (1921): 150; Buescu 346; Soubiran 1975: 75; Kenney (1984) ad *DRN* 3.314–18. Discussed in Ch. 4 pp. 103–4 above.	

3.413 *at si*	245 *at si*

Note: This may look like the most jejune formulaic repetition, but note context. Both collocations occur in passages about light and darkness, in C. of the sky, in L. of the eye. Compare *Arat.* 245–9,

at si nocturno convisens tempore caelum,
cum neque caligans detergit sidere nubes
nec pleno stellas super ardet lumine luna,
vidisti magnum candentem serpere circum,
Lacteus hic nimio fulgens candore notatur.
—with *DRN* 3.413–5,

at si tantula pars oculi media illa peresa est,
occidit extemplo lumen tenebraeque sequuntur,
incolumis quamvis aliqui splendidus orbis.

Note: *Orbem* also occurs later, at the end of *Arat.* 250; compare the line-end *orbis* in *DRN* 3.415. Comparison of the two passages, provoked by 'threadbare' repetition, creates a meaningful analogy between the blinding of the eye, and the image of the setting sun.

3.433 *nam procul*	186 *nam procul*
3.529 *inde pedes*	388 *inde pedes*

Note: in L. the collocation is used in a context of gradual death; in C. of the gradual rising of Canis. Perhaps see above on 3.218 and 3.309.

3.557 *conexu corpus adhaeret*	292
	Hydra tenet flexu, Creterra et Corvus adhaerent

Note: The phrase in L. is used of the mind/body connection; in C. connection between different celestial elements. For the possibility of thematic significance, see above on 3.218.

(continued)

209

Lucretius	Cicero, *Aratea*
3.610 *in certa regione locatam*. For the line-end, cf. 4.102 *in . . . regione locatam.*	193 *sub media caeli regione locatam*
3.657–9 *quin etiam tibi si lingua vibrante minanti* / *serpentis cauda procero corpore †utrumque†* / *sit libitum in multas partis discidere ferro,* / *omnia iam sorsum cernes ancisa recenti* / *vulnere tortari et terram conspargere tabo,* / *ipsam seque retro partem petere ore priorem,* / *vulneris ardenti, ut morsu premat, icta dolore.*	149–52 *hunc Orionis sub laeva cernere planta* / *serpentem poteris, proceraque vincla videbis* / *quae retinent Pisces caudarum a parte locata* / *Flumine mixta retro ad Pistricis terga reverti.*
Note: The soul, here characterized as distributed throughout the body, functions as do the constellations: elements, distinct in themselves, are nonetheless integrally connected to one another when they form figures ('bodies'). For the allusive link between the soul and the stars in the wider context of *DRN* 3, see note above, on 3.218. See also 3.825 and 829 below. There is a complex of Ciceronian reference here.	
3.822 *quia quae*	228 *quia quae*
3.825 *saepe futuris*	*Prog.* fr. 3.1–2 *atque etiam ventos praemonstrat saepe futuros* / *inflatum mare . . .*
Note: The context in C. is weather prediction; in L., the premonitory capacity of the soul. For other references to the *Prog.*, see on 1.9, 39, 128, 252–3, 413; 2.1122; 3.304; 5.298–9; 6.504; for references to fr. 3 in particular, 1.2, 39, 191. 1034; 2.296, 367; 4.210, 577.	

3.829 *mergitur undas*	381 *mergitur unda*
Note: The metaphorical 'setting' of the soul, as it is engulfed in the blackness of depression, is thematized by the setting of the stars. NB: See on 3.218 above.	
3.845–6 . . . *qui comptu coniungioque / corporis atque animae consistimus uniter apti*	242–3 *tum magnos orbis magno cum lumine latos, / vinctos inter se et nodis caelestibus aptos.*
Note: No one previously has noticed the correspondence between the initial summary of the celestial circles in Cicero, and L.'s vision of the soul/body. There is a conjunction of imagery between the soul/body entity in L. and the celestial circles in C. Both represent a totality. There is precedent for this idea of the human totality as analogous to the cosmic structure, although from a very different philosophical perspective, in Plato's *Timaeus* 44d3–6, where the secondary gods create the human entity on the analogy of the cosmos. L. may be engaging with this tradition here, as well as, or through, that of the *Aratea*.	
3.849 *atque iterum nobis fuerint data lumina vitae*	287–8 *in quo autumnali atque iterum sol lumine verno / exaequat spatium lucis cum tempore noctis.*
Note: On L.'s use of Cicero in this passage in particular see previous n., on 3.845. See above, n. on 3.218, for the pattern of imagery across the soul/body discussion of *DRN* 3. If the echo of *atque iterum* here seems less than conclusive, it may be strengthened by the fact that L. might have this passage in mind elsewhere. He uses *tempore verno* (*Arat.* 287–8) at 5.688 *[anni] nodus nocturnas*; likewise he imitates C.'s description of the equator (the passage at stake here) at 5.802; likewise he imitates C.'s description of the equator (the passage at stake here) at 5.802, *exaequat lucibus umbras.* A conflation of Ciceronian imagery from this particular passage is spread across the *DRN*. This is similar to the phenomenon noted above, Ch. 4 pp. 94–8, on L.'s 'thematic' use of C.'s Sirius passage.	
3.882 *proiecto corpore*	330 *proiecto corpore [Taurus]*
3.1006 *cum redeunt*	233 *cum redeunt* (in the same *sedes*)

(continued)

Lucretius	Cicero, *Aratea*
Note: This reference might look 'formulaic,' but the context is revealing. In C. it is about the planets and the Long Year (*Arat.* 232–3): *hae faciunt magnos longinqui temporis annos* *cum redeunt ad idem caeli sub tegmine signum . . .* In L. it is the seasons (*DRN* 3.1005–6): *quod faciunt nobis annorum tempora, circum* *cum redeunt fetusque ferunt variosque lepores . . .* Note: For L.'s use of *Arat.* 232–3 elsewhere, see on 2.147–8; for L.'s use of Cicero's *planets* elsewhere, and their significance, see above on 1.1061.	
3.1011 *iam vero* Note: For L.'s use of *Prog.* fr. 5 elsewhere, see on 1.191, 252–3.	*Prog.* fr. 5.1 *iam vero*
3.1012 *Tartarus horriferos eructans faucibus aestus* Cf. 1.724 *faucibus eruptos iterum vis ut vomat ignis.* Note: If there is a similarity in these lines, it consists in sound and context (Sirius again; see Ch. 4 pp. 94–8).	110–12 *nec vero toto spirans de corpore flammam* *aestiferos validis erumpit flatibus ignes:* *totus ab ore micans iacitur mortalibus ardor.*
4.136 *[nubes] aera mulcentes motu* Note: Uniquely, it seems, both C. and L. transfer the epic metaphor of 'stroking' or 'sweeping' (as by a ship, of the sea) to air (see Buescu 1941 'Loc. Sim.' ad *Arat.* 88).	88 *[Aquila] igniferum mulcens tremebundis aethera pinnis*
DRN 4	

4.171 *caeli complesse cavernas* cf. *DRN* 6.252; 4.391, *sidera cessare aetheriis adfixa cavernis*	252 *caeli lustrare cavernas*
4.189–90 *lumine lumen . . . fulgure fulgur*	299–300 *extremis extremos . . . a medio media*

Note: Buescu (1941): 'Loc. Sim.' ad *Arat.* 299 has noted this for the repeated polyptoton; however, if one examines the passages there is an additional point of possible similarity in the repetition of *lumen* (*DRN* 4.189/*Arat.* 298 and 301). How does the motion of L.'s elements compare with the craftsmanship of C.'s celestial circles? Are both reflected in verbal interweaving?

4.208 *lumina caelum*	113 *lumina caeli*; 405 *lumina caeli*; *Prog.* fr. 4.10 *lumina caeli*

Note: A Cicernonian termination: see above, 1.9.

4.210 *celeri motu*	*Arat.* fr. 3.1 *celeri . . . motu*

Note: There could well be Ciceronian reminiscence here: look at the whole passage (*DRN* 4.210–13):

quam *celeri motu* rerum simulacra *ferantur,*
quod simul ac primum sub diu splendor aquai
ponitur, extemplo *caelo* stellante serena
sidera respondent in aqua radiantia mundi.

With *Arat* fr. 3.1–2

Cetera labuntur *celeri* caelestia *motu,*
cum *caeloque* simul noctesque diesque *feruntur.*

Cicero's passage is about stars; Lucretius, discussing the reflection of stars on water, verbally 'reflects' Cicero.

4.213 *sidera . . . radiantia mundi*	*Arat.* fr. 9.4 *radianti sidere*

(continued)

Lucretius	Cicero, *Aratea*
Note: The likelihood of this being a Ciceronian reference is perhaps militated for by the fact that L. evokes the following lines of this same passage, *obstipum caput, a tereti cervice reflexum, lobtutum . . .,* at the beginning of *DRN* 1 (see above on 1.35), and by the Ciceronian context of 4.210.	
4.368 *lumine cassus* Cf. 5.719 *cassum lumine;* 5.757 *cassum . . . lumine*	369 *non cassum lumine*
Note: The Ciceronian phrase is about Orion's sword. L. may also have been thinking of this line of C. at 2.25, *manibus retinentia dextris* (see n. above). If so, there is a verbal correspondence between Cicero's Orion passage and three loci in L., in Books 2, 4, and 5. See on 6.311.	
4.377 *spoliatur lumine terra*	473 *vestivit lumine terras* (shared line-end)
Note: The shared collocation may generate an opposing but related metaphor: in L. the earth 'sloughs off' (*sibi abluit*) the shadows; in C., Aquarius 'clothes' the earth in light.	
4.391–4 *Sidera cessare aetheriis adfixa cavernis* *cuncta videntur, et adsiduo sunt omnia motu,* *quandoquidem longos obitus exorta revisunt,* *cum permensa suo sunt caelum corpore claro.*	337 *signa revisunt*
4.493 *quandoquidem longos obitus exorta revisunt*	57 *obitus . . . vissit*
4.394 *corpore claro*	365 *claro cum corpore* 386 *claro corpore*

4.404	402 *erigit alte*
iamque rubrum tremulis iubar ignibus erigere alte	

Note: There is a complex of Ciceronian reference in *DRN* 4.391–6, a passage about the perceptive gap between the apparent movements of the heavenly bodies and their real movements (note *videtur* in 395). It is highly appropriate, in this context, that L. should engage with the salient passage of C. on the zodiac. For *aetheriis . . . cavernis* in 4.391, see also above, on 4.171.

Note: The shared collocation comes in the same *sedes*, and is used of the rising of heavenly bodies, in both authors. For the imagery, perhaps also compare *Arat*. fr. 22.3, *magni' Leo tremulam quatiens e corpore flammam*, and cf. 5.697.

4.437 *navigia aplustris fractis obtulier undie*	*Arat*. fr. 24
Cf. 2.555 *fluitantia aplustra* with n. below.	*navibus absumptis fluitantia quaerere aplustra.*
4.444 *tempore nocturno, tum splendida signa videntur*	223 . . . *quae visens nocturno tempore signa*

Note: For further discussion of this passage, see above, Ch. 4 pp. 105–7. This is one of the clearest instances of Lucretian allusion to Cicero outside the astronomical passage of Book 5. The two authors share four elements in one line. Here Lucretius is describing, not just the ostensibly wandering motions of the planets, but the apparent wandering of *all* the constellations. But in doing so, he draws on Cicero's description of the planets, allusively ascribing 'planetary' motion to all the stars. Quotation is an appropriate gesture towards the philosophical differences between the 'Stoic' universe of Cicero's poem and the Epicurean one of Lucretius'. Lucretius interposes the Epicurean understanding of nature between himself and his model: for Lucretius it makes no difference whether the planets wander, or all the heavenly bodies do. Lucretius refers to this passage of Cicero in several other places in the *DRN*: for instance, to *Arat.* 224, *legitimo cernes caelum lustrantia cursu*, at *DRN* 5.79, *libera sponte sua cursus lustrare perennis* (an important programmatic passage for L.'s astronomy: see Ch. 3 p. 58) and Buescu 1941 'Loc. Sim.' *ad Arat.* 227). Likewise *Arat.* 227, *simili ratione*, appears in several significant loci in L. (see above on 1.1061 and Buescu 1941 'Loc. Sim.' *ad Arat.* 227).

4.456 *caligine caeca*	345 *caeca caligine*

Note: For the collocation see above, 3.304. L. may use this same passage at 6.448–9 *montis . . . lofficere* (compare *Arat.* 344 *officiens mons*).

(continued)

Lucretius	Cicero, *Aratea*
4.564 *ab ore*	113 *ab ore* (Sirius)
4.577 *reddere voces*	*Prog.* fr. 3.4 *reddere voces*

Note: the wider context is enlightening. Consider *Prog.* fr. 3.3–6—

saxaque cana salis niveo spumata liquore
tristificas certant Neptuno reddere voces,
aut densus stridor cum celso e vertice montis
ortus adaugescit, scopulorum saepe repulsus.

—with 4.572–9:

quae bene cum videas, rationem reddere possis
tute tibi atque aliis, quo pacto per loca sola
saxa paris formas verborum ex ordine reddant,
palantis comites cum montis inter opacos
quaerimus et magna dispersos voce ciemus.
sex etiam aut septem loca vidi reddere voces,
unam cum iaceres: ita colles collibus ipsi
verba repulsantes iterabant dicta referri.

In addition, the fact that L. uses this passage of the *Prog.* widely elsewhere strengthens the case for its influence here. For other references to *Prog.* fr. 3, see 1.2, 39, 191. 1034; 2.296, 367; 4.210. In particular, for the incohative verb *adaugescit* at *Prog.* fr. 3.3–6, see above on 2.296. Such verbs are arguably a Ciceronian idiom in the *Prog.*, imitated by Lucretius in appropriate contexts (for the general phenomenon, see on 1.191).

4.587 *semiferi capitis [Panos]*	59 *corpore semifero [Capricorni]*
See on 2.702 above.	

4.734 *quorum morte obita tellus amplectitur ossa*	116 *nam quorum stirpis tellus amplexa prehendit*
Note: See above on 1.135 for the tissue of references to Cicero's Sirius passage in the *DRN*, and their significance.	
4.825 *lumina . . . oculorum* Cf. 6.1180–1 below	479 *oculorum ardentia lumina*
4.904 *atque gubernaculum* (cf. the following line)	137 *inde gubernaculum* 157 *atque gubernaculum*
4.905 *pondere magno*	132 *magno cum pondere*
Note: There may be an aggregation of reference to Cicero's Argo (*Arat.* 126–138).	
4.933 *aeriis quoniam vicinum <u>tangitur auris</u>*	253 *quorum alter <u>tangens</u> Aquilonis vertitur <u>auras</u>*
4.987 *equos fortis* cf. *DRN* 2.264; 3.8, 764; 5.397.	54 and 57 (see above on *DRN* 3.8)
4.992 *redducunt naribus aures*	*Prog.* fr. 4.11 *naribus . . . duxere ex aere sucum*
Note: Compare the whole context of *DRN* 4: *venantumque canes in <u>molli saepe quiete</u>* [999] *iactant crura tamen subito vocisque repente* [991] *mittunt et crebro <u>redducunt naribus auras</u>* with *Prog.* fr. 4.10–11: *mollipedesque boves, spectantes lumina caeli,* *naribus umiferum <u>duxere ex aere sucum</u>.* On L.'s use of the *Prog.* elsewhere, see for instance on 2.296, 5.298–9 and for fr. 4, on 5.1 and 6.504, 890. The material preserved in this particular fragment was also used by Varro of Atax and Virgil: see Williams (1968): 255–9; Thomas (1988): ad *Geo.* 1.374–87.	

(*continued*)

	Lucretius	Cicero, *Aratea*
	4.1087 *corpore flammam* cf. *DRN* 5.906 (of a Chimaera)	*Arat.* fr. 22.3; 110
DRN 5	**5.1** *pectore carmen*	*Prog* fr. 4.4 in the same *sedes*
	Note: For Lucretius' use of Cicero in the proem to *DRN* 5, see above, Ch. 4, section 4.1.3.	
	5.33 *corpore serpens*	215 *corpore serpens*
	Note: This is an appropriate allusion, since it refers to the serpent of the Hesperides in L., the Hydra in C. (cf. the same collocation, also of Hydra, *Arat.* 286). The thematic connection lies in mythical serpents. See next reference below. See also 6.660 *corpore serpens*, with n. below.	
	5.34 *arboris amplexus stirpem*	116 *quorum stirpis tellus amplexa prehendit*
	Note: This is the second of two Ciceronian allusions in as many lines. For the use of Sirius references to signal unnatural things in the *DRN* see on 1.135 and discussion in Ch. 4 section 4.2.1.	
	5.76 *lunaeque meatus*	*Prog.* fr. 1.1, *luna means*
	Note: For the collocation, see above on 1.128, below on 5.774. On Lucretius' engagement with Cicero in his exposition of astronomy at 5.76–81, see above, Ch. 3. p. 58.	
	5.79 *libera sponte sua cursus lustrare perennis*	225 *legitimo cernes caelum lustrantia cursu*
	Note: The intertextuality here presents a clear case of anti-Stoic polemic. Lines 76–9 take a swipe at the Stoic position, with *natura gubernans* in 77, the intelligent design concept, is replaced in 107 by *fortuna gubernans* in the same *sedes*. Cf. on 5.122 below.	

5.122 *divino a numine*	305 *divino numine*
Note: Lucretius refers here, in a polemical context, to Cicero's programmatic passage on the Craftsman. On this passage as polemic, see above, Ch. 3. p. 79. It forms a sequel to Lucretius' polemic against the use of the heavenly bodies as evidence of the divine (5.114–6); a few lines later, in 122, he chooses to echo a phrase in which Cicero extols the divine craftsmanship. Cf. the denial of *divina numina* in a different context at *DRN* 4.1233.	
5.261 *quod superest . . . flumina fontes*	177 *quod superest . . . flumine fontes*
5.288 *inferior pars*	99 *pars inferior*
	188 *inferiore in parte*
Note: Consider the whole context of 5.286–8: *quod simul ac primum nubes succedere soli* *coepere et radios inter quasi rumpere lucis,* *extemplo inferior pars horum disperit omnis* with *Arat.* 99–100: *at pars inferior Delphini fusa videtur* *inter solis iter . . .*	
5.298–9 *ignibus instant /instant*	*Prog.* fr. 4.5–6 *et matutinis acredula vocibus instat,* *vocibus instat . . .*
Note: On Lucretius' use of *Prog.* fr. 4 at this point in the *DRN*, see above, Ch. 4 section 4.1.3. See also 6.1159 below.	
5.319 *amplexu terram* Cf. 5.34	239 *amplexi terras*

(continued)

Lucretius	Cicero, *Aratea*
5.327 *cecinere poetae* cf. 5.405 *ut veteres Graium cecinere poetae*	33 *ut veteres statuere poetae*
Note: On these passages see above, Ch. 4 section 4.1.3 above.	
5.387 *ex alto gurgite ponti*	*Prog.* fr. 3.7 *e gurgite ponti*
5.432 *solis rota* Cf. 5.564	281 *rota fervida solis* Cf. 'Quintus Cicero' zodiac fragment 15 *rota fulgida solis*
5.459 *ignifer . . . ignis* Cf. 5.498 *aether ignifer*	458–9 *aether lignifer . . . ignis* cf. 88 *igniferum . . . aethera*
5.472 *matutina*	*Prog.* fr. 4.5 *matutinis*
Note: The word is not exclusively Ciceronian, but we have evidence that L. had this particular passage of Cicero in mind elsewhere: see for instance on 5.298–9 *instant linstant*.	
5.509 *motibus astrorum*	*De consulatu suo* fr. 2.11 *astrorum motus*
Note: Although the *Cons.* falls outside the strict ambit of this appendix, the speech of Urania in Cicero's later epic represents near-contemporary 'rational' astronomy. For a comparison of Cicero's 'planets' passage in the *Aratea* with fr. 2 of the *Cons.*, see above, Ch. 5 pp. 119–21. In date the *Cons.* may be almost contemporary with Cicero's *Prognostica* (see above, Ch. 3 pp. 63–4). This run of Ciceronian astronomical signposts begins at the outset of Lucretius' astronomical programme (see on 5.76). See also n. on the following line.	
5.510 *caeli . . . orbis*	314 *caeli . . . orbem*
Note: Both authors give panoramic (and programmatic) pictures of the heaven.	

5.575 *lumine lustrans* cf. 5.693, 1437, etc.	332 *lumine lustrans* 237 *lustrantes lumine*
5.612 *fulgore notatus*	*Arat.* fr. 9.2 *fulgore notata* cf. 249 *fulgens candore notatur*

Note: Lucretius here puts the Epicurean side using Ciceronian (Stoic) phrasing: a case of appropriation. The Epicurean argument for the sizes of heavenly bodies 5.564–613 contains two Ciceronian identifiers adjacent to its beginning and end (575 and 612). L. could well have *Arat.* fr. 9 in mind here. Consider the Lucretian passage about the sun (5.610–13)—

> *forsitan et rosea sol alte lampade* <u>*lucens*</u>
> *possideat multum caecis fervoribus ignem*
> *circum se, nullo qui sit* <u>*fulgore notatus*</u>,
> *aestifer ut tantum* <u>*radiorum*</u> *exaugeat ictum.*

—with *Arat.* fr. 9.1–5 (Draco):

> *hiuc non una modo caput ornans stella* <u>*relucet*</u>,
> *verum tempora sunt duplici* <u>*fulgore notata*</u>,
> *e trucibusque oculis duo* <u>*fervida lumina flagrant*</u>,
> *atque uno mentum* <u>*radianti sidere lucet*</u>;
> *obstipum caput, a* <u>*tereti cervice reflexum*</u> . . .

L. has this passage in mind elsewhere: for *tereti cervice reflexum* see on 1.35; for *ornans* see on 5.695.

5.616 *brumalis adeat flexus* cf. 5.640 *brumalis usque ad flexus*	61 *brumali flectens* 282 *brumali tempora flexu*

Note: For the collocation, see also above on 2.147–8. Here, both authors refer to the tropic of Capricorn. However, in L. it's an anti-Stoic argument and technique, that of multiple explanation (see 5.614–20). On this same passage of Lucretius, see the following note below.

(continued)

Lucretius	Cicero, *Aratea*
5.628 *fervida signa*	281 *rota fervida solis* *Arat.* fr. 9.3, *fervida lumina flagrant.*

Note: This is L.'s explanation of Democritus' theory about the movement of the sun back and forth between the tropic signs (621–36). His explanation is not the Platonic/Stoic one of the obliquity of the ecliptic, but is to do with the distance from the earth of the heavenly bodies. All the same it is marked by Ciceronian expression. L. has *Arat.* 280–3 in mind throughout this whole passage, and elsewhere. There are two significant collocations:

hunc a clarisonis auris Aquilonis ad Austrum
cedens postremum tangit rota fervida solis:
exinde in superas, brumali tempore, flexu
se recipit sedes . . .

With *rota fervida solis* compare also *DRN* 5.432, 564, 628, 642; with *brumali tempore flexu*, *DRN* 5.616, 640. *Aestifer* in 5.642 is also possibly Ciceronian (see *Arat.* 330, *aestifer est pandens ferventia sidera Cancer*, of the zodiac, the point at issue in this passage of L.).

Lucretius	Cicero, *Aratea*
5.636 *signa revisunt*	337 *signa revisunt* (zodiac)
5.644 *quae volvunt magnos in magnis orbibus annos* Cf. 1.1029; 5.648 *magnos orbes* Munro (1894) ad loc. 'Lucretius imitates Cicero . . .'	232–6 (planets) *hae faciunt magnos longinqui temporis annos,* *cum redeunt ad idem caeli sub tegmine signum;* *quarum ego nunc nequeo tortos evolvere cursus:* *verum haec, quae semper certo [e]voluntur in orbe* *fixa.* . . .

5.648 *magnos orbes*	236 *magnos orbes*
5.664 *dispersos ignes orienti lumine cerni*	137 *disperso lumine fulgens*
5.665 *conficere orbem*	250 *conficit orbem*
Note: L. is perhaps also thinking of this passage at 4.391 *sidera cessare aetheriis adfixa cavernis*, with *Arat.* 252 *caeli lustrare cavernas.*	
5.684 *in partis . . . dividit*	268 *in partes divisum*
Note: This is a collocation which could happen by chance, but the Ciceronian passage on the celestial circles is one which L. draws on a lot at this point, increasing the likelihood that this expression also originates there.	
5.688 *nocturnas exaequat lucibus umbras*	288 *exaequat spatium lucis cum tempore noctis*
Note: Both authors refer to the sun's intersection with the equator.	
5.689 *flatus aquilonis et austri*	280 *auris Aquilonis ad austrum*
5.691 *signiferi . . . orbis*	318 *signiferum orbem* (cf. 340, 363)
Note: This designation for the zodiac is probably a Ciceronian coinage, first in *Aratea* (317–8): *Zodiacum haec Graeci vocitant, nostrique Latini* *Orbem signiferum perhibebunt nomine vero. . . .* Cicero glosses it at *Div.* 2.42.89 *signifero in orbe, qui Graece ζῳδιακός dicitur* (cf. *DND* 2.20.52).	
5.692–3 *annua sol in quo concludit tempore serpens* *obliquo terras et caelum lumine lustrans*	332–3 *haec sol aeterno convestit lumine lustrans* *annua conficiens vertentia tempora cursu*

(*continued*)

Lucretius	Cicero, *Aratea*
Note: For the Ciceronian parallels in these lines see also Munro (1894) ad loc. There is a general cross-hatching of Lucretian parallels with *Arat.* 332–7 which goes beyond the immediate passage. As well as the lines above, L. uses the same passage of C. elsewhere. For *convestit* see also 2.148 with n. above. For *Arat.* 335, *tantundem pandens supera mortalibus edit*, see 2.556, 6.359. For *Arat.* 336–7, *sex omni semper cedunt labentia nocte / tot caelum rursus fulgentia signa revisunt*, see both *labentia signa* in *DRN* 1.2 and *signa revisunt* at 5.636.	
5.694 *loca caeli*	130 *caeli . . . loca*
5.694–5 *ut ratio declarat eorum qui loca caeli* *omnia dispositis signis ornata notarunt*	162–6 *haec ille astrorum custos ratione notavit* *Signaque dignavit caelestia nomine vero;* *has autem quae sunt parvo cum lumine fusae,* *consimili specie stellas parilique nitore,* *non potuit nobis nota clarare figura.* (Cf. *Arat.* fr. 9.1 *ornans*)
Note: On 5.680–695, see above, Ch. 3 pp. 76–80. In this passage there is a constellation of Ciceronian parallels, culminating with a response to Cicero's programmatic passage on the first namer of stars. The Ciceronian parallels peter out somewhat after line 695. In 680–95 L. presents an argument in which he expressly engages with the Stoics, followed by one in lines 696ff, signalled by *aut quia*, in which he does not.	
5.708 *[luna] pleno lumine fulsit*	137 *disperso lumine fulgens* (see above, 5.664) 247 *nec pleno stellas super ardet lumine luna*

Note: L. may combine two passages of C., as we've seen him do before, for instance in his use of *Arat.* 54 and 57 in 3.8 (above).	
5.712 *labitur ex alia signorum parte per orbem* See above, on 1.2, below, 5.766.	226 *signorum labier orbem*
5.719 *cassum lumine fertur* Cf. above, 4.368, *lumine cassus*, and below 5.757.	301 *lumine fertur* (zodiac)
5.721 *candenti lumine* Cf. 6.1197	*Prog.* fr. 2 *ast autem tenui quae candet lumine Phatne*
5.742 *etesia* See below, on 6.716.	*Arat.* fr. 23 *hoc motu radiantis etesiae in vada ponti*
5.757 *cassum labatur lumine* (M 153, B 338) cf. 5.766 *perlabier orbem*[4]	37 *labentes lumine* 226 *labier orbem* 329 *lumine labens* 390 *labens per caeli lumina*
Note: In Cicero the verb *labor* is characteristic of the movement of the heavenly bodies (see on 1.2; 5.712, 766); the collocation with *lumen* is also a Ciceronian signature.	
5.774 *lunaeque meatus* See above on 5.76	*Prog.* fr. 1.1 *luna means*
5.906 *de corpore flammam*	110 *nec vero toto spirans de corpore flammam*
Note: This is a reference to Cicero's Sirius; see also on 2.705; 5.1099. For the thematic use of Sirius in Lucretius, see above, Ch. 4 pp. 94-8.	

(continued)

Lucretius	Cicero, Aratea
5.1092 *mortalibus ignem*	*Arat.* fr. 26.2 *mortalibus ignem* Cf. 112 *mortalibus ardor*
5.1099 *emicat interdum flammai fervidus ardor*	107–112 (Sirius): *namque pedes subter rutilo cum lumine claret* *fervidus ille Canis stellarum luce refulgens.* *hunc tegit obscurus subter praecordia vepres,* *nec vero toto spirans de corpore flammam* *aestiferos validis erumpit flatibus ignes:* *totus ab ore micans iacitur mortalibus ardor.*
Note: 5.1091–1104 may be compared with Cicero's whole Sirius passage, quoted above. On Sirius, see above on 2.705; previous n. on 5.1092.	
5.1138 *praeclarum insigne*	*Arat.* fr. 2.2 *praeclara insignia caeli*
5.1193 *murmura magna minarum* See on 1.68; Ch. 3 pp. 73–6.	71 *minitanti murmure*
5.1205 *stellis micantibus aethera fixum*	*Arat.* fr. 16.3–4 *. . . subter praecordia fixa videtur /stella micans radiis . . .* fr. 20.1–2 *. . . adfixa videtur /stella micans*
5.1293 *ferreus ensis* For discussion see Ch. 2 pp. 52–3.	*Arat.* fr. 18.1–2 *ferrea . . . /ensem*
5.1333–6 *terram consternere casu . . . /vulneribus*	432–3 *vulnera . . . /constravit corpore terram*

Note: The context in Lucretius is the death of horses in the bizarre war of beasts which took place at an earlier stage of human development; in Cicero the death of the giant bellicose constellation Orion. See on 6.311 for other uses of this passage in L.	
5.1399 *caput atque umeros*	417 *caput atque umeros*
5.1402 *pede pellere*	52 *pede pellere*
5.1437 *lustrantes lumine circum*	237 *lustrantes lumine mundum*
See above on 5.692–3	
Note: *DRN* 5.1436–9 is the beginning of the book's *peroratio*. L. begins his astronomical signoff to Book 5 with a reference to a characteristic Ciceronian passage which he has used elsewhere. Compare these lines of Lucretius—	
at vigiles mundi magnum versatile templum	
sol et luna suo lustrantes lumine circum	
perdocuere homines annorum tempora verti	
et certa ratione geri rem atque ordine certo	
—with *Arat.* 332–3	
haec sol aeterno convestit lumine lustrans,	
annua conficiens vertentia tempora cursu.	

DRN 6	**6.91** *divino numine*	305 *divino numine* (craftsman simile)[5]
	Cf. 4.1233 *divina . . . numina*; 5.122 *divino a numine*	On this passage, see above Ch. 3 pp. 78–80.
	6.99 *caeli de parte*	360 *caeli de parte*
	6.237 *fervore corusco*	96 *ore corusco*
	6. 252 *magnus caeli complesse cavernas*	252 *caeli lustrare cavernas*

(*continued*)

Lucretius	Cicero, Aratea
Note: On L.'s use of the Ciceronian *lustrare* elsewhere, see nn. above on 2.147–8 and 5.692–3.	
6.283–4 *omnia luminibus lustrans loca percitus ardor* *[fulmen] coruscis* cf. 5.692–3 with n. above	96 *ore corusco* 332 *haec sol aeterno convestit lumine lustrans*
6.295 *vis venti incidit . . . flamine*	198 . . . *inciderit vehementi flamine ventus* cf. 100–1
Note: Here we have a triple (near-quadruple) collocation with *variatio* of the fourth element. See following reference.	
6.311 *vementi perculit ictu*	431 *hic valido cupide venantem perculit ictu* (Orion)
Note: L. seems to have favoured C.'s purple passage on Orion: see also 2.25, 1114; 4.368; 5.1333–6. L. seems to have C.'s Orion passage in mind particularly in Book 6: as well as 6.311 *vementi perculit ictu* with *Arat.* 431 *hic valido cupide venantem perculit ictu*, we have 6.819–20 *mortiferum vinn, de terra quae surgit in auras, lut spatium caeli quadam de parte venenet* with *Arat.* 432 *mortiferum in venas figens per vulnera virus*; 6.857 *corpore terram* with *Arat.* 433. Perhaps Cicero's Orion serves Lucretius well in the increasing tenor of violence in Book 6, leading up to the Plague.	
6.334 *celeri . . . impete labens* Cf. 4.210 (*celeri . . . motu . . . ferantur*)	*Arat.* fr.3 *cetera labuntur celeri caelestia motu,* *cum caeloque simul noctesque diesque feruntur.*
Note: In the original (*Arat.* fr. 3) the context is one of stasis vs. dynamism. In L. the phrase is used of the thunderbolt. The Ciceronian reference is appropriate here, of this most mobile of celestial phenomena.	
6.359 *et cum tempora se veris florentia pandunt*	39–40 *propterea quod aestatis primordia clarat,* *et post, hiberni praepandens temporis ortus*

Note: For *pando*, see the Quintus Cicero fragment, line 4; see also *Arat.* 330, *aestifer est pandens ferventia sidera Cancer* (both connected with the zodiac).	
6.389 *iaciunt ignem*	*Arat.* fr. 24.2 *iaciunt mortalibus ignem* Cf. 331 *et Gemini clarum iactantes lucibus ignem*
6.446 *hic ubi se* Cf. 6.140, 524, 686, 836	113 *hic ubi se*
Note: Is this a Ciceronian formula? According to *BTL* the threefold collocation is found only in Cicero and Lucretius.	
6.448–9 *montisque necessest lofficere in terris*	344 *officiens . . mons*
6.455 *haec faciunt*	232 *hae faciunt*
Note: This doesn't at first look like a convincing parallel, but one may wish to take into account *variatio* in the rest of the line. L. reads *haec faciunt primum parvas consistere nubis*; C. *hae faciunt magnos longinqui temporis annos*. In *DRN* 6, we have passed from big things (stars) to small things (weather signs). This passage of Cicero is one favoured elsewhere by L. (see on 1.1029), perhaps making more likely its use here.	
6.461 *nubis caligine crassa*	345 *caeca caligine nubes*
6.660 *corpore serpens* cf. 5.33.	215 *corpore serpens* cf. 286
Note: In Book 6 the collocation may anticipate use of Aratean borrowing in the Plague (e.g., *serpere coepit*, 6.1120).	
6.716 *anni tempore eo qui etesiae esse feruntur* Cf. 1.200.	*Arat.* fr. 23 *hoc modo radiantis etesiae in vada ponti*

(continued)

229

Lucretius	Cicero, *Aratea*
Note: This is a key instance of Lucretian reminiscence of Cicero, not picked up by Merrill (1921), but mentioned by Soubiran (1975): 75. Both Cicero and Aratus have the same word, and the same hiatus, in the same place in the verse: see *Ph.* 152 τῆμος καὶ κελάδοντες Ἐτησίαι εἰρέι πόντῳ. There is a possible aggregation of parallels here: see also *anni tempore* with *Arat.* 69 sed tamen iam labuntur anni tempore toto.	
6.754 *Graium ut cecinere poetae* Cf. 5.405, 6.424 6.90 *ut veteres Graium cecinere poetae*	33 *ut veteres statuere poetae*
Note: L. may have Cicero's programmatic Pleiades passage in mind at several points in the *DRN* where he takes issue with myth: see on 2.600. On the connected theme of naming, see on 6.908.	
6.780 *aspectu fugienda . . . tristia*	*Arat.* fr. 31.2 *Andromeda, aufugiens aspectum maesta parentis*
6.819–20 *mortiferam vim . . . lut . . . venenet*	432 *mortiferam in venas figens per vulnera virus* (Orion)
Note: For references to Cicero's Orion, see n. on 2.25 above.	
6.852 *caligine texit*	194 *caligine tectam* *Prog.* fr. 1.2 *caeca caligine tecti*
Note: The collocation *caligo + tego* is only in L. and C. (*BTL*). See also *validis viribus, Arat.* 195, with 1.287.	
6.856 *superum lumen*	185 *superum . . . lumen*
6.857 *corpore terram* See above, n. on 2.1114.	433 *corpora terram* 435 *corpora terris* 438 *corpore terras*

6.881 *taedaque consimili ratione accensa per undas*	*197 per undas* *227 simili ratione*
Note: Again, there may be two passages of Cicero combined in one line of L. For a near-quadruple collocation shared with one of the present passages of the *Arat.* (line 198), see above, on 6.295. For *consimili ratione*: see above, n. on 1.1061.	
6.890 *dulcis aquai*	*Prog.* fr. 4.1 S., *aquai dulcis alumnae*
Note: for further reference to the *Prognostica* see above on 2.296, 5.298–9, and 6.504.	
6.908 *nomine Grai*	*Arat.* fr. 14 *nomine Grai*
Note: For the (Ciceronian) theme of naming, see also *DRN* 1.830–2; 2.629–30; 6.298, 424 with *Arat.* fr. 14.	
6.957 *in caelum*	26 and 407 (both in the same *sedes*)
6.1159 *assidue comes et gemitu commixta querela*	*Prog.* fr. 4.6 *vocibus instat et adsiduas iacit ore querelas*
Note: It is almost certain that L. had this line in mind at 5.298–9 (n. above). It is equally certain L. is using the same fragment at 1.191 (n. above). For *querel[l]a* at the line-end, see also *DRN* 6.16.	
6.1180–1 *. . . ardentia morbis* *lumina versarent oculorum expertia somno* Cf. 4.825	479 *. . . oculorum ardentia lumina vestit*
Note: This is a triple collocation shared between Cicero and Lucretius. In the *Aratea*, the Hydra is obscured by darkness; in Lucretius the eyes of the dying person cannot close. Perhaps this is a continuation, heading into the climax of Book 6, of the thematic use of the setting of a star to represent the dying soul (see above on 3.218).	

APPENDIX C

Text and Translations of Aratus' Proem and Avienus' Proem

Aratus, Proem (ed. Kidd)	Translation (Kidd)
ἐκ Διὸς ἀρχώμεσθα, τὸν οὐδέποτ' ἄνδρες ἐῶμεν ἄρρητον. μεσταὶ δὲ Διὸς πᾶσαι μὲν ἀγυιαί, πᾶσαι δ' ἀνθρώπων ἀγοραί, μεστὴ δὲ θάλασσα καὶ λιμένες· πάντη δὲ Διὸς κεχρήμεθα πάντες. τοῦ γὰρ καὶ γένος εἰμέν· ὁ δ' ἤπιος ἀνθρώποισι 5 δεξιὰ σημαίνει, λαοὺς δ' ἐπὶ ἔργον ἐγείρει μιμνήσκων βιότοιο, λέγει δ' ὅτε βῶλος ἀρίστη βουσί τε καὶ μακέλῃσι, λέγει δ' ὅτε δεξιαὶ ὧραι καὶ φυτὰ γυρῶσαι καὶ σπέρματα πάντα βαλέσθαι. αὐτὸς γὰρ τά γε σήματ' ἐν οὐρανῷ ἐστήριξεν 10 ἄστρα διακρίνας, ἐσκέψατο δ' εἰς ἐνιαυτὸν ἀστέρας οἵ κε μάλιστα τετυγμένα σημαίνοιεν ἀνδράσιν ὡράων, ὄφρ' ἔμπεδα πάντα φύωνται. τῷ μιν ἀεὶ πρῶτόν τε καὶ ὕστατον ἱλάσκονται. χαῖρε, πάτερ, μέγα θαῦμα, μέγ' ἀνθρώποισιν ὄνειαρ, 15 αὐτὸς καὶ προτέρη γενεή. χαίροιτε δὲ Μοῦσαι, μειλίχιαι μάλα πᾶσαι· ἐμοί γε μὲν ἀστέρας εἰπεῖν ᾗ θέμις εὐχομένῳ τεκμήρατε πᾶσαν ἀοιδήν. **The Layout of the Universe** οἱ μὲν ὁμῶς πολέες τε καὶ ἄλλυδις ἄλλοι ἐόντες	'Let us begin with Zeus, whom we men never leave unspoken. Filled with Zeus are all highways and all meeting-places of people, filled are the sea and the harbours; in all circumstances we are all dependent on Zeus. [5] For we are also his children, and he benignly gives helpful signs to men, and rouses people to work, reminding them of their livelihood, tells when the soil is best for oxen and mattocks, and tells when the seasons are right both for planting trees and for sowing every kind of seed. [10] For it was Zeus himself who fixed the signs in the sky, making them into distinct constellations, and organised stars for the year to give the most clearly defined signs of the seasonal round to men, so that everything may grow without fail. That is why men always pay homage to him first and last. [15] Hail, Father, great wonder, great boon to men, yourself and the earlier race! And hail, Muses, all most gracious! In answer to my prayer to tell of the stars in so far as I may, guide all my singing. **The Layout of the Universe** The numerous stars, scattered in different directions, [20] sweep all alike

232

Avienus, Proem (ed. Soubiran)	Translation (my own)
Carminis incentor mihi Iuppiter: auspice terras linquo Iove, excelsam reserat dux Iuppiter aethram, imus in astra Iovis monitu, Iovis omine caelum et Iovis imperio mortalibus aethera pando. hic statio, hic sedes primi patris. iste paterni 5 principium motus, vis fulminis iste corusci, vita elementorum, mundi calor, aetheris ignis astrorumque vigor, perpes substantia lucis et numerus celsi modulaminis. hic tener aer materiaeque gravis concretio, sucus ab alto 10 corporibus caelo, cunctarum alimonia rerum, flos et flamma animae: qui discurrente meatu molis primigenae penetralia dura resolvens implevit largo venas operatus amore, ordinis ut proprii foedus daret. iste calorem 15 quo digesta capax solidaret semina mundus inseruit. rite hunc *primum*, medium *atque secundum* vox secreta canit: sibi nam permixtus utrimque et fultus sese geminum latus, unus et idem est	'Jupiter inspires my poem. Under the prophetic guidance of Jupiter I leave the earth, Jupiter as leader unlocks the lofty ether, we enter the stars under instruction from Jupiter, under the omen and the order of Jupiter I lay open the ether to mankind. [5] This is the guardpost, this the seat of the First Father. He is the beginning of generative motion, he the power of the scintillating lightning bolt, the life-force of the elements, warmth of the world, strength of the etherial fire and of the stars, the never-ending material of light, and the number of celestial harmony. He is the gauzy air and the weighty coagulation of matter [10], he is moisture for bodies from the high heaven, nutriment of all things, flower and flame of the soul. Dissolving the solid inner parts of the primeval mass by running through it on his path, he did the work of filling its veins with broad-spreading love, [15] in order to confer the treaty of initial order. He himself instilled the heat by means of which the world, full of potential, might amass the disjunct seeds of things. It is right that the awed voice sings him first, middle and following. For combining with himself on one side and the other, and

Aratus, Proem (ed. Kidd)	Translation (Kidd)
οὐρανῷ ἕλκονται πάντ᾽ ἤματα συνεχὲς αἰεί· 20 αὐτὰρ ὅ γ᾽ οὐδ᾽ ὀλίγον μετανίσσεται, ἀλλὰ μάλ᾽ αὕτως ἄξων αἰὲν ἄρηρεν, ἔχει δ᾽ ἀτάλαντον ἀπάντῃ μεσσηγὺς γαῖαν, περὶ δ᾽ οὐρανὸν αὐτὸν ἀγινεῖ. καί μιν πειραίνουσι δύω πόλοι ἀμφοτέρωθεν· ἀλλ᾽ ὁ μὲν οὐκ ἐπίοπτος, ὁ δ᾽ ἀντίος ἐκ βορέαο 25 ὑψόθεν ὠκεανοῖο.	across the sky every day continuously for ever. The axis, however, does not move even slightly from its place, but just stays forever fixed, holds the earth in the centre evenly balanced, and rotates the sky itself. Two poles terminate it at the two ends; [25] but one is not visible, while the opposite one in the North is high above the horizon.

Avienus, Proem (ed. Soubiran)		Translation (my own)
auctor agendorum propriique patrator amoris	20	supporting himself on both flanks, one
et mundi vere sanctus *pater*. hic chaos altum		and the same [20] he is the instigator of
lumine perrupit, tenebrarum hic vincula primus		things to be done, and the accomplisher of
solvit et ipse parens rerum fluvitantia fixit;		his own love, indeed the holy father of the
hic dispersa locis statuit primordia iustis,		universe. He exploded deep chaos with his
hic digestorum speciem dedit; iste colorem	25	light, he is was who first loosed the chains
imposuit rebus, sexuque immixtus utroque		of darkness, and, in his own generative
atque aevi pariter gemini simul omnia lustrans,		role stabilized what was in flux; he set the
sufficit alterno res semine. rerum opifex hic,		scattered particles in their right places, [25]
hic altor rerum, rex mundi, celsa potestas		he gave shape to what had been sepa-
aetheris atque Erebi, pigra inclinatio nodi,	30	rated; he conferred colour on things, and,
insocabilium discretio iusta deorum,		containing an admixture of the two sexes
cuius et extremum tellus opus, ignea cuius		and encompassing all matters of double
lumina sunt late, sol et soror, ille diei		generation equally at the one time, he was
tendat ut infusi rutilum iubar, altera noctis		capable of creating the universe from the
ut face flammanti tenebrosos rumpat amictus.	35	seeds of both.[1] He is the craftsman of the
nec defit genitis pater ullo in tempore rebus:		universe, the one who brings it to fruition,
istius ille *anni* pulcher chorus, alta ut hebescat		king of the world, supreme power [30]
terra gelu, ver ut blandis adrideat arvis,		of both the ether and the underworld,
pulverulenta siti tellurem ut torreat aestas		the gentle incline of the ecliptic,[2] the just
et gravis autumni redeat fetura parentis.	40	mediator between warring gods. The earth
hoc duce per tumidi ferimur freta gurgitis, *isto*		was his final work, lit far and wide by its fi-
praeceptore solum gravibus versamus aratris.		ery lights, the sun and his sister, so that the
iste modum statuit signis, hic rebus honorem		former should proffer the ruddy beam of
infudit; tenebris hic interlabitur aethrae		outflowing day, [35] while the latter should
viscera et aeternos animat genitalibus artus.	45	rip the shadowy cape of night with her
denique ne longum marcentia corda iacerent		flaring torch. Nor does the Father desert
mundanique ortus mens immemor omnia sensim		his creation at any time. His is the beauti-
vilia conciperet neque se subduceret umquam		ful dance of the year, which brings it about
		that the deep loam grows stiff with frost,
		that gentle spring laughs upon the fields,
		that dusty summer parches the earth with
		thirst [40] and the heavy offspring of fruit-
		ful autumn returns. Under his guidance
		we are borne across the straights of the
		swelling sea, under his instruction we turn
		the earth with resilient ploughs. He placed
		a limit on the signs, he imbued everything
		with its own status, he interweaves his
		shadowy form into the innards of the
		ether and vivifies its everlasting limbs as
		a creative force. [45] Finally, so that our
		hearts should not lie in a long sleep and
		our mind, forgetful of its celestial origin,

Aratus, Proem (ed. Kidd)	Translation (Kidd)

Header navigation top right: "Appendix C } 237"

Avienus, Proem (ed. Soubiran)	Translation (my own)
fontis in aeterni primordia, quo, velut amnis quem festina citis urget natura fluentis, 50 lapsa continuo ruiturae in corpora nostra prorumpunt animae seriemque per aethera nectunt, hic primum Cnidii radium senis intulit astris mortalemque loqui docuit convexa deorum: cur Hyperionis Nepa circumflecteret ignes 55 autumni reditu, cur sub gelido Capricorno bruma pruinosi iuga tristia solveret anni, cur spatium lucis, madidae cur tempora noctis Libra celerique Aries dimenso pondere Olympi aequarent, qua parte polus sublimior alto 60 cardine caeruleas Thetidis non tangeret undas, quis polus umbrifero lateat declivis in axe et vaga palanti cur signa errore ferantur. que rursum ingenio numerisque Solensibus idem Iuppiter efferri melius dedit, incola Tauri 65 Musa ut Cecropios raperetur et Aonas agros. me quoque nunc similis stimulat favor edere versu *tempora cum duris versare ligonibus arva* *conveniat,* cum velivolo dare carbasa ponto et cum viticomo crinem tondere Lyaeo. 70 O mihi nota adyti iam numina Parnasei! *O per multa operum mea semper cura, Camenae!* iam placet in superum visus sustollere caelum atque oculis reserare viam per sidera. maior, maior agit mentem solito deus, ampla patescit 75 Cirrha mihi et totis Helicon inspirat ab antris. **The Layout of the Universe** omnia quae flammis pingunt radiantibus aethram nox agit et verso ceu fixa trahuntur Olympo.	conceive unworthy things, and thus never approach the source of the eternal spring, by means of which, just like a river [50] which impatient nature drives forth in rapid jets, souls burst forth in a continuous stream, intending to flow into our bodies, and line up in the ether – he first directed the instrument of Eudoxus to the stars and taught him, though mortal, to describe the vaults of the gods: [55] why Cancer turns the beams of the sun around at the return of autumn, why under chilly Capricorn the winter solstice relieves the frosty year of its gloomy yoke; why Libra and swift Aries, dividing the weight of heaven, make equal the portion of day and the time of dewy night; [60] in what part the more lofty pole with its high turning-point fails to touch the indigo waters of Thetis; which pole lies hidden way down on the axis out of sight, and why the roaming stars are carried about in their wandering meander. [65] That same Jupiter, in turn, gave greater facility in telling these things to the intelligent verses of Aratus, so that the Muse who lives in the Taurus Mountains should speed across the fields of Aonian and Athenian poetry. Likewise his indulgence now drives me to set forth in verse the times when it is proper to turn the earth with hardy mattocks, when to raise the canvas to the sea apt for sails, [70] and when to trim the hair of vine-bearing Bacchus. O deities of the Parnassan grotto, already known to me! Muses, always my concern throughout many works! Now I am pleased to raise my gaze to highest heaven and lay bare with my eyes a path through the stars! [75] A greater – yes, a greater – god than usual galvanizes my mind, broad Cirrha is open to me, and Helicon breathes upon me from all its caves. **The Layout of the Universe** Night drives all those stars which decorate the ether with their flickering flames, and

Aratus, Proem (ed. Kidd)	Translation (Kidd)

Avienus, Proem (ed. Soubiran)	Translation (my own)
at non cuncta tamen signorum in lege putanda: pars numeris et honore caret. micat omnibus ignis 80 et rutilo cunctis flagrat coma flammea crine, sed quia non certa formarum in luce notantur omnia, sideribus cassum fit cetera volgus. mobilis en etiam mundi se machina versat, ponderis et proprii trahit inclinatio caelum. 85 *sed non axis* item curvi vertigine *fertur* aetheris, ut stilus instabili convolvitur orbi: *iuge manet*, tenuisque procul sacra viscera caeli perforat et mediae molem terrae tenet. illum non prolixa dies, non incumbentis Olympi 90 cursus agit motatve loco labor, ut semel haerens constitit et ferri se circum cuncta remisit. nec minus extremo dispar polus: Oceano pars sublime erigitur, subit altera, mersa sub undas, pars Erebum et nigri iacet haec ut conscia Ditis. 95 hic Notus, horriferis Aquilonibus illa rigescunt, ac teres in gemina stridit vertigine cardo. *alter in obtutum facilis, latet alter et alto deprimitur barathro.*	they are dragged along by the sky as it turns, as though fixed to it. However, not all of the heavenly bodies should be thought of as under the rule of law: [80] part lacks rhyme and reason. In every one of the stars the fire flickers, and on all of them a fiery coif flames with reddish hair, but because they can't all be recorded using the indisputable elucidation of figures, a crowd devoid of constellations becomes the remainder. Look how the mobile mechanism of the sky turns itself, and the momentum of its own weight drags the heaven. But the axis is not similarly carried along by the turning of the concave ether, as a shaft is turned by an unstable disk: it remains constant, and though slender, runs though the holy entrails of heaven from top to bottom and holds the mass of the earth in the middle. [90] Neither long-drawn-out time nor the movement of the sky resting upon it, or effort, can push it or shift it from its place: it stands as though stuck once and for all, and permits everything to be carried around it. The poles at its extremities could not be more diverse: one is lifted high up from Ocean, [95] this other one lies underneath, subsumed under the waters, as though an associate of Erebos and dusky Dis. On the one hand is the South wind, on the other, they grow stiff with the shivery North wind, and the smooth pivot rings in its twin turning-point. One is easy to see, the other lies hidden, weighed down in the deep abyss.

NOTES

Introduction

1. 'Copernicus may be regarded as one of the last, and one of the most accomplished, astronomers in the Ptolemaic tradition,' Evans (1998): 26; cf. Kuhn (1957): 135: 'In every respect except the earth's motion [Copernicus'] *De Revolutionibus* seems more closely akin to the works of ancient and medieval astronomers and cosmologists than to the writings of the succeeding generations who based their work upon Copernicus' and made explicit the radical consequences that even its author did not see in his work.' For details of the relationship between Copernicus and Ptolemy, see Kuhn (1957): 64–73.

2. For the basic parameters, see recently Cusset, 'Aratos,' *EANS*, pp. 123–24. Best on the issues, and the debates surrounding them, is Kidd (1997) Introduction, pp. 1–68. Kidd's thorough account cannot be bettered. Some excellent introductory essays on Aratus have come out in recent years, notably Volk (2010) and Taub (2010). On Stoicism, still standard is Effe (1977): 40–56, now watered down by some, for instance Fantuzzi and Hunter (2004): 226–27 (see below, Ch.6 p. 000). On Aratus' use of Hesiod, Fakas (2001) is seminal.

3. Collected by Martin (1998): xi–xlviii.

4. On Aratus' 'sources', see Volk (2010): 198.

5. Sale (1966): 160. A history of the question from Lewis (1992) and recently Taub (2010) and Volk (2010).

6. Taub (2010): 121; cf. Courtney (2003): 150: 'There must have been a strong urge to win Aratus for Latin when Germanicus (*Phaen.*) and Ovid (fr. 1–2; *Phaen.*) repeated Cicero's efforts (cf. also Cinna fr. 11 and the Ephemeris of Varro Atacinus).' Despite specifying four translations, Taub (2010): 120 refers primarily to the three extant ones, Cicero, Germanicus, and Avienus. Lewis (1992): 95–97 has a more comprehensive list, as does Volk (2010): 208–9 (translations: Cicero, Varro of Atax, Ovid, Germanicus, Avienus; adaptations: Virgil, *Georgics*, Manilius, Ovid, *Fasti*). For a full list of translations, commentaries and editions, see Kidd (1997): xii–xiv and Introduction Sections V–VII, pp. 36–60.

7. For Varro of Atax's date, see Ch.3 p. 65.

8. See for instance Farrell (1991): 79–83; 157–62.

9. Courtney (2003) Ovid frr. 1–2. On Ovid's translation see Gee (2000): 69 and n.8.

10. On *Ast*. 1.255–808, see Volk (2009): 188–92. On the date of the *Ast.*, see Volk (2009): 137–61, the latest contribution to a long-running debate.

11. Probably first half of the eighth century: see Kidd (1997): 52–55; Reeve (1983a); de Bourdellès (1987).

12. On Ceporinus, see Ludwig (2003). On Camerarius and Buchanan, see Gee (2008). On Buchanan and the wider context of Renaissance astronomical poetry, see Naiden (1952) and Haskell (1998).

13. Poochigian (2010). Poochigian gives this rationale: 'Like Aratus' original, my translation endeavours not only to teach the constellations and weather signs, but also to help the reader understand why this knowledge is important' (p.ix). On Poochigian, see my review in *CR* 62 (2012): 433–5.

14. The Cinna epigram is printed as the epigraph to this book, and discussed in Ch.3 p. 65. On Callimachus and Aratus see Lewis (1992): 97 and Volk (2010): 199–200; on Cinna and Aratus, Lewis (1992): 98. For other epigrams in praise of Aratus by Leonidas of Tarentum, and by Ptolemy, see Lewis (1992): 111, and Kidd (1997): 36–37.

15. Volk (2010): 197 also cites Quintilian's verdict.

16. This area of Aratean studies still rests almost exclusively on the works of Maass (1898) and Martin (1956 and 1974). A synthesis of the two scholars' work is needed, perhaps with particular attention to the introductory texts appended to Aratus' text.

17. Kidd (1997): 18–21 and 45.

18. Kidd (1997): 43.

19. Martin (1956): 69; (1974): IV–V; Kidd (1997): 44. Also putatively from the third century is the introductory work ascribed to 'Achilles'. The edition is Maass (1898): 27–85; see Di Maria (1996); Kidd (1997): 48. This is a general work which came to be used as an introduction to Aratus.

20. *Iulii Firmici Astronomicorum libri octo integri & emendati, ex Scythicis oris ad nos nuper allati. Marci Manilii astronomicorum libri quinque. Arati Phaenomena Germanico Caesare interprete cum commentariis & imaginibus. Arati eiusdem phaenomenon fragmentum Marco. T. C. interprete. Arati eiusdem Phaenomena Ruffo Festo Auienio paraphraste. Arati eiusdem Phaenomena graece. Theonis commentaria copiosissima in Arati Phaenomena graece. Procli Diadochi Sphaera graece. Procli eiusdem Sphaera, Thoma Linacro Britanno interprete.* Venetiis in aedibus Aldi Romani, 1499. On the Aldus edition see Kidd (1997): xii.

21. Volk (2010): 197, 'As far as modern readers are concerned, Aratus is a poet undone by his own success.'

22. 'It is a revolution-making rather than a revolutionary text' (Kuhn 1957: 135). See the Epilogue to this book for further remarks about Copernicus.

23. Hipparchus ed. Manitius (1894). Kidd (1997): 161 cites the Hipparchus passages. The 'Hipparchan tradition' of Aratus' relationship with Eudoxus is more often assumed than acknowledged: see for instance Taub (2010): 119. This tradition has a very long shelf-life: already Cicero (reading Hipparchus?) cited it at *Republic* 1.22:

> dicebat enim Galus, sphaerae illius alterius solidae atque plenae vetus esse inventum, et eam a Thalete Milesio primum esse tornatam; post autem ab Eudoxo Cnidio, discipulo ut ferebat Platonis, eandem illam astris quae caelo inhaererent esse descriptam; cuius omnem ornatum et descriptionem, sumptam ab Eudoxo, multis annis post non astrologiae scientia sed poetica quadam facultate versibus Aratum extulisse (text of Powell 2006).

> 'Galus said that that another type of sphere, which was solid all the way through, was an old invention, and that Thales of Miletus had first made one of the kind afterwards made by Eudoxus of Cnidus, a pupil, so they say, of Plato. This same one was engraved with the stars which are attached to the heaven. Many years later Aratus took the whole arrangement and order from Eudoxus and set it out in verse, not with any great knowledge of astronomy, but with poetic facility' (my trans.).

See Kidd (1997): 16–17. St Augustine too is, despite himself, an heir of the 'Hipparchan tradition', even as he tries to do down Aratus and Eudoxus and the 'pagan' scientific thought they represent: *postremo universum stellarum numerum comprehendisse et conscripsisse iactantur sicut Aratus et Eudoxus vel si qui alii sunt, eos libri huius contemnit auctoritas* ('Finally, the authority of [the bible] condemns those like Aratus and Eudoxus and others who claim to have grasped and recorded the complete number of the stars', *Civ. Dei* 16.23; see Lewis 1992: 99). In the fourth century the same tradition is worked into the proem of the *Phaenomena* itself by Avienus, who artificially forces Eudoxus and Aratus into sequence, as the twin founders of astronomy. Avienus' *Phaenomena* thus becomes a reflective work, binding together in one 'translation' the textual and paratextual traditions.

24. www.wikipedia.org/wiki/Phenomenon, accessed 07/12/11, 13.04 pm UK Time.

25. On the wider issue of 'reality' and 'realism' in the history of science, see Kennedy (2002): 1–63.

26. These terms also include 'data' and 'observation', both connected conceptually with the establishment of 'phenomena' (Bogen and Woodward 1988: 314).

27. 'We expect phenomena to have stable, repeatable characteristics which will be detectable by means of a variety of different procedures, which may yield quite different types of data' (Bogen and Woodward 1988: 317).

28. Bogen and Woodward (1988): 305–6.

29. Bacon, *Adv. Learn.* 2 I 3r and 2 I 4r (Kiernan 2000).

30. Bacon was agnostic about the 'truth' of the theories themselves. On Bacon's attitude to astronomy, see Pérez-Ramos (1990).

31. *Oxford Francis Bacon* XV, p. 55.27–30.

32. Morgan (2000): 287 n.76: 'Aristotle himself does not use the formulation "saving the phenomena"; it appears repeatedly in Simplicius' commentary on Aristotle's *De Caelo*, and also in Plutarch, Theon of Smyrna, John Philoponus, and Proclus.'

33. See Vlastos (1975): 59–60; 110–11.

34. Simplicius *Cael.* 488.14–24 ed. Heiberg, trans. Mueller (2005).

35. Kuhn (1957): 3 describes the Copernican revolution 'an episode in the development of planetary astronomy.'

36. Kuhn (1957): 169.

37. Kuhn (1957): 224, my emphasis.

38. *LSJ* φαίνω B.II.2.

39. Plato uses ὁράω and its cognates to designate the objects of *sense*-perception, for instance ὁρώμενα at *Rep.* 530b4. He uses αἰσθάνομαι to distinguish the 'perceptible' from the intelligible (and therefore more real) world, for example τῶν αἰσθητῶν, *Rep.* 529b8–9.

40. For the 'saving' of the myth in Plato, see Segal (1978); Howland (1993): 30–31; Morgan (2000): 281–89.

41. Morgan (2000): 287 comments, 'What we choose to save in any instance is indicative of our approach to the world. Plato chooses to save the argument, whereas Aristotle chooses to save the phenomena, that is, the appearances of the sensible world.'

42. Morgan (2000): 202–4.

43. See Ch. 6.

44. The planets for instance: Aratus did not mention their 'explanation' in the theory of 'homocentric spheres' developed by his model Eudoxus.

45. Kuhn (1957): 3.

46. For instance, the view attributed to the Stoic speaker in Cicero, *DND* 2.110 (*ita dimetata signa sunt ut in tantis descriptionibus divina sollertia appareat*, 'The star-signs are measured out in such a way that divine intelligence is revealed in such great patterns,' my trans.). On 'intelligent design' in antiquity, and its opponents, see Sedley (2007).

47. Kuhn (1957): 76–77 refers to '*the* ancient tradition of astronomical research', and '*the* astronomical tradition' (my emphasis).

48. Kuhn, for instance (1957): 7, talks of '. . . the two main scientific cosmologies of the West, the Ptolemaic and the Copernican.'

49. Of the writings of the 'master,' only Epicurus' *Letters, Principal Doctrines* and *Vatican Sayings* (epitomes of his philosophy preserved in Diogenes Laertius, writing in the third century AD) are extant. The edition with English translation and notes is Geer (1964).

50. He puts his own position in *Tusc. Disp.* 4.7: *sed defendat, quod quisque sentit; sunt enim iudicia libera: nos institutum tenebimus nullisque unius disciplinae legibus adstricti, quibus in philosophia necessario pareamus, quid sit in quaque re maxime probabile, semper requiremus* ('But let everyone defend their own beliefs. Opinions are free. I will stick to my principle and, unfettered by any particular school of thought, always seek out what is the position of greatest probability,' my trans.).

51. See Ch. 3 below.

52. The evidence is stark: there were no manuscripts of Lucretius written between the ninth century and the fifteenth (Reeve 2007: 206).

53. Greenblatt (2011). This book tries to make a fairly arcane area of classical and humanist studies accessible to a wider audience. It has made something of a splash in the wider literary world, where it has been variously received (the reviews of Black at http://www.historyextra.com/book-review/swerve-how-renaissance-began (accessed 12/11/12), and Grafton in the *New York Review of Books*, December 8, 2011, exemplify differences in its reception).

54. On the role of Lucretius in the history of modern science see Johnson and Wilson (2007).

55. Kuhn (1957): 123.

56. Kuhn (1957): 103; 109–11.

57. Kuhn (1957): 27, my emphasis.

58. Kuhn (1957): 235–36.

59. Kuhn (1957): 41–43.

60. F.9v of the first ed. of Copernicus *De rev.*, held in the rare books collection of St Andrews University Library, reproduced with thanks.

61. See chapters 3 and 4.

62. 'The mission of the Richard Dawkins Foundation for Reason and Science is to support scientific education, critical thinking and evidence-based understanding of the natural world in the quest to overcome religious fundamentalism, superstition, intolerance and suffering' (http://richarddawkins.net) accessed 12/12/11, 13.57 pm UK Time. Compare Lucretius, *De rerum natura* 1.102–11: 'You will yourself some day try to defect from us, overcome by the terrifying words of priests. It's true—for how many dreams can they now invent for you, which can overturn the rational principles of life and poison all your futures with fear! And with good reason: because if men saw that a limit has been set to troubles, somehow they would find the strength to defy the rumour-mongering of the priests. But as

things stand there is no means of resistance and no power, because they are scared of everlasting punishments after death' (my trans.). Likewise, Dawkins' genetic reductionism (*The Selfish Gene* 30th Anniversary Edition, 2006, pp. 12–20) finds a parallel in the mechanistic causality of *DRN* 2.1059–62, 'Of their own accord, by knocking together by chance, forced together in many ways without rhyme, reason or rationale, at length [the primary particles] formed those things which, thrown suddenly together, could become every time the beginnings of large things . . .' Lucretius' 'Primary Particles' and Dawkins' 'Replicators' (p. 15) are conceptually interchangeable. On Lucretius and the genetics of Dawkins (among others), see Kennedy (2002): 79–84.

63. Kuhn (1957): 4–5.

64. On Camerarius, see Gee (2008).

65. For the date, see Kidd (1997): 4.

66. The terminus post quem is Lactantius' *Divinae institutiones* (c.310 AD) in which Avienus is not mentioned among the translators of Aratus at I.21.38 and 5.5.4–5; the terminus ante quem Jerome *Comm. Epist. ad Tit.* 1.12 (c.386 AD), in which he is (see Soubiran 1981: 7–8). For the knotty questions of the name, *gens* of the author, and his geographical origin, see Soubiran (1981): 15–29; Cameron (1995b).

67. Most recently Van Noorden (2009); Volk (2012): 223, 'an intricate amalgam of themes from Hesiod.' For further bibliography, see below, Ch. 1 n.7.

68. Morgan (2000): 208.

69. So, for instance, Possanza (2004), on Germanicus.

70. Alongside another intelligent design model, namely Plato. On the interactions between Lucretius and Plato's *Timaeus*—the archetypal intelligent design text-in particular, see Sedley (1998).

71. Avienus was (probably) a member of the Roman aristocracy from Volsinii. He translated both Aratus and the geographical work, the *Periegesis*, of Dionysius the Periegete, and wrote a geographical poem, the *Ora Maritima*.

72. 'Aratus' readers took the *Phaenomena*—and made it into whatever they pleased' (Volk (2010): 208.

Chapter 1

1. Hipparchus' commentary, c.150 BC. See Taub (2010): 126–27.

2. On allegorical interpretations of epic, see for instance Lamberton (1986).

3. On this passage the bibliography is extensive: the most recent contribution I know of, with extensive notes and bibliography, is Halliwell (2011): 154–207, 'To Banish or Not to Banish? Plato's Unanswered Question about Poetry.'

4. A pithy but insightful interpretation of this myth is in Morgan (2000): 204–10.

5. 'It is no accident that the myth of Er follows so soon after the dismissal of the poets. In response to Socrates' call for the lover of poetry to defend it in prose, Plato presents not a defence, but a replacement', Morgan (2000): 208.

6. It is safe to postulate, both here and later in this book, that Aratus and his Roman followers, even those earlier ones who were not avowed Neoplatonists, were also readers of Plato or at the very least had good access to the Platonic texts. Alline (1915) chapter 3, 'Le texte de Platon à l'époque hellénistique' is still standard on the reception of Plato in Aratus' time. Alline comments (p. 77) that the great success and rapid diffusion of Plato's dialogues

was not always best for the state of the text, a phenomenon partially rectified during the course of the third century BC with the advent of the critical approach. It was in this century, also Aratus', that readership became especially widespread; at the same time, with the development of textual criticism, Plato's text was studied and improved in intellectual circles in the main Hellenistic centres (Athens, Alexandria, Pergamum, Rhodes). On the reception of Plato in later periods see Dillon (1977) for the first century BC and the first two centuries AD; comprehensively, Gersh (1986); for the later periods in particular Tarrant (2000), and the papers collected in Tarrant and Baltzy (2006). See also below, Ch. 6, on Avienus, Aratus, and Neoplatonism. The comments of Fowler (2000a): 141 on Lucretius' use of Plato are salient ('. . . Any intertext will be present in the target text both in itself, contextualised within the original work, and also with its accumulation of later uses'). In a sense it is a non-question whether our authors (Aratus here, Virgil in the following chapter) used Plato directly or indirectly, consciously or subconsciously: the Platonic stratum lends meaning to *our* reading.

7. Commentaries on or studies of the passage include Hopkinson (1988): 140–42; Kidd (1997); Martin (1998). Some of the many voices in its interpretation include Kaibel (1894): 85–86; Porter (1946); Ludwig (1963): 441; Solmsen (1966); Gatz (1967) 58–63; Erren (1967): 36–39; Schwabl (1972); Effe (1977): 40–56; Hutchinson (1988): 223–24; Fakas (2001): 149–75; Hunter (1995/2008): 178–81; Landolfi (1996); Kidd (1997): 8–10; Hunter (2004): 238–42; van Noorden (2009); Volk (2012): 223–25.

8. See Erren (1967): 39.

9. On the works of Empedocles and the surrounding debate, see recently Sedley (1998): 2–10, and Inwood (2001): 8–21.

10. There exists a partial precedent for reading Hesiod's myth as cyclical in the rereading of its structure in Vernant (1965): 13–97; see now Vernant (2006): 25–52; 53–88; 89–114. For instance: 'Just as generations of men succeed one another within one race, and just as the races succeed one another within the total cycle of the ages, so the cycles might well succeed one another,' Vernant (2006): 80–81; or again, 'The succession of races in time reflects a permanent, hierarchical order in the universe. The ages succeed one another to form a complete cycle that, once finished, starts all over again, either in the same order, or, more probably, as in the myth in Plato's *Statesman*, in reverse order . . .' Vernant (2006): 28–29. Some remain unconvinced by Vernant: among others, Clay (2003): 83–85, maintains the view that Hesiod's myth is sequential. Nonetheless, Vernant's interpretation is useful for us in that it does not just make the myth sequential, but allows for the the coexistence of linear and cyclical time within a single myth,.

11. Plato's speaker also nods to tradition in the run-up to the *Politicus* myth (*Pol.* 269b4 καὶ τοῦτο ἓν τῶν πάλαι λεχθέντων, 'and this was the sole version of the ancient mythographers'). As in Aratus' case, this is a reference to the tradition of Hesiod, which Plato follows in the *Politicus* myth (see below, Ch. 2 section 2.1). Plato himself may be another 'source' of report for Aratus, an intermediary between Hesiod and Aratus in a threefold sequence.

12. See appendix A for the details of Hesiodic reminiscence in Aratus' *Dike* myth. The critical mass of reminiscences lies with the Myth of Ages (*WD* 109–201), closely followed by Hesiod's passage on *Dike* (*WD* 217–73). The combination of these two Hesiodic passages in Aratus' account has long been recognized. See Solmsen (1966): 125–26, who noted that 'it is evident that Aratus has introduced into his account of the Golden Age (vv.100–114) motifs

of Hesiod's just city'; Luck (1976): 227–28: 'Aratus combines two different contexts in Hesiod: (a) the departure of Aidos and Nemesis in the Iron Age (*Erga* 197ff); (b) the active role of Dike on earth, even now, together with the guardians appointed by Zeus (*Erga* 248ff). . . . Thus he creates the tradition which we find in Cicero, *Aratea* fr.XVIIIff; Verg. *Ecl.* 4.6, *Georg.* 2.474; Germanicus 103ff, Avienus 273ff.' On the assumption by *Dike* of the role of Hesiod's Aidos and Nemesis (*WD* 97–201) see especially Ludwig (1963): 441. On the Hesiodic context, see also Gatz (1967): 59–60; Schiesaro (1996): 16, Kidd (1997), Introduction, p. 9; Fakas (2001): 151–52.

13. Kidd (1997) introductory n. ad *Ph.* 96–136: 'A. does not follow Hesiod into the Heroic and Iron Ages, because his need goes only as far as the ascent of Justice into the sky'; cf. Hunter (1995/2008): 179; Schiesaro (1996): 11 and 22 (going one step further, to incorporate Catullus 64, with only two ages); Hunter (2004): 240; Van Noorden (2009a): 259.

14. See Franchet d'Espèrey (1997): 176.

15. See Luck (1976): 224–25 and West (1978) ad loc. for reminiscences of the Golden Age in Hesiod's Isles of the Blest.

16. Callataÿ (1996): 30 postulates that the Golden Age in Plato's *Politicus* (on which see Ch. 2) lasts for half of the entire world-cycle. We might add here that Aratus' own interpretation of it may follow or parallel Plato. See also Franchet d'Espèrey (1997): 177: 'On peut dire . . . que les poètes latines tendent vers une bipolarisation age d'or/age de fer, effaçant le role des races intermediaries.'

17. See Kidd (1997) ad loc.; Solmsen (1966): 126; Johnston (1980: 16), who flags Aratus' innovation: 'In Hesiod's poem, the golden age and agriculture are both prominent factors, but they are set in opposition to each other. These two topics are not joined until Aratus . . . depicts Dike and the ploughing-ox working together to provide sustenance for the golden race.' Fantuzzi/Hunter (2004): 240 maintain that Aratus 'placed agricultural labour in the golden age not just in deference to Stoic doctrine, but because agriculture is itself a manifestation of divine ordering and justice.'

18. Johnston (1980): 22, 'Hesiod's successors, particularly Aratus, Varro and Virgil, tend to merge certain details of Hesiod's just society and of his metallic myth, so that Justice becomes the important deity in the myth of the golden age.' See also Gatz (1967): 61 n.20; Schiesaro (1996): 13; Fakas (2001): 155–56.

19. For the convergence, see Fakas (2001): 152.

20. On the connections between the Prometheus myth and the myth of the races which follows it, see in particular Vernant (1966) = Vernant (2006): 62–66 and (2006): 98–99: 'Not only is this mythical theme repeated and enriched from one story to the next; there is also a shift in emphasis. The emphasis is no longer on the pair formed by good and evil Eris but on a different, though still symmetrical pair—the opposed powers of *dike* and hubris' (p. 66).

21. Kidd (1997) ad loc.

22. Compare this to Virgil's practice in *Ecl.* 6 where, in the Song of Silenus, Prometheus is made to follow the *Saturnia regna*, Hesiod's Golden Age: 'Vergil has here fused myths which in Hesiod are distinct . . . Vergil rearranges Hesiod's chronology, thereby revealing his own conception of the chronology surrounding a golden age' (Johnston 1980: 9). Aratus is Virgil's direct precedent in his treatment of the Hesiodic myths, both in terms of combining sequential myths, and in terms of chronological recurrence (see further chapter 2 section 2.1).

23. On *Dike*'s paternity in *Ph.* 99, see for instance Solmsen (1966): 125; Schiesaro (1996): 14; Kidd (1997) ad *Ph.* 99; Fakas (2001): 170; Possanza (2004): 130–31, 162 n.48.

24. On the mythology, see Gundel (1949) and Gatz (1967): 28–51; Martin (1998) ad loc. On the astrology, see Gundel (1949): 1953–7.

25. Erren (1967): 36.

26. Kidd (1997) ad loc.

27. Kidd (1997) ad loc.

28. 'Between Hesiod and Aratus lie many different reconstructions of human history. . . . Of particular importance will have been Empedocles' account of the "Golden Age"' (Hunter, 2004: 239 and n.178).

29. Maass (1893) ad *Ph.* 108–9 was the first to identify the Empedoclean reminiscence in these lines of Aratus. See Ludwig (1963): 446–47; Traglia (1963): 385–87; Fakas (2001): 156 and n.26.

30. Kidd (1997) ad loc. notes that ox-eating is an Aratean innovation under the influence of Empedocles fr. 128.8. Virgil follows the Aratean innovation at *Geo.* 2.536–40, on which see chapter 2 section 2.1.

31. On Empedocles, see *KRS* pp. 280–321; Wright (1981); Viano (1994); Inwood (2001). I have here used Inwood's second edition, which postdates the publication of the Strasbourg Papyrus (Martin and Primavesi 1999). On Aratus and Empedocles, see Traglia (1963), Ludwig (1963) 445–47, and Steinmetz (1966): 459.

32. 'Tutto qui è empedocleo, concetti e forma', Traglia (1963): 385.

33. As for instance at Empedocles fr. 25/17.7–8 Inwood, ἄλλοτε μὲν φιλότητι συνερχόμεν' εἰς ἓν ἅπαντα, /ἄλλοτε δ' αὖ δίχ' ἕκαστα φορεύμενα νείκεος ἔχθει, 'at one time all coming together by love into one, and at another time again all being borne apart separately by the hostility of strife' (Inwood).

34. See for instance Inwood frr. 21/8, 22/9, 28/26, 65/59. According to Inwood (2001): 43, total mixture is formed by the complete domination of Love; the reign of Strife is the total separation of all the elements from each other.

35. See Traglia (1963): 387–93. The Strasbourg papyrus (n.31 above), which is particularly relevant in Inwood's reconstruction of the latter part of fr. 17, has not yet been brought to bear on interpretations of Empedocles in Aratus. Other relevant fragments include Inwood 21/8, 22/9, 28/26, 61/35, and 65/59.

36. Traglia (1963): 392.

37. The problem is not dissimilar from that involved with the Platonic reinterpretation of Hesiod's Myth of Ages in the *Politicus* (El Murr (2010): 294–95), which we shall explore in the next chapter, and points the way to later reinterpretations such as that of Virgil. Closer to hand, a morally neutral two-stage cycle would have been familiar from Stoicism, since most Stoics espoused a two-stage cosmic cycle involving evolution towards *ekpyrosis*, after which the world begins again (on *ekpyrosis* and its theoretical nuances in Stoicism, see Bénatouïl 2009).

38. '. . . Despite Empedocles' positive valuation of Love and the sphere, we must be clear that it is only with complete separation under Strife that the world's superficial and underlying structures form a perfect match. If the ultimate reality of the world is that there are four roots, Love and Strife, and if mixture is in a sense a deceptive state of affairs, then only when mixture is completely banished is the world in its natural and ontologically-transparent state' (Inwood 2001: 46–47).

39. Halliwell (1998): 71–73.

40. Few modern scholars have made the connection between Aratus' *Dike* and the Muses. In general terms, van Noorden (2009: 272) characterizes *Dike* as '. . . a "Muse" of a

different kind, insofar as her story provokes Aratus' own didactic project.' But there is at least one ancient reading of her as a Muse-like figure. She is invoked at the opening of Germanicus' translation of Aratus' *Dike* myth, c.14–17 AD; see Germanicus, *Ph.* 98–102 (and chapter 2 section 2.2, on Germanicus' version of *Dike*).

41. West (1966) ad loc. notes several features of the Muses in Hesiod's *Theogony* which he identifies as 'traditional'. These include: (i) 'A poet, prophet, or lawgiver receives instructions in an encounter with a god' (ii) 'The encounter takes place on a mountain where the god lives' (iii) 'The god who appears (or the prophet inspired by him) addresses mankind in strongly derogatory terms'. All of these features recur in Aratus' *Dike* myth, serving to tie it in with the tradition.

42. Luck (1976): 222: the 'chanting' of the laws may be an archaic touch in keeping with the picture of *Dike* as 'an Archaic ruler-figure'.

Chapter 2

1. On this passage of Plato's *Republic* and its Hesiodic background, see in particular van Noorden (2010): 195–99.

2. On the topos, see Vegetti (2005) ad loc.

3. In Plato's other revision of Hesiod's Myth of Ages, *Politicus* 273c-d, ἀνωμαλία and ἀναρμοστία constitute the condition of the world in extreme disorder.

4. A connection between Hesiod's sequence of myths in the *WD*, and civil war, may be anticipated by Heraclitus fr. 82, the first in a long series of rereadings of the *Dike* passage of Hesiod's *WD*. In the words of Kahn (1979): 205, 'The symmetrical confrontation of two sides in battle now becomes a *figura* for the shifting but reciprocal balance between opposites in human life and the natural world.'

5. I have found most useful here the explanation of the sun's motions using epicycles and deferents, Kuhn (1957): 59–60, although it is anachronistic in respect of Plato (see Vlastos 1975: 47).

6. Rowe (1995) ad *Pol.* 271c4–7 comments on the 'problematical' nature of this passage in respect of the sense of 'turning' (τροπή).

7. Scholars are in agreement as to the newness of the idea of retrogression: '. . . Virgil seems to have been the first poet to conceive the *Saturnia regna* not as belonging exclusively to the irrecoverable past but as something destined to return to the earth in the future' (Coleman 1977, Introduction p. 29); 'There is no extant precedent for the idea that the sequence could be repeated or reversed', (Coleman 1977 ad loc.); 'One of the crucial distinctions between Vergil's conception of a golden age and that of his predecessors is the fact that Vergil's golden age can recur (Johnston 1980: 8); 'The ancients conceived of no such prodigious birth or rebirth; for them the golden age was a mythical paradise irretrievably lost' (Clausen 1994, Introd. note ad *Ecl.* 4, p. 121).

8. For a cross-section of bibliography on the *Politicus* myth, see Viano (1994); Rowe (1995a), Introduction pp. 11–13 and notes ad loc.; Rowe (1995b): 349–98; Annas and Waterfield (1995): xiv–xvi; Morgan (2000): 253–61; El Murr (2010); Rowe (2010). See also the very interesting section in Callataÿ (1996): 16–21, in the context of the argument about world cycles in general, with further bibliography at p. 16 n.41. None of these authors discuss the myth's possible relationship with Virgil's texts; nor, to the best of my knowledge, does anyone integrate Virgil's reading of Plato with his reading of Aratus. Implied in this argument is of course the notion of Virgil as an attentive reader of Plato (see above, Ch. 1 n.6).

9. I leave aside Virgil's selective translation of Aratus' weather signs in the first book of the *Georgics*, on which work has already been done: see, for instance, Farrell (1991): 79–83; 157–62.

10. As in Platonic scholarship (n.8 above), so in Virgilian scholarship the *Pol.* as a model for Virgil has gone almost unnoticed. Coleman (1977 ad *E.* 4.36) adduces Plato briefly: 'The retrogression from iron to heroic to golden age does not belong to the cyclic conceptions of history alluded to earlier but recalls rather the pendular movement of the world to and from god, which is depicted in the myth of Plato's *Politicus*. . . .'

11. Bibliography is extensive: see fundamentally Mayor, Warde Fowler, and Conway (1907); for modern bibliography, Clausen (1994) ad loc.

12. Thus Clausen (1994) Introd. note ad *Ecl.* 4 (p. 119): '[Virgil] unhesitatingly identifies the last age . . . with reference to Hesiod and Aratus as the mythical golden age', and ad loc.: 'Virgil assumes a knowledge of the story which Aratus tells in describing the constellation of the Virgin (Παρθένος, Virgo).' See also Coleman (1977) ad *Ecl.* 4.6: 'Aratus took up a hint from Hes. *Op.* 200–1. . . .'

13. See Coleman (1977) ad line 36, who refers to 'the regression from Iron to Heroic to Golden Age in this part of the poem. . . .'

14. Coleman (1977) and Clausen (1994) ad line 32. Aratus also comes immediately to mind in lines 38–39, *cedet et ipse mari vector, nec nautica pinus /mutabit merces*, where *merces* is Aratus' βίου in *Ph.* 111.

15. On this passage of *Georgics* 2, helpful (but by no means exhaustive) are Johnston (1980): 50–61; Farrell (1991): 146–47; Morgan (1999): 108–11; Gale (2000): 38–45; Gee (2000): 50–54.

16. Thomas (1988) ad *Geo.* 473–74: 'V. refers to Arat. *Phaen.* 96–136 (as at 537 . . .).' Gale (2000): 38 notes that 'The paragraph is framed by Aratean allusions: lines 459–60 recall the account of the golden age in *Phaen.* 108–13, and the gradual departure of *Iustitia* ("Justice", 473f) is evidently based on Aratus' more extended narrative.' Cf. Farrell (1991): 161–62.

17. Johnston (1980) makes much of the innovative nature of Virgil's connection between agriculture and the Myth of Ages in the *Georgics*; see for instance p. 49: 'Vergil's gradual removal, in the *Georgics*, of the golden age from the realm of mythology into a somewhat more visible milieu may reflect the increasing stability of the Roman state as Octavian gained control and finally defeated Antony. The essential modification, whereby the golden age becomes agricultural, takes place in the *Georgics*. . . .' Much has also been made of the supposed contradictions between the 'golden age' picture of agriculture at the end of *Geo.* 2 and the picture of the farmer's existence elsewhere in the work (a useful summary of the issues in Thomas 1988, Introductory note ad *Geo.* 2.458–540; cf. Farrell 1991: 161).

18. Used in the latter sense in Cicero, *Aratea* 228, for instance.

19. Note Germanicus' tendency toward prolepsis, and his intimations of finality at the end of the Golden Age (see section 2.2); Virgil may be of influence here.

20. Elsewhere I have shown how Virgil here enacts, in lines 475–82, the writing in astronomical didactic poetry in miniature, 'being Aratus' as it were, even before the *recusatio* of lines 483–86 (Gee 2000: 50–54). Virgil has, of course, already 'been Aratus' with his translation of the '*Diosemeiai*' in *Georgics* 1 (see n.9 above).

21. On Lucretius' exposition itself, and the tradition of Aratus, see Ch. 3 below.

22. On these lines see Johnston (1980): 50; Farrell (1991): 146–47; Gale (2000): 38–45.

23. Dicte in Crete was, in the mythic tradition, one of the sites of Jupiter's birth (see for instance Callimachus, *Hymn to Zeus* line 4).

24. The two-stage cycle becomes clearest in Ovid's account at *Met.* 1.113–14, where the point of transition from one stage of the cycle to the other is after the Silver Age. On Ovid's account, see Gatz (1967): 70–77. Germanicus presumably read Ovid as well as Virgil, but the only clear reminiscence is Germ. 104–5 (with *Met.* 1.149).

25. For the complexities of the debate about the number of phases involved, see Brisson (1994); Viano (1994): 408 n.11; Rowe (2010). Like Viano, I retain the traditional two-phase interpretation. Both Viano and El Murr note that what is placed in a chronological framework in Plato may in fact be simultaneously present, though contradictory, tendencies of the world: 'Even though Plato depicted an indefinite alternation of cosmic cycles, the two worlds within the myth may well be intended as no more than two contradictory aspects of one and the same world, our world' (El Murr, op. cit.: 296); cf. Viano (1994): 410, 'Platon y développe, en les faisant succéder périodiquement et en sens contraire, deux aspects du monde qui coexistent: l'élément eternel et intelligible et l'élément corporel et corruptible.'

26. See further El Murr (2010): 283–90 for the allusions to Hesiod in Plato's terminology.

27. στάσις here is the same term as we have noted in *Rep.* 545d7–e1; see Ch. 1 p. 35.

28. For the moral ambiguity in both stages of Plato's cycle, see El Murr (2010): 294–95 (and above, Ch. 1 p. 00 n.00).

29. For the allegory see Rowe (1986) ad *Phdr.* 246e4ff. The Neoplatonic commentator Hermeias renders it specific: see below, Ch. 6 p. 152.

30. Coleman 1977 ad loc. (*pace* Clausen 1994 ad loc.).

31. A fascinating study of the Great Year as a progress from unity to multiplicity and back again is de Callataÿ (1996).

32. Thomas (1988) comments ad loc., 'they enjoy the spontaneous beneficence of the Saturnian age—a sense guaranteed by every word in the two lines.'

33. In addition, φέρει ζείδωρος ἄρουρα also exactly echoes the formula as applied to the afterlife of the heroic men at *WD* 173. See above, Ch. 1 p. 25. For the ambivalence, we might compare Germanicus. Different notions of the Golden Age are seen in *colonus* and *sponte sua* in Germanicus *Ph.* 117 and 118, respectively. *Colonus*, 'farmer', predicates the idea of working for food; but *sponte sua*, like *Geo.* 2.501, reflects Hesiod's spontaneously producing earth. This is a supposed *translation* of Aratus, unlike Virgil's *Georgics*. The ambiguity is therefore present in the direct tradition of Aratus as well as in Virgil's selective paraphrases.

34. The best index of comparison for the role of Zeus in Aratus' universe is the Zeus of the contemporary *Hymn to Zeus* by the Stoic Cleanthes, on which see James (1972); Hopkinson (1988): 27–29 and 131–36; Thom (2005).

35. One might also compare the idealized philosophical life at Lucretius 2.29, *cum tamen inter se prostrati in gramine molli, . . .*

36. Commentaries on this passage of Germanicus include Bresig (1967), le Boeuffle (1975); Gain (1976), Maurach (1978), and Bellandi et al. (2001). Further interpretation: Steinmetz (1966): 457–65; Gatz (1967): 65–67; Santini (1987); Franchet d'Espèrey (1997); Possanza (2004): 128–45; Landolfi (1990) and (1996); Bellandi (2000). Steinmetz (1966): 463 was the first to suggest a possible connection between the catasterism of *Iustitia* in Germanicus and the goddess *Iustitia* to whom Augustus dedicated a temple in 13 AD, probably a year or so before Germanicus commenced his translation of Aratus; most recently, see

Possanza (2004): 137; Bellandi et al. (2001): 28, 85–86; Franchet d'Espèrey (1997): 182; Weinstock (1971): 246–47. Sources are *Fasti Praenestini, CIL* I², 306, and Ovid, *Pont.* 2.1.33; 3.6.25–26.

37. Unless otherwise stated, all references to Cicero's *Aratea* are to the text of Soubiran (1972), especially important to note for the ordering of the fragments; all translations are my own.

38. On Aratus' mixing of the races, see above, Ch. 1 pp. 24–5.

39. Possanza (2004): 142.

40. On the thematic ligatures between the endings of *Geo.* 1 and 2, see Gale (2000): 41.

41. Possanza (2004): 136; cf. Franchet d'Espèrey (1997): 183.

42. Steinmetz (1966): 459 sees three terms in Germanicus (*rabies* 112; *discordia* 113, and *avaritia* 115–16), parallel to Aratus' three.

43. Cf. *Geo.* 2.459 *discordibus.* Other instances of 'civil-war' usage are recorded at Bellandi et al. (2001) ad loc., and Possanza (2004): 136.

44. Thus also the description of the civil wars at the end of Virgil, *Geo.* 1, *et curvae rigidum falces conflantur in ensem* (*Geo.* 1.508), with *ensem* at the line-end.

45. It is just possible that the Roman translators are following a prompt in Aratus' account of the *Bronze* Age. In *Ph.* 125, there is a paradox, as Kidd (1997) notes ad loc. that the adjective ἀνάρσιον usually suggests enemies, the noun αἷμα, kinsmen, thus implying a paradox. Even if this is so, it remains for the Roman authors fully to articulate the civil-war theme.

46. On Lucretius and the Myth of Ages, see Johnston (1980): 32–33. Johnston notes that the two extreme conditions of mankind represented by Lucretius are 'parallel to the two extremes, in Hesiod's *Works and Days*, of the age of gold and the age of iron.' Costa also notes that 'traces of the "Golden Age" theme survive in the occasional references to the earth producing *sponte sua*' (Costa 1984: introd. n. ad *DRN* 5.925–87; see also p. xix).

47. For the structure see Costa (1984): xviii; Sedley (1998): 152–54.

48. Sedley (1998): 152 sees this section of the *DRN* as mirroring Epicurus' response to *Timaeus* 28b–41a: 'one can imagine' that Epicurus, in developing his own account of the world's origin in *On Nature* XI–XIII felt the need to respond point-by-point to the *Tim.*' (see also his chart on p. 136).

49. Sedley (1998): 153–54 also invokes in support of his argument the ordering of the Proem to Book 5, in which astronomy comes last.

50. Sedley (1998): 154.

51. Perhaps Virgil also has this passage in mind in his description of the Roman civil wars at the end of *Georgics* 1. Compare *paribus . . . telis* in *Geo.* 1.489 and *et curvae rigidum falces conflantur in ensem* in *Geo.* 1.508 with *exaequataque . . . certamina belli* in 1296 and *versaque in opprobrium species est falcis ahenae, DRN* 5.1294; although the expression is somewhat different, the two ideas, of the level playing-field and of the commutation of agricultural implements into instruments of war, correspond. The origin of all war is, in a sense, civil, a levelling of weaponry used to inflict wounds on members of the same species.

52. Lucretius uses the same passage of Cicero elsewhere in the *DRN.* This strengthens the possibility that it is being used in the present context. Close to Cicero in its collocation, for instance, is *DRN* 1.187, *e terraque exorta repente arbusta salirent.* In fact, the context fits here too: *DRN* 1.184–91 form part of Lucretius' refutation of creation *ex nihilo* in *DRN* 1. Lucretius argues that it is impossible for the earth to produce things from nothing, nor can

just anything arise from just anything else: fixed 'seeds' are required. Lucretius' account characteristically uses a phrase from Cicero's rendition of a conflicting account in which the god creates the races. For more on Lucretius' use of and opposition to Cicero, see Ch. 3.

53. This is also a formulation in Cicero's *Aratea*: see *Arat.* 281 *rota fervida solis.*

54. We recall Plato's approach to the Myth of the Races in *Rep.* 547a, in which the mixing of the races is a kind of civil war.

55. Bailey (1947) ad *DRN* 5.381; see Bailey's introd. note ad 380–415 for Empedoclean influence. On Lucretius and Empedocles in general (although not on this passage) see Trépanier (2007). The material is brilliant, but I do not agree with his conclusions (see Introduction to Ch. 3 below).

56. For the civil-war ramifications of the term, see Costa (1984) ad loc.: 'Because they are all *membra* of the world the elements' strife is called civil war, *pio nequaquam bello*. We regularly find *impius* (or the equivalent) used of civil war: Virg. *A.* 1.294, 6.613, Hor. *C.* 3.24.25, Lucan 1.238.' On the parallel between Lucretius' concept and Manilius' 'war of the planets' (*Ast.* 1.805) see below, Ch. 5 p. 122.

57. For other parallels between this and the passage of Book 5 under discussion, see Costa (1984) ad *DRN* 5.793–94; 937–38.

Chapter 3

1. Costa (1984) ad *DRN* 5.1437, *lustrantes lumine*: 'This may be another example of the influence on L. of Cicero's translation of Aratus.'

2. Lucretius also uses *lunaeque meatus* at *DRN* 1.128 and 5.76 and 774. See appendix B, nn. on these references.

3. For example, *DND* 2.15, *statuat necesse est ab aliqua mente tantos naturae motus gubernari;* note also the multiple uses of *administrari* and cognate terms at *DND* 2.86.

4. I am arguing here for the presence of Cicero's *Aratea* in Lucretius' text. But there is also a more direct overlap with Aratus' Empedoclean project, in the relationship of Lucretius with Empedocles. On the latter, see Sedley (1998): Ch. 1.

5. See Asmis (1995), Sider (1995), and Wigodsky (1995) on the relationship between Epicurean philosophy and poetry. The relationship was an ambivalent one, as Asmis points out: 'The ancient quarrel between philosophy and poetry seems to have played itself out in an extreme paradox in Epicureanism. Epicurus has the reputation of being the most hostile to poetry of any Greek philosopher. But some of his later followers were clearly devoted to poetry, and one of them, Lucretius, achieved a remarkable reconciliation between philosophy and poetry' (Asmis 1995: 15).

6. *Ad QF* 2.10(9).3 (Feb. 54 as dated by Shackleton Bailey 1980).

7. Helm (1956): 149.20–26. See Munro (1864): vol. 2 pp. 1–5; Soubiran (1972): 2; Costa (1984): ix.

8. For the debate and related issues, see Munro (1893 ed.): 17–19; Boyancé (1963): 22–26, with the bibliography on pp. 332–33; Soubiran (1972): 2; 76–77; Costa (1984): Sedley (1998): 1–2.

9. Cameron (2011): 430–31, discussing usages of the verb *emendo* in manuscript subscriptions contemporary with Jerome.

10. Costa (1984): ix.

11. Would it be impish to ask whether Cicero might have added a few of his own resonances to the *DRN* during the process of editing?

12. Commentaries on the *Aratea* are by Ewbank (1933), Buescu (1941), and Soubiran (1972). Interpretative work on the *Aratea* is scattered: close readings of some passages are available in (for instance) Kubiak (1981) and Clausen (1986) (both on Orion) and Kubiak (1990) (*Prog.* fr.4). For contextual readings of the *Aratea*, see Gee (2001) and (2007). For the full intertextual data see appendix B.

13. '. . . Between, let us say, his seventeenth and his twenty-second year,' Pease (1958) ad *DND* 2.104. Cicero was born in 106. Soubiran (1972): 9 gives 90–89 BC.

14. On Aratus' elision of the planets, see Volk (2009): 56–57: 'There is something uncanny about the planets . . . Aratus does not want them in his description of the universe'.

15. See Gee (2001): 527–36.

16. Camerarius in his 1535 translation apparently recognized the affinity between Aratus and Cicero's *De consulatu*. He integrates the latter into his translation of the former, in the proem with which he replaces Aratus' 'Hymn to Zeus'. Lines 78–79 of his translation read:

> omnibus at tu animum *curis* Daniele *relaxa,*
>
> > et mecum hac coeli moenia scande via.
>
> 'Daniel, absolve your mind of all cares, and scale with me the walls of heaven by this road' (my trans.).

Lines 77–78 of Cicero's *Cons.* fr. 2 (ed. Soubiran) read:

> tu tamen anxiferas *curas* requiete *relaxans*
>
> > quod patriae vacat, id studiis nobisque sacrasti.
>
> 'But you, dissolving your anxious cares in rest, devoted what the Fatherland left of you to our studies' (my trans.).

The context fits too: Cicero here is being addressed by his didactic instructor Urania as a student of the Muses, specifically astronomy (her own subject, *studiis nobisque*, which I have translated as zeugma); Camerarius in the role of Urania, as celestial guide, is addressing the young Daniel Stibar. On Camerarius, see Gee (2008).

17. Kuhn (1957): 59.

18. Lucretius himself was not uninfluenced by Cicero's *Cons.* as well as his *Aratea*. On Lucretius and Cicero's *Cons.*, see Soubiran (1972): 76–77.

19. On the date, see Shackleton Bailey (1965): p. 343. On the *Prognostica*, SB, ad *Att.* 2.1.11 comments, 'C.'s youthful version of Aratus' Προγνώσεις (Διοσημεῖαι), the second part of his Φαινόμενα. He evidently regarded it as a separate poem. There is no need to see in this a reference to a revision or a new work.' In other words, according to SB, Cicero was merely sending his old work to Atticus.

20. Pease (1917); Buescu (1941): 28–34; Pease (1958) ad *DND* 2.104; Soubiran (1972): 9–16; Kubiak (1990); Murphy (1998).

21. Hollis (2007) p. 42: 'We can gauge the popularity of Aratus at Rome from Cicero's early *Aratea* and a stream of subsequent translators or imitators (eg. Varro Atacinus . . ., Virgil, *Georgics* 1, the *Aratea* of Ovid and Germanicus, to go no further). Equally significant is the ringing testimonial to the poetic qualities of Aratus given by the docti in 55BC (perhaps very soon after the composition of this epigram), "*constat inter doctos . . . ornatissimis atque optimis versibus Aratum de caelo stellisque dixisse*" (Cicero, *De Oratore* 1.69).' On this passage of the *De orat.*, see above, Introduction p. 6.

22. On this passage see Kidd (1997): 16–17.

23. Courtney (1993) fr. 11/Hollis (2007) fr. 13. On the date, see Hollis (2007): p. 19. The Cinna Epigram calques Callimachus, *Epigram* 27 Pfeiffer:

Ἡσιόδου τό τ' ἄεισμα καὶ ὁ τρόπος· οὐ τὸν ἀοιδῶν
ἔσχατον, ἀλλ' ὀκνέω μὴ τὸ μελιχρότατον
τῶν ἐπέων ὁ Σολεὺς ἀπεμάξατο· χαίρετε λεπταί
ῥήσιες, Ἀρήτου σύμβολον ἀγρυπνίης.

'The song is from Hesiod, as is the form. To be sure, the poet of Soli did not copy every last word, but only the very sweetest. Hail charming utterances, the sign of Aratus's wakefulness' (my trans.).

On the Callimachus epigram and the critical tradition on Aratus, see Lewis (1992): 97–101, 111–12; Cameron (1995): 374–79; Kidd (1997): 36.

24. Two second-century kings of Bithynia were named Prusias (see Courtney 2003 and Hollis 2007 ad loc.).

25. The first four lines of fr. 14 Courtney/121 Hollis correspond to Aratus 942–45, last 3 to Aratus 954–57. It is possible that two separate passages which we now have as fr. 121 were run together in scholia (see Courtney 2003: 244, who prints a lacuna between them, and Hollis 2007: 194, who does not). I have elsewhere postulated a similar phenomenon in relation to the astronomical fragment attributed to Quintus Cicero (see Gee 2007). In Varro's case, however, it seems to me more natural to posit the selective translation characteristic of the Roman interpreters of Aratus.

26. Varro's earliest poem may have been the *Bellum Sequanicum* celebrating Caesar's campaign of 58 BC, probably written not long after that (Hollis 2007: 177–79). In this, and in Varro's *Saturae*, scholars have seen an 'adherence to an old Roman style of poetic composition' (Hollis 2007: 177). Jerome *Chron.* for 82 BC, recording Varro's birth, adds *qui postea XXXV annum agens Graecas litteras cum summo studio didicit* ('who afterwards in his 35th year took to Greek letters with the greatest enthusiasm,' Helm 1956: 151.15–17, with my trans.). This may imply, as Courtney thinks, that 'his translation of Apollonius Rhodius, his adaptations of Aratus in the *Eph.*, and the knowledge of Alexander of Ephesus shown in the geographical *Chorographia*, all postdate 47 BC' (Courtney 2003: 236), although Hollis is sceptical that the poems of Varro which display Hellenistic influence were all 'crammed into the last dozen years of his life' (Hollis 2007: 178).

27. Munro (1864) ad *DRN* 5.619. Büchner (1939): 1242 provides a useful synopsis of the debate.

28. Norden (1926) p. 371. Soubiran (1972): 73–74 gives a further history of the Ennian debate.

29. Merrill (1921): 144.

30. Merrill (1921): 145; cf. Merrill (1924): 306.

31. Merrill (1921): 143.

32. Kenney (1971) ad *DRN* 3.314–18: '. . . In view of the close resemblance we may reasonably guess that L. was borrowing from Cicero.'

33. Costa (1984): xiii 'The importance of Aratus [for Lucretius] can be seen indirectly through Cicero's verse translation of his astronomical poem, *Phaenomena*; there is clear evidence that Lucretius knew and used this work, which in spite of Cicero's pedestrian rendering must have been of considerable technical interest and assistance to him.' Cf. Costa (1984) nn. ad *DRN* 5.108, 1016, 1437.

34. Courtney (1993): 150: 'Lucretius himself read the *Aratea* with care and was greatly influenced by its versification and language.'

35. For instance, Kenney and Clausen (1982): 176, '. . . No account of the genesis of the "new" poetry of Catullus and his school should omit mention of Rome's greatest orator.' On changing attitudes to Cicero's poetry in general, see Kubiak (1990): 198. On the 'negative copy' from antiquity, see for example Ewbank (1933): 27–31; Gee (2013).

36. Conte (1986): 52. Cf. Fowler (2000a): 155: 'To attempt to define too closely what is and is not a relevant interaction is doomed to failure.'

37. Conte (1986): 66.

38. Conte (1986): 91–92.

39. Fowler (2000a): 148.

40. Fowler (2000a): 144: 'The text constantly shocks the reader by appropriating to its own very different purposes the language and imagery of religion and theist philosophy.'

41. Sedley (1998): 84–85.

42. Costa (1984) ad loc.

43. Costa 1984 ad loc.

44. Sedley 1998: 119–20 and 136.

45. Sedley (1998): 83.

46. Trépanier (2007): 281.

47. Fowler (2000a): 142: 'The passages in question were thus clearly from early on read philosophically as well as literarily. . . .'

48. See Bailey (1947) ad *DRN* 2.1031: *palantia sidera* are not the planets, πλάνητες ἀστέρες, but all the stars, 'for according to Lucretius they all move in the *turbo*'.

49. On the Platonic passage (the myth of the cave and the sun from the *Republic*) see above, Introduction p. 00.

50. See Bailey (1947) introd. n. ad 2.1048–66.

51. Bailey (1947) ad 2.1058–61.

52. Compare Manilius 1.492–3: *quis credat tantas operum sine numine moles / ex minimis caecoque creatum foedere mundum?* It is the opinion of Volk (2009): 217, that in this passage Manilius 'is . . . specifically attacking the Epicurean philosophy of Lucretius.' My view is that Manilius finds precedent for his attack in the debate which already existed and is exemplifed by Cicero's reactions to Epicureanism in the *DND*. Note that Manilius' passage ends (1.531) *non casus opus est, magni sed numinis ordo. Casus* is a keyword in the debate.

53. On this passage see Gee (1997): 21–40 and Gee (2001): 527–36.

54. For *temere* used in philosophical polemic, this time by an Epicurean speaker, see Cicero, *DND* 1.43; see also my discussion in the next chapter of *DRN* 3.1–8.

55. Some have seen allusion to Aratus' *Dike* in these lines: 'Lucretius, when he first praises Epicurus for freeing mankind from the tyranny of Religion, gives an explanation which is almost a complete inversion of Aratus' account of the race of bronze and the departure of Dike from the presence of mortals. . . . Thus, Aratus' Dike, whose favourable disposition toward mortals turned into loathing . . . in Lucretius's account becomes *Religio*, the scowling tyrant who shrivels into nothing when she encounters the courage and intelligence of Lucretius' Epicurus,' Johnston (1980): 30.

56. For the Ciceronian parallels, see Munro (1864) ad *DRN* 5.619. Best on the progression of subjects, and their explanation, is Bailey (1947) ad loc.

57. Bailey (1947) ad *DRN* 5.682–95; cf. Munro (1894) ad *DRN* 5.619 'It is evident that Lucretius had studied this translation of Cicero; other parts of which are imitated in other

parts of this poem.' See also Soubiran (1972): 76; Büchner (1939) 1243–44. For a full list of parallels, refer to my appendix B.

58. Compare Epicurus' similarly aporetic approach to the sun and weather signs at *Letter to Pythocles* 98a–99a:

μήκη νυκτῶν καὶ ἡμερῶν παραλλάττοντα καὶ παρὰ τὸ ταχείας ἡλίου κινήσεις γίνεσθαι καὶ πάλιν βραδείας ὑπὲρ γῆς <ἢ καὶ> παρὰ τὸ μήκη τόπων παραλλάττοντα καὶ τόπους τινὰς περαιοῦν τάχιον ἢ καὶ βραδύτερον, ὡς καὶ παρὰ ἡμῖν τινα θεωρεῖται, οἷς συμφώνως δεῖ λέγειν ἐπὶ τῶν μετεώρων. οἱ δὲ τὸ ἓν λαμβάνοντες τοῖς τε φαινομένοις μάχονται καὶ τὸ ᾗ δυνατὸν ἀνθρώπῳ θεωρῆσαι διαπεπτώκασιν. ἐπισημασίαι δύνανται γίνεσθαι καὶ κατὰ συγκυρήσεις καιρῶν, καθάπερ ἐν τοῖς ἐμφανέσι παρ᾽ ἡμῖν ζῴοις, καὶ παρ᾽ ἑτεροιώσεις ἀέρος καὶ μεταβολάς· ἀμφότερα γὰρ ταῦτα οὐ μάχεται τοῖς φαινομένοις· ἐπὶ δὲ ποίοις παρὰ τοῦτο ἢ τοῦτο τὸ αἴτιον γίνεται οὐκ ἔστι συνιδεῖν.

'The varying lengths of day and night may be due to the sun's moving over the earth now quickly, now slowly, either because of the changing length of his journey or because he crosses certain places with greater or less speed, as is seen to be the case with some things on earth in accordance with which we must give our explanations about things above. But those who insist on a single cause oppose the evidence of the senses and have wandered far from the way in which a man may learn. Weather signs may be due to mere coincidence, as is the case with signs from animals about us, or they may be due to actual alterations and changes in the air, for both are in harmony with phenomena; but we cannot tell under what conditions a sign is due to this cause or that' (trans. Geer 1964; text of Arrighetti 1973).

59. Bailey (1947 ad loc.). For further speculation as to the identity of these men, see Costa (1984) ad loc.

60. Elsewhere in the *Aratea* Cicero describes the stars themselves using the same term, for instance fr. 9.1 Soubiran, *huic non una modo caput ornans stella relucet*.

61. Gee (2000): 86–90; Gee (2001): 528–31.

62. It is consistently used this way, for instance, in Balbus' argument in the second book of Cicero's *DND* (Gee 2001: 528–31).

63. Lucretius' anti-divine-workmanship agenda is thoroughgoing: cf. for instance, his denial of *divina numina* at *DRN* 4.1233.

64. Arguably, the craftsman simile is always emblematic of the intelligent design universe of Plato's *Timaeus*, whence it originates (see *Tim.* 36c-d with Cornford 1937 ad loc.). Cornford believes Plato's description of the construction of the world soul is with reference to an actual physical model, an armillary sphere.

65. On the Namer and his connection with divine artistry, see Gee (2000): 87.

Chapter 4

1. Selectivity of examples is a common problem in appraisals of Lucretius' debt to the *Aratea*. For instance, Büchner's examples (1939: coll. 1243–44) all pertain to Lucretius' astronomical passage, more precisely to *DRN* 5.680–95, with the single exception of 3.316, which Büchner is inclined to impute to chance.

2. *DRN* 1.135, 1.351–53, 1.724, 2.700–706, 3.1012, 4.734, 4.1087, 5.34, 5.906, 5.1099, and possibly elsewhere (see appendix B).

3. On the significance of the 'Epicurean' proems, and in particular the structural importance of Proems 1.3 and 5, see Kenney (1984): 12–13, and introd. n. ad *DRN* 3.1–30.

4. On the formula, see Merrill (1921): 145, Buescu (1941): 343. Merrill cites 18 other parallels in Lucretius. The expression is clearly first in Cicero: it occurs once in the *Aratea* as extant, in line 177. A similar case of the pre-appearance of a characteristically 'Lucretian' formula in Cicero might be *principio* (passim in L., e.g., 1.503; with the incipit of Cicero's didactic Muse Urania in *De consulatu suo* fr. 2.1 Soubiran).

5. Munro (1894) ad *DRN* 1.2.

6. Cicero's *labuntur* in *Aratea* fr. 3 translates Aratus' ἕλκονται (*Ph.* 20). See also *Arat.* 329 and 390, and *DRN* 1.1003–4 *fulmina . . . /labentia;* 1.1034, *labentes aetheris ignes*; 4.443–46, *caelum . . . signa . . . /labier*; 5.712, *labitur ex alia signorum parte per orbem*, and 766, *. . . perlabier orbem;* 6.334, *celeri volat impete labens.*

7. The fifth-foot *lumine/lumina* shortly after, in *DRN* 1.9, is also a Ciceronian signature: see *Arat.* 113 *lumina caeli;* 405 *lumina caeli; Prog.* fr. 4.10 S., *lumina caeli.*

8. Lucretius has many other references to Cicero's passage on the planets: see for instance 1.1029, 1061; 2.296–99, 4.444.

9. For the *figura etymologica, errare vagae*, and the possible Lucretian echo of it in *DRN* 1, see section 4.2.4 below.

10. See below, on 4.444. Compare Aratus' use of Empedocles to underscore the idea of motion and stability, discussed above in Ch. 1 pp. 30–1.

11. *Ictu* in the final foot of the hexameter may also be a Ciceronian mannerism: compare with our passage *Arat.* 431, *hic valido cupide venantem perculit ictu,* and also with *DRN* 6.311 *vementi perculit ictu.*

12. On this passage, see also below, Ch. 5 pp. 119–20.

13. Appendix B, nn. on 3.218, 3.529, 557, 657–59, 829, 845–6, 849.

14. Cf. Aratus *Phaenomena* 10–13.

15. On this passage see also Gee (2008): 486–89.

16. Katarina Volk also notes that the swallow and the swan fit into a complex of pre-existing metaphors for comparison of great and lesser poets (Volk 2002:108–9). On Greek and Latin idioms in this passage, see further Sedley (1998): 57–58.

17. So Schiesaro (1990): 101; Fowler (2000a): 148.

18. Kenney (1984) ad *DRN* 3.4: 'The phrases *ficta vestigia* and *pressa signa* hardly differ in meaning, and this emphasises the fidelity with which L. follows the tracks of his master.'

19. See Gee (2000): 164–67 for the apotheosis of heroes in the Stoic tradition.

20. 'Ironically enough, Epicureans like Lucretius similarly venerated Epicurus as a god-like figure' (Walsh 1997 ad *DND* 1.38). On the divinity of Epicurus, see further Costa (1984) ad *DRN* 5.8; Pease (1955–58) ad *DND* 1.43.

21. On *utilitas* in Stoicism, see for instance Pease (1955-8) ad *DND* 1.38.

22. Buescu (1941): 'Loci Similes', ad fr. 14.4 (Buescu's numbering).

23. See the cover-image to this book, the vivid illustration in Harley 647, a manuscript of Cicero.

24. It is worth emphasizing that it is clear that Lucretius was reading Cicero's *Prognostica* as well as his *Aratea*. For references to the *Prog.* elsewhere in the *DRN*, see 1.39, 1.191, 1.413, 2.296, 2.367, 2.1122, 3.304, 3.825, 4.210, 4.577, 5.76, 5.298–99; 6.890 (appendix B).

25. Another Ciceronian hapax: a bird—or maybe a tree-frog. See Soubiran (1972) ad *Prog.* fr. 4.5; Kidd (1997) on Aratus' ὀλολυγών, *Ph.* 948.

26. *BTL* gives only Lucr. and Cic., and late grammarians quoting these passages.

27. Reference to this same passage of Cicero is unequivocal elsewhere in the poem, in fact in this very book (see 5.298–99, *ignibus instant /instant,* with *Prog.* fr.4.5–6, *vocibus instat, /vocibus instat*).

28. For *de corpore flammam,* also of Chimaeras, see *DRN* 5.906. The hexameter-end collocation *corpore flammam* is also used at *DRN* 4.1087.

29. For *aestiferos,* see *DRN* 6.721 (proximate to one of the strongest of all Ciceronian references in the *DRN,* at 6.716).

30. For Cicero's hexameter opening *hic ubi,* used in a similar context of the death of trees, see *DRN* 6.140. It is likely that Lucretius had this same passage in mind there as here: the twofold reference as well as the similarity in context supports his use of it in both places.

31. On the death of heroes in *DRN* 3.1024–52, see Reinhardt (2004): 30–31.

32. On Hercules as a Stoic hero, see Bailey (1947) ad *DRN* 5.22; Costa (1984) introd. n. ad 5.1–54, and n. ad 5.22ff; and above all Cicero, *DND* 2.62, with Pease (1955–8) and Walsh (1997) ad loc.

33. For the Stoicism of *DND* 2.62 in particular, see Pease (1955–8) ad *DND* 1.119, '. . . this must be considered as a characteristically Stoic tenet' (citing the evidence at length). The divinization of heroes, also known as euhemerism (as Cicero's Epicurean speaker Velleius contemptuously tells us at *DND* 1.38) was introduced into Stoicism by Persaeus, a pupil of Zeno. On the views of Persaeus, which may represent only one modulation of Stoic views on the divine, see Pease (1955–8) ad *DND* 1.38.

34. One might also compare 'Quintus Cicero's' poem on the zodiac, lines 6, *languificosque Leo proflat ferus ore calores* (with Lucretius 2.705, *ore Chimaeras*), and 12, *bruma gelu gelans iubar est spirans Capricorni* (for the Lucretian usage *spirantis*). On Quintus' poem, see Gee (2007).

35. We might also note Plato, *Rep.* 588c as part of the conceptual underlay to Lucretius' nexus between hybridism and the underworld. In *Rep.* 588c the soul itself is a hybrid. Howland (1993): 154 aptly refers to the 'psychic menagerie'. Reinhardt (2004): 32 interprets Lucretius Book 3 as a 'symbolic katabasis', in which the reader is led through a series of underworld-like scenes: 'The very purpose of this katabasis is, paradoxically, to assure us of the non-existence of the underworld, by way of explanation or reinterpretation of some of the stages a visitor of the underworld would go through.' Reinhardt's emphasis is on judgment rather than hybridism: but the important point *for us* is that Lucretius populates his 'underworld' with mythical creatures *modelled on Cicero's constellations.*

36. Lucretius also uses the same line of Cicero at 5.34 *arboris amplexus stirpem.*

37. Fowler (2000a): 148 (not on this passage): 'Language itself . . . only exists because of intertextuality, because of the traces of past speech in the present, just as the *textura* of the world is made up of atoms reused from previous combinations.'

38. Merrill and Buescu cite Ennius *Ann.* 602, *aplustria,* but the collocation with *fluvitantia* is only in Cicero and Lucretius (*BTL*).

39. Soubiran (1972) takes *Arat.* fr. 24 as Cicero's translation of Aratus line 159, where it presumably expanded Aratus' κεδαιομένους ἀνθρώπους, men in trouble at sea under the sign of the Kids. Buescu (1941) situates it differently, with Cicero's translation of Aratus' Ara, a constellation which also engenders a storm-at-sea set piece (Aratus *Ph.* 402–30), this one containing the bizarre image of ships sailing on, submerged (*Ph.* 425). Either way works for my interpretation of the significance of its resonance in Lucretius.

40. Lucretius and Cicero are the earliest attested instances of the collocations *fluctus canos* and *minitanti murmure* (*BTL*).

41. The text of this line is corrupt: see the apparatus of Bailey (1921) ad loc.

42. This passage of Cicero is alluded to elsewhere in Lucretius. Lucretius' consistent use of it may support the collocation at *DRN* 3.242 (see appendix B on *DRN* 1.50, and 5.261, *quod superest, umore novo mare flumina fontes*, a *four-fold* collocation with *Arat.* 177, *quod superest . . . flumine fontes*).

43. I have adopted the reading '*Aquai*' in my translation.

44. On this passage, see further Ch. 5 p. 123. The retrograde or unpredictable motions of the constellations accompanies civil turmoil. Lucan's *meatus* takes us, intentionally I think, given Lucan's celestial preoccupation at this point, into the Ciceronian–Lucretian tradition (compare Lucan's line-end *signa meatus* with *DRN* 1.128 *solis lunaeque meatus*, and Cic. *Prog.* fr. 1.1 Soub., *luna means*).

45. In Lucretius, war (even civil war) is good: it enables the universe to form (see my discussion of *DRN* 5.380–81 and 5.432–40 on pp. 108–9); in *DRN* 5 it is part of the development of man.

46. '. . . In view of the close resemblance we may reasonably guess that L. was borrowing from Cicero,' Kenney (1984) ad *DRN* 3.314–18.

47. Possible instances of Lucretius' use of this same passage (*Arat.* 223–36) elsewhere, include *DRN* 1.1029, 1.1061, 5.79, 5.635, 5.644, etc. (see appendix B).

48. On this passage see Gee (2000): 87, and the discussion in Ch. 5 below.

49. For another passage in which Lucretius may make use of the Namer of stars, this time in opposition, to describe the explicable form of the atom, see *DRN* 2.379, *certam formam*, with *Arat.* 159 *formam . . . certam*.

50. In the next chapter we shall look at a third rogue element, that of celestial change.

51. Compare also *DRN* 5.643, *quae volvunt magnos in magnis orbibus annos*, and see Bailey (1947), introd. n. ad *DRN* 5.643–49, and n. ad 5.644. In both cases, Bailey (1947) ad loc. strenuously denies that the 'Long Year' is implicated. Costa (1984) ad DRN 5.643–44, remarks, 'The Great Year, with its mystic and astrological implications, seems alien and irrelevant to L[ucretius]'s thinking'. On the Great Year see Callataÿ (1996).

52. On these lines, see further Ch. 5 pp. 119–20 below.

53. See the (helpful if brief) comments by Fowler (2000a): 140 on the ways in which the question of anti-Stoic polemic has been framed.

54. The intelligent design debate, of course, goes much further back than the Hellenistic schools: see Plato, *Laws* 889b1–c6, with the comments of Vlastos (1975): 23–24.

55. See above, Ch. 3 pp. 119–20 for the full context.

56. See also *palantia sidera*, *DRN* 2.1031, with Ch. 3 n.48.

57. 'We regularly find *impius* (or an equivalent) used of civil war: Virg. *A.*1.294, 6.613, Hor. *C.*3.24.25, Lucan 1.238' (Costa 1984 ad loc.).

Chapter 5

1. Tarrant (1985): p. 204, Introd. n. ad Seneca, *Thyestes* Chorus IV: 'The notion of a universe on the point of collapse is a potent metaphor for moral anarchy, both within the play and also in the Roman world to which the play implicitly relates.'

2. See below, Ch. 6 pp. 169–70 for further discussion of this passage of Plato.

3. A Homeric word (Kidd 1997 ad loc.). Homer is perhaps the source of Plato's military imagery of Zeus leading the celestial parade of the gods at *Phdr.* 246e4–247a7. On the link between Namer and Craftsman in Aratus, see Gee (2000): 84–90.

4. Hunter (1995/2008): 164.

5. Volk (2009): 57.

6. Vlastos (1975): 54, on Plato's exposition of the planets at *Timaeus* 38c–39e: '[Plato] hypothesizes that the motions of the sun, moon and planets are in every case compositions of *un*wandering circular motions proceeding in different planes in different directions at different velocities. . . . The conceptual kernel of this hypothesis . . . is that the composition of postulated regular circular motions may account for irregular phenomenal motions.'

7. The same contrast between appearance and reality is at work in Simplicius *Cael.* 488. 14–24, quoted in the Introduction, p. 9. Simplicius may have had the *Laws* passage in mind.

8. No more did they for Plato as for Copernicus. The 'false' use of the term by the Copernicans is noted by Kuhn (1962): 127–8: '. . . The Copernicans who denied its traditional title "planet" to the sun were not only learning what "planet" meant or what the sun was. Instead, they were changing the meaning of "planet" so that it could continue to make useful distinctions in a world where all celestial bodies, not just the sun, were seen differently from the way they had been seen before.'

9. 'Incommensurability' is where the meaning of a word has become divorced from its etymology, as a result of an intervening change of paradigm. The phenomenon was defined by Kuhn in the 1969 'Postscript' to Kuhn (1962): see Kuhn (1970): 198–204. In the case of 'atom', for instance, the word means in Greek 'uncuttable': the most basic particle below which we cannot go. For us, however, the atom is not 'uncuttable', rather the reverse; yet we still use the term, despite the ineptitude of its etymological foundation. See Kennedy (2002): 37, '. . . Repetition always brings about a subtle, or sometimes not so subtle, reconfiguration. On the micro level, from the perspective of re-presentation, the atom of Lucretius is not the atom of Dalton, the atom of Dalton is not the atom of Rutherford, and so on. In each case, the textual trace has been reconfigured in its new context toward a new argumentative end.' The case of 'planet' is analogous: the term is from the Greek verb 'to wander', but the heavenly body so designated is no longer seen as 'wandering'.

10. Note the conjunction in this passage between the topics of planetary motion and namelessness.

11. Cornford (1937): 116. On Plato's knowledge of Eudoxus, see Cornford (1937): 92–3.

12. On the theory of 'homocentric spheres', see Kuhn (1957): 55–9.

13. On this passage see Volk (2009): 109–15.

14. See Ch. 4 pp. 100–2 for Lucretius' use of this passage.

15. On this passage, see Ch. 2 n.1 and p. 37 above.

16. After Kuhn (1957): 45–77, 'The problem of the planets' and Volk 2009: 53–7, 'The puzzle of the planets'.

17. Kuhn (1957): 59.

18. On the date, see Goold (1977) Intro. p. xii. For the ordering of these lines, see Goold (1977) ad loc.; Volk (2009): 48–9.

19. On these passages, see above, Ch. 4 pp. 108–9.

20. See above, Ch. 3 p. 109.

21. In this tradition, the fifth-century Neoplatonist Proclus ascribes a 'life-period' to each planet (*in Tim.* 38c, 256A, Diehl 1903–6, p. 56.10–11): ἔπεται γὰρ ἄλλα ἄλλων ἀποκαταστάσεσι καὶ κατ' ἄλλα μέτρα τὰς ἑαυτῶν συμπεραίνει ζωάς. 'For different effects

follow from the *apokatastasis* of the different planets, which according to different measures, bring their own lives to a period.' The periods of the planets correspond to 'planet lives' or planet years, on the analogy of different lifespans for different creatures on earth. The idea of celestial concurrence and the end of the world cycle is also mirrored in Proclus (*in Tim*. 39d, 271A, Diehl 1903–6, p. 93.5–11): καὶ ἔοικε μία τις μνημονεύεσθαι ἀποκατάστασις, διὸ καὶ λέγουσιν ὡροσκόπον εἶναι τοῦ κόσμου τὸν Καρκίνον, καὶ καλοῦσι τὸν ἐνιαυτὸν τοῦτον κυνικόν, διότι τῷ Καρκίνῳ συνανατέλλει τῶν ἀπλανῶν λαμπρὸς ἀστὴρ ὁ τοῦ Κυνός. πάλιν οὖν ἐὰν κατὰ ταὐτὸν τοῦ Καρκίνου σημεῖον συνδράμωσιν, ἔσται περίοδος αὕτη μία τοῦ παντός. 'It seems that one certain *apokatastasis* has been singled out: they say that Cancer is the horoscope of the world (ὡροσκόπον . . . τοῦ κόσμου). This year is called "of the Dog", because the bright star among the fixed stars, the star of the Dog, rises with Cancer. If therefore the planets should again meet in the same point of Cancer, this same concurrence will represent one full circle of the universe.'

22. Lucan's phrasing here also anticipates the language of cosmic mixture in Nigidius' speech, at 1.648, *omnis an infusis miscebitur unda uenenis?*

23. On the historical backdrop of Statius, see for instance Dominik (1994); Newlands (2002).

24. Used this way in Cicero, *Arat*. 347, *ortus atque obitus omnis cognoscere possis* and Germanicus 442 *occasus ortusque* (of the planets). See further on *ortus* Tarrant (1985) ad Seneca, *Thyestes* 787.

25. War between brothers—*fraternas acies* (Statius, *Theb*. 1.1)—is a trope for civil war in Rome (see for example Virgil, *Geo*. 2.496, with my comments, Ch. 2 p. 50 above), whose founding myth is that of fratricide, as Lucan, writing about the civil wars between Caesar and Pompey, is aware (*Pharsalia* 1.92–5):

> nulla fides regni sociis, omnisque potestas
> impatiens consortis erit. nec gentibus ullis
> credite nec longe fatorum exempla petantur:
> fraterno primi maduerint sanguine muri.

> 'Loyalty [will] be impossible between sharers in tyranny, and great [power] will resent a partner. Search not the history of foreign nations for proof, nor look far for an instance of Fate's decree: the rising walls of Rome were wetted with a brother's blood' (Duff).

Rome's foundation plays itself out time and again in the civil wars of Sulla and Marius, the Catilinarian conspiracy, Caesar and Pompey, Octavian and Antony. Likewise, in the Roman tradition, there is no sharp distinction between civil war which is 'historical' and civil war which is 'mythical'. When Roman poets like Statius write about *myths* of civil war, the political context is always immediate.

26. See Tarrant (1985) ad *Thy*. 830–5. Tarrant tends to emphasize *Stoic* influence, citing the equivalency of *Natura* and god in Stoic thought, e.g., Seneca, *Ben*. 4.7.1, *quid enim aliud est natura quam deus et divina ratio toti mundo partibusque eius inserta?* On Stoic cycles in general, the most nuanced study I have found is Bénatouil 2009. I would not deny Stoic influence, merely add the influence of Plato's *Politicus* as a further interpretative tool, in line with our interpretations in Ch. 2.

27. Compare Manilius *Astronomica* 2.579–607. This outburst on human evil follows Manilius' discussion of 'inimical' signs in astrology. Here also the sun disappears on the assassination of Caesar (594–5): *ipse deus Caesar cecidit, qua territus orbi /imposuit Phoebus*

noctem terrasque reliquit ('. . . even the god Caesar fell victim to deceit unspeakable, whereat in horror on the world Phoebus brought darkness and forsook the earth,' Goold). The passage concludes with the 'civil wars' of earth and heaven: *utque sibi caelum sic tellus dissidet ipsa*, 'just as is heaven, earth is at war with itself', trans. Goold).

28. Seneca may gesture toward golden-age tradition (see Chh. 1 and 2 above). Compare *Thy.* 878–81—

> in nos aetas
> ultima venit? o nos dura
> sorte creatos, seu perdidimus
> solem miseri, sive expulimus!

'Has the final age come upon us? We drew the short straw in the lot of life, whether we lost the sun in our misfortune or exiled him' (my trans.)
—with Hesiod *WD* 174–8:

> μηκέτ' ἔπειτ' ὤφελλον ἐγὼ πέμπτοισι μετεῖναι
> ἀνδράσιν, ἀλλ' ἢ πρόσθε θανεῖν ἢ ἔπειτα γενέσθαι.
> νῦν γὰρ δὴ γένος ἐστὶ σιδήρεον· οὐδέ ποτ' ἦμαρ
> παύσονται καμάτου καὶ ὀιζύος οὐδέ τι νύκτωρ
> φθειρόμενοι· χαλεπὰς δὲ θεοὶ δώσουσι μερίμνας.
> ἀλλ' ἔμπης καὶ τοῖσι μεμείξεται ἐσθλὰ κακοῖσιν.

'If only then I did not have to live among the fifth men, but I could have either died first or been born afterwards! For now the race is indeed one of iron. And they will not cease from toil and distress by day, nor from being worn out by suffering by night, and the gods will give them grievous cares' (trans. Most 2006).

29. On the passage of Seneca studied here, though a very different reading from mine, see Volk (2006).

30. On which see Gee (2007).

31. Tarrant (1985) ad *Thy.* 867–74: 'In its clarity and balance the passage mirrors the regularity of the heavens, celebrating the cosmic order that is doomed to pass away.'

32. Lucretius *DRN* 6.535–607, especially 577–84 for the 'flatulence theory' of earthquakes; on parallels for Statius see further Smolenaars (1994) ad loc.

33. On the Bears in Germanicus, see Possanza (2004): 117–19.

34. *Fasti* 2.153–92, *Met.* 2.401–530; see Gee (2000): 174–87.

35. Feeney (1991): 381 discusses the personification (although not the '*katasterism*') of *Mors*.

36. 'Both active and passive senses of *aspectus* seem at work: the sun averts its gaze, and so can no longer be seen,' Tarrant (1985) ad *Thy.* 793.

37. These myths of Hesiod were already combined by Aratus: Statius is reading through the tradition. See Ch. 1 pp. 24–9 above.

38. Franchet d' Espèrey (1997): 184, 'On notera que la choix de *Pietas* est particulièrement heureux, puisque son role des d'empecher le duel fratricide entre Etéocle et Polynice, le crime par excellence, le comble de l'impiété.' An association between *Dike* (Virgo) and Pietas already exists in Manilius, who uses the alternative version of the myth of the constellation Virgo. In *Astronomica* 2.31–2, Virgo is Erigone, a girl who killed herself on learning of her father's death. In Manilius, she is *pietate ad sidera ductam / Erigonen*. It is by *pietas* (towards her father) than Erigone is catasterised. The relationship between Piety and

Justice, expressed in familial terms, also occurs much later, in the Emperor Julian's *Hymn to Helios* 70d, ἔστι γὰρ ὁσιότης τῆς δικαιοσύνης ἔκγονος. On Julian's *Hymn to Helios*, see Ch. 6 pp. 162–71 below.

39. See above, Ch. 4 p. 108.

40. Ch. 2 p. 40.

41. Used in the latter sense in Cicero, *Aratea* 228, *[stellae] quae faciunt vestigia.*

42. See Kuhn (1957): 206–8, on Tycho Brahe's observations of the Nova of 1572 and its sceptical reception among his contemporaries.

43. The series of such invocations in the Roman tradition extends from Virgil to Statius. See also Lucan *Phars.* 1.45–59 (the potential apotheosis of Nero). In addition, Germanicus in his *Phaenomena* 558–60 assimilates the deceased Augustus to the zodiacal constellation Capricorn (on Augustus and Capricorn, see Gee 2000: 138 and n.37; Schmit 2005: 19–30, and Volk 2009: 146–61).

44. Callataÿ (1996): 122–7. By the time of Dante, the planets can stand as indices of *order*, not chaos (*Paradiso* 10.16–21).

Chapter 6

1. On the author's name and probable identity, about which little is known, see above, Introduction n.66. Smolak (1989) summarizes all we know; the most comprehensive treatment is still Soubiran (1981): 7–29. See also Cameron (1967), (1995), and (2011): 241–42; Fiedler (2004): ix n.ii; *EANS* pp. 181–82. Contributions to the study of Avien<i>us' *Phaenomena* are few ('scanty', Cameron 2011: 565): see Gatz (1967): 67–70; Soubiran ed. (1979); Soubiran ed. (1981); Weber (1982 and 1986); Zehnacker (1989); Bellandi et al. (2001, on the *Iustitia* episode only; on which see also Gatz (1967): 67–70; and Fiedler (2004, on lines 367–746). On the current state of research, see Fiedler (2004): xi–xii with the bibliography given on pp. xxi–ii.

2. Zehnacker (1989): 325. The fullest discussion of date is still Soubiran (1981): 7–29, and 38–39. Fiedler (2004) recapitulates (p. IX n.II).

3. Soubiran (1981): 30–32.

4. Soubiran (1981): 39; Bellandi, Berti, Ciappi (2001): 89.

5. For a recent synopsis of the fourth century and its concerns, see Mitchell (2007): 55–100. On the cultural and literary conditions of the fourth century, see Kaster (1988); Swain and Edwards (2004); Scourfield (2007); Cameron (2011). Avienus' *Phaenomena* might be characterized as a product of the age of the compendium. Late antiquity, especially the late fourth century and the beginning of the fifth, was a time of scholarly activity which concerned itself with collection and completion to the point of exhaustiveness: Nonius Marcellinus, Martianus Capella, Ausonius, Augustine, Macrobius, and Servius exemplify the period, among others. Scholia on classical authors originate or crystallize at this time, most notably Donatus on Virgil (c.350), Servius on Virgil (c.420) (Cameron 2004: 341–42). On Servius and his intellectual environment, see Kaster (1988): 169–97; Cameron (2011) Ch. 16. On Macrobius and Servius, with earlier bibliography, see Cameron (2011) 231–72.

6. Cameron (2011): 565.

7. *LRE* I: 83.

8. These terms are the tools of modern debate: see North (2005/2011): 496: 'The terms "monotheism" and "polytheism" are not translatable into Greek or Latin and they cannot therefore represent the terms in which ancient pagans themselves thought about these

matters.' The recent debate about 'pagan' monotheism can be said to have begun with Athanassiadi and Frede (1999); cf. North (2005/2011). The debate is both summarized and moved on by Mitchell and van Nuffelen (2010): 1–15. For our purposes, see especially the highly nuanced contribution of Frede (2010) in that volume. Frede's comments (pp. 70–75) on the Stoic 'monotheism' of Chrysippus are particularly relevant here. As regards the related issue of 'syncretism' (see North's barbed comment, 2005/2011: 493), we might define it as the fusion of unitary figures, for instance of Mithras with the sun-god, or the Stoic deity with the (Neo)platonic demiurge-figure (for this definition see Mitchell and van Nuffelen 2010: 10–11).

9. The seminal contribution to the modern understanding of the pagan–Christian dichotomy is, of course, Lane-Fox (1986). For a more recent, nuanced assessment of the issues, see Mitchell (2007): 225–55.

10. Weber (1986b); Zehnacker (1989).

11. See further below, section 6.2.2.

12. In an earlier work (Gee 2000: 66–91), I have shown how the ideas and expression of the proem continue to resonate across the work, which I see as 'Stoic' in a thoroughgoing sense. This is a brand of Stoicism accessible to every cultured reader. Cf. Zehnacker (1989): 317 and Fantuzzi-Hunter (2004): 226–27.

13. Like Avienus, Firmicus was of aristocratic and Italian (or rather Sicilian) origin (Monat 1992-7: vol.1: 7–9). Again like Avienus' *Phaenomena*, his *Mathesis* may or may not have been written under Christian influence. It (or at least the orientation given to each book) is broadly Neoplatonist in outlook. On the author and work, see my entry on 'Iulius Firmicus Maternus' in the Routledge *Encyclopedia of Ancient Natural Scientists*, with further bibliography; the edition, with introduction, is Monat (1992-7); translation and useful introduction in Bram (1975). Cameron (2011): 565 describes the *Mathesis* as 'little more than a translation of various Greek astrological treatises', which, though it quotes both Plotinus and Porphyry, does so 'only for their relevance to his astrological themes.' As in the case of Avienus, this does not do Firmicus justice.

14. On Julian, see *LRE* I: 119–24; Browning (1975); Bowersock (1978); Athanassiadi-Fowden (1981); Smith (1995); Tougher (2007); Mitchell (2007): 73–79 and especially 263–88, on Julian's Platonism and 'paganism'; Carrié (2009). Bibliography on his intriguing and poorly annotated work is not extensive: see Dillon (1998-9); Athanassiadi (1977); Athanassiadi-Fowden (1981): 147–53; Gnoli (2009); Smith (1995): 139–63.

15. The collection was probably compiled in 389 by Pacatus, the author of the latest in date,. See Nixon and Rodgers (1994): 6–7; Cameron (2011): 228, and below for my discussion of the panegyric of Julian by Mamertinus, delivered in 362.

16. On the cultural conditions of literature in the fourth century, see for example Cameron (2004) and Cameron (2011) Ch. 15; Rees ed. (2004) and Scourfield ed. (2007). Cameron (2004): 350–51 speaks of a fourth-century 'renaissance' or 'revival' in Latin poetry: 'The revival of the whole range of early imperial Latin poetry is a central feature of western elite culture at this time . . .'. At the same time, he argues emphatically for a lack of first-hand knowledge of much classical literature outside the classroom (2011, Ch. 15).

17. Precise points of contact are shown in appendix C.

18. *Substantia* is a word favoured by Firmicus Maternus (eg. *Math.* 1.1.4, *ignes, qui ex Aetnae vertice erumpunt, quae natura eorum quaeve substantia*); and passim. The word also occurs in Nazarius' *Panegyric of Constantine* 4.14.2 (ed. Nixon and Rodgers 1994): *et quamvis caelestia sub oculos hominum venire non soleant, quod crassam et caligantem aciem*

simplex illa et <u>inconcreta substantia</u> naturae tenuis eludat . . . ('And although heavenly things are not in the habit of coming before men's eyes, because the unmixed and incorporeal substance of their subtle nature eludes our dull and darkened vision . . .'). This is interesting, given our twofold contextualization of Avienus' *Ph.* alongside both theology (as Firmicus) and panegyric.

19. *OLD 'concretio'* I.

20. Usages cover both incline and trajectory. See *TLL 'Inclinatio'* I B 2 c (= κλίμα, as glossed by Vitruvius 10.1.10, *inclinationes caeli, quae Graeci* κλίματα *dicunt*); and II B (= *motus*), under which rubric the authors of the *TLL* situate our passage. Avienus uses the word again, with *caelum*, at 85.

21. *OLD 'discretio'* I.

22. Cicero, *Leg.* 1.23 makes a similar association between *societas* and *ius*:

> est igitur, quoniam nihil est ratione melius eaque <est> et in homine et in deo, prima homini cum deo rationis societas; inter quos autem ratio, inter eosdem etiam recta ratio {et} communis est; quae cum sit lex, lege quoque consociati homines cum dis putandi sumus; inter quos porro est communio legis, inter eos communio iuris est . . . (text of Powell 2006).

> 'It's the case, then, since nothing is better than reason, and that exists both in man and in god, that man's primary connection with god is that of reason. Those who have reason in common must necessarily have correct reason in common. Since law is a form of this, we must also think that men are associated with the gods through law. Further, among those for whom there is a common law, there must also be a common justice . . .' (my trans.).

For the political terminology, cf. Avienus 79, *in lege*.

23. The Emperor Julian proposes a similar spread of topics at *Hymn to Helios* 132b, as characteristic of *encomium*: ἢ δῆλον ὅτι περὶ τῆς οὐσίας αὐτοῦ καὶ ὅθεν προῆλθε καὶ τῶν δυνάμενων καὶ τῶν ἐνεργείων διελθόντες, ὁπόσαι φανεραὶ ὅσαι τ᾿ ἀφανεῖς, καὶ περὶ τῆς τῶν ἀγαθῶν δόσεως, ἣν κατὰ πάντας ποιεῖται τοὺς κόσμους, οὐ παντάπασιν ἀπάδοντα ποιησόμεθα τῷ θεῷ τὰ ἐγκώμια; ('Or is it not evident that if I describe his substance and his origin, and his powers and energies, both visible and invisible, and the gift of blessings which he bestows throughout all the worlds, I shall compose an encomium not wholly displeasing to the god?', trans.Wright 1980).

24. *tenebrae* are a theme of Avienus' proem: see also *tenebrarum* . . . *vincula* . . . /*solvit*, 22–23 (the rupture of the primal darkness by **Jupiter**, but surely also the coming to light of philosophy), mirrored by the action of the **sun**, *tenebrosas rumpat amictos*, 35. The contrast between light and shadow adds drama, as in Lucretius' third proem in praise of Epicurus, beginning *e tenebris tantis tam clarum extollere lumen* . . .

25. Weber (1986a) ad loc. references this passage but does not enlarge on its interpretation.

26. Should we already see a reception of the *Phdr.* passage in Aratus' proem? τετυγμένα occurs in *Phdr.* 247a2, and in Aratus 11–13, ἐσκέψατο δ᾿ εἰς ἐνιαυτὸν /ἀστέρας οἵ κε μάλιστα τετυγμένα σημαίνοιεν /ἀνδράσιν ὡράων ('[Zeus] organised stars for the year to give the most clearly defined signs of the seasonal round to men', Kidd). Perhaps we can see Avienus' 'Platonic' rewriting as signalled by a layer of Platonic interpretation already embedded in the Aratean text itself?

27. Hermeias ed. Couvreur (1901): 136.10–13.

28. Yunis (2011) ad loc.: 'Beauty's radiance and S[ocrates]'s glimpse of it are likened to the ἐποπτεία (ἐποπτεύοντες, 250c3), the Eleusinian cult's highest grade of initiation, in which the light of sacred torches . . . breaks upon the night to put the cult's hidden, sacred objects suddenly in view (ὄψιν τε καὶ θέαν, 250b5, φάσματα, c3).'

29. Weber (1986a) ad loc. also contends that Avienus' *vox secreta* is a Latinization of μυστὶς φωνή, but cites Orphic sources without mentioning either Plato or Firmicus.

30. For an additional connection between fruitfulness and leadership, in panegyric, see for instance *Panegyrici Latini* 4.2.4 and 4.3.5 (and section 6.2.5 below).

31. All translations of Firmicus in this chapter are my own.

32. We shall see in addition below how Avienus mirrors concepts also present in the Emperor Julian's *Hymn to King Helios*, namely the demiurgic power of the sun's light.

33. Note also *animus divina inspiratione formatus* at 5 pr. 6.

34. Monat (1992–7) ad *Math.* 5 pr. 3 speaks of 'le syncrétisme néoplatonicien de Firmicus'. For a definition of 'syncretism', see n.8 above.

35. Above, ch. 3, p. 00.

36. Cf. Aratus 10–12, αὐτὸς γὰρ τά γε σήματ᾽ ἐν οὐρανῷ ἐστήριξεν /ἄστρα διακρίνας, ἐσκέψατο δ᾽ εἰς ἐνιαυτὸν/ἀστέρας . . . ('For it was Zeus himself who fixed the signs in the sky, making them into distinct constellations, and organised stars for the year'), where ἐν οὐρανῷ ἐστήριξεν represents Zeus' establishment of *ordo*, ἐσκέψατο δ᾽ εἰς ἐνιαυτὸν his establishment of the stars' *cursus*. Firmicus is following the twofold division of divine activity.

37. E.g., Soubiran (1981): 75; contra, Cameron (2011): 565.

38. *Math.* 1.13; see Monat (1992–7): Introd., vol. 1, p. 8. For views on the possible influence of Christianity on Firmicus, see Monat (1992–7) Introd. p. 22. Monat somewhat hedges his bets, seeing the work (like Avienus') as pagan, without excluding Christian currents of thought: 'Nous dirions, pour notre part, que la *Mathesis*, toute païenne qu'elle est, a pu naître dans l'environnement teinté de christianisme, de ce christianisme mêlé et ambigu que connaissait la cour de Constantin.'

39. Monat (1992–7): Introd., vol. 1 p. 21.

40. 'S'il reprend volontiers les thèmes de la diatribe Stoïcienne, il s'est, par Plotin et Porphyre, imprégné de néoplatonisme' (Monat 1992–7 Introd., vol. 1 p. 21).

41. On features of Avienus's translation said to be Christian or designed for a Christian audience, see in particular Weber (1986b): 327–28.

42. On Neoplatonism and fourth-century literature in general, the classic treatment is Courcelle (1943).

43. Weber (1986a) ad loc. seems to agree with this interpretation.

44. For discussion of this passage of Lucretius and its Ciceronian antecedents see above, Ch. 3 pp. 00–00.

45. Bailey (1947) ad loc. Cf. Costa (1984) ad loc.: '*Nodus* . . . is a technical term for the point at which the ecliptic cuts the celestial equator.'

46. There are two instances of *nodus* at the hexameter end in astronomical poetry, both in Cicero: *Arat.* fr.32.4S, *aeternum ex astris cupiens conectere nodum* ('desiring to join an everlasting knot from the stars'), and *Arat.* 17, *quem veteres soliti caelestem dicere nodum* ('which those of old were accustomed to call a knot'). Although the meaning in these cases is apparently different (one star shared by two astral figures), it is possible that Avienus is imitating this mannerism of astronomical didactic here.

47. As Goold points out ad loc. both the tropic (Cancer and Capricorn) and the equinoctial signs (Aries and Libra) are included under the designation *tropici* (cf. 2.178).

48. In line 58 of Avienus there is a demonstrable parallel with Cicero, making it more likely that Avienus is thinking of Cicero elsewhere in his proem. Avienus' *spatium lucis* is adopted from Cicero *Arat.* 288. In fact, the two passages are very similar, both describing the equinoxes (note also, for instance, *aequarent* in Avienus line 60 with *exaequat*, Cic. *Arat.* 288). Eudoxus as he is described by Avienus apparently learned his astronomy not so much from Jupiter as from Cicero.

49. Kuhn (1957): 34.

50. Courtney (1993): 433: 'This poem was widely known and much imitated.'

51. Courtney (1993): 335 cites Avienus line 6, *vis fulminis iste corusci.*

52. See especially Dillon (1998–9): 107–8.

53. See Kuhn (1957): 34–35.

54. Soubiran (1981) ad loc. favours the reading of *discretio iusta* as the 'harmonic ratio' that separates the orbits of the planets, which do not themselves intersect (*insociabilium*). Weber (1986a), on the other hand, takes *insociabilium deorum* as the elements, and *discretio iusta* as a description of the role of Jupiter in '*Diakrisiskosmogonie*'.

55. Perhaps this is the meaning of *deorum* in Avienus line 54, *convexa deorum*, an expression followed by the list of zodiacal constellations; *convexa deorum* might mean 'the vaults of the gods [which inhabit them]', i.e., the constellations. A precedent might be Plato's description of the heavenly bodies as οὐράνιον θεῶν γένος at *Tim.* 39e11–40a1 (and cf. *Rep.* 508a4, where the heavenly bodies are called τῶν ἐν οὐρανῷ θεῶν). In the fourth-century AD context, Julian may also support the idea of the constellations-as-gods. At *HH* 148c, describing the arrangement of the zodiac by the Demiurge, he says: τοὺς τρεῖς γὰρ τετραχῇ τέμνων διὰ τῆς τοῦ ζῳοφόρου κύκλον πρὸς ἕκαστον αὐτῶν κοινωνίας τοῦτον αὖθις τὸν ζῳοφόρον εἰς δώδεκα θεῶν δυνάμεις διαιρεῖ . . . ('For as he divides the three spheres by four through the zodiac, which is associated with every one of the three, so he divides the zodiac also into twelve divine powers . . .'). θεῶν δυνάμεις = lit. 'forces of gods'. Perhaps cf. Manilius 2.434–47 (an Olympian god is assigned to each constellation).

56. My thanks to Katharina Volk for confirming by email, from a position of greater astrological expertise, my suspicion that Cancer and Capricorn as signs of the zodiac are *insociabiles*: '. . . Generally these signs can well be considered inimical: Cancer and Capricorn are in opposition to one another, as are Aries and Libra, and that is often considered a cause of hostility; and all four signs belong to the same hexagon (a.k.a. are in quartile aspect), which is also typically a reason for enmity.' In terms of the natives of these constellations, *in Cancro genitos Capricorni semina laedunt* (Manilius 2.547).

57. Soubiran (1981) ad Avienus 1552–6: 'Le *Discours sur Hélios-Roi* de l'empereur Julien (fin déc. 362) est exactement contemporain d'Aviénus . . .'

58. Zehnacker (1989): 325, 329.

59. Dillon (1998–9): 103–4: Julian's *HH* 'constitutes an attempt to define the essence both of his own religious belief, and of the revived, rationalised religious system he wished to impose on the Empire;' Athanassiadi-Fowden (1981): 148: 'The Hymn to King Helios . . . can be regarded as Julian's definitive attempt to crystallise the Roman religion.'

60. Julian can address a hymn to Helios as supreme god because of the 'incontestable solar affinities' (Athanassiadi-Fowden 1981: 179) of the second Flavian dynasty. We might

note the description of Constantine, who promoted the cult of *Sol Invictus* first established by Aurelian, in *PanLat* 4.12.3. On Helios and the Flavian dynasty, see Barnes (1981): 36–37.

61. The sun as mediator between the cosmic levels was a Neoplatonic idea shared with Mithraism (see Dillon 1998–9: 107–8; Athanassiadi-Fowden 1981: 150). The idea also lies behind Tiberianus line 20 (above, p. 160).

62. All translations of Julian's *HH* hereafter are from Wright (1980).

63. Soubiran (1981) ad loc. 'On songe à la philosophie d'Empedocle . . . Mais le "premier moteur" d'Aristote, dont a vu une mention probable au v.5 . . . n'est pas étranger non plus à cette notion d'amour . . .'

64. Dillon (1998–9): 111: The μέσστης of Helios 'does not . . . consist . . . in the mere fact of being equally remote from two extremes, but rather in being that which unifies and links together what is separate (ἐνωτικὴ καὶ σθνάγουσα τὰ διεστῶτα), like Empedocles' *harmonia.*'

65. Dillon (1998–9): 112. Iamblichus, the third- to fourth-century Neoplatonist, is Julian's avowed source for much of his theology (cited, e.g., at *HH* 146a, 150d, etc.). Note here how Julian, like Avienus, cites two chronologically separate sources, in Avienus' case Eudoxus and Aratus, in Julian's case, Plato and Iamblichus.

66. This appears to anticipate the heliocentric system: see (for a surprisingly close resonance) Copernicus 1.10: 'So the sun sits as upon a royal throne ruling his children the planets which circle around him', discussed below, Epilogue. In fact in Julian, Helios is the middle *planet*, ἐν τοῖς πλανωμένοις μέσης 135c; in *HH* 148a he is not only the middle of the planets, but the middle of the 'three kosmoi' (τριῶν . . . τῶν κόσμων) of Neoplatonism. Needless to say, this is not the same as the middle of the *solar system.*

67. And see Rowe (1986) ad *Phdr.* 246c7–d1 and e4ff.

68. Given the Platonic flavour, I am almost tempted to translate *sensim* as '[led astray] by sense perception'; see Weber (1986a) ad loc., who glosses *sensim* as αἰσθετικῶς, i.e., in the world of αἴσθησις as opposed to that of νόησις.

69. On *flos et flamma* see Weber (1986a) ad loc.

70. Note also the metaphor of irrigation at *HH* 137d, ἐποχετεύων.

71. ὁρατὸν δὲ ὅλως εἴη ἂν τὶ μὴ φωτὶ πρῶτον ὥσπερ ὕλη τεχνίτη προσαχθέν, ἵν' οἶμαι τὸ εἶδος δέξηται; ('For what, speaking generally, could be seen, were it not first brought into touch with light, in order that, I suppose, it may receive a form, as matter is brought under the hand of a craftsman?' *HH* 134c).

72. For a variety of readings see Soubiran (1981) ad loc.

73. The rationale is similar to Julian *HH* 137c, ἃ δὲ ἡμᾶς ἔοικεν αὐτὸς ὁ θεὸς διδάσκειν ὑπέρ τε αὐτοῦ καὶ τῶν ἄλλων, ἐκεῖνα ἤδη διέλθωμεν ('And let me now relate what the god himself seems to teach us, both about himself and the other gods').

74. See also below, on *HH* 152b–c (an important passage for our understanding of the rationale of the *Hymn*).

75. Cf. Avienus' *numerus* at line 9.

76. Compare Avienus *Ph.* 32–33.

77. Athanassiadi-Fowden 1981: 151. See especially *HH* 139d: δύο δὴ ταύτας οὐσίας συνοχῆς αἰτίας . . ., quoted with translation Ch.6 p. 168.

78. See also 133c; 139d; 140a–b; 145d (ὁ φαινόμενος ἐξ αἰῶνος κόσμος).

79. *ab Iove principium magno deduxit Aratus. /carminis at nobis, genitor, tu maximus auctor, /te veneror tibi sacra fero . . .* ('Aratus began with mighty Jupiter. My poem, however,

claims you, father, greatest of all, as its inspirer. It is you that I reverence; it is to you that I am offering sacred gifts . . .,' Germ. *Ph.* 1–3, trans. Gain). On the identity of the *genitor*, see Gain (1976): 20. For an earlier equation between the rule of Octavian on earth and of Jupiter in heaven, see Horace *Odes* 1.12.51–60. In the specifically astral context, Manilius also assimilates 'Caesar' with the ruler of the universe: *hunc mihi tu, Caesar, patriaeque princeps paterque, /qui regis augustis parentem legibus orbem /concessumque patri mundum deus ipse mereris . . .* (Manilius *Ast.* 1.7–9).

80. Compare the term, and the concept, to 'intertextual polemic', used of Lucretius in Chh. 3 and 4.

81. See Tougher (2007): 20–21 on Julian's attitude to, and revivification of, the identification between the emperor and Helios in the *HH* and in his panegyrics.

82. Note the vatic ᾄδειν (on which see above, Ch. 1 pp. 33–4)—even though Julian's utterances are in prose.

83. His second oration frequently quotes verbatim from Plato (*Menex.* 247e at *Or.* 2, 68c–d; *Tim.* 90a at *Or.* 2.69a; *Apol.* 30d at *Or.* 2.69b, *Laws* at *Or.* 2.81a, etc.).

84. The corpus of *Panegyrici Latini* (henceforward *PanLat*) was compiled in the fourth century, probably by the Gaul Pacatus Drepanius, who delivered the panegyric to Theodosius in 389 (Cameron 2011: 227–28; 404). On the *PanLat* see Nixon and Rodgers (1994) and Rees (2002).

85. E.g., Athanassiadi-Fowden (1981): 179: Constantine, despite his Christianity, had encouraged the diffusion of the cult of *Sol Invictus*, 'whose terrestrial image he was.'

86. On Zeus as 'father', see Kidd (1997) ad loc. ἤπιος is characteristic of a father (Kidd 1997 ad line 5). Perhaps a 'political' hint lies in the Homeric λαούς, usually used of the people as opposed to their leaders (Kidd 1997 ad line 6). Zeus in rousing the people to work takes on the role of such a leader. On the 'father' tradition, see also Fowler (2000b).

87. Schol. Arat. *Ph.*1 (Martin 1974 p.38.12).

88. On the formation of the connection between emperor and god in earlier panegyric and historiography up to Pliny's *Panegyricus* in 100 AD, see Levene (1997). Hesiod already adumbrated the connection in his *dictum* ἐκ δὲ Διὸς βασιλῆες at *Theog.* 96. One of the earliest characterizations of Zeus as βασιλεύς may be Empedocles, fragment 128 (= Inwood 122/128).2, Ζεὺς βασιλεὺς (see Ch. 1 n.31 above).

89. Even closer is Avienus' *parens rerum* in *Ph.* 23.

90. Cf. Germanicus *Ph.* 2, where the poet's *genitor* is also the *carminis auctor.*

91. Compare Avienus' *perpes substantia lucis* in *Ph.* 8.

92. Compare *imperio*, Avienus line 4.

93. Text and translation of the *PanLat* from Nixon and Rodgers (1994) throughout this chapter.

94. Nixon and Rodgers (1994) ad loc.

95. There is a similar raft of terms for the godhead in Nazarius, *Panegyric of Constantine*: see Nixon and Rodgers (1994): 336. As Nixon and Rodgers point out, this god is not necessarily Christian: 'Although this is the vocabulary of monotheism, these are only words, not an affirmation of faith.'

96. Nixon and Rodgers (1994) ad loc. comment, '. . . to speak of Constantine's *numen* being present is risky, however traditional it be, in what appears to have been a changed atmosphere.' The topos of the emperor as a '*praesens deus*' permeates the *PanLat*: see for instance 6.1.5, 6.22.1, of Constantine, and Nixon and Rodgers (1994): 292–93 and 336.

97. Cf. Avienus 6, *vis fulminis iste corusci.*

98. 'The orator has not given up on comparing emperor to deity, a device that the panegyrist of 289, and others, used effectively' (Nixon and Rodgers 1994 ad loc.).

99. Specific commentaries on *PanLat* 3, in addition to Nixon and Rodgers (1994) are Lieu (1989), Ruiz (2006), and Gutzwiller (1942).

100. See n.57 above.

101. Nixon and Rodgers (1994): 392.

102. Gutzwiller (1942) ad loc. adduces Pliny's *Panegyricus* as precedent: 'Vergleiche des Kaisers mit Jupiter finden sich ferner bei Plinius, *Paneg.* 80.4.'

103. Ruiz (2006) ad loc. believes *poetae ferunt* is a formula of safe distancing from the divinization of the emperor. In the case of Julian this is unnecessary, given that he was apparently comfortable with the solar affinites of the dynasty: more likely it is a signifier of the literary tradition. On similar references to the tradition of Hesiod in Aratus, see above, Ch. 1 p. 24.

104. Above, Ch. 1 p. 46.

105. De Boeft et al. (1995) ad Ammianus Marcellinus 22.10.6 (see following note) for parallels, which include Symmachus, *Or.* 3.9, *caelo rediisse Iustitiam*, and *Or.* 4.15, *haec est illa Latii veteris aetas aureo celebrata cognomine qua fertur incola fuisse terrarum necdum moribus offensa Iustitia* (text of Callu 2009).

106. See Ammianus Marcellinus 22.10.6, recording Julian himself, in the course of his law-giving activities, as playing on Aratus and the Roman tradition of *Iustitia*: *et aestimabatur per haec et similia, et ipse dicebat assidue, vetus illa Iustitia, quam offensam vitiis hominum, Aratus extollit in caelum, imperante eo reversa ad terras* . . . ('. . . these and similar instances led to the belief, as he himself constantly affirmed, that the old goddess of justice, whom Aratus takes up to heaven because she was displeased with the vices of mankind, had returned to earth during his reign . . .' (trans. Rolfe 1940). De Boeft et al. (1995) ad loc. confess aporia as to the precise meaning and context of the reference, although they note its affiliations to Aratus *Ph.* 133–34, and are tempted to ascribe it propagandistic value: 'There is unfortunately no other evidence of what appears to be imperial propaganda in the making. . . . It could be that Julian indeed had Aratus 96 sqq. in mind and wished to believe that the goddess in question had decided to return to earth'. If true, this would add another interesting aspect to my argument about the role of Aratus in the fourth century. I do not agree with de Boeft et al. that 'the lack of undisputed references or allusions in the text prescribes a "non liquet" concerning such ideas in Julian's days.' Ideas such as these can be situated through examination of the literary tradtions in which they find their context, as has been done in this chapter.

Epilogue

1. Martin (1974) p. 42.9–18.

2. Copernicus 1.10 (1543 ed. ff.9v–10r), consulted in the rare books collection of St Andrews University Library, with thanks to Norman Reid. F.9v, reproduced by courtesy of St Andrews University Library, is the endpiece to this book.

3. On the (surprising) Neoplatonism of Copernicus, see Kuhn (1957): 131, '[Copernicus'] authorities are immediately Neoplatonic'; cf. pp. 141 and 181.

Appendix A

1. Ludwig (1963) 441 n.1; Hunter (1995/2008): 179 n.79; Schiesaro (1996): 10; Fakas (2001): 153.

2. Fakas (2001): 153. On this passage, along with *WD* 252, see Hunter (1995/2008): 179 n.79.

3. Ludwig (1963) 441 n.1, Fakas (2001): 154–55.

4. Solmsen (1966): 125; for the reading ἀπέκειτο see West (1978) ad loc.

5. Fakas (2001): 153.

6. Fakas (2001): 153, also noting the *oppositio in imitando* between *Ph.* 114, γαῖα γένος χρύσειον ἔφερβεν, and *WD* 121, τοῦτο γένος κατὰ γαῖα κάλυψεν.

7. Fakas (2001): 158.

8. Ludwig (1963) 441 n.1. Contrast Hesiod's use of the same formula for the Silver Age men, *WD* 142 δεύτεροι, ἀλλ' ἔμπης τιμὴ καὶ τοῖσιν ὀπηδεῖ (with Fakas 2001: 158).

9. Fakas (2001): 158.

10. Fakas (2001): 158, adding also *WD* 145–46 οἷσιν Ἄρεος /ἔργ' ἔμελε στονόεντα καὶ ὕβρεις.

11. Ludwig (1963) 441; Solmsen (1966): 125; Fakas (2001): 158–59.

12. Fakas (2001): 159.

13. Fakas (2001): 159. Compare also the wordplay in *Ph.*130–31, χαλκείη . . . | . . . ἐκαλκεύσαντο with *WD* 150–51, χάλκεα . . . χάλκεοι . . . | χαλκῷ. However, Aratus substitutes μάχαιραν for one of Hesiod's group of three (χάλκεα).

14. Identified by Ludwig (1963) 441; cf. Fakas (2001): 160.

15. Ludwig (1963) 441.

16. Kidd (1997) ad loc.

17. Fakas (2001): 154.

18. Fakas (2001): 156; see also *WD* 113 νόσφιν ἄτερ τε πόνου καί ὀϊζύος (with Fakas 2001: 156); cf. (conceptually) *WD* 115 and 119.

19. Ludwig (1963) 441 n.1; Solmsen (1966): 126; Fakas (2001): 156.

20. Ludwig (1963) 441 n.1; Solmsen (1966): 125; Fakas (2001): 158.

21. Kidd (1997) ad *Ph.* 123–26.

22. Solmsen (1966): 126–27; Fakas (2001): 160 n.40.

23. See Fakas (2001): 158 n.34, connecting the adjective with temporal progression (with ὑποδείελος) in Aratus.

Appendix B

1. For the numbering of the fragments I have followed Soubiran (1972).

2. Conte (1986): 52.

3. On the reading *umbra* in this line, and the construction, see Kenney (1984) ad loc.

4. Following this line, there is a hiatus in Merrill's collocations until 5.915. Did he not find any, or did he not look, not expecting to find any after the astronomical section?

5. Ω reads *lumine* (see Soubiran 1972, apparatus ad loc.).

Appendix C

1. This expression is extremely obscure. I have taken it to follow from the reference to the two sexes in line 26, and translated '*aevum*' as 'generation'. The interpretation of Soubiran

(1981): n. ad loc. is different. He says '. . . *geminum aevum* ne peut signifier que le passé et l'avenir' ('*geminum aevum* can only signify the past and the future'). On this reading, which I find attractive in itself, you might translate line 27 'and perceiving at the one time equally everything pertaining to past and future . . .' I did not eventually adopt this interpretation, however, because it seems to me to square less well with what immediately precedes and follows, i.e., the references to Jupiter's ability to reproduce alone because of his bisexual nature.

2. See Ch. 6, pp. 158–60, for my comments on this reading of *pigra inclinatio nodi*.

BIBLIOGRAPHY

Adams, J.N. and R.G. Meyer (1999), *Aspects of the Language of Latin Poetry* (Proceedings of the British Academy 93), Oxford: Oxford University Press.

Algra, K., M. Koenen, and P. Schrijvers edd. (1997), *Lucretius and his Intellectual Background*, Amsterdam/Oxford: Koninklijke Nederlandse Akademie van Wetenschappen.

Alline, H. (1915), *Histoire du texte de Platon*, Paris: Édouard Champion.

Annas, J. and R. Waterfield, edd. (1995), *Plato: Statesman*, Cambridge: Cambridge University Press.

Arrighetti, G. (1973), *Epicuro. Opere*, 2nd edn., Turin: Einaudi,

Asmis, E. (1995), 'Epicurean Poetics,' in Obbink (1995): 15–34.

Athanassiadi, P. (1977), 'A contribution to Mithraic Theology: the emperor Julian's *Hymn to King Helios*,' *JThSt* 28: 360–71.

Athanassiadi, P. and M. Frede (1999), *Pagan Monotheism in Late Antiquity*, Oxford: Clarendon Press; New York: Oxford University Press.

Athanassiadi-Fowden, P. (1981), *Julian and Hellenism: an Intellectual Biography*, Oxford: Clarendon Press.

Bakhouche, B. (2002), *L'astrologie à Rome*, Louvain: Editions Peeters.

Bakhouche, B. (2009), 'La subversion du genre romanesque dans le *De nuptiis Philologiae et Mercurii* de Martianus Capella,' in Carrié (2009): 375–82.

Bailey, C. (1921), *Lucreti de rerum natura libri sex*, Oxford: Clarendon Press, second edition.

Baldwin, B. (1981), 'The Authorship of the Aratus Ascribed to Germanicus', *Quaderni urbinati di cultura classica* 36: 163–72.

Barnes, T. (1981), *Constantine and Eusebius*, Cambridge MA: Harvard University Press.

Bartalucci, A. (1983), 'Il neopitagorismo di Germanico,' *Studi classici e orientali* 33: 133–69.

Barton, T. (1994), *Power and knowledge: astrology, physiognomics, and medicine under the Roman Empire*, Ann Arbor: University of Michigan Press.

Beaujeu, J. (1979), 'L'astronomie de Lucain,' in Soubiran ed. (1979): 209–24.

Bellandi, F. (2000), 'Arato, Cicerone e il mito della Vergine,' *Paideia* 55: 37–73.

Bénatouil, T. (2009), 'How industrious can Zeus be? The extent and objects of divine activity in Stoicism,' in Salles (2009a): 23–45.

Bernard, H. (1997), *Kommentar zu Platons Phaidros: Hermeias von Alexandrien*, Tübingen: Mohr Siebeck.

Bing, P. (1988), *The Well-Read Muse: Present and Past in Callimachus and the Hellenistic Poets*, Göttingen: Vandenhoeck and Ruprecht.

Bing, P (1990), 'A pun on Aratus' name in verse 2 of the *Phainomena*?' *HSCP* 93: 281–85.

Bing, P. (1993), 'Aratus and his audiences,' *Mega Nepios: the Addressee in Didactic Epic*, *Biblioteca di MD* 31: 99–109.

Blass, F. (1887), *Eudoxi ars astronomica qualis in charta Aegyptia superset*, Keil: Universität Kiel, ex officina Schmidtii et Klaunigii, repr. in *ZPE* 115(1997): 79–101.

Blumenthal, H.J., and E.G. Clark, edd. (1993), *The Divine Iamblichus: Philosopher and Man of Gods*, Bristol: Bristol Classical Press.

Boccuto, G. (1985), 'Weather Forecasting in Vergil and Aratus,' *Atene e Roma* 30: 9–16.

Bogen, J., and J. Woodward (1988), 'Saving the Phenomena', *The Philosophical Review* 97: 303–52.

Bouché-Leclercq, A. (1899), *L'Astrologie greque*, Paris: E. Leroux.

Bowersock, G. (1978), *Julian the Apostate*, London: Duckworth.

Boyancé, P. (1963), *Lucrèce et l'Épicurisme*, Paris: Presses universitaires de France.

Boys-Stones, G. and J. Haubold (2010), *Plato and Hesiod*, Oxford: Oxford University Press.

Bram, J.R., ed. (2005), *Ancient astrology: theory and practice, Matheseos libri VIII by Firmicus Maternus*, Bel Air: Astrology Center of America.

Bresig, A., ed. (1899), *Germanici Caesaris Aratea cum scholiis*, Leipzig: Teubner.

Brisson, L. (1994), 'Interprétation du mythe du *Politique*,' in Rowe (ed.) (1995b): 249–63.

Browning, R. (1975), *The Emperor Julian*, London: Weidenfeld and Nicolson.

Büchner, K. (1939), 'M. Tullius Cicero', *PW* vol.VII: 1242–45.

Buescu, V. (1941), *Cicéron, Les* Aratea, Bucarest, repr. Hildesheim: Georg Olms 1966.

Bureau, O. (1979), 'La cosmologie Lucrétienne,' in Soubiran ed. (1979): 185–94.

Burnet, J., ed. (1900), Platonis opera, vol. 1, Oxford: Clarendon Press.

Burnet, J. (1902), Platonis opera, vol. 4, Oxford: Clarendon Press.

Callu, J.-P., ed. (2009), *Symmaque, Tome V, Discours-Rapports*, Paris, Les Belles Lettres.

Camerarius, Joachim (1536), *Ioachimi Camerarii Quaestoris Opuscula aliquot elegantissima*, Basel: per Balthasarem Lasium, et Thomam Platterum.

Cameron, A. (1967), 'Macrobius, Avienus, and Avianus,' *CQ* 17: 385–99.

Cameron, A. (1970), *Claudian*, Oxford: Clarendon Press.

Cameron, A. (1972), 'Callimachus on Aratus' Sleepless Nights', *CR* 86: 169–7. (1995a), *Callimachus and his Critics*, Princeton NJ, Princeton University Press.

Cameron, A. (1995b), 'Avienus or Avienius?' *ZPE* 108: 252–62.

Cameron, A. 'Poetry and Literary Culture in Late Antiquity', (2004) in Swain and Edwards (2004): 327–54.

Cameron, A. (2011), *The Last Pagans of Rome*, Oxford: Oxford University Press.

Campbell, M. (1988), *Index verborum in Arati Phaenomena*, Hildesheim: Olms

Carrié, J.-M. (2009), *L'empereur Julien et son temps (Antiquité tardive 17)*, Brepols: Turnhout.

Cervellera, M.A., and D. Liuzzi, edd. (1989), *L'astronomia a Roma nell' età augustea*, Testi e studi (Università degli studi di Lecce), Galatina: Congedo.

Clausen, W. (1981), 'Cicero and the New Poetry,' *HSCP* 90: 159–70.

Clay, J. (2003), *Hesiod's Cosmos*, Cambridge, New York: Cambridge University Press.

Coleman, R. (1977), *Vergil: Eclogues*, Cambridge: Cambridge University Press.

Conte, G.B. (1986), *The Rhetoric of Imitation*, trans. C. Segal, Ithaca: Cornell University Press.

Costa, C.D.N., ed. (1984), *Lucretius* De rerum natura V, Oxford: Clarendon Press.

Courcelle, Pierre (1948), *Les lettres grecques en Occident: de Macrobe à Cassiodore*, Paris: E. de Boccard; trans. by Harry E. Wedeck (1969) as *Late Latin Writers and their Greek Sources*, Cambridge, MA: Harvard University Press.

Courtney, E. (1969), 'Some passages of the Aratea of Germanicus,' *CR* 19: 138–41.

Courtney, E. 'Aratea' in *OCD³*.

Courtney, E. (1993), *The Fragmentary Latin Poets*, Oxford: Oxford University Press; second edn. 2003.

Couvreur P. (1901), *Hermiae Alexandrini in Platonis Phaedrum scholia*, Paris: Librairie Emile Bouillon.

Cramer, F. (1954), *Astrology in Roman Law and Politics*, Philadelphia: American Philosophical Society.

Cusset, C. (1995), 'Exercises rhétoriques d'Aratos autour du terme ἠχή,' *RPh* 69: 245–48.

Cusset, C. (2002), 'Poétique et onomastique dans les *Phénomènes* d'Aratos,' *Pallas* 59: 187–96.

Dalzell, A. (1996), *The Criticism of Didactic Poetry: Essays on Lucretius, Virgil and Ovid*, Toronto: University of Toronto Press.

Danielewicz, J. (2005), 'Further Hellenistic Acrostics: Aratus and Others,' *Mnemosyne* 58: 321–34.

de Boeft, J., J. Drijvers, D. den Hengst, and H. Teitler (1995), *Philological and Historical Commentary on Ammianus Marcellinus XXII*, Groningen: Egbert Forsten.

de Bourdellès, H. (1987), *L'Aratus Latinus: étude sur la culture et la langue latine dans le nord de la France au VIII e siècle*, Peritia: Brepols.

de Callataÿ, G. (1996), *Annus Platonicus: a study of world cycles in Greek, Latin and Arabic sources*, Louvain-la-Neuve: Université Catholique de Louvain.

de Callataÿ, G. (2005), 'Il numero geometrico', in Vegetti (2005): 167–87.

Defradas, J. (1965), 'Le mythe hésiodique des races: essai de mise au point,' *L'information littéraire* 4: 152–56.

Della Casa, A., ed. (1962), *Nigidio Figulo* 'astrologo e mago': testimonianze e frammenti, Lecce: Milella.

di Maria, G., ed. (1996), *Achillis quae feruntur astronomica et in Aratum opuscula*, Palermo: Facoltà di Lettere e Filosofia dell'Università di Palermo.

Diehl, E., ed. (1903–6), *Proclus Diadochus in Platonis Timaeum commentaria*, 3 vols., Leipzig: Teubner.

Dihle, A. (1994), *Greek and Latin Literature of the Roman Empire*, London, New York: Routledge.

Dillon, J. (1998–9), 'The Theology of Julian's Hymn to King Helios,' *Itaca* 14–15: 103–15.

Dillon, J., ed. (1973), *Iamblici Chalcidensis in Platonis dialogos commentariorum fragmenta*, Leiden: Brill.

Dillon, J. (1977), *The Middle Platonists: a Study of Platonism 80 BC to AD 220*, London: Duckworth.

Dominik, W.J. (1994), *The mythic voice of Statius: Power and Politics in the Thebaid*, Leiden & New York: Brill.

Duff, J.D. (1928), *Lucan: The Civil War*, Cambridge, MA, London: Harvard University Press.

Eastwood, B. (2007), *Ordering the Heavens: Roman Astronomy and Cosmology in the Carolingian Renaissance*, Leiden: Brill.

Effe, B. (1970), 'Προτέρη γενεή: eine stoische Hesiod-Interpretation in Arats *Phainomena*,' *RhM* 113: 167–82.

Effe, B. (1977), *Dichtung und Lehre: Untersuchungen zur Typologie des antiken Lehrgedichts*, München: Beck.

El Murr, D. (2010), 'Hesiod, Plato and the Golden Age: Hesiodic motifs in the myth of the *Politicus*,' in Boys-Stones and Haubold (2010): 276–97.

Erren, M. (1967), *Die Phainomena des Aratos von Soloi: Untersuchungen zum Sach- und Sinnverständnis*, Wiesbaden: F. Steiner.

Erren, M., ed. (1971), *Aratus Phaenomena: Sternbilder und Wetterzeichen*, Munich: Heimeran.

Erren, M. (1994), 'Arat und Aratea 1966–1992', *Lustrum* 36: 299–301.

Esposito, P. (1998), 'I *Phaenomena* di Ovidio', in *Ovidio: da Roma all'Europa*, edd. I. Gallo & P. Esposito, Università degli studi di Salermo, Quaderni del dipartimento di scienze dell' antichità 20, Napoli: Arte tipografica: 55–69.

Evans, J. (1998), *The History and Practice of Ancient Astronomy*, New York/Oxford: Oxford University Press.

Fakas, C. (2001), *Der hellenistische Hesiod: Arats Phainomena und die Tradition der antiken Lehrepik*, Wiesbaden: L. Reichert.

Fantuzzi, M. and R.L. Hunter (2004), *Tradition and Innovation in Hellenistic Poetry*, Cambridge: Cambridge University Press.

Farrell, J. (1991), *Virgil's Georgics and the Traditions of Ancient Epic*, New York/Oxford: Oxford University Press.

Feeney, D.C. (1991), *The Gods in Epic: Poets and Critics of the Classical Tradition*, Oxford: Clarendon Press.

Feeney, D.C (1998), *Literature and Religion at Rome*, Cambridge: Cambridge University Press.

Feeney, D.C. (2007), *Caesar's calendar: ancient time and the beginnings of history*, Berkeley: University of California Press.

Fiedler, M. (2004), *Kommentar zu V. 367–746 von Aviens Neugestaltung der Phainomena Arats*, Stuttgart: Saur.

Fontanella, F. (1991), 'A proposito di Manilio e Firmico,' *Prometheus* 7: 75–92.

Ford, A. (2010), 'Plato's two Hesiods,' in Boys-Stones and Haubold (2010): 133–56.

Fordyce, C.J., ed. (1961), *Catullus: a Commentary*, Oxford: Clarendon Press.

Fowden, G. (1986), *The Egyptian Hermes: A Historical Approach to the Late Pagan Mind*. Princeton: Princeton University Press.

Fowler, D. (2000), *Roman Constructions*, Oxford: Oxford University Press.

Fowler, D (2000a), 'Philosophy and literature in Lucretian intertextuality', in Fowler (2000): 138–54.

Fowler, D. (2000b), 'God the Father (Himself) in Vergil,' in Fowler (2000): 218–34.

Franchet d'Espèrey, S. (1997), 'Les metamorphoses d'Astrée,' *RÉL* 75: 175–91.

Frede, M. (2010), 'The case for pagan monotheism in Greek and Graeco-Roman antiquity,' in Mitchell and van Nuffelen (2010): 53–81.

Freese, J.H. (1926), *Aristotle, the "Art" of Rhetoric*, London: Heinemann, New York: Putnam.

Gain, D.B. (1976), *The Aratus ascribed to Germanicus Caesar*, London: Athlone Press.

Gale, M. (1994), *Myth and Poetry in Lucretius*, Cambridge; New York: Camrbridge University Press.

Gale, M. (2000), *Virgil on the Nature of Things: the Georgics, Lucretius, and the Didactic tradition*, Cambridge; New York: Cambridge University Press.

Gale, M. (2005), 'Didactic Epic' in S. Harrison ed., *A Companion to Latin Literature*, Malden, MA; Oxford: Blackwell Publishing: 101–15.

Gale, M. (2009) ed., *Lucretius*, De rerum natura V, Warminster: Aris and Phillips.

Gale, M., ed. (2004), *Latin epic and didactic poetry: genre, tradition and individuality*, Swansea: Classical Press of Wales.

Garcia Ruiz, M.P. (2006), *Claudio Mamertino Panegírico (Gratiarum actio) al Emperador Juliano*, Pamplona: EUNSA.

Gatz, B. (1967), *Weltalter, goldene Zeit und sinnerwandte Vorstellungen*, Hildesheim: G. Olms.

Gee, E. (1997), '*Parva figura poli*: Ovid's Vestalia and the *Phaenomena* of Aratus', *PCPhS* 43: 21–40.

Gee, E. (2000), *Ovid, Aratus and Augustus: Astronomy in Ovid's Fasti*, Cambridge: Cambridge University Press.

Gee, E. (2001), 'Cicero's Astronomy', *CQ* 51: 520–36.

Gee, E. (2002), 'Vaga signa: Orion and Sirius in Ovid's *Fasti*', in G. Herbert-Brown ed., *Ovid's Fasti: Historical Readings at its Bimillennium*, Oxford: Oxford University Press: 47–70.

Gee, E. (2007), 'Quintus Cicero's Astronomy?', *CQ* 57: 565–85.

Gee, E. (2008), 'Astronomy and Philosophical Orientation in Classical and Renaissance Didactic Poetry,' in J. Ruys ed., *Didactic Literature in the Medieval and Early Modern Periods*, Turnhout: Brepols: 473–96.

Gee, E. (2009), 'Borrowed Plumage: Literary Metamorphosis in George Buchanan's *De Sphaera*' in *George Buchanan: Poet and Dramatist*, Philip Ford and Roger Green edd., Swansea: Classical Press of Wales: 35–58.

Gee, E. (2013), 'Cicero's Poetry,' in K. Steel ed., *The Cambridge Companion to Cicero*, Cambridge: Cambridge University Press: pp. __.

Geer, R. (1964), *Epicurus: Letters, principal doctrines, and Vatican sayings*, Indianapolis: Bobbs-Merrill.

Gersh, S. (1986), *Middle Platonism and Neoplatonism: the Latin Tradition*, 2 vols, Indiana: Notre Dame Press.

Gillespie, S. and P.R. Hardie, edd. (2007), *The Cambridge Companion to Lucretius*, Cambridge: Cambridge University Press.

Giomini, R., ed. (1975), *M. Tullius Cicero Fasc. 46: De divinatione, de fato, Timaeus*, Leipzig: Teubner.

Glei, R. (1990), 'Der Zeushymnus des Kleanthes,' in L. Hagemann and E. Pulsfort edd., *"Ihr alle aber seid Bruder": Festschrift für A. Th. Khoury zum 60. Geburtstag*, Würzburg: Echter; Altenberge: Telos: 577–97.

Gnoli, T. (2009), 'Giuliano e Mitra', in Carrié ed. (2009): 215–34.

Godwin, J., ed. (1995), *Catullus: Poems 61–68*, Warminster: Aris and Phillips.

Goldberg, S. (1995), *Epic in Republican Rome*, New York, Oxford University Press.

Goldschmidt, V. (1950), 'Theologia,' *REG* 63: 33–39.

Grafton, A., and M. Williams (2006), *Christianity and the Transformation of the Book: Origen, Eusebius, and the library of Caesarea*, Cambridge, MA: Belknap Press of Harvard University Press.

Gundel, W. (1907), *De Ciceronis poetae arte capita tria*, Leipzig, Univ., phil. Diss., Leipzig: Noske in Borna

Gundel, W (1949), 'Parthenos' (1), in *PW* XVIII.2.II.

Guthrie, W. (1939), *Aristotle, On the Heavens*, Cambridge MA: Harvard University Press.

Gutzwiller, H. (1942), *Die Neujahrsrede des Konsuls Claudius Mamertinus vor dem Kaiser Julian (Basler Beiträge zur Geschichtswissenschaft 10)*, Basel: Helbig und Lichtenhahn.

Gutzwiller, K. (2007), *A guide to Hellenistic literature*, Oxford: Blackwell.

Hacking. I, (1983), *Representing and intervening: introductory topics in the philosophy of natural science*, Cambridge: Cambridge University Press.

Hahm, D.E. (1977), *The Origins of Stoic Cosmology*, Columbus: Ohio State University Press.

Halliwell, F.S. (1973), *Aristotle, the* Poetics, Cambridge, MA: Harvard University Press.

Halliwell, F.S. (1987), *The Poetics of Aristotle*, London: Duckworth.

Halliwell, F.S. (1998), *Aristotle's* Poetics, London: Duckworth, 2nd edition.

Halliwell, F.S. (2011), *Between Ecstasy and Truth: Interpretations of Greek Poetics from Homer to Longinus*, Oxford: Oxford University Press.

Hamilton, R. (1989), *The architecture of Hesiodic poetry*, Baltimore: London: Johns Hopkins University Press,.

Haskell, Y.A. (1998), 'Renaissance Latin Didactic Poetry on the Stars: Wonder, Myth and Science', *Renaissance Studies* 12: 495–522.

Haslam, M. (1992), 'Hidden Signs: Aratus' "Diosemeiai" 46ff, Vergil "*Georgics*" 1.424ff', *HSCP* 94: 199–204.

Haubold, J. (2010), 'Shepherd, Farmer, Poet, Sophist,' in Boys-Stones and Haubold (2010): 11–30.

Haury, A., (1964) 'Cicéron et l' astronomie,' *RÉL* 42: 198–212.

Heath, M. (1985), 'Hesiod's didactic poetry,' *CQ* 35: 245–63.

Heiberg, J. (1894), *Simplicii in Aristotelis de caelo commentaria (commentaria in Aristotelem Graeca 7)*, Berlin: Reimer.

Helm, R., ed. (1956), *Eusebius Werke, seibenter Band: die Chronik des Hieronymus (Hieronymi Chronicon)*, Berlin: Akademie Verlag.

Heniger, S.K. (1977), *The Cosmographical Glass: Renaissance Diagrams of the Universe*, San Marino, California: Huntington Library.

Hershbell, J. (1970), 'Hesiod and Empedocles,' *CJ* 65: 145–61.

Hine, H. (2010), *Seneca, Natural Questions*, Chicago and London: University of Chicago Press.

Horsfall, N. (1999), 'The Prehistory of Latin Poetry,' *RFIC* 122: 50–75.

Hopkinson, N. (1988), *A Hellenistic anthology*, Cambridge: Cambridge University Press.

Housman, A.E. (1900), 'The *Aratea* of Germanicus,' *CR* 14: 26–39.

Housman, A.E. ed. (1926), *M. Annaei Lucani bellum civile*, Oxford: Blackwell.

Howland, J. (1993), *The* Republic: *the Odyssey of Philosophy*, New York: Twaine Publishers.

Hunter, R.L. (1995, repr. in Hunter 2008b), 'Written in the stars: poetry and philosophy in the *Phaenomena* of Aratus,' first published in *Arachnion* 1.2 (1995), online at http://www.cisi.unito.it/arachne/num2/hunter.html, repr. in Hunter, R.L. (2008), *On coming after: studies in post-classical Greek literature and its reception*, Berlin: Walter De Gruyter: vol. 1 pp. 153–88.

Hutchinson, G.O. (1988), *Hellenistic poetry*, Oxford: Clarendon Press.

Ihlemann, C. (1909), *De Avieni in vertendis Arateis arte et ratione*,.Göttingen Phil. Diss. Göttingen: Dieterich.

Inwood, B. (2001), *The poem of Empedocles: a text and translation with an introduction*, Toronto: University of Toronto Press.

Irigoin, J. (1997), *Tradition et critique des textes grecs*, Paris: Belles Lettres.

Jaeger, M. (2002), 'Cicero and Archimedes' Tomb,' *JRS* 92: 49–61.

James, A.W. (1972), 'The Zeus Hymns of Cleanthes and Aratus,' *Antichthon* 6: 28–38.

Jacques, J.M. (1960), 'Sur un acrostiche d'Aratos (*Phén.*, 738–787),' *RÉA* 62:48–61.

Johnson, M. and C. Wilson (2007), 'Lucretius and the history of science,' in Gillespie and Hardie (2007): 131–48.

Johnston, P.A. (1980), *Vergil's Agricultural Golden Age: a Study of the Georgics*, Mnemosyne suppl. 60, Leiden: Brill.

Kaibel, G. (1894), 'Aratea,' *Hermes* 29: 82–123.

Kaster, R. (1988), *Guardians of Language: the Grammarian and Society in Late Antiquity*, Berkeley, Los Angeles, and London: University of California Press.

Katz, J. (2008), 'Vergil Translates Aratus: *Phaenomena* 1–2 and *Georgics* 1.1–2,' *MD* 60: 105–23.

Kauffmann, G. (1888) *De Hygini memoria scholiis in Ciceronis Aratum Harleianis servata: scripsit scholia apparatu critico et notis instructa et catalogum stellarum adhuc ineditum*, Vratislaviae: G. Koebner.

Kenney, E.J. and W. Clausen, edd. (1982), *Cambridge History of Classical Literature* vol. 2, Cambridge: Cambridge University Press.

Kennedy, D. (2002), *Rethinking Reality: Lucretius and the Textualization of Nature*, Ann Arbor: University of Michigan Press.

Kerlouegan, F. (1988), 'Aratus Latinus: a Study of the Culture and the Latin Language in Northern France during the C8th', *Revue de philology, de litteraire et d' histoire anciennes* 62: 185–87.

Keydell, R. (1960), review of reprint of Maass 1898, *Gnomon* 32: 369–70.

Kidd, D. (1981), 'Notes on Aratus, *Phaenomena*,' *CQ* 31: 355–62.

Kidd, D. (1997), *Aratus*: Phaenomena, Cambridge: Cambridge University Press.

Kiernan, M. (2000), *Francis Bacon, the Advancement of Learning*, The Oxford Francis Bacon IV, Oxford: Clarendon Press.

Klotz, A., ed. (1973), *P. Papini Stati Thebais*, Leipzig: Teubner.

Kubiak, D. (1981), 'The Orion Episode of Cicero's *Aratea*,' *CJ* 77: 12–22.

Kubiak, D.D. (1990), 'Cicero and the Poetry of Nature,' *SIFC* 8: 198–214.

Kuhn, T. (1957), *The Copernican Revolution: Planetary Astronomy in the Development of Western Thought*, Cambridge, MA: Harvard University Press.

Kuhn, T. (1962), *The Structure of Scientific Revolutions*, Chicago and London: University of Chicago Press.

Kuhn, T. (1970), *The Structure of Scientific Revolutions*, 2nd., enlarged, Chicago and London: University of Chicago Press.

Lamberton, R. (1986), *Homer the Theologian: Neoplatonist Allegorical Reading and the Growth of the Epic Tradition*, Berkeley and Los Angeles: University of California Press.

Landolfi, L. (1990), 'Virginis inde subset facies (Germanico 96–139): rivisitazione di un mito aratea,' *Orpheus* 11: 10–20.

Landolfi, L. (1996), *Il volo di Dike (da Arato a Giovenale)*, Bologna: Pàtron.

Lane-Fox, R. (1986), *Pagans and Christians in the Mediterranean World from the Second Century AD to the conversion of Constantine*, Hammondsworth: Viking.

Le Boeuffle, A., ed. (1975), *Germanicus, des Phénomènes d'Aratos*, Paris: Les Belles Lettres.

Le Boeuffle, A. (1983), 'Le destin astrale d'après Germanicus, auteur des *Phénomenes*, in *Visages du destin dans les mythologiques: mélanges Jacqueline Duchemin*, Actes du Colloque du Centre de Recherches Mythologiques de l'Univ. de Paris X de Chantilly, 1er-2 mai 1980, ed. François Jouan, Paris: Les Belles Lettres.

Le Boeuffle, A. (2010), *Les noms latins d'astres et de constellations*, 2nd ed., Paris: Les Belles Lettres.

Lee, D. (2007), *Plato: the Republic, rev.* ed., London: Penguin.

Leggatt, S (1995), *Aristotle: On the heavens, I and II*, Warminster: Aris & Phillips.

Lehoux, D. (2007), *Astronomy, weather, and calendars in the ancient world: parapegmata and related texts in classical and Near Eastern societies*, Cambridge; New York: Cambridge University Press.

Levene, D. (1997), 'God and Man in Classical Latin Panegyric', *PCPhS* 43: 66–103.

Levitan, W. (1979), 'Plexed Artistry: Aratean Acrostics,' *Glyph* 5: 55–68.

Lewis, A. (1983), 'From Aratus to the Aratus Latinus: a comparative study of Latin translation,' PhD thesis, *Open Access Dissertations and Theses* Paper 3199, http://digital commons.mcmaster.ca/opendissertations/3199.

Lewis, A. (1985), 'Aratus Ph. 443–9: Sound and Meaning in a Greek Model and its Translations,' *Latomus* 44: 804–10.

Lewis, A. (1988), 'Rearrangement of motif in Latin translation: the emergence of a Roman *Phaenomena*', in C. Deroux (ed.) *Studies in Greek and Latin Literature and Roman History IV*, Coll. Latomus, Bruxelles: Latomus: 210–33.

Lewis, A. (1992), 'The Popularity of the *Phaenomena* of Aratus', in *Studies in Latin Literature and Roman History VI*, ed. C. Deroux, Coll. Latomus, Bruxelles: Latomus: 94–118.

Lieu, S. (1989), *The Emperor Julian, panegyric and polemic: Claudius Mamertinus, John Chrysostom, Ephrem the Syrian*, Liverpool: Liverpool University Press.

Liuzzi, D. (1988), 'Echi degli *Aratea* di Ciceroni negli *Astronomica* di Manilio,' *Rudiae* 1: 115–59.

Lloyd, G.E.R. (1968), 'Plato as a Natural Scientist,' *JHS* 88: 78–92.

Lombardo, S. (1983), *Sky Signs: Aratus' Phaenomena*, Berkeley: North Atlantic Books.

Long, A.A. (1985), 'The Stoics on World-conflagration and Everlasting Recurrence,' *Southern Journal of Philosophy* supplementary volume XXIII: 13–38.

Long, A.A. (1992), 'Stoic Readings of Homer', in R.D. Lamberton and J.J. Keaney edd., *Homer's Ancient Readers*, Princeton, N.J Princeton University Press: 41–66.

Luck, G. (1976), 'Aratea,' *AJPh* 97: 213–34.

Ludwig, W. (1963), 'Die Phainomena Arats als hellenistiche Dichtung,' *Hermes* 91: 425–28.

Ludwig, W. (1968), 'Anfang und Schluss der Aratea des Germanicus,' *Philologus* 112: 217–21.

Ludwig, W. (2003), '*Opuscula aliquot elegantissima* des Joachim Camerarius und die Tradition des Arat,' in *Joachimus Camerarius (Leipziger Studien zur klassischen Philologie, n.s. 1)*, ed. by Rainer Kössling and Günther Wartenberg, Tübingen: Gunter Narr Verlag: 97–132.

Maass, E., ed. (1893), *Arati Phaenomena*, Berlin: Weidmann.

Maass, E, ed. (1898), *Commentariorum in Aratum reliquiae*, Berlin: Weidmann.

Manitius, K., ed. (1894), *Hipparchi in Arati et Eudoxi Phaenomena commentariorum libri tres*, Leipzig: Teubner.

Marcone, A. (1983), 'L'imperatore Giuliano tra politico e cultura: a proposito di due libri recenti,' *Rivista storica Italiana* 95: 504–9.

Marcotte, D. (2000), 'Avienus, temoin de Julien: pour une interpretation et une datation nouvelles de la *Descriptio orbis terrae*,' *RÉL* 78: 195–211.

Marinone, N. (1997), *Berenice da Callimacho a Catullo: testo critico, traduzione e commento*, 2nd ed., Bologna: Pàtron.

Marinone, N. (2004), *Cronologia ciceroniana*, 2nd ed., Bologna: Pàtron.

Martin, A. and O. Primavesi (1999), *L'Empédocle de Strasbourg*, Berlin and New York: de Gruyter.

Martin, J. (1956), *Histoire du texte des Phénomenes d'Aratos*, Paris: Librairie C. Klincksieck.

Martin, J. (1998), *Aratos: Phénomènes*, Paris: Les Belles Lettres.

Mastandrea, P. (1979), *Un Neoplatonico Latino: Cornelio Labeone: testimonianze e frammenti*, Leiden: Brill.

Maurach, G. (1977), 'Aratus and Germanicus on Altar and Centaur,' *AClass* 20: 121–39.

Maurach, G. (1978), *Germanicus und sein Arat*, Heidelberg: Winter.

Mayor, J.B., W. Warde Fowler, and R.S. Conway (1907), *Virgil's Messianic Eclogue: its Meaning, Occasion, and Sources*, London: J. Murray.

McGurk, P. (1973), 'Germanici Caesaris Aratea cum scholiis: A New Illustrated Witness from Wales,' *National Library of Wales Journal* 18: 197–216.

Merrill, W. (1921), 'Lucretius and Cicero's Verse', *University of California Publications in Classical Philology* 5: 143–54.

Merrill, W. (1924), 'The Metrical Technique of Lucretius and Cicero,' *University of California Publications in Classcial Philology* 7: 293–306.

Mitchell, S. (2007), *A history of the later Roman Empire, AD 284–641: the transformation of the ancient world*, Malden, MA: Blackwell.

Mitchell, S. and van P. Nuffelen (2010), *One God: Pagan Monotheism in the Roman Empire*, Cambridge: Cambridge University Press.

Momigliano, A. (1975), *Alien Wisdom: the Limits of Hellenization*, Cambridge: Cambridge University Press.

Monat, P. (1999), 'Astrologie et pouvoir,' in *Pouvoir, divination, prédestination dans le monde antique*, Élisabeth Smadja and Évelyne Geny edd., Paris: Les Belles Lettres: 133–36.

Monat, P., ed. (1992–7), *Firmicus Maternus: Mathesis*, 3 vols., Paris: Les Belles Lettres.

Montanari-Caldini, R. (1973), 'L'Astrologia nei Prognostica di Germanico', *SIFC* 45: 137–204.

Montanari-Caldini, R. (1981), 'Virgilio, Manilio e Germanico: memoria poetica e ideologia imperiale,' *Quaderni di filologia Latina*: 71–114.

Montanari-Caldini, R. (1984), 'Cicerone, Firmico e la dittatura di Scipione Emiliano,' *Prometheus* 10: 19–32.

Moraux, P. (1981), 'Anecdota Graeca Minora IV: Aratea', *ZPE* 42: 47–51.

Morel, W. (1943), 'Germanicus' *Aratea*', *CR* 57: 106–7.

Morgan, L. (1999), *Patterns of Redemption in Virgil's Georgics*, Cambridge: Cambridge University Press.

Morrison, A. (2007), *The narrator in Archaic Greek and Hellenistic poetry*, Cambridge: Cambridge University Press.

Most, G. (1989), 'Cornutus and Stoic Allegoresis: a Preliminary Report,' *ANRW* II.36.3: 2014–65.

Most, G. (2006), *Hesiod: Theogony, Works and Days, Testimonia*, Cambridge MA; London: Harvard University Press.

Morgan, K. (2000), *Myth and Philosophy from the Presocratics to Plato*, Cambridge: Cambridge University Press.

Mueller, I. (2005), *Simplicius On Aristotle On The Heavens 2.10–14*, London: Duckworth.

Munk-Olsen, B. (1982), *L'étude des auteurs classiques latins aux XI et XII siècles, I: catalogue des manuscripts classiques latins copies du XI au XII siècle*, Paris: éd. de CNRS.

Munro H.A.J. (1864), *Titi Lucreti Cari De rerum natura libri sex*, Cambridge: Deighton Bell and Co.

Murphy, T. (1998), 'Cicero's first readers: epistolary evidence for the dissemination of his works,' *CQ* 48: 492–505.

Naiden, J.R. (1952), *The Sphera of George Buchanan (1506–1582): A Literary Opponent of Copernicus and Tycho Brahe*, Philadelphia, privately printed.

Nappa, C. (2005), *Reading After Actium: Vergil's Georgics, Octavian, and Rome*, Ann Arbor: University of Michigan Press.

Netz, R. (2009), *Ludic Proof: Greek Mathematics and the Alexandrian Aesthetic*, Cambridge: Cambridge University Press.

Newlands, C. (2002), *Statius' Silvae and the Poetics of Empire*, Cambridge: Cambridge University Press.

Nixon, C., and B. Rodgers, edd. (1994), *In Praise of Later Roman Emperors: the Panegyrici Latini*, Berkeley: University of California Press.

Norden, E. (1903), *P. Vergilius Maro Aeneis Buch VI*, Leipzig: Teubner.

Norden, E. (1926), *P. Vergilius Maro Aeneis Buch VI, 3rd ed.*, Leipzig: Teubner.

North, J. (2005/2011), 'Pagans, Polytheists and the Pendulum', in W. Harris ed. (2005), *The Spread of Christianity in the First Four Centuries: Essays in Explanation*, Leiden, Boston and Köln: Brill: 125–43, repr. in J. North and S. Price edd. (2011), *The Religious History of the Roman Empire: Pagans, Jews and Christians*, Oxford: Oxford University Press: 479–502.

Nuzzo, G. ed. (2003), *Gaio Valerio Catullo: Epithalamium Thetidis et Pelei (c.LXIV)*, Palermo: Palumbo.

Obbema, P., B. Eastwood, F. Mütherich (1985), *Aratea* (Faksimile Verlag Luzern Schweiz, facsimile of & commentary on Leiden Voss. Lat. Q.79, Germanicus' *Aratea*).

Obbink, D., ed. (1995), *Philodemus and poetry: poetic theory and practice in Lucretius, Philodemus, and Horace*, New York: Oxford University Press.

Obrist, B. (2004), *La Cosmologie médiévale, Textes et Images I: Les fondements antiques*, Firenze: Edizioni del Galluzzo.

Olivieri, A. (1898), 'Sulla traduzione di R. Festo Avieno dei v. 1–732 di Arato,' *Riv. Di Storia Antica* 3, 2–3: 132–35.

Panichi, E. (1969), *Gli Aratea e i Phaenomeni*, Milan: Soc. ed. Dante Alighieri.

Pease, A.S. (1917), 'Were there two versions of Cicero's *Prognostica*?' *CP* 12: 302–4.

Pease, A.S., ed. (1955–8), *M Tulli Ciceronis de natura deorum libri III*, Cambridge, MA: Harvard University Press, vol. 2.

Pendergraft, M. (1987), *Aratus as a poetic craftsman*, Ann Arbor: University Microfilms International.

Pendergraft, M. (1990), 'On the Nature of the Constellations: *Aratus* Ph. 367–85', *Eranos* 88: 99–106.

Pendergraft, M. (1995), Euphony and Etymology: Aratus' *Phaenomena*,' *SyllClass* 6: 43–67.

Pérez-Ramos, A. (1990), 'Francis Bacon and Astronomical Inquiry,' *BJHS* 23: 197–205.

Piganiol, A. (1951), 'Sur le calendrier brontoscopique de Nigidius Figulus', in P.R. Coleman-Norton et al. edd. (1951), *Studies in Roman Ecomonic and Social History in Honour of Allan Charter Johnson*, Princeton: Princeton University Press: 79–87.

Pohlenz, M., ed. (1982), *M. Tullius Cicero: Tusculanae disputationes*, Stuttgart: Teubner.

Pöhlmann, E. (1973), 'Charakteristika des römischen Lehrgedichts,' *ANRW* I.3: 813–901.

Poochigian, A. (2010), *Aratus: Phaenomena, translated with an Introduction and Notes*, Baltimore: Johns Hopkins University Press.

Porter, H. (1946), 'Hesiod and Aratus,' *TAPhA* 77: 158–70.

Possanza, M. (2004), *Translating the heavens: Aratus, Germanicus, and the Poetics of Latin Translation*, New York: Lang.

Powell, J.G.F., ed. (2006), *M. Tulli Ciceronis de re publica, de legibus, Cato Maior de senectute, Laelius de amicitia*, Oxford: Clarendon Press.

Rawson, B. (1985), *Intellectual Life in the Late Roman Republic*, London: Duckworth.

Rees, R. (2002), *Layers of Loyalty in Latin Panegyric AD 289–307*, Oxford; New York: Oxford University Press.

Reeve, M.D. (1980), 'Some astronomical manuscripts,' *CQ* 30: 508–22.

Reeve, M.D. (1983), 'Aratea,' in L.D. Reynolds ed. *Texts and Transmission: a Survey of the Latin Classics*, Oxford: Clarendon Press (1983): 18–24.

Reeve, M.D. (2007), 'Lucretius in the Middle Ages and Early Renaissance: transmission and scholarship,' in Gillespie and Hardie (2007): 205–13.

Reinhardt, T. (2004), 'Readers in the Underworld: Lucretius, *De rerum natura* 3.912–1075,' *JRS* 94: 27–46.

Reydams-Schils, G. (1999), *Demiurge and Providence: Stoic and Platonist Readings of Plato's Timaeus*, Turnhout: Brepols.

Rinaldi, M. (2002), *Sic itur ad astra*, Napoli: Loffredo editore.

Rolfe, J. (1940), *Ammianus Marcellinus*, Cambridge MA: Harvard University Press; London: Heinemann, 3 vols.

Rosen, E., and J. Dobrzkcki, edd. (1978), *Nicholas Copernicus on the Revolutions*, Nicholas Copernicus Complete Works vol.2, Polish Scientific Publishers; London: Macmillan.

Ross, D.O. (1980), *Virgil's Elements. Physics and Poetry in the Georgics*, Princeton, N.J.: Princeton University Press.

Ross, W.D. (1959), *Aristotelis ars rhetorica*. Oxford: Clarendon Press, (repr. 1964).

Rotman, B. (2010), 'Mathematics', in B. Clarke and M. Rossini edd., *The Routledge Companion to Literature and Science*, London: 157–68.

Rouse, W.H.D., ed. (1975), *Lucretius: De Rerum Natura*, Cambridge MA: Harvard University Press.

Rowe, C., ed. (1986), *Plato*: Phaedrus, Warminster: Aris and Phillips.

Rowe, C., ed. (1995a), *Plato*: Statesman, Warminster: Aris and Phillips.

Rowe, C., ed. (1995b), *Reading the Statesman: Proceedings of the III Symposium Platonicum*, Sankt Augustin: Academia Verlag.

Rowe, C. (2010), 'On Grey-haired Babies,' in Boys-Stones and Haubold (2010): 298–316.

Schiesaro, A. (1990), *Simulacrum et Imago*, Pisa: Giardini.

Sale, W. (1966), 'The Popularity of Aratus,' *CJ*: 160–64.

Salles, R. (2005), 'Ἐκπύρωσις and the goodness of god in Cleanthes,' *Phronesis* 50: 56–78.

Salles, R., ed. (2009a), *God and Cosmos in Stoicism*, Oxford: Oxford University Press.

Salles, R. (2009b), 'Chrysippus on conflagration and the indestructibility of the cosmos,' in Salles (2009): 118–34.

Santini, C. (1977), *Il segno e la tradizione in Germanico scrittore*, Rome: Cadmo.

Santini, C. (1987), '"Quam te, diva, vocem?": Germanico e la Virgo,' in G. Bonamente and M. Segoloni edd., *Germanico: La persona, la personalità, il personaggio nel bimillenario della nascita*, Atti del convegno, Macerata-Perugia, 9–11 maggio 1986, Roma: Giorgio Bretschneider: 133–51.

Santini, C. and Schivoletto, N., edd. (1990), *Prefazioni, prologhi, proemi di opere tecnico-scientifiche latine*, Rome: Herder.

Schiesaro, A. (1996), 'Aratus' Myth of Dike', *MD* 37: 9–26.

Schmit, A. (2005), *Augustus und die Macht der Sterne: antike Astrologie und die Etablierung der Monarchie in Rom*, Köln: Böhlau.

Schwabl, H. (1972), 'Zur Mimesis bei Arat: Prooimion und Parthenos,' in R. Hanslik et al. ed., *Antidosis: Festschrift für Walther Kraus zum 70. Geburtstag*, Vienna: Böhlau: 336–56.

Scourfield, J.H.D., ed. (2007), *Texts and culture in late antiquity: inheritance, authority, and change*, Swansea: Classical Press of Wales.

Sedley, D. (1997), 'How Lucretius composed the De Rerum Natura', in K. Algra, M. Koenen and P. Schrijvers edd., *Lucretius and his Intellectual Background*, Amsterdam: North-Holland: 1–19.

Sedley, D. (1998), *Lucretius and the transformation of Greek wisdom*, Cambridge: Cambridge University Press.

Sedley, D. (2007), *Creationism and its Critics in Antiquity*, Berkeley and Los Angeles: University of California Press.

Segal, C. (1978), '"The myth was saved": reflections on Homer and the mythology of Plato's *Republic*,' *Hermes* 106: 315–36.

Selter, B. (2010), 'Through the Looking Glass of Memory: Reading Avienus,' *Quaderni urbinati di cultura classica* 95: 113–30.

Semanoff, M. (2006), 'Undermining authority: pedagogy in Aratus' *Phaenomena*,' in M. Harder, R. Regtuit, and G. Wakker edd., *Beyond the Canon*, Leuven; Dudley, MA: Peeters: 303–18.

Seznec, J. (1953), *The survival of the pagan gods: the mythological tradition and its place in Renaissance humanism and art*, translated from the French by Barbara F. Sessions, New York: Pantheon Books.

Shackleton Bailey, D.R., ed. (1965), *Cicero's Letters to Atticus*, Cambridge: Cambridge University Press, vol. 1.

Shackleton Bailey, D.R., ed. (1980), *Cicero: Epistulae ad Quintum fratrem et M. Brutum*, Cambridge: Cambridge University Press.

Shaw, B. (1985), 'The Divine Economy: Stoicism as Ideology', *Latomus* 44: 16–54.

Shaw, G. (1995), *Theurgy and the Soul: The Neoplatonism of Iamblichus*, Pennsylvania: Pennsylvania State University Press.

Sider, D. (1995), 'Epicurean Poetics: Response and Dialogue,' in Obbink (1995): 35–41.

Sier, K. (1990), 'Zum Zeushymnos des Kleanthes,' in P. Steinmetz ed., *Beiträge zur hellenistischen Literatur und ihrer Rezeption in Rom*, Stuttgart: Steiner: 93–108.

Skutsch, O., ed. (1985), *The* Annals *of Quintus Ennius*, Oxford: Clarendon Press.

Slings, S., ed. (2003), *Platonis res publica*, Oxford: Clarendon Press.

Smith, R. (1995), *Julian's Gods: Religion and Philosophy in the Thought and Action of Julian the Apostate*, London: New York: Routledge.

Smolak, K. (1989), Postumius Rufius Festus Avienus, in R. Herzog and P.L. Schmidt, edd. (1989), *Handbuch der lateinischen Literatur der Antike vol. 5: Restauration und Erneuerung: Die lateinische Literatur von 284 bis 374 n. Chr.*, München: Beck, S. 320–327 = Herzog, R.

ed. (1989), *Nouvelle histoire de la littérature latine: Restauration et Renouveau 284–374*, Turnhout: Brepols: no. 557, 'Aviénus'.

Smolenaars, J. (1994), *Statius, Thebaid VII: A Commentary*, Leiden: Brill.

Solmsen, F. (1966), 'Aratus on the Maiden and the Golden Age', *Hermes* 94: 124–28.

Soubiran, J., ed. (1972), *Cicéron:* Aratea, Fragments poétiques, Paris: Les Belles Lettres.

Soubiran, J. (1979), *L'astronomie dans l'antiquité classique*, Paris: Les Belles Lettres.

Soubiran, J. (1979a), 'Les *Aratea* d'Aviénus: critique des textes et histoire des sciences,' in Soubiran (1979): 225–44.

Soubiran, J. (1981), *Aviénus: les Phénomènes d'Aratos*, Paris: Les Belles Lettres.

Springer, C. (1984), 'Aratus and the Cups of Menalcas', *CJ* 79: 131–34.

Steinmetz, P. (1966), 'Germanicus, der Römische Arat', *Hermes* 94: 450–82.

Swain, S. and M. Edwards, edd. (2004), *Approaching Late Antiquity: the Transformation from Early to Late Empire*, Oxford: Oxford University Press.

Swoboda, A., ed. (1964), *P. Nigidii Figuli Operum reliquiae*, Vindobonae: Tempsky; repr. Amsterdam: A.M. Hakkert, 1964.

Szidat, J. (1982), 'Der Neuplatonismus und die Gebildeten im Western des Reiches,' *MusHelv* 39: 132–45.

Tantillo, A. (2003), 'L'impero della luce: riflessioni su Costatino e il sole,' *MÉFRA (Mélanges de l'école Francais à Rome)* 115: 985–1048.

Tarrant, H. (2000), *Plato's First Interpreters*, London: Duckworth.

Tarrant, H. and D. Baltzy, edd. (2006), *Reading Plato in Antiquity*, London: Duckworth.

Tarrant, R. (1985), *Seneca's Thyestes*, Atlanta, Georgia: Scholars Press.

Taub, L. (2010), 'Translating the Phainomena across genre, language and culture' in A. Imhausen, and T. Pommerening edd., *Writings of early scholars in the Near East, Egypt, Rome and Greece*, Berlin and New York: de Gruyter.

Thom, J.C., ed. (2005), *Cleanthes' Hymn to Zeus*, Tübingen: Mohr Siebeck.

Thomas, R.F. (1982), 'Catullus and the Polemics of Poetic Reference,' *AJPh* 103: 144–64.

Thomas, R.F. (1986), 'Unwanted Mice (Aratus, Phaenomena 1140–1) and the textual criticism of Aratus' *Phaenomena*,' *HSCP* 90: 91–92.

Toohey, P. (1996), *Epic Lessons: an introduction to ancient didactic poetry*, London/New York: Routledge.

Tougher, S. (2007), *Julian the Apostate*, Edinburgh: Edinburgh University Press.

Traglia, A. (1963), 'Reminiscenze empedoclee nei "Fenomeni" di Arato', in *Studi Alessandrini in memoria di A. Rostagni*, Torino: Bottega d'Erasmo: 382–93.

Traglia, A. (1966), 'Aratea I', *Stud. Class. e Orientali* XV: 250–58.

Traglia, A. (1978), 'Germanico poeta-astronomo,' *C&S* 68: 32–38.

Traglia, A. (1984), 'Germanico e il suo poema astronomico,' *ANRW* II.32.1: 321–43.

Traina, A. (1970), *Vortit barbare: Le traduzioni poetiche da Livio Andronico a Cicerone*, Roma: Edizioni dell'Ateneo.

Trépanier, S (2007), 'The didactic plot of Lucretius' DRN and its Empedoclean model,' in Richard Sorabji and Robert W. Sharples edd., *Greek and Roman philosophy, 100 BC-200 AD*, London: Institute of Classical Studies: 243–82.

Tsantsanoglou, K. (2009), 'The λεπτότης of Aratus,' *Trends in Classics* 1: 55–89.

van Noorden, H. (2009), 'Aratus' Maiden and the Source of Belief,' in M.A. Harder, R.F. Regtuit, and G.C. Wakker, edd., *Nature and Science in Hellenistic Poetry*, Leuven: Peeters: 255–75.

van Noorden, H. (2010), '"Hesiod's races and your own": Socrates' "Hesiodic" project,' in Boys-Stones and Haubold (2010): 176–99.

Vegetti, M., ed. (2005), *Platone, la Reppublica*, vol. VI, Napoli: Bibliopolis.

Verkerk, C. (1980), 'Aratea: a review of the literature concerning MS Voss. Lat. Qu. 79 in Leiden University Library,' *Journal of Medieval History* 6: 245–87.

Verkerk, C. (1984), 'The Heliocentric Planetary Configuration of the Leiden *Aratea*,' *Journal of Medieval History* 10: 145–47.

Vernant, J.-P. (1960), 'Le mythe hésiodique des races: essai d'analyse structurale,' *Revue de l'histoire des religions* 157: 21–54.

Vernant, J.-P. (1969), *Mythe et pensée chez les grecs, Paris:* F. Maspero, *second edition, translated as Vernant, J.-P. (2006), Myth and Thought Among the Greeks*, New York; London: Zone.

Vernant, J.-P. (1966), 'Le mythe hésiodique des races: sur un essai de mise au point,' *Revue de philologie* 40: 247–76.

Vernant, J.-P. (1985), 'Méthode structurale et mythe des races,' in J. Brunschwig, C. Imbert, and A. Roger edd., *Histoire et structure: à la mémoire de Victor Goldschmidt*, Paris: J. Vrin: 43–60.

Veyne, P., (1979) 'The Hellenization of Rome,' *Diogenes* 106: 1–27.

Viano, C. (1994), 'Aristote, *De Coel.* 1.10: Empédocle, l'alternance et le mythe du Politique,' *RÉG* 107: 400–413.

Vlastos, G. (1975), *Plato's Universe*, Oxford: Clarendon Press.

Voit, L. (1984), 'Arat und Germanicus über Lyra, Engonasin und Kranz', *Würtzburger Jahrbücher für die Altertumswissenschaft* n.f. 10: 135–44.

Volk, K. (2002), *The Poetics of Latin Didactic: Lucretius, Vergil, Ovid and Manilius*, Oxford; New York: Oxford University Press.

Volk, K. (2006), 'Cosmic Disruption in Seneca's *Thyestes*,' in K. Volk and G. Williams edd., *Seeing Seneca Whole: Perspectives on Philosophy, Poetry, and Politics*, Leiden; Boston: Brill: 183–200.

Volk, K. (2009), *Manilius and his intellectual background*, Oxford.

Volk, K. (2010), 'Aratus,' in J.J. Clauss and M. Cuypers edd., *A Companion to Hellenistic Literature*, Oxford: Blackwell: 197–210.

Volk, K. (2012), 'Letters in the Sky: Reading the Signs in Aratus' *Phaenomena*,' *AJP* 133: 209–40.

Walsh, P.G. (1997), *Cicero: The Nature of the Gods*, Oxford: Clarendon Press.

Warden, J. (1998), 'Catullus 64: Structure and Meaning,' *CJ* 93 (1998): 397–415.

Watt, W. (1994), 'Eight Notes on Germanicus' Aratea', *RhM* 137: 73–77.

Weber, D. (1986a), *Aviens Phaenomena, eine Arat-Bearbeitung aus der lateinischen Spätantike*, Vienna: VWGÖ.

Weber, D. (1986b), 'Et nuper Avienus: Religiöse Tendenzen in Aviens "Phainomena"-Übersetzung,' *Eos* 74: 325–35.

West, M., ed. (1978), *Hesiod: Works and Days*, Oxford, Clarendon Press.

Wigodsky, M. (1995), 'The Alleged Impossibility of Philosophical Poetry,' in Obbink (1995): 58–68.

Williams, G. (1968), *Tradition and Originality in Roman Poetry*, Oxford: Clarendon Press.

Winston, R. and C. Winston, trans. (1970), *The Glass Bead Game: Hermann Hesse*, London: Johnathan Cape.

Woestijne, P. van de (1961), *La Descriptio Orbis Terrae d'Aviénus: astronomie et idéologie*, Bruges: de Tempel.

Wresniok, R. (1907), *De Cicerone Lucretioque Ennii imitatoribus*, Breslau, Univ., Diss.,: Vratislaviae: R. Nischkowsky.

Wright, M.R., ed. (1981), *Empedocles: the extant fragments*, New Haven and London: Yale University Press.

Wright, W.C. (1980), *The Works of the Emperor Julian*, Cambridge, MA: Harvard University Press; first printed 1913.

Zehnacker, H. (1989), 'D'Aratos à Aviénus: Astronomie et idéologie,' *Illinois Classical Studies* 44: 317–29.

INDEX

INDEX LOCORUM

Note: references in bold type are to passages of text; references in roman type are to page numbers in this book. In the case of Lucretius' *DRN*, I have noted all passages referred to in the main text; where references run sequentially by book and line in Appendix B, they have not been noted individually here.

net, in quo terram cum orbe lunari tanquam epicyclo contineri diximus. Quinto loco Venus nono mense reducitur. Sextum deniq; locum Mercurius tenet, octuaginta dierum spacio circu currens. In medio uero omnium residet Sol. Quis enim in hoc

pulcherimo templo lampadem hanc in alio uel meliori loco po neret, quàm unde totum simul possit illuminare? Siquidem non inepte quidam lucernam mundi, alij mentem, alij rectorem uocant. Trimegistus uisibilem Deum, Sophoclis Electra intuentê omnia. Ita profecto tanquam in solio re gali Sol residens circum agentem gubernat Astrorum familiam. Tellus quoq; minime fraudatur lunari ministerio, sed ut Aristoteles de animalibus ait, maximâ Luna cū terra cognationê habet. Concipit interea à Sole terra, & impregnatur annuo partu. Inuenimus igitur sub hac